Democracy and Elections

Democracy and Elections

RICHARD S. KATZ

New York • *Oxford* • *Oxford University Press* • 1997

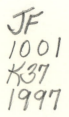

Oxford University Press

Oxford   New York

Athens   Auckland   Bangkok   Bogota   Bombay   Buenos Aires
Calcutta   Cape Town   Dar es Salaam   Delhi   Florence   Hong Kong
Istanbul   Karachi   Kuala Lampur   Madras   Madrid   Melbourne
Mexico City   Nairobi   Paris   Singapore   Taipei   Tokyo   Toronto   Warsaw

and associated companies in
Berlin   Ibadan

Library of Congress Cataloging-in-Publication Data
Katz, Richard S.
Democracy and elections / Richard S. Katz.
p.   cm.
Includes bibliographical references and index.
ISBN 0-19-504429-0
1. Elections.   2. Political parties.   3. Democracy.   I. Title.
JF1001.K37   1997
324.6—dc21   96-46292

1 3 5 7 9 8 6 4 2

Printed in the United States of America
on acid-free paper

Preface

The subjects of this book—what it means for a polity to be democratic and how democracy can be institutionalized—are massive and intricate. Many of the theoretical and normative questions raised have plagued political thinkers for millennia. I would like to say that I have solved at least some of them, but that would be carrying hubris beyond the point at which tragedy becomes farce. I do hope, however, that I have been able to clarify many of the issues involved and to suggest interesting and productive ways of thinking about them. In particular, I have tried to show how systematic empirical analysis can be applied to questions that have most often been addressed only in theory, and how the questions raised by normative theory can direct empirical research. It is said that prior disclosure excuses a multitude of sins, and so this is the place to acknowledge that this is an incomplete effort. Questions are raised that in principle could be addressed with data but are not; strings are left hanging, holes unplugged. In one respect this is just as well; if all of these problems were solved, many political scientists would be out of business. In reality, however, it is my private interest rather than the public good that dictates the incomplete nature of much of the analysis and argument. It was simply time to let go, and move on to other things.

One of the early frustrations in doing research such as that reported in this volume is the discovery that all of the work that has gone before is riddled with factual errors. I also would like to say that this book is an exception, but the effort to correct old errors leads quickly to the realization that they are inevitable. Many of the primary materials (laws, regulations, official reports) on which tables ultimately are based are not available outside of their home countries, and those that are, quite naturally, are in many more languages than any individual could master, especially in their technical nuances. Thus one must rely on secondary sources, and although these can be checked against one another, on closer inspection they often lead, like the branches of a tree, back to a single root. Moreover, many of the facts themselves are in constant flux; what was correct when I wrote it, or when it was published in the work in which I found it, may no longer be true. To cite but one example, the laws governing local councils in many countries tie their size to population; as populations change, so do the numbers of local officials. To these, of course, must be added the usual errors of typography and transcription, translation and interpretation. While I have tried to make this book as accurate as possible, consulting with local experts and diligently comparing with original sources, both humility and deference to the principles of inductive research that underlie most of what we claim to know in the social sciences require me to admit that some errors certainly remain. To the usual absolution given to those who were kind enough to check and confirm my "facts" and the customary (because it is true) statement that the remaining sins of commission and omission are the sole responsibility of the author must be added a strong caveat lector.

This book began as an upper-level undergraduate course at The Johns Hopkins University. Its first critics were the students, whose discussions often showed me what needed to be clarified, expanded upon, or omitted, and who reminded me that what was clear to me might appear so only because I had missed important complications. As the book was in preparation, many colleagues either volunteered to read the manuscript or had large chunks of it inflicted upon them. Among those who have been so generous with their time and insights are Milton Cummings, Munroe Eagles, Richard Friedman, Bernard Grofman, Arend Lijphart, Kirstie McClure, and Peter Mair. Various pieces of the book, or papers derived from it, have been presented at a variety of conferences, and I have benefitted greatly from the comments and suggestions of those participating. Although my debt to all of these people is enormous, it pales in comparison to what I owe my wife, Judith. Beyond her intellectual (and clerical, and library-professional) contributions, she has supported and encouraged, nagged and cajoled, and resisted what must have been the nearly overwhelming temptation to wash her hands of the whole business. She has allowed me to drag her to Buffalo, and then back to Baltimore. The end product is not as good as she deserves, but I dedicate it to her nonetheless because it is the best I could do.

Contents

Democracy and Elections

Values and Institutions

Elections are the defining institutions of modern democracy. Although some communities make some decisions in "town meetings," and although direct decision of occasional issues through referendum is possible in many countries, in all modern democracies most public decisions most of the time are made by elected representatives. Even such microstates as Liechtenstein and San Marino are ruled by elected parliaments rather than directly by the people. Likewise, elections have been regular fixtures in "people's democracies" and "guided democracies" no less than in western "liberal democracies."

Democracy is a normative as well as a descriptive term, and the propriety of delegating authority to elected officials has been one of the enduring questions of democratic theory. To some, elections are the device that makes democracy possible in societies so grown in scope and complexity that direct rule by the assembly of all citizens is impossible. Indeed, some conclude that government by elected representatives is more truly democratic than direct popular rule. To others, elections are an impediment to the achievement of democracy, a device for elites to control the people rather than the reverse.

Although theorists on both sides of this debate agree that elections are key institutions in modern democracies, they have had remarkably little to say about the differences among electoral systems and practices. Instead, they have tended to regard elections as a genus whose species are substantially interchangeable. This literature has focused on the "true" meaning of democracy and the impact of elections in general on its achievement, with little attention devoted to the possibility that some democratic values may be better achieved, or more seriously undermined, by one variety of electoral system rather than another.

There have, of course, been extensive studies of the impact of electoral systems. There is, however, an ironic symmetry between this literature and that of democratic theory. These authors have recognized the linkage between elections and democracy and, indeed, have justified the conduct of elections and their own concern about them in precisely these terms. The opening paragraph of Graham

Gudgin and Peter J. Taylor's investigation of the relationship between seats and votes provides a particularly explicit but otherwise typical example.

> The word democracy means, literally, 'government by the people.' Up until the eighteenth century the term was restricted to describing political systems in which the population governed directly through large meetings. . . . Such 'pure' democracy is difficult to imagine in complex societies. Hence an 'indirect' or representative form of democracy has evolved whereby government is by the *elected representatives* of the people. Such systems of government raise a whole host of problems. . . . This book treats one of these problems in some detail: we investigate how the votes cast for a political party are translated into seats for the party's candidates in the legislature, parliament, or assembly. This is a key relationship which lies at the very heart of modern representative democracy.[1]

This paragraph, however, is virtually the only reference to democracy in the entire book. Just as democratic theorists have tended to treat elections generically, so these authors tend to regard democracy as an undifferentiated whole.

Democratic theory and the study of elections are two fields of inquiry that ought to be connected intimately but that, in fact, have tended to proceed independently, each acknowledging the importance of the other and then blithely ignoring it. In this book, I take steps toward connecting them. The two subjects of the book are political elections and political democracy, but my real purpose is to explore the relationship between them.

The Problem of Definition in Democratic Theory

The debate over the value and place of elections in modern democracy stems from the problem of defining democracy itself. There is agreement that the prototypical democracy was Athens in the age of Pericles. There is also agreement that the Athenian constitution, even if sanitized by the emancipation of women and the abolition of slavery, could not be implemented in toto in the modern world. There is agreement that the task of the modern democrat is to devise a constitution that will, as nearly as possible, achieve at least some of the same values that Athenian democracy strove to achieve. The agreement begins to break down when one tries to determine those values and disappears when one tries to assign them relative weight or to specify adequate or feasible levels of attainment.

Nearly every country claims to be democratic, or at least to be laying the foundations for an eventual democracy. Nearly every political theorist claims to be arguing for true democracy. Yet one realizes that the problems of politics and political philosophy have not been solved as soon as the range and variety of democracies and of democratic theories are considered. To be sure, there are some common themes. At least as an ideal, some attention must be given to the basic equality of all citizens and to the people as the ultimate source of legitimate authority if any etymologically valid claim to the Greek roots of the word is to be maintained. But this is the fundamental point. The agreement that democracy is good is more semantic than substantive.

There are many conceptions of democracy. That one conception may have a claim to the term that is etymologically, historically, or logically superior to another's is only of secondary importance. People do not value a political system because it legitimately is called democratic; they call it democratic because it satisfies their particular set of ethical criteria. To find the "true" meaning of democracy in the modern world is a task akin to cleaning the Augean stable and will not be attempted here.

We must still consider the problem of defining democracy, however, to identify the values implicit in use of the term, an important task in an analysis of the relationship between democracy and elections for three reasons. First, political arrangements can be evaluated only if the standards to be applied are clear. Once the individual values summarized in particular conceptions of democracy are isolated, they can serve as the basis for judgment, or at least define the dimensions for comparison.

Second, the nature of the connection between democracy and values varies among different "democracies." Is democracy a means to some end, or is it an end in itself? If democracy is a means, it is relatively easy to judge the democraticness of institutions, but not obvious that democraticness is desirable. Rather, preference for democracy must be based on the additional assertion that democratic means yield valued ends. Likewise, normative judgments must be based less on the democraticness of the institutions per se, and more on the interaction between the institutions and the environment in which they operate. Alternatively democracy may be considered an end, a social condition that, by definition, entails the achievement of particular values. Thus, under the first view, a political system can be democratic and undesirable; under some conditions, democracy must be limited if a desirable social state is to be obtained. In the second view, democracy is synonymous with virtue, so any shortcomings of society must indicate failure to democratize fully, not a failure of democracy.

Third, a detailing of the values involved in debates over the meaning of democracy is necessary if the politics and outcome of institutional reforms are to be understood. Reforms are advocated because they are expected to produce desired results. Often those results are the protection or advancement of the self-interests of those advocating them. The arguments, however, usually include appeals to higher values made in the expectation that others will be influenced by them. Moreover, while they may originate as the rankest hypocrisy, over time they are likely to take on a life of their own, even for those making them. The values themselves thus become inputs into the political process, affecting both the likely shape of institutional reforms and the functioning of the institutions.

Not only are differing sets of values implicit in differing conceptions of democracy but each individual conception of democracy usually entails several values not always mutually compatible, although the theorists involved have often tried to make them so with dubious empirical assertions. Quite typically, both majority rule and freedom of conscience are regarded as democratic values, but what happens if, as in Schumpeter's famous mental experiment, the majority decides to persecute religious dissent?[2] Very few democrats are so attached to majority rule that they are prepared to support the persecution of minorities, but, conversely, few are so committed to protecting the individual that they would support universal application of the "liberum veto."

If, as is generally conceded, democracy is in one sense an ideal that cannot be fully realized in the world, translation of that ideal into real terms requires two varieties of compromise. First, each of the individual values encompassed in the ideal is likely inherently unattainable—an aspiration rather than an achievable state of the world. Rule by the people is a common democratic ideal, but, quite aside from definitional problems, obviously the people cannot decide every detail of every public question. Similarly limited is the notion of the development of each citizen's human potential. To achieve this would leave no room for any person to develop more fully, an absurd possibility and one that no advocate of personal development as a democratic ideal would admit. Although no one committed to such a goal can ever be satisfied in the sense of ceasing to strive for fuller attainment, differences in degree of attainment must be recognized as significant unless one is to call all potentially realizable systems equally undemocratic.

Second, because the values encompassed in any conception of democracy are likely to be mutually incompatible beyond a certain point, a compromise will have to be struck among them. While some situations may be more democratic than some others in all respects, more often reforms that make society more democratic in one respect will make it less so in others. The problem is to determine the most desirable of the feasible combinations of values.

If it is not possible or desirable to specify a single definition of democracy against which to judge alternative electoral systems, what can be done? No definite conclusions that one electoral system is superior to another can be advanced. Instead, one can inventory possible democratic values and assess the efficacy of different electoral systems in achieving them. Thus a reader with a well-articulated set of values and schedule of acceptable compromises among them might deduce a single "best" electoral system for him- or herself, but must always recognize that another reader, with a different set of values, may reach a different, but equally valid, conclusion.

Institutions and Values

The systems of government for which political philosophers argue can be given life only by political institutions. Athenian democracy required the institutions of the assembly, sortition, the Council of 500, and so forth in order to operate. Its character changed as these institutions evolved. In the same way, modern democracy has its own host of institutions—parties, legislatures, cabinets, bureaucracies, and, above all, elections. Each of these institutions is subject to many variations. What difference do variations in electoral institutions make to the character of modern democracy? More immediately, what concerns must be paramount in considering the relationship between institutions and values?

One way of conceptualizing the relationship between values and institutions is in terms of the functions that those institutions are expected to perform. This does not imply a functionalist or a structural-functionalist analysis in the technical sense of those terms.[3] Rather than suggesting that any particular function *must* be performed in any political system, or that it must be associated with a *specific* structure, I use the term more loosely, referring to claims that elections ought to do, or are likely to do, something, allow something to be done, or produce some identifiable result. If institutions are supposed to make a difference to outputs, then the production of that difference is their function.

Institutions embody the value commitments of a polity. This is especially clear where the framers of constitutions have left a record of their deliberations, but it is also indicated by the value-laden debate surrounding more limited institutional reforms. Those who see society as composed of organic communities likely espouse representative institutions in which localities are key units, while those who see society based on geographically dispersed social classes likely oppose territorially based representation. Similarly, adherents of the brand of liberalism that sees the primary threat to freedom as unrestrained government power likely support institutions that afford many opportunities for minority vetoes, while others may be looking for ways to increase the likelihood of majority rule.

Not only values shape institutions, however. Institutions are not politically neutral. They affect the distribution of effective political power and thus the likely output of the political system as well as the relative ability of different groups to influence that output. Although expectations of likely gainers and losers from institutional reforms may prove, after the fact, incorrect, that they are believed at the time can make constitutional reform a most contentious political issue—what is at stake is not just one decision but the ability to influence all future decisions.

The impact of an institutional change depends on how people react to it as much as on the "objective logic" of the change itself. While the "objective" institution may constrain behavior and the consequences of behavior, the choices people make on the basis of their perceptions of reality are usually more important, and political reality is sufficiently ambiguous to allow wide variations in understanding. Debate over the Equal Rights Amendment provides a contemporary American example. For both sides, the question was more symbolic than substantive, yet both expected that the message sent by ultimate passage or rejection of the amendment would influence subsequent behavior.

Institutions create or foreclose opportunities; they do not guarantee that anyone will be willing and able to exploit them. Institutions alter the relative value of many political resources; they do not create their initial distribution. Moreover, the meaning of an institution is defined in part by culture; institutions may influence political culture but they are not alone. A full account of the consequences of institutions therefore must consider their context.

The product of this book should be a firm basis for evaluating electoral systems in terms of democratic values and for understanding the possibility and consequences of electoral reform. To address these problems requires a three-step approach.

The first step is to explore the role of elections in modern democracy. Here two classes of questions must be addressed. What are the values implicit in democracy? And, according to various democratic theories, what role will elections play in the furtherance of those values?

These questions are raised in chapters 3–6. In detail, there appear to be at least as many conceptions of democracy, and hence as many sets and rankings of democratic values, as there have been theorists. In more general terms, however, it is possible to distinguish four types, each based on the priority of a single value. Chapter 3 concerns treatments of democracy that give primacy to popular rule in the sense of government in which "the will of the people" is carried into effect. In this popular sovereignty view of democracy, government should be an instrument of the people, who exercise positive control over it. A second type, here called liberal democracy, assigns principal weight to democracy as a means of preventing tyranny. Thus the protection of minority (and majority) rights *against* government is valued over popular direction *of* government. This variety of democratic theory is the subject of chapter 4. Both popular sovereignty and liberal democracy focus concern on policy. The third type, participationist democracy, primarily concerns the effect of the political system on the human development of the citizens. Although stressing its connection to Periclean democracy and certainly with roots in Rousseau and Bentham, this variety of democratic theory, discussed in chapter 5, is a reaction to the perceived elitism of apologists for modern representative government. The fourth variety of democratic theory, the subject of chapter 6, emphasizes the development of political community. While one subtype of communitarian democracy is closely related to participationist democracy and is meant to be relevant to western societies, this category also encompasses the democracies of the third world and communist bloc.

The second step of the analysis, and the task of chapters 9–14, turns to empirical material to see how the functions assigned to elections by various democratic theories can best be performed. This part is organized around the major sets of questions defining an electoral system. The first of these involves the translation of votes into a distribution of offices among candidates. The central question concerns the choice of electoral formula—plurality, majority, or proportional—but related topics include the size of electoral districts, apportionment of representatives among districts, and the process of drawing district lines. These topics are discussed in chapters 9 through 11. The second cluster of topics (chapter 12) involves the nature of the choice voters are allowed to make. In terms of earlier formulations, the principal distinctions involve the nature of the interparty choice—whether it is categoric (requiring a choice of one party only) or ordinal (allowing votes for candidates of more than one party or an ordering of preferences)—and whether an intraparty choice is allowed.[4] Also involved here are questions of ballot form and decisions regarding the types of officials elected and the timing of those elections. The third cluster (chapter 13) concerns access to the ballot box. Historically, the central question has been franchise extension. Other questions include voter registration and the possibility of making voting compulsory. The final cluster, access to the ballot and control of candidates, is the subject of chapter 14. How does one become an officially recognized candidate, both in terms of qualification for office and formal nominating procedures, and are some candidates "more equal than others"? What restrictions are placed on the fund-raising and spending activities of candidates and what forms, if any, of public support do they receive?

The last step, and the task of chapter 15, is to bring these strands together and ask in a more systematic way which electoral systems are best suited to which conceptions of democracy. To anticipate the conclusion, chapter 15 suggests that there is no single "best" or "most democratic" electoral system, but rather that the choice of an electoral system is, in effect, a choice among competing definitions of democracy itself.

Before considering where we might go, however, it will be helpful to look at where we have been. Chapter 2 turns attention to the past.

Early Voting and Elections

The primary purpose of this book is to explore the relationship between elections and democracy. Of course, such a relationship is not necessary. Aristotle regarded elections as an undemocratic feature of the Athenian constitution, since they entail rule by the best people rather than rule by all the people.[1] Indeed, the rise of Athenian democracy was accompanied by the widespread replacement of elections with selection by lot, while its decay saw the reverse.[2] For roughly 2,000 years after the fall of Athens, democracy was rejected roundly by all serious thinkers. Nonetheless, elections continued to be held within various institutions and polities.

A brief review of the history of elections is vital, however, if current electoral systems are to be understood. Contemporary democracies were not established overnight with new institutions derived solely from rigorous logical analysis. In general, governments were democratized, not replaced. Even where change was revolutionary, existing institutions normally were modified and adapted. Thus many features of contemporary institutions reflect the needs and values of earlier political systems. Moreover, although before the nineteenth century elections often were designed to serve aims quite apart from democracy, many of the problems they raise continue to be relevant.

A complete treatment of the history of elections is impossible here. Instead, this chapter consists of four "snapshots" or "film clips," each concerned with the functions and procedures of elections in a particular setting. To put the conclusions at the beginning, these four, and the associated primary purpose served by elections, are the democracy of Athens (prevention of tyranny); the Roman Republic (confirmation of authority through consent); the medieval Catholic church (discovery of a divinely ordained choice); and thirteenth- through eighteenth-century England (selection of "attorneys" to act for the community). At least if one takes "divinely ordained choice" to be a special case of any choice whose correctness does not depend on the will of the choosers, these are all concerns—albeit usually not the principal concerns—in the design of electoral systems today.

Athens

The origins of popular decision by means of voting in Athens appear to lie in the reforms of Solon. Solon divided the citizen population into four classes based on annual income, with public offices open to those in the upper classes, while those in the fourth class were given "only a share in the Assembly of the People and in the law courts."[3] While hardly democratic, these reforms for the first time established a popular assembly in which any citizen could speak and popular courts to which any citizen could take his grievance. Moreover, the replacement of birth by wealth as the qualification not only opened office to the most successful of the upper middle class, but also introduced a standard that could be adjusted in the future.

Aristotle also credits Solon with having given the Athenians "the power of electing to office and of calling the magistrates to account."[4] In particular, "Solon established the rule that the magistrates were to be appointed by lot out of candidates previously selected by each of the four tribes."[5] Exactly how these passages are to be construed is in dispute, but regardless of the precise method, clearly voting played a significant role at some stage in the selection process.

The Solonic system was supplanted by the tyranny of Peisistratus. According to Aristotle, the tyrant's "rule was more like a constitutional government than like a tyranny."[6] The use of the lot in selection of archons was suspended and they again were elected. That these elections were manipulated is evidenced both by Thucydides' account of the period and by a fragmentary list of eponymous archons that shows a distribution among the leading families inconsistent either with lot or with free popular choice.[7]

The real birth of Athenian democracy followed the tyranny and was introduced by the reforms of Cleisthenes. The most fundamental of these was a complete reorganization of the Athenian population. In place of the four tribes based on kinship, 10 artificial tribes defined by territory were created. Many new citizens were enrolled, which certainly expanded the sphere of participation and may have defused a potentially dangerous crisis of legitimacy. The new tribes were constructed so as to cross-cut the major political cleavage of the day, that between the shore, the city, and the interior. This reform may have been intended to mitigate this conflict, but it also allowed Cleisthenes to break up the areas of aristocratic strength and to "gerrymander" the tribes to his own advantage. A central feature of Cleisthenes' constitution was to entrust power to boards of officials on which each tribe was represented equally, thus minimizing the possibility of a cabal seizing power.

At the height of Athenian democracy during the fifth century BC, selection for most offices was by lot. For major offices, selection was from among candidates previously nominated by the demes (roughly neighborhoods). In the case of minor officials, apparently lots were drawn among the demes for the right, or duty, to fill particular posts. In either case, a rough proportionality was maintained, with the more populous demes given more nominees or a greater than equal chance of being selected to fill an office. In this way, each citizen would have an equal chance of being selected regardless of the population of his deme.

Any citizen who met the necessary age and income qualifications—which gradually were relaxed—could seek office. However, people were discouraged by a strict scrutiny of the official-designate's background and character before he assumed his position. There is some suggestion that the original purpose of this scrutiny, aside from verification of the candidate's eligibility in the technical sense, was to mitigate the worst potential dangers of sortition. Most positions involved purely routine duties and were shared among boards of officials. Further, a corps of state slaves was available to assist. Still, although the Athenians may have believed that the majority were competent to discharge most offices, they hardly can have believed that every citizen could perform adequately in every office.[8] Later, the scrutiny was used to challenge the would-be official's commitment to democracy and his general moral worth. A further check was the requirement that officials give an accounting of their performance at least nine times during the year.

The guiding principle in the selection of Athenian officials seems to have been the taming of power, and the principal fear that a permanent oligarchy of some kind would develop. Use of the lot was one way to avoid this end.[9] Additionally, power was divided among boards rather than being entrusted to a single individual, providing some protection against the less than fully competent as well. The key protection, however, was rotation in office and short tenure. Officials usually were ineligible to succeed themselves, and in some cases a citizen could hold a particular office only once during his lifetime. Thus any Athenian citizen who chose to be a candidate would have had a reasonable expectation of holding some major office at least once.

Practicality dictated that these principles be violated for some offices that required judgment and technical skill, most notably membership of the board of generals, or *strategoi*. These were elected by show of hands. Before 501 BC, the strategoi were elected, one from each tribe, in the tribal assemblies. After 501, the election took place in the full assembly, but still with one strategos elected from each tribe. This was counter to the general trend of Athenian practice and must have contributed to the eventual political as well as military dominance of the strategoi.

By the age of Pericles, the Assembly, which originally had met only at the call of the nobility, and then 10 times per year, met at least 40 times annually and possessed full legislative authority. Although only 2,000 to 3,000 of the estimated 50,000 to 60,000 eligible citizens (at the time of Pericles) would attend an average assembly, many votes would be taken so any method of recording votes more time-consuming than a show of hands would have been impossible. The votes may have been counted by tribe, but only the grand total of individual votes cast for each side determined the outcome. Thus the result would be unaffected by the tribe to which any particular group of voters belonged.

Votes to ostracize were held in a special assembly (with an extraordinary quorum of 6,000), which was called only after a regular assembly voted to invoke the law of ostracism. Votes were cast by scratching the name of the proposed victim on a bit of pottery and could, if the voter wished, be kept secret. On the other hand, there was nothing to prevent a citizen from revealing his vote, and citizens could use *ostraka* prepared in advance by others. Similarly, considerable ingenuity went into the creation of voting tokens that allowed a secret vote in the courts. Apparently the Athenians valued a secret ballot in questions concerning the rights of individual citizens but were prepared to accept—or perhaps preferred—open voting on questions of public policy, notwithstanding the possibility of pressure on some citizens or a "bandwagon" effect.

There can be little doubt that one important reason for the development of democracy in Athens was that the people appeared a useful ally to one faction in an elite struggle. Naturally, democracy was not justified in this way later. What were its principal values from the point of view of the Athenians?

As has already been suggested, the central value appears to have been prevention of tyranny. This value would appeal to insecure elites—since if they were the potential tyrants they were also those with the most to lose from tyranny by others—as well as to ordinary citizens. The organization of the population into, and division of offices among, artificially created tribes as well as selection of officials by lot, short tenure, and rotation in office were all designed to prevent an entrenched elite, no matter how competent or popular, from monopolizing office and supplanting the Assembly as the ultimate authority. The institution of ostracism similarly was aimed at the potential tyrant. By temporarily banishing one, but only one, politician, a leader whose popularity was growing dangerous could be disposed of without threat to his followers. Indeed, leaders who had been elected frequently as strategoi were among the most prominent victims of ostracism. At the same time, however, Athenian democracy frequently was dominated by "leaders of the people" (the original demagogues). As Moses Finley notes, "The historical root of ostracism lay in tyranny and the fear of its recurrence, but the practice owes its survival to the almost intolerable insecurity of political leaders, who were driven, by the logic of the system, to try to protect themselves by removing from the scene physically the chief advocates of an alternative policy."[10]

The Athenians clearly valued the active involvement of citizens in the life of the *polis*. Nowhere is this expressed more eloquently than in Pericles' Funeral Oration: "Here each individual is interested not only in his own affairs but in the affairs of the state as well: . . . we do not say that a man who takes no interest in politics is a man who minds his own business; we say that he is a man who has no business here at all."[11] In the same vein, Aristotle attributes to Solon "a special law . . . enacting that whoever, in a time of political strife, did not take an active part on either side should be deprived of his civic rights and have no share in the state."[12] On the other hand, one should not exaggerate the degree to which this ideal was reflected in practice. If 5,000 was an exceptionally large attendance for an Assembly, the reason was that the vast majority of those eligible did not attend. No friend of the poor, Aristotle attributes the introduction of pay for the Assembly to the need of the elite to increase attendance rather than to a desire by the poor to make free with the public purse.[13] Of those who did attend, very few exercised their right to speak. The use of the lot in preselection of nominees for a final sortition was as much to conscript candidates as to control competition. While any citizen could involve himself in public affairs, apparently most citizens, most of the time, did not. Participation, perhaps, was less a virtue in itself than it was simply doing one's share of the dirty work of administering the polis. Nonetheless, even if the primary decision-making bodies—the Assembly, the courts, and the Council of 500—were arenas in which practiced orators competed for the favor of the people rather than forums in which ordinary citizens spoke regularly, the essence of the democracy was that the people retained the final right to decide.

Rome

Rome was never a democracy in the Greek sense nor, unless one takes communist criticisms of liberal democracy at face value, in the modern sense either. Magistrates (except for the *interreges* required when the terms of one set of magistrates expired before their successors could be elected) could take office only on election by the people. Legislation required the approval of the people and "[i]t was admitted that when the whole People met to legislate, their assent was a command, their refusal to assent a prohibition."[14] Nonetheless, Rome remained an oligarchic timocratic state. Even when a choice was allowed in elections, the choice was tightly controlled by the presiding magistrate. Legislative votes were simply "yes" or "no" decisions on a question with no amendments possible. In addition to the limits on the people's freedom of choice, the presiding magistrate in particular, and the ruling class in general, had a variety of institutional and procedural devices by means of which they could control the outcome of a vote. The Republican constitution conformed well to Cicero's description of the centuriate assembly, whose structure he ascribed to Servius Tullius.

> Servius so disposed the centuries in the classes that the votes were under the control of the rich and not of the masses. He accepted the principle, to which we must forever adhere in the Republic, that the majority should not have the strongest voice. . . . No one was deprived from the right of suffrage, and yet he who had the most to gain from the well-being of the state could use his vote to the greatest effect.[15]

Like the Athenians, the Roman population ultimately was categorized in a number of ways. The most important difference was that in Greece, even if votes were counted by groups, the overall majority of individual votes determined the result, whereas in Rome the result was determined by the vote of the majority of groups. Naturally this opened the door to the functional equivalent of the modern gerrymander as well as to various other manipulatory techniques familiar to the managers of modern elections.

The Romans had three types of voting assemblies of the whole people, based on the kinds of units into which the population was divided. The oldest of these was the *comitia curiata*, with 30 *curiae*, 10 for each of the three traditional clans of Rome. The comitia curiata passed the *lex de imperio* annually, but whether this was the formal grant of *imperium* (the right to command) to the newly elected consuls and praetors or merely confirmed their right to take auspices is unclear. By 443 BC, the comitia curiata already was of secondary importance and when the office of censor was created in that year, even the grant of the right of auspices came from the centuries rather than the curiae.

The second type of assembly, the *comitia centuriata*, was of military origin, but began to assume a political role at the end of the monarchy. It eventually was supplanted in the field of legislation by the tribal assemblies, but it continued to elect the consuls, praetors, and censors throughout the Republican period. Until the middle of the fifth century, the comitia centuriata simply gave or withheld assent to a number of nominees exactly equal to the number of places to be filled; after that time there was a real, if often controlled, choice.

The third type of assembly was based on the territorial tribes. There were two tribal assemblies, the *concilium plebis*, presided over by a tribune and from which patricians theoretically were excluded, and the *comitia populi tributa*, presided over by a curule magistrate and with all citizens eligible to vote. The concilium plebis appears to have begun voting by tribes in 471 BC, and plebeian acceptance of the group vote in what was an antiestablishment assembly suggests that it was seen either as legitimate or as administratively necessary, notwithstanding its potential for distorting the outcome. The concilium plebis elected the 10 tribunes of the plebs. They also could enact resolutions that acquired legal status if sanctioned by the patricians. In 287 BC, however, acts of the concilium plebis (*plebiscita*) were made binding on the whole population and from that time the concilium plebis was the principal legislative assembly of the Republic.

All Roman voting assemblies were weighted in favor of the rich, but this was particularly true of the centuriate assembly. In the early Republic, this assembly consisted of 18 centuries of aristocratic cavalry, 80 centuries of infantry from the first census class, 20 centuries from each of the next three classes, 30 from the fifth class, and five centuries of noncombatants, including all citizens with too little property to be enrolled even in the fifth class. There was, thus, great overrepresentation of the first order, who, together with the cavalry centuries, constituted a majority until the third century. Even after that, they still were radically overrepresented.

The advantage the rich enjoyed in the centuriate assembly by virtue of their overrepresentation was made even greater by the privilege of voting first. This benefit was particularly important because of the Roman practice of considering the votes of a majority of units to be sufficient as well as necessary for election. As soon as a candidate reached the required majority, he was declared elected; as soon as a sufficient number of candidates reached a majority, the election was over and no further units were called to vote. Thus, if the upper classes were reasonably united, the lower classes would not be called to vote at all.

Although it would not be apparent because the announcement of results stopped as soon as enough candidates reached a majority, one result of this electoral system is that the candidate who was the choice of the most centuries might not be elected. For example, in an election for the two consuls, 386 votes could be cast (two by each century) so three candidates could have at least the 97 votes (i.e., one vote from each of a majority of the 193 centuries) required for election.

Rather than declaring the two with the largest relative majorities elected, the Romans declared elected the first two to reach absolute majorities. These, of course, need not be the same. Suppose that after the first three classes had voted, candidates A and B each had 97 votes, leaving 82 to candidate C. Then by the Roman procedure A and B would be elected and the voting would stop. If, however, it continued with A and C receiving the two votes of half the remaining centuries and B and C the votes of the other half (with the odd century voting for B and C), the final result would have been 124 votes for A, 125 votes for B, and 137 votes for C, so by relative majorities B and C rather than A and B would have been elected.

In elections of magistrates, the tribes appear to have voted simultaneously (as did the centuries within a single census class), thus denying any tribe an advantage analogous to that enjoyed by the centuries of the first census class. On the other hand, the vote of the first voter in each tribe was announced before his fellow *tribules* voted and could set a trend. This individual, who was always a prominent member of the tribe, was nominated by the presiding magistrate and thus invariably supported his position.

Since people were assigned to tribes on the basis of residence rather than wealth, the tribal assemblies incorporated less institutionalized overrepresentation of any economic class. Several devices led to elite domination nonetheless. In the fifth century, there were 21 tribes, four for the city and 17 for the surrounding *agra Romana*. As the population grew and citizenship was extended to new territories, the number of tribes was increased to 35, but the number of urban tribes, and thus the voting strength of the urban proletariat—which was growing with the development of large estates and consequent depopulation of the countryside—remained at four. Moreover, until late in the Republican era, freedmen could only be enrolled in the urban tribes.

Once the number of tribes became fixed, new territories were added to the existing tribes. Often these additions were not contiguous. The assignment process led to considerable political jockeying and influence for the censors, who made the assignments, as politicians attempted to have areas favorable to their interests added to marginal tribes and hostile areas assigned where they could do no harm.

Rural voters were more likely than their urban counterparts to be under the influence of a local patron. To maximize the benefits of this, which clearly was a neighborhood rather than a tribal phenomenon, aspiring politicians might purchase villas in several tribal areas; Cicero, for example, had six. Further, while it would be relatively easy for urban voters to cast their ballots, they were concentrated in only four tribes. The journey to Rome would be far more difficult for the more valuable rural voters, most of whom would attend only at the behest, and perhaps at the expense, of a patron. Roman culture stressed the obligation of the recipient of a *beneficium* to be loyal to his patron. It was considered perfectly proper for a rich Roman to provide hospitality to his fellow tribesmen when they came to Rome for an election, and the beneficiaries of this largess naturally would follow their host's lead in voting. As this description implies, the senatorial class was an exception to the rule that city dwellers were registered in the urban tribes. These rich individuals, although generally registered on account of their estates in a rural tribe, nonetheless usually resided in the city.

In all assemblies, the presiding magistrate had a variety of devices available to control the outcome. A citizen became an official candidate only on acceptance of his *professio* by the presiding magistrate, who could refuse to take any notice of votes cast for candidates without his sanction. Although elections of the major magistrates were fixed in July, assemblies met to vote on legislation at the call of the magistrate, who could time the vote to his own advantage. For all votes, the magistrate could suspend the proceedings at any time on account of unfavorable auspices or omens.[16]

Voting by units had the advantage of preserving the equality of tribes whose territories were distant from Rome and therefore were unlikely to have large numbers of voters in attendance. Occasionally, however, almost no one might turn out to represent a unit. This was particularly true of the middle census classes in the centuriate assembly after the concentration of land ownership had proletarianized most of the small holders. If fewer than five voters appeared for a unit, the presiding magistrate could make up that number by temporary transfers (of his political allies). After the written ballot was introduced, he also named three *custodes* for each unit who voted with the unit they were supervising, rather than the unit to which they ordinarily belonged.

Voting assemblies were preceded by meetings called to present the issue to be voted upon. In the case of legislative or judicial votes, there would be more than one meeting to present the issues. Especially for legislative votes, the magistrate calling the vote had complete control over who could address the meeting, although he could be pressured to allow certain opponents to speak by the threat that a rival magistrate would convene his own meeting. For electoral assemblies, the candidates would not be called upon to speak, so that oratorical skill could not be used to influence the vote. Indeed, the promulgation of legislative edicts ultimately was forbidden during the period leading up to an election, both to prevent the influx of voters into Rome for the election from influencing the legislative vote and to deny the candidates the opportunity to sway the electoral vote by taking positions on policy.

Election campaigns, thus, were not based on issues. Cicero's brother advised him to avoid taking any political stand during the campaign for fear of making enemies.[17] They were, nonetheless, protracted and intense. Typically, Cicero began his campaign for the consulship a year in advance. The basic campaign tool, aside from mobilization of one's own friends and clients, was the *commendatio*, a written endorsement in which a leading citizen pledged his support and invited others to join him. A variant would be "campaign posters" of the kind found for municipal elections in Pompei: "M. Cerrinus Vatia is supported for the aedilate by Nymphodotus and Caprasia" or the less friendly announcement that "Vatia is supported for the aedilate by all the petty thieves."[18] The function of the campaign was to mobilize one's friends to mobilize their clienteles actually to come to vote. Thus, if the "formal" campaign might last a year, more generally campaigning was a lifetime occupation of forming alliances and of building one's clientele by doing favors and providing largess.

Roman voting assemblies never were deliberative bodies analogous to the Athenian Assembly. Instead, they were summoned by a magistrate to answer a specific question put by him—to approve or reject a bill he proposed, to convict or acquit a defendant he charged, or to choose among candidates he recognized. Elections were a trial of strength among rival candidates and their clienteles, rather than tests of the popularity of leaders or of their positions on public questions. The Roman Republic was government with the consent of the people, but in no real sense was it government by the people.

The Medieval Church

With the collapse of the Roman Republic, elections ceased to be the accepted way of choosing political leaders. Gradually force and heredity came to be the principal avenues to public office. During the early Middle Ages, the church was the only western institution to hold regular elections or to be concerned with the participation of the governed in the selection of those who would govern them. At least until the revival of classical scholarship, the church was the main source both of the theory and of the experience on which European political institutions were built. The church either invented or revived a variety of modern electoral devices, including relative, absolute, and qualified majority voting as well as the use of a secret ballot.[19] Additionally, the church was the originator of modern concern with strict procedural regularity.

The church was an important political actor in the Middle Ages. Monasteries often held vast tracts of land. Bishops, in addition to holding land, exercised through their courts a variety of powers that would now be considered governmental. The choice of an abbot or bishop, thus, was important not only religiously but also temporally, so it was natural that the important political actors of the day—the great feudal families, kings and their ministers, neighboring bishops—would all have candidates for an ecclesiastical vacancy. Indeed, the right of appointment to ecclesiastical office was one of the most hotly contested and enduring political questions of the Middle Ages.

In this context, the right of election became an important weapon of self-defense for the church against lay interests and for monasteries against both lay interests and the interests of the diocesan bishop. Unable to appeal either to principles of heredity or to pure force, the church tried to take refuge in scrupulous attention to legal detail. In this, it was not always successful. Many medieval bishops and abbots were named by the king with no pretense of election; in other cases, a pro forma election would be held to ratify the king's nomination.[20] Many monasteries, however, obtained or retained the right of election. In this regard, the monastery's right to have an abbot named from among the monks, and in particular to avoid the imposition of a secular abbot interested only in its wealth, was more important than the right to choose a particular individual.

Although politically important, canonical elections in the Middle Ages differed both from ancient and from modern elections in two important respects. First, while canonical elections often involved a choice, the choice itself did not confer authority. The authority of an abbot or bishop came not from his election, but in theory from God and in practice from his appointment by canonical superiors. Thus confirmation is an integral part of canonical election,[21] and if there was a disputed election the superior would have discretion in deciding the true choice of the community. Second, especially in the early and medieval church, the purpose of election was less to allow a free choice to the electors than to provide a vehicle through which the will of God could be expressed.[22]

Early episcopal elections involved both the clergy and people of the city and the bishops of neighboring sees. The exact procedure is not known and probably was not institutionalized. In some cases, the crowd would play a decisive role, and the chronicles repeatedly speak of parties forming among the people and threatening violence. For example, in 374 the Milanese community was divided. "Accordingly Ambrose, in his official capacity as Governor of the province, went in person to the church and spoke some soothing words. Suddenly a voice (a child's voice, it is said) rang out: 'Ambrose Bishop!' The whole congregation instantly took up the cry."[23] A similar story (a divided population, divine revelation, universal acclamation) is recounted by Gregory of Tours concerning the election of Rusticus as bishop of Auverge in 471.[24] More often, the choice would be made by the visiting bishops and presented to the people for their approval. It appears that they could, at least in theory, veto an unpopular choice.[25]

Since the purpose of elections, and of church councils, was to discover divine rather than human will, the choice naturally ought to have been unanimous. Since irreconcilable differences could mean only that God was failing to speak to at least one party, minorities would be under strong pressure to concede. Failing conversion, small minorities might be excommunicated, as happened to two dissenting bishops at the Council of Nicea (325), thus restoring unanimity among those who remained. For elections, the principle was St. Leo's dictum that "He who is to preside over all must be elected by all."[26] The first clear example of a pope elected without general assent was Innocent II in 1130, and his election led to a schism. Unanimity was especially important for the monasteries. By definition, the community should live in perfect harmony. A division of voices, if frequent or persistent, was considered reprehensible. Moreover, it would open the door to outside interference.

The formal election would be preceded by nomination and discussion aimed at eliminating discord. Especially in smaller houses, a consensus was likely to have formed in advance, and in any case there was a strong expectation of consensus that would encourage deference to the first candidate supported. Failing this kind of spontaneous agreement, considerable pressure might be put on a minority to come around. It mattered little that the unanimity was often more apparent than real. It represented the minority's acceptance, with more or less good grace, of their defeat. In some cases, majority rule was a device for achieving unanimity, which might be no more significant than contemporary motions to "make the vote unanimous."

Of course, persuasion and conversion were not always successful, and unanimity, no matter how much desired, might not be obtained. Unlike questions of doctrine, elections could not be postponed indefinitely. In response to this dilemma, the church evolved the principle of *sanioritas*, which was central to the theory of canonical elections for at least 600 years, and to which one finds occasional reference in political discussions even in the mid-twentieth century.[27] Although earlier traces can be found, its roots lie in the rule of St. Benedict, which decreed that an abbot should be chosen unanimously by the monks on the basis of his merit, but failing unanimity, the new abbot should be the choice of that "part of the community who, however few, in view of their judgment are the most wise."[28]

Although it is not clear precisely when the formula *maior et sanior pars* made its appearance, by the twelfth century there was a clear preference for the maior (larger) and sanior (wiser) parts of the congregation to agree.[29] Two problems, however, naturally arose. First, the two principles logically are not commensurable; if the larger and wiser parties did not agree, only an arbitrary choice between them would be possible. Second, it is not readily apparent, especially to their opponents, that one party is the wiser. Both these problems were resolved by appeals to the superior.

In the case of papal elections, however, there was no superior to whom appeals could be made. This problem became apparent in the election following the death of Honorius II in 1130. On the night he died, a hastily convened conclave, including a minority of the cardinals, elected Gregorio Papareschi. Papareschi took the name of Innocent II. The leader of the opposing party, Piero Pierleoni, succeeded in having himself named Pope Anacletus II by the 23 cardinals excluded from the original conclave, a party of the Roman nobility, the lesser clergy, and the people. The case ultimately was laid before St. Bernard who decided in favor of Innocent, as the candidate who was *dignior*, whose electors were sanior, and whose ordination was *ordinabilior*.[30]

Clearly, the church could not count on a leader of the stature of St. Bernard always to be available to resolve disputed elections. The solution adopted by the Third Lateran Council in 1179 was to continue the principle of election by maior et sanior pars, but with the explicit assumption that a qualified majority of two thirds included the sanior part. For offices other than the papacy, this presumption could be challenged through appeal to a superior; in papal elections, however, the presumption was absolute. The principle of two thirds majority vote was extended to chapter elections with the same force it had for papal elections by the Council of Lyons (1274).

A variety of electoral techniques developed that were systematized by the Fourth Lateran Council in 1215. This council recognized three means of election. The first was unanimity by quasi-inspiration; a name would be proposed that would meet with general acclamation. This technique was most like the earliest forms of election; although unanimity was required, it was not the formal unanimity of a written ballot (after 1523 a formal confirming ballot was required) and might be achieved through prior consultation or pressure.

The second technique, and especially for monastic elections the most common at the time, was election by compromise. The whole electorate would select a small number of individuals to make a choice, pledging in advance to accept whomever the compromisers chose. In a sense, unanimity was preserved, because even a single dissenter could prevent the appointment of compromisers, but the compromisers themselves could use any of a variety of decision rules ranging from unanimity to absolute majority.

The final means of election recognized was by formal ballot. This method is now the norm but then was far less common. Election could be unanimous, by qualified majority, or by *maior et sanior pars*. In all cases, votes had to be given freely and absolutely; qualified or conditional votes were excluded.

The development from the principle of *sanioritas* to simple counting of votes occurred in several steps. The first was the conjunction of *sanior* and *maior* parts. This obviously was inconvenient. The Lateran Council took the next step in codifying the presumption that overwhelming numbers (i.e., two thirds) implied *sanioritas*. The third step was the Council of Lyons' decision making the presumption of *sanioritas* for two thirds majorities unappealable; moreover, failing an appeal based on the principle of *sanioritas*, an absolute majority was decreed sufficient. The final step was taken by the Council of Trent, which required a secret ballot, thus making appeals based on the quality of the voters impossible.

Pre-Reform England

The English, later the British, parliament developed in general terms from three roots. The oldest was the *Curia Regis*, or court of the king's feudal vassals. Its members were summoned individually, so the question of election did not arise with this body, which developed into the House of Lords.[31]

The second root was the king's need for information from, and communication with, his subjects. The practice of taking testimony from representatives of the local communities was established in the compilation of Domesday Book. The novelties were the summoning of such individuals to meet with the king rather than his legates and to meet together. This occurred first when King John in 1213 summoned four discreet knights of each shire to meet with him at Oxford.[32]

The third root was financial. In feudal theory and English law, the king was entitled to various dues and other payments. Additionally, he had vast royal estates to provide his income both for public and private purposes. If this income proved inadequate, he could ask for aid from his subjects, but they had to consent. A lord could be taken to represent his vassals, but "as early as 1254 the lay baronage had refused to commit the lesser laity to general taxation, forcing the government to summon four knights from each shire 'to provide . . . what sort of aid they will give us.' "[33] From the latter two roots grew the House of Commons.

The knights summoned by John were representatives of the country in the sense that collectively they knew what was happening throughout the realm; it was not necessary that they be able to act for their counties in any corporate sense. If they were to consent to taxation on behalf of the county, however, such authority is precisely what was required. Accordingly, between 1264 and 1295, a variety of formulas were tried before it was finally settled that knights and burgesses of Parliament should come with "full and sufficient power to do and consent to those things which then and there by the Common Council of Our said . . . Kingdom . . . shall happen to be ordained upon the aforesaid affairs, so that for want of such power . . . the aforesaid affairs may in no wise remain unfinished." The representatives thus were to come as attorneys of those who elected them.[34] Moreover, they were attorneys for corporate communities, not just for particular individuals.

The first legislative regulation of parliamentary elections came in 1406 with a statute enacted in response to complaints that many sheriffs had returned themselves or their friends without consulting the county. This statute declared that the election of knights should be in the full county court by "all they that be there present."[35] The broad franchise of this statute apparently reflected an attempt by the lords to flood the polls with their retainers rather than a democratic impulse and was repealed by the "disenfranchising statute" of 1430, which limited the county franchise to "People dwelling and resident in the same [counties] whereof everyone of them shall have free [Land or] Tenement to the Value of Forty Shillings by the Year at the least above all Charges."[36] With the exception of temporary restrictions like the religious tests, a few minor exclusions, and the desuetude and ultimate repeal of the residence requirement, this remained the basic county franchise into the nineteenth century. Its meaning changed, however, with inflation.

The statute of 1430 also recognized the majority principle and made provision for a poll of the electors, but for the purpose of verifying their qualifications rather than counting their votes. As late as 1555, the chief justice could say that a candidate challenging an election did not need to assert actual numbers of votes, "[f]or election might be by voices, or by hands, or by such other way, wherein it is easy to tell who has the majority, and yet very difficult to know the certain number of them."[37] Although this provision appears to have established relative rather than absolute majority as the decision rule, the medieval pressure for unanimity was such that as late as 1626 a second election might be held to confirm "unanimis assensibus et consensis" the result of a contested election.[38] Moreover, both the provision for majority election and the poll were relevant only if there was a contested election. There certainly were disputes over who would represent the counties, on occasion leading to violence, but these did not often result in more than two candidates being presented for choice by the county court.

In Tudor times, a seat in the Commons, especially as a knight of the shire, was highly prized and this resulted in more competition. The basis of this competition was the local following would-be members could produce, and electoral outcomes often either reflected or determined status within the county. This did not always mean a contested election, however. In many counties the prestige of a single family might be such that they virtually "owned" one or both seats. In other cases, the leaders of the gentry would settle the matter among themselves before the meeting of the county court; there is, indeed, at least one case recorded in which the candidates drew lots to avoid a public contest.[39]

Unlike the counties, the boroughs had no uniform franchise, but most were extremely oligarchic. There were four basic types. Most oligarchic, but also most reflective of the idea that the borough as a community was the object of representation, not individual voters, were the corporation boroughs. In these towns, the borough's governing body elected the members itself. Only somewhat less oligarchic, and most numerous, were the boroughs with a "freeman" franchise. Freedom was usually hereditary but could also be acquired, in various places, by apprenticeship to a freeman, marriage, or purchase. Freedom could also be granted by the borough corporation, which was rarely reticent about creating new freemen if they feared their candidate might be defeated. The third type was the burgage borough, in which the right to vote was tied to ownership of specific pieces of property. Finally, some boroughs had relatively liberal taxpayer or household franchises.

As the population of the cities grew and ownership of rural land became more concentrated, the electorate declined dramatically. In 1640, approximately 30% of the adult men in England and Wales could vote; by 1832, the figure was closer to 10%. In Scotland, the franchise was even more restrictive. In every Scottish borough the right to elect members of Parliament was vested in a self-perpetuating corporation. The county franchise was restricted to owners of feudal "superiorities" of £400 annual value; of 2,000,000 residents in 1823 only 3,000 could vote. At one election "for the county of Bute, which had not more than twenty-one electors, of whom but one was resident, that resident, together with the sheriff and the returning officer, constituted the meeting; and having taken the chair, moved and seconded his own nomination, put the question to the vote, and elected himself."[40]

By the end of the eighteenth century, a large number of members of the House of Commons owed their seats to patrons. Nominated members might hope to make careers in politics but usually voted as they were told.[41] Other seats were bought and sold. In 1767–1768, nominations for Honiton, Melbourne Port, and Reading were advertised in the newspapers. Obviously, a member who bought a seat could be as independent as he liked. For example, Antony Henly, MP, is reputed to have written to his "constituents":

> Gentlemen:
> Yours I received, and am very much surprized at your Insolence in troubling me about the Excise. You know what I know very well; that I bought you. I know what perhaps you think I don't know, that you are about selling yourselves to somebody else; and I know what perhaps you don't know; that I am about buying another Borough_____And now may the curse of God light upon you all; and may your Houses be as common to Excise-Men, as your Wives and Daughters were to me, when I stood Candidate for your Corporation.[42]

As the number of nominated members and purchased seats rose, ultimately to more than one third of the total membership of the House, the place of the Commons in the British constitution changed, and with it the rationale for the system by which its members were chosen. In Tudor England, the earlier idea that the king was the embodiment and interpreter of the national interest was maintained and developed. The monarch governed while the Commons consented to supply and petitioned for redress of specific grievances. For these purposes, members who served as attorneys for recognized communities were entirely appropriate. And this hierarchical conception of society carried over to the local level, where it was likewise appropriate for the leaders of the community to "ar-

range" an election with the average elector consenting to their choice, or supporting one leader or another if there were factional disputes.

By the eighteenth century, three major developments opened this conception
of government to challenge. First, the system of nomination and purchase of seats
expanded and took on a more national organization. When one man controlled
many seats in various parts of the country, it became hard to claim that communities were represented or consent obtained. Second, the balance of the British
economy began to shift decisively in favor of trade and industry. New and important cities grew up that were represented in Parliament only by the knights of
the counties in which they were located. Third, the role of the Commons in
government changed to coequal with the Lords and the monarch in representing
the national will. All this required a new justification for the electoral system. In
the first place, the expanded role of the Commons required that it be a "deliberative assembly of one nation" rather than a "congress of ambassadors." This change
required both independence and talent. One defense of the system of "rotten
boroughs" was that it allowed members with these qualities to find and keep seats.
Accompanying this was the idea of virtual representation. Since the job of the
Commons was to find the national interest, not just to speak for local interests,
what was important was diversity, rather than that each town or city be represented directly. This argument also made diversity of franchise a virtue, since it
led to diversity of representation.

The first step toward eliminating this system was taken by the Reform Act of
1832. Many rotten boroughs were eliminated, and new towns were given representation. The electorate was not significantly increased in size, but it was "rational-
ized," introducing reason into a field that had previously been governed entirely
by tradition. With this reform, Britain was clearly on the road toward a modern
democratic electoral system, but its incremental nature illustrates how earlier institutions and practices exert effects long after their original justifications become
obsolete.

Modern Parallels

There is an obvious parallel between Athenian democracy and modern manifesta-
tions of direct democracy such as the extensive use of the referendum in Switzerland or the New England town meeting. And the Athenians' problem of poor
turnout finds reflection in these modern situations as well. Perhaps more significant, however, are the less obvious parallels. The Athenian belief in turnover in
office has its modern parallel in the movement in the United States for short
terms of office and severe limitations on reelection. While ostracism has no modern parallel, the problem it addressed, the inability of one set of insecure leaders
to tolerate the presence of its rivals, has been one of the major reasons why newly
established democracies have collapsed into authoritarianism.

Roman elections, and the problems the Romans confronted, have striking
resonance in twentieth-century America, but even more in nineteenth-century
Europe. The advice given by Cicero's brother to avoid taking a stand on the
issues for fear of making enemies is precisely the advice given by many twentieth-

century admen attempting to "merchandize" a candidate. Cicero's own justification of the plutocratic features of the centuriate assembly is repeated in justifications of a property requirement for voting throughout Europe in the nineteenth
century and is especially mirrored in the system of plural voting in force in Belgium in 1893, whereby although the majority of adult men could vote, the majority of votes were cast by the minority possessing more than one vote. In a system
based on clientelism, the Romans were pioneers in the area of campaign finance
legislation similar in concern, if not in detail, to contemporary legislation. And,
of course, the Romans were masters of the gerrymander.

The church was the originator of such devices as qualified majority voting
used, for example, in the procedures to amend the American constitution. The
strongest parallel to church elections is, however, not to be found in the west, but
in the people's democracies of the second world and the guided democracies of
the third. In all three, there is presumed to be a single "correct" resolution to
questions, whether it be defined by God, historical/economic science, or the spirit
of the nation. Thus in all three there is an obsession with unanimity, and thus in
the modern cases dissent becomes barely distinguishable from treason, just as the
dissenters at the Council of Nicea could be dealt with only by excommunication.
And again underlying all this is the notion that elections are held to confirm, not
to determine, decisions.

Of the four electoral systems discussed here, only the British was concerned
with the choice of representatives. As such, it is the precursor of many of the
modern problems of representation. In particular, the idea that representatives
are chosen to speak for communities, not just for isolated individuals, continues
to be raised as a counterargument to demands for strict population equality in
single-member districts. On the other hand, the idea of virtual representation
finds resonance in the idea that guaranteeing the election of minority candidates
in a few districts will somehow solve the problem of minority representation
overall.

Obviously, these few suggestions of connections between historical and modern electoral systems barely scratch the surface. Underlying them is a fundamental continuity. In the modern west, attention tends to focus on either or both
(often apparently ignoring their potential incompatibility) of two functions of
elections: to produce a stable government controlled by the wishes of the people
and to produce a legislative body accurately reflecting the distribution of opinions
and interests found among the people. Nonetheless, the values that were primary
in earlier systems continue to be reflected in the institutions inherited from them
and continue to play an important, if now secondary, role in modern assessments
of democratic institutions.

Popular Sovereignty

H ere, the People rule." It would be hard to find a better epigram to sum up the idea of popular sovereignty. But what does it mean for the people to rule? One immediately may distinguish two quite different answers. The first takes ruling as a physical act to be performed by the people themselves, rather than being delegated to a smaller political class. This Athenian sense of democracy was supported as a means of avoiding tyranny. Direct popular participation has also been supported as the best way to advance a variety of other values. One is the human development of the citizens, and rule by the people in the sense of their direct participation in governing will be a central concern of chapter 5. In this case, the benefit is presumed to lie in the process of governing, not in what is done but in the fact that the citizens do it.

Alternatively, the people could be said to rule if policy is made and implemented so that "the will of the people" is carried into effect. Here democracy is a property of outcomes rather than of processes. This answer assumes that government is a matter of will or free choice, although not necessarily simply the aggregation of raw preferences. The problem is whose will is to prevail. Clearly for a democrat, it must be the will of the people.

What then is meant by the will of the people? In broad terms, there are two families of answers based on different conceptions of society. On one hand is the collectivist tradition. Society is an organic whole in which each person has a proper place. Legitimate differences are based on functional differentiation, with each segment making an equally necessary contribution to the whole. In some conceptions, groups may be structured hierarchically while other conceptions will accept only horizontal differentiation. In either view, these differences contribute to the uniting of groups into the social organism and to its survival, rather than to its disintegration. The social organism has an interest that, when the society is democratic, that is, when its component members are fundamentally equal, is the popular will, or in Rousseau's term the general will. The supposed existence of this single popular will does not preclude the possibility of disagreements about what ought to be done. These, however, are attributed to two pathologies: ignorance and self-interest. In the first place, people are not equal in their knowledge and foresight, and so they may disagree about their common interest or how to pursue it. In the second place, the long-term common interest of all may not coincide with the short-term private interest of each. The collectivist democrat believes that under the proper conditions, individuals would identify themselves so firmly with the collectivity that they would prefer the common interest. The popular will that ought to prevail is the will the people would express in circumstances that allowed them to rise above their self-interests in order to find the common interest.

The other family springs from an individualistic tradition. Society is no more than the sum of its members. Real conflicts of interest cannot be obviated by some deeper understanding. Self-interests are the only interests. The so-called national interest is simply the aggregation of the private interest of each citizen. The "popular will" is merely an aggregation of the individual wills of the people. The problem of government is not to transcend private interests but to cope with them.

The individualistic conception of society has its most immediate intellectual roots in nineteenth-century liberalism. Its fundamental assumptions—an atomistic view of society and the belief that individuals can, do, and should pursue their private interests—are shared by capitalist economics. One might expect this to lead naturally to a liberal theory of democracy, the subject of the next chapter.

That people pursue individual self-interest does not mean, however, that they must pursue it individually, nor does it necessarily entail a minimalist state. Some things that might be valued by some people are by nature public goods. One characteristic of public goods is that they are likely to be underprovided, or not provided at all, if left to voluntary agencies, even if everyone would like to see the public good provided.[1] One way to overcome this problem is to use the power of the state to compel cooperation. Thus even a unanimous citizenry may want an active state. If expression of the popular will requires less than unanimous support, the possibility that its implementation will require government is even more obvious.

Further, "the people" may want to use the state to do things other than produce public goods. The classical economic defense of liberalism is that in a free market the pursuit of individual self-interest will produce the greatest possible total value of goods and services. This is self-evidently good only within the economic paradigm. People may pursue many other goals, and it is not clear that liberty will maximize their attainment. Nor is it clear that total value, irrespective of distribution, is the only proper evaluative standard. To say this, or to say that people ought not to be able to use public power to pursue private goals, requires attention to values beyond popular sovereignty.

Another way of approaching the meaning of the popular will suggests a metaphor. Both the collectivist and the individualist conceptions of popular sovereignty equate the popular will with the decision the people would make in an idealized "town meeting." What they mean by this and what they expect the outcome to be differ. For the collectivist, the idealized aspect of the town meeting metaphor is the regular participation of rational citizens in the collective task of governing themselves, which, it is postulated, will produce in citizens a sympathetic involvement in one another's welfare. Through intensive interaction, each citizen will perceive the common interest as his own so that unanimity that reflects a true meeting of minds will result. In this ideal case, the collectivist need not worry about aggregating conflicting preferences, and the resultant unanimous decision is the popular will.

Discussion is important for the individualist as well since it allows people to assess possibilities and to understand the likely consequences of alternative courses of action. It may even convince some people to change their preferences. It is not, however, the crucial part of the metaphor. That comes after the discussion, when the problem is to arrive at a single collective decision. The central requirements are that each individual be able to act for his own interests and that each individual have equal weight in determining the final outcome.

These town meetings represent ideal models; they obviously are unrealizable. Even in Athens, most citizens did not attend most assemblies. In a modern state, the problems of allowing direct debate and decision by the citizens are insurmountable. While modern means of communication might make the physical assembly of the citizens unnecessary,[2] sheer weight of numbers renders the idea impractical; if only 1% of a population of one million were to speak for only one minute each, it would take over 10 16-hour days. In addition, to acquire even a superficial knowledge of the number and complexity of questions that governments currently are expected to manage is a full-time occupation. Citizens cannot devote all their time to studying public issues if anything else is to be accomplished. The first problem in devising political institutions that will allow the people to rule is to devise a decision-making process that approximates the results of these idealized assemblies yet requires no actual meeting of everyone.

One solution might be to empower a subset of citizens selected by lot. In a very limited sense, this process is institutionalized in the ever growing prominence of the sample survey. Surveys, however, do not allow for interaction among respondents; they are more likely to tap individuals' private wills than the general will, and indeed questions usually are framed with precisely this intent. Even from the individualist perspective, their value is limited since each respondent is constrained by a fixed question format. Moreover, surveys leave the real decision-making authority with officials who are free to decide for themselves whether to take the popular advice or ignore it.

This last problem is cured by the binding referendum, which allows the citizens to make authoritative decisions, but faces many of the other problems of the sample survey. Voters can respond only to a set question. Although a campaign likely surrounds a referendum, it more likely revolves around factional interests than the general will, so the result will be of questionable legitimacy from the collectivist perspective. And both the frequency and number of referenda are limited for practical reasons. Thus, while the referendum may be a valuable supplement to other institutions, it can be no more than a corrective device for decisions ordinarily made elsewhere.

If these devices are impractical, what then is left? The virtually universal answer has been government by elected representatives. One justification for representative government is exactly this kind of ex adverso argument. John Stuart Mill, for example, is not atypical in mentioning representation only once in a chapter entitled "That the Ideally Best Form of Government is Representative Government," and that in the final sentence—"But since all cannot, in a community exceeding a single small town, participate personally in any but some very minor portions of the public business, it follows that the ideal type of a perfect government must be representative."[3] This is not the only justification, however. The town meeting metaphors are predicated on a number of empirical assumptions that are, in fact, false. Representative institutions also have been justified as means of overcoming these deficiencies and arriving at decisions that are more like those that the ideal people would have reached in an ideal assembly than are those that the actual people would reach even if they could be assembled.

Because representative government is expected to solve problems beyond the impossibility of direct democracy, representation becomes a complex concept in democratic theory. At least in part, to choose an appropriate meaning of representation is to say what elections ought to do; to specify the function of elections is to define representation. The choice depends both on the values to be served and on the presumed nature of the world. At this point, each of the two major approaches to popular sovereignty divides into a number of specific theories.

Collectivist Popular Sovereignty

If the intellectual roots of individualist popular sovereignty theories lie in nineteenth-century liberalism, those of the collectivist tradition go back to the medieval conception of a society composed of classes or estates rather than atomistic individuals. In theory, decisions should have been made with unanimity *within* the estates, although not necessarily with the unanimous assent of every member of every estate. In fact, only the rich and well born counted; most people were excluded from the nation in whose interest they were ruled. The medieval system of estates was based on a fundamental inequality of men; democracy assumes a basic equality of worth. A democratic "nation" must include everyone.

How could the medieval notion of a single national interest be extended to a democratic nation? In highly simplified terms, there have been two answers. One is adaptation of the Roman principle that the will of the majority is the will of the collectivity. This interpretation goes beyond simple majority rule in which the majority, by virtue of their greater numbers, are entitled to prevail. Instead, the majority *is* the collectivity, just as if the minority did not exist at all. This view developed into the plebiscitarian system that few currently would accept as democratic.

The other answer came through the gradual adaptation of medieval politics, by broadening the base of participation and by expanding the scope of the nation. Competitive elections, ultimately with mass suffrage, became the hallmark of democracy. The underlying assumption of a single national interest remained, as

did the notion that this interest has an existence independent of private preferences so that some—in medieval terms the sanior pars—might be better able than
others to perceive it.

This version of popular sovereignty theory has been most influential in Britain. Of course, many features of the British models are reflected in other ideas
about democracy, and others reflect concerns beyond popular sovereignty. Nonetheless, the apologists for and activists in the major British parties have constructed two unusually developed and distinctive collectivist conceptions of popular sovereignty and how it can be institutionalized.

Tory Popular Sovereignty

Only in the ideal town meeting would everyone be able to perceive the general
will. That variant of collectivist popular sovereignty theory most clearly associated
with the British Conservative Party (at least until the ascension of Margaret
Thatcher to the leadership) is based fundamentally on this observation coupled
with a belief in "the need for strong and stable government first."[4] The task, thus,
is to put those who are best able to identify and pursue the national interest into
office with sufficient independence to do so. The system is democratic because
the authority of the government rests on the consent of the people, but it is not
government by the people.

The role assigned to the ordinary citizen by Tory popular sovereignty theory
is reactive rather than active. The argument for limited popular participation goes
beyond the negative assertions that governments must have independence to be
effective and that the people are not able to decide issues intelligently. In addition, leadership is required to call the will of the people into being. Thus the
outcome of this frankly elitist system, in which leaders pursue their own views of
the national interest, can be defended as being more democratic—in the sense of
rule in accordance with the national interest or general will—than could be expected were popular opinion to play a more directive role.

The idea that the government "is an independent body which on taking
office assumes the responsibility of leading and directing . . . the nation in accordance with its own judgement and convictions"[5] is the modern democratic
translation of ideas dating from the Middle Ages. Governing—making and implementing policy—is the function of the Crown.[6] This is as true today as it was in
Tudor times, although control over the exercise of the power of the Crown has
shifted from the monarch to the cabinet. This evolution has been gradual, continuing into the current century, but fundamentally it was a predemocratic development.

Accompanying this process, however, was a shift in the body to whom those
exercising the power of the Crown are accountable. Initially, the Crown was accountable only to the monarch, who personally judged the national interest; the
Parliament's role was to act as the agents of the people in consenting to taxes and
in voicing grievances. Later, the unreformed Parliament became the voice of the
nation, with the government accountable to it. The range of issues over which
consent was required broadened to include all legislation, but the function of the

Parliament in the Tory view remained to consent to, or withhold consent from, the initiatives of the Crown (ministry), not to initiate or direct policy itself. Finally, the system became democratic when the ministry became accountable to the people at large through elections with universal suffrage.

This theory denies both the possibility, and the desirability, of equality of political influence. Governing is not necessarily the highest human calling, but it "is a task requiring high and exceptional talents in the governor. To govern . . . is a 'specialized vocation' requiring a 'habit of mind' which can be acquired only by 'specialized preparatory training' in home and school."[7] There must be, therefore, a political class, with sufficient economic and social security to take an enlightened, but detached, view of the public interest and able to rule "with the effortless grace which inspires loyalty without loss of self-respect in those who are ruled."[8]

In practice, this argument may be only special pleading on behalf of those currently on top. The claim that the political class must have certain privileges in order to rule responsibly can turn easily into the claim that those who are better off have a right to rule, just as the claim that ability to govern must be cultivated can become an argument for a hereditary and closed political caste. If, however, one takes a more open and meritocratic view of the political class— denying, for example, that an upper-class education is necessary and sufficient proof of fitness to govern—it is simply the argument that the public interest is best served if those who have the necessary aptitude govern.

This system gives the voters power, but it is the power to choose a government rather than the power to choose a line of policy. Opinions regarding the policies pursued by the government in office may influence a voter's decision to support or oppose it, but the real question is its prospects for success in handling the unforeseen crises of political life and in pursuing the national interest. The decision to retain or dismiss a government is primarily a matter of confidence in the abilities and judgment of those who govern.

The Tory ideal would be characterized by a deferential electorate, interests represented by and channeled through the established institutions of society, and no structured parties. Having accepted the institutions of twentieth-century politics—mass suffrage, interest groups, and organized parties—the Tory conception of democracy still has a number of implications for the organization of politics and the conduct of campaigns. The first is the requirement of two parties. On one hand, this implication follows from the natural division between government and opposition, that is between those whose function is to exercise the power of the Crown and those whose function is to criticize and claim that they could do better. On the other hand, commitment to a two-party system follows from the importance of strong and stable government. The government must command a secure majority; only a two-party system can provide an organized alternative to the party in power while guaranteeing a party with a majority.

The second implication is that parliamentary parties ought to be cohesive and loyal. This does not mean passive acceptance of everything the leader proposes; suggestions and constructive critiques are part of the job of loyal subordinates, and ultimately the party may withdraw the consent by which the leader holds his position. Short of this option, however, the final decision rests with the leader.

If the role assigned to the parliamentary party in setting policy is limited, the role of the extraparliamentary party is even more so. Mass suffrage made it necessary for leaders to organize their supporters in the electorate. Nonetheless, they remain supporters of the party, but do not assume control of it. The leader should emerge from a consensus of the parliamentary party as interpreted by its most prominent members[9] and has the primary responsibility for setting party policy. Although the mass party, like the parliamentary party, is free to debate policy and to adopt resolutions, its resolutions are only advice to the leader.

It is the function of the electorate to judge the relative fitness of alternative teams of leaders. A fourth implication, thus, is that the competition between parties ought to be based on confidence rather than policy promises. To try to attract supporters by catering to their whims would be to abdicate the responsibility of office. The question for the voter is which team has the greater capacity to serve the nation, not which will pursue the policies he or she would adopt personally.

From this perspective, the role of Parliament is to act as a training ground and recruitment pool for future leaders, an automatic transmission belt for putting into office that team of leaders who have won the support of a majority of the constituencies, and a forum for competing leaders to conduct a permanent electoral campaign. This role reflects the Parliament's displacement by the electorate as the body to which governments are responsible. Rather than making the Parliament superfluous, however, this frees it better to exercise its historic function of voicing grievances and speaking for the various "interests" that constitute society. One of the most important interests is the local community, and each MP should speak for the interests of his or her community. Constituencies ought to be real communities with coherent interests, not just areas defined because they contain a certain number of voters. Furthermore, the MP should represent all the residents of a constituency, not just those who support the MP's party.

Socialist Popular Sovereignty

Even though society naturally is divided into classes in the Tory view, there is no natural conflict of interest among them. It makes sense, therefore, both practically and in terms of democratic theory, for the people to leave "predominant political control in the possession of those who are by descent, by character, by education, and by experience best fitted to exercise it."[10] The fundamental premise of the socialist theory of popular sovereignty is that both these claims are false. Although differences of ability in politics are inevitable, not only would all citizens see the national interest in an ideal world, but all citizens can contribute to its identification in the real world.

Socialists also reject the assumption of harmony among the classes. Instead, contemporary society is divided into two major classes, the bourgeois and the proletarian, whose interests naturally conflict. On its face, this disharmony would appear to exclude this theory from the collectivist tradition that posits a single general will. The answer is that, although there are two conflicting interests, only one is legitimate, and the true national interest is precisely the interest of the working class.

If the working class embodies the true will of the people, what is the status of the other class? In broad terms, there are two possible responses. The extremist approach would be, in effect, to declare the bourgeois class excommunicate and anathema. On the other hand, one can take a less personal stance. Although the bourgeois interest is illegitimate, as is the private ownership of capital on which it rests, the capitalists themselves are not beyond redemption; those in error can be converted. The vanguard working class represents the entire society, so that although it is rooted sociologically in a single class and advocates policies in the immediate interest of that class at the immediate expense of others, a working-class party "is not a sectional party; it represents the long-term interests of all the constructive elements in the community." [11]

This distinction has obvious implications for strategy in achieving the socialists' objectives. The view that the supporters of capitalism are implacable enemies is difficult to reconcile with competitive politics. The implications of this view are considered in chapter 6. The alternative position is that socialism can and should be achieved through competitive elections, which would legitimize socialist rule, even among its erstwhile opponents. [12]

The socialist conception of society is basically bipolar. Those who do not live solely by labor or solely by rents represent intermediate cases, not additional interests. Further, although there are differences within each class, the conflicts of interest these engender are trivial in comparison to the overwhelming common interest of the members of one class as opposed to the other. Party is the political manifestation of class. Hence, the bipolar nature of the class system implies two parties.

The party program is fundamentally important to socialist popular sovereignty theory. The program of the working-class party is to be the "will of the working class," which, because of the identity of the interest of the working class with the interest of society, is the general will. The party exists primarily to articulate, to agitate for, and to implement its program. Unlike the Tory, who expects the electorate to choose a set of leaders, the socialist expects the electorate to choose a program. Hence, electoral competition should be primarily programmatic. Moreover, the program must be spelled out with sufficient clarity and detail that the voters can know what they are choosing and that the party, therefore, can claim a specific mandate and can add to its assumption that its program represents the general will the further claim that its program is the preference of the majority.

Of course, problems will arise that were not foreseen in the party's manifesto, and the manifesto may promise policies found unworkable in practice. The party must seek a more general mandate to govern, but always in accordance with its general principles and program. Elections are not primarily contests among leaders, and even less among local candidates. They are contests between alternative programs, with leaders committed to implement their programs and candidates pledged to support their programs and leaders. Clearly, the party's personnel in government ought to be united, since it is the party rather than any individual member that has been given a mandate.

From where does the program to which all must give loyal support come? Here the other difference between socialist and Tory theory comes into play. While for the Tory the ultimate source of policy is the leader, for the socialist it is the working class, and in particular its political arm, the mass party. Thus, where for the Tory the mass membership association is merely the organized supporters of the leadership, for the socialist it is the party's authoritative policymaker.

In principle, this belief means that the party conference and the executive that it elects have the right to dictate policy to party members in public office. In practice, this right has been a continuing point of dispute between the party in Parliament and the leaders of the party conference, with the former pointing to their responsibility to the public and the latter to the party's constitution. In terms of the socialist theory of popular sovereignty, the problem resolves into three subquestions. First, who has the authority to establish the party program? Second, who has the authority to decide precisely what the party program means in practical terms and how it ought to be put into effect? Third, does the membership have the authority to impose policies on its elected officials that were not articulated in the party program at the time they were elected? Only on the first point is the answer relatively clear. Here, authority clearly lies with the mass party, although they may judge it prudent to heed the advice of the party's officeholders and candidates. The latter are not obliged to adhere to the program if they think it imprudent, but then they ought not to stand as party members, and the party executive would be justified in expelling them. The second question is the most difficult. Even if the officeholder is primarily an agent of his party, one can argue consistently that the parliamentary party is the proper *party* organ to interpret the manifesto on which they stood. With regard to the third question, the argument that the party is entitled to impose its policies on society because they were specifically approved by the electorate cannot be applied to policies that were not part of its manifesto. Although the conference or the executive may be the proper bodies for articulating party policy, the party has no mandate for policies that were not part of the manifesto. Thus the parliamentary party can claim that their public responsibility as elected officials entitles them to use their own judgment even if they were elected as party representatives. Of course, in both these cases the party remains free to expel its parliamentary representatives.

Like the Tory version, the socialist version of popular sovereignty is a type of responsible party government. The meaning of responsibility is different, however. For the socialist, it is loyalty to the party and its program so that voters can exercise prospective control by choosing one party or the other. The official exercises his individual responsibility in deciding whether to be a party candidate in the first place.

On the function of elections in collectivist popular sovereignty theories, the Tory and socialist theories share a crucial perspective. In neither case are general elections the way to discover the common interest or popular will. For the Tory, the common interest is articulated by the ruling class. For the socialist, it is articulated by the working class, organized in a political party. For each party, the electoral victory of the other does not negate the legitimacy of its own position; it merely means that the electorate is mistaken.

If elections do not determine the popular will, and if they entail the risk of loss to reprehensible opponents (for the socialists, to the party of the exploiters and promoters of the haves over the have-nots; for the Tories, to the party of sectional interest over the national interest), why have them? For both sides the reason is fear of the alternative. If they agree on nothing else, both parties agree that the alternative to continuing the system of competitive elections is revolution, dictatorship, repression, and the use of terror as a weapon.

What, then, do elections accomplish? First and most important, they legitimize a government by demonstrating that it has the consent of a majority. For both these theories, this means a single party with a coherent program (socialist) or a cohesive team of leaders (Tory) and an absolute majority of seats in Parliament. The electoral system must be perceived as sufficiently fair that those who are unhappy with the outcome of a particular election nonetheless accept the winner's mandate as legitimate. This requirement extends beyond the simple translation of votes into seats to all aspects of the electoral system.

Second, elections must allow for turnover in office. Aside from the fear that one party might be the permanent opposition, both theories are compromises based on the belief that permanent dominance by one party would lead to violence by the other. More importantly, a party securely in a permanent position of power would lose the incentive to stay in touch with the public and to act responsibly.

Third, elections result in representatives who become channels of access to the central government. For the Conservatives, this means having representatives of the major established interests, whereas for Labour it has meant putting at least a sprinkling of "real" workers into Parliament.

Finally, it will be useful to return to the ends, in addition to determining the general interest, that elections are not expected to accomplish. They are not expected to produce a Parliament that mirrors the distribution of opinion in the country, nor are they expected to allow individuals to express the full complexity of their opinions. They are not expected to force accountability by individual MPs to individual constituencies or to allow the people to determine party policy or to choose among individuals or shades of opinion within a single party. Instead, they are expected merely to give the people a choice between alternative conceptions of the public interest.

Individualist Popular Sovereignty

In collectivist theories of popular sovereignty, elections do not define the popular will. For them, the popular will does not depend on the preferences individuals express in society as currently structured. Individualist theories, on the other hand, define the popular will in terms of the individual preferences or interests of the citizens. (The distinction between preferences and interests made in collectivist theories breaks down here because each person acts as the only judge of his or her own interests, which, by assumption, he or she must prefer. On the other hand, a distinction sometimes must be drawn between preferences and expressed preferences.) Elections provide the institutional framework for aggregating expressed preferences into a collective decision. In place of the collectivist question "Who knows the popular will?" is the central individualist question "How can individual preferences be aggregated into the popular will?" This problem would exist even in a town meeting, and so this discussion can begin without reference to problems of representation.

The problem of popular sovereignty is to specify a decision rule for which the input is an expression of citizens' preferences and the output is a single social choice. The rule that seems most obvious for a democracy is simple majority rule,[13] which counts everyone equally. Given a choice between two alternatives and barring exact ties, it always produces a unique decision. If more than a majority is required, neither alternative may be adopted; if less than a majority is sufficient, both alternatives may have the required support. Simple majority rule is neutral with regard to the status quo, which is important since a "nondecision" is in fact a choice of that alternative. Finally, as a consequence of the other properties, simple majority rule maximizes the expected number of citizens who win.[14]

On the other hand, simple majority rule has at least three important problems.[15] First, it uses only the preference order of the voters, ignoring their intensity of feeling. Thus, although it maximizes the number of voters who expect a net increase in utility, it may not be utilitarian in the full sense. The majority who win may be nearly indifferent, whereas the defeated minority may be nearly as large and feel very strongly.

Second, with more than two possible choices, simple majority rule, which is a binary choice procedure, cannot be applied directly to choose among them. Extension of the majority principle to these cases involves more problems than the possibility that the votes may be split so that no one choice obtains a majority. The most consistent extension of simple majority rule to choice among several possibilities is the Condorcet criterion—that possibility which can defeat each of the others in a series of pairwise contests under simple majority rule is the Condorcet majority choice. But no such possibility may exist. If there are three possibilities, A, B, and C, and three voters—one who prefers A to B to C, a second who prefers B to C to A, and a third who prefers C to A to B, then by successive votes of two to one, A is chosen over B, C over A, B over C, A over B, etc. This problem is not limited to simple majority rule, for as Arrow has shown, no social decision rule other than dictatorship or complete social indifference always will produce a transitive social ranking of possibilities from transitive individual preference rankings while simultaneously satisfying minimal ethical criteria.[16] Nor is it limited to artificially constructed and unbelievable sets of preference rankings. Instead, unless severe restrictions are placed on allowable individual preference orders, cyclical majorities will almost certainly appear and include the social "first" choice.[17]

Cycles rarely appear in practice because comparisons of all pairs of possibilities are rarely made. Although most politicians may be unaware of the theoretical basis of the paradox of voting, however, skillful ones are all too aware that by manipulating the agenda, they can manipulate the outcome. The choice of a majority has very little claim to legitimacy if it rests primarily on the order of voting.

Third, the votes cast may not reflect true preferences. In the example above, if the third voter's preference ranking of choices A and B were reversed (i.e., C preferred to B preferred to A), B would be the majority choice over either A or C, both by votes of two to one. Suppose the order of voting is A against B and then the winner against C. Clearly, B should win the first round of voting and then win the second as well. But the third voter can induce a result more to his or her liking by concealing his or her true preference on the first vote, choosing A instead of B. Then A wins the first vote and is defeated by C on the second. Thus the third voter, by voting for his or her last choice on the first vote gets his or her first choice on the second, even though B is the Condorcet choice. Just as the popular will should not depend on the agenda, neither should it depend on skill in playing political games.[18]

These problems are not unique to the decision-tree method of adapting majority rule to the case of several possibilities. Two other methods are sufficiently widespread to deserve special comment. The first is the run-off system. Each voter chooses one of the possibilities. If one receives an absolute majority of the votes, it is chosen (and must be the Condorcet choice if everyone votes sincerely). If not, a second vote is taken between the top two vote-getters from the first round, thus ensuring one of an absolute majority. This only assures selection of a possibility preferred by a majority to *one* alternative; it might lose by a majority to every other alternative.

The second system, simple plurality rule, suffers from exactly the same difficulties. Even if there is a potential Condorcet choice, it may be defeated by a possibility that is the first preference of very few and the second preference of no one at all. Supporters of any possibility except one of the two they expect to be the most popular are encouraged to desert the possibility they really approve to vote for the less obnoxious of the possibilities they think might be selected. In cases where choice is to be made from among many alternatives, this system depends on rather sophisticated guesswork by the voters, each of whom must try to anticipate the reactions of all the others. Even after this strategic voting, however, there is no guarantee that either of the two top vote-getters—the choices for which strategic voters have deserted their real preferences—actually are popular.

Binary Democracy

The easiest way to minimize the importance of the paradox of voting is to deny the legitimate existence of situations in which the problem would arise. Most simply, one could assume that social choice is binary. As Duverger put it, "the two-party system seems to correspond to the nature of things, that is to say that political choice usually takes the form of a choice between two alternatives. A duality of parties does not always exist, but almost always there is a duality of tendencies. Every policy implies a choice between two kinds of solution."[19] In this case, simple majority rule will guarantee selection of the solution that has the best claim—still ignoring the problem of intensity of opinion—to be called the popular will.

Translated into the institutions of representative democracy, this argument leads to yet another version of the responsible two-party government model. Clearly there must be exactly two parties; one party would give the voters no choice, while restricting choice to two parties assures a majority choice. Each party is to represent one of the two tendencies that Duverger posits. They should, therefore, take clear and distinctive positions on public questions. Although the voice of the sovereign people is not "limited to 'Yes' or 'No' " as in Schattschneider's formulation,[20] it is limited to "this" or "that." But since "this" and "that" are *the* two alternatives, this vocabulary is adequate to give the people control over government policies.

The control envisioned here is both prospective and retrospective. On one hand, voters choose a party on the basis of their relative preferences for the policies they expect it will pursue in office, based in part on its promises for the future, and in part on its performance in the past. On the other hand, voters also can punish parties for failures of policy or failures to honor their promises. Even this retrospective control should have prospective consequences, however. First, it provides an incentive for parties to keep their word; the threat of retrospective punishment in the future encourages responsibility in the present. Second, although it may not be fair to punish a party for unsatisfactory outcomes that were not its fault as well as for breaches of faith that were, punishing it nonetheless both relieves voters of the obligation of determining whether disaster was the result of bad management (in which case they should vote for the other party), bad policies (in which case they should vote for other policies, but the party in power may change its stand as well), or bad luck (in which case no conclusion can be drawn) and gives parties an incentive to improve the beneficence, as well as the popularity, of their programs.

Nothing can be put into practice, however, unless each party is united. Only by acting together can party members control all the levers of power and enact their program. Moreover, if the party is not cohesive, how can it, or any of its officeholders, be called to account? Each can blame the others. Not only may too many cooks spoil the broth, it becomes impossible to blame any one of them for the foul taste and pointless to try to improve it by changing one cook at a time.[21]

Only what Austin Ranney has called the "little civil war about 'intraparty democracy' " is left.[22] Should the party's leadership determine its policies, or should its mass members or supporters?[23] If one opts for internal democracy, the result is very much like socialist popular sovereignty, except that there is no implied connection between the party and a single social class and the party program gains its legitimacy only through electoral victory. As in the socialist theory, this need not mean that members control everyday decision making. Nonetheless, the leadership must be held accountable. Unless party organizations are democratic, the popular will, through the perversity or ignorance of the party elite, may not be presented as an alternative. Also, an uncontrolled party oligarchy, acting through campaigns and traditional loyalties, could distort opinion so that a determination of the autonomous popular will becomes impossible.[24]

The alternative view is based on a number of arguments. One suggests that internal democracy is incompatible with party cohesion, another that internal democracy will confuse the voters, in part because the party will appear to speak with many voices, and in part because, as majorities shift within the party, its position will change. A third argument supposes that leaders are better able than their followers to formulate effective, popular policies in the public interest. Finally, some have argued that internal democracy is impossible but that its sham appearance is more dangerous than to accept democracy as free competition between two avowed oligarchies. To pretend that party members can rule the party diverts their attention from that which they can do, control the government.

Downsian Democracy

Although many public questions are two-sided—whether to build an MX missile, whether to provide public support for religious schools, whether to provide government-funded health care—many are not. Indeed, even these examples lead immediately to questions that do not involve only two sides: how many missiles should be built, how quickly, and at what cost? What schools should be supported, at what level, and with what conditions? What level of health care should be provided, to whom, and how should it be organized? If possibilities like these are allowed, a new solution to the problem posed by the paradox of voting is required.

Suppose that all possible outcomes can be arrayed along a single dimension so that each voter's preference ranking of those outcomes is single-peaked.[25] If each voter, given a choice between two alternatives, always votes for the one he or she more prefers, then there is a Condorcet choice and, if the voters are ordered along the same dimension according to their first preferences, it is the first preference of the median voter. Since this is the best majoritarian definition of the popular will, the problem becomes designing institutions that will ensure its adoption.

Suppose that voters and issues satisfy these conditions and suppose further that parties compete by each associating itself with one point in the unidimensional issue space. The last implies that each party must be cohesive. Each party's point, or platform, represents the policy it promises to pursue if elected. Each voter then chooses the party that offers him or her the highest expected return on the investment of a vote. In the full Downsian model, this is represented by a complex calculation involving the desirability of the party's platform, its credibility, and the probability that the voter's vote will make a difference to the outcome, but here we can use Downs' simplest model, in which each voter chooses the party whose platform he or she most prefers, only bearing in mind the credibility qualification as providing an incentive for a victorious party actually to implement its platform.

The final assumption of the Downsian model is that parties are single-minded seekers of office. Platforms are adopted solely for their electoral utility; a party is presumed to change platforms if it sees a chance to increase its likelihood of success. In most democratic theories, this kind of unprincipled votemongering would be a cause for condemnation; Downs turns it into a virtue, arguing that if two parties compete, desire for electoral success will lead them to converge on the policy that is the Condorcet choice. This result depends on precisely two parties; with more than two parties, there will not be a stable equilibrium at the Condorcet choice. Thus, like the binary model, Downsian democracy calls for two cohesive and policy-oriented parties, although in the binary model the policy orientation of the parties is inspired by ideological commitment whereas here it is purely instrumental to office seeking. Moreover, where the binary model assumes voters will choose between two parties with distinctive platforms, when the Downsian model is working ideally, the parties' platforms will be virtually identical.

The driving force of the Downsian model is that while voters are motivated by policy, parties are motivated by office. Policy motivation on the part of politicians is an impediment to achieving the popular will, since it may restrain parties from converging on the Condorcet choice. For this reason internal democracy is incompatible with Downsian democracy. While it may be reasonable to assume that those who, if victorious, will assume office are motivated themselves primarily by that concern, it is not reasonable to extend this assumption to ordinary voters who could not hope to share substantially in the private advantages of victory. As Downs himself says, if a party is internally democratic, "actions taken by the party as a whole are likely to form a hodge-podge of compromises—the result of an internal power struggle rather than any rational decision-making." [26] Alternatively, if one simply extends the Downsian argument to the intraparty case, the best one could hope is that each party will be frozen at the first preference of its own median voter.

Ostrogorskian Democracy

The assumption of a single underlying dimension is a gross oversimplification. Likewise, even if there are only two sides to each issue, there are not the same two sides to all issues. Although perhaps a single dimension could so predominate that one could proceed as if the Downsian model (or the binary model) applied in full, this is still a very strong assumption. If one abandons it and allows for several important but independent bipolar issues or issue dimensions, however, there will be a Condorcet choice only under the most fortuitous circumstances. Nonetheless, if the majority principle is to be retained, some acceptable system of making popular decisions must be found. Basically, two approaches are possible—to deal with issues in the electoral arena one at a time or all at once. In either case, one is led to give up the ideal of two cohesive and durable parties.

The case for dealing with issues one at a time was made by Moisei Ostrogorski as the conclusion to his monumental study of nineteenth-century democracy in England and the United States. He was disturbed by the degree to which permanent parties became frozen in their organization and policy positions, which, in becoming antiquated, also became both blurred and irrelevant. Most fundamentally, Ostrogorski rejected the idea that a single party could represent adequately the popular will over a range of issues. His solution was to eliminate permanent parties, replacing them with organizations created by citizens to deal with a single problem and dissolved by them once that problem was settled. The problem of citizens being forced to choose between one of two overall policy composites would be solved and a different majority might decide each issue. "Party holding its members . . . in a vice-like grasp would give place to combinations forming and re-forming spontaneously, according to the changing problems of life and the play of opinion brought about thereby."[27]

The Ostrogorski theory makes heavy demands on "amateur" politicians among society's leaders. They are required to recognize a problem, decide on a solution, organize with other like-minded citizens, campaign, and if victorious put their solution into effect. Moreover, as soon as a new problem arises, all this effort is to be abandoned and the process renewed. The theory also is based on an extremely optimistic view of the capacities of ordinary citizens. Without the cues provided by standing loyalties to party or leaders, they must understand and decide each issue.[28] It also assumes that government can be controlled by a series of amateur administrations. But if each administration is replaced as soon as a new problem arises, "what is to prevent the constant replacement of elective officials from leading to sheer chaos, or, failing that, to a situation in which the real power of government will come to vest in permanent, irresponsible administrative officials, who alone can promise the continuity and cohesiveness necessary for the conduct of the affairs of a great nation?"[29] Moreover, it assumes that problems will arise singly at a leisurely pace, each amenable to a discrete solution after which it will politely disappear. At least in the twentieth-century context of managed economies and large-scale social service and regulatory programs, such an assumption is untenable.

Legislative Democracy

If voters cannot resolve multiple issues one at a time, the only alternative is for them to confront several issues simultaneously. This task still could be done with a "responsible two-party system" in the sense that, if each party took a stand on each issue, the inevitable majority victory of one or the other of them would settle all the questions, at least until the next election. That qualification points, however, to the first problem with this system. While at any single election between two parties one or the other must achieve a majority, over time this is the scenario for the paradox of voting. Thus, that one party achieves a majority neither legitimizes its program nor provides any stable resolution of issues, leaving policy in a constant state of flux. Moreover, a majority of voters could choose a party whose platform represents the minority view on *every* issue.[30]

Imagine a small number of citizens assembled in a town meeting. If they tried to adopt a single resolution to decide simultaneously a number of independent issues, they would confront immediately the paradox of voting with its cyclical majorities and all the attendant problems just discussed. Likely, however, they would not attempt to do so. Rather, they would, as Ostrogorski proposes, manage issues one at a time. In this case, assuming that each issue involved preferences that were either binary or single-peaked, they would avoid cyclical majorities, although the other problems associated with simple majority rule would remain. They would also face two further avenues of manipulation.

The first concerns the definition of issues. Consider the relatively simple problem of establishing budget allocations for two discrete areas, defense and education, for example. Although these budgets can be specified variously in terms of two issues, two ways seem especially reasonable. One method would be to decide the allocation for defense and then to decide the allocation for education (or conversely). The other method would be first to establish a total budget for the two items and then to divide the total. The problem, as illustrated in Figure 3.1, is that the two methods do not produce the same results. Assuming sincere voting, with the first method the Condorcet choice for education is six million while for defense it is five million. With the second method, however, the Condorcet choice for the total budget is 12 million rather than 11 million, with that figure divided equally between the two areas.

The second possible manipulation involves vote trading. Suppose in this example that C feels far more strongly about a high defense budget than he or she does about a low education budget while F feels more strongly about a high education budget than a low defense budget. In this case, each can secure an outcome more to his or her liking by trading votes; C supports F's position on education and receives in return F's support for defense. As this example is constructed, the outcome under either decision strategy is for each policy area to receive a budget allocation of seven million. Of course, this is not the only trade possible.

Is this a problem which institutions must face, or is it a strength of direct democracy that ought to be carried over to representative institutions? One view is that vote trading is a positive process that solves the problem of intensities by allowing each citizen to exchange his or her influence on an issue about which he or she cares little for the influence of another on an issue about which he or she cares more.[31] Thus, after a series of trades, the total welfare of the citizens ought to be maximized.

Critics claim that this argument ignores a fundamental difference between a market in votes on public issues and a market in economic goods and services. While ignoring externalities (costs imposed on individuals by actions not under their control) is possible in economic analysis, it is not analogously possible in political analysis. In particular, in classical economics one can assume the consent of all parties affected by a transaction. The deduced beneficence of the market depends on this assumption; all transactions benefit someone and hurt no one or they would not have been entered into.[32] On the other hand, the changes in public policy brought about by vote trading affect everyone and, if decisions are made by majority rule, need not have the consent of everyone. Externalities imposed on nontraders may be significant. Indeed, a series of trades could be entered into, each beneficial to those who make it, but the aggregate result would be harm to everyone.[33] Individuals acting rationally in their own interests nonetheless bring ruin on all.

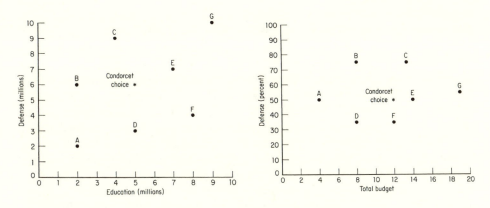

FIGURE 3.1
Allocation of Defense and Education Budgets Under Alternative
Agendas

Moreover, in a sense this debate is irrelevant to the subject under discussion here. Logrolling may produce decisions that are not Pareto optimal in comparison to majority rule without vote trading, but so may majority rule in comparison to the status quo. In neither case does suboptimality lessen the majoritarian claim that the resulting decision be called the popular will.

If vote trading or other forms of compromise across issues would affect the outcome of a town meeting, allowance must be made for them in the representative institutions designed to discover and implement the popular will in a mass democracy. This requires a representative assembly that is, in effect, the entire citizenry in microcosm. With only one issue to be resolved, it was necessary only that the right party have a majority. Whether it was a bare majority or totally excluded the minority was beside the point.[34] If, however, the deals struck in the assembly are to duplicate those struck in a town meeting, the actual distribution of opinion among the citizens must be reflected in the assembly.

Vote trading does not eliminate the problem of the paradox of voting, and indeed under certain conditions is its logical equivalent.[35] Decision making by constantly shifting coalitions of representatives does not solve the problems associated with majority rule; it merely displaces them from the electoral arena to the legislative. This shift has a number of implications for the organization and operation of representative institutions. The previous discussions tacitly have assumed a parliamentary system, but would be compatible with a presidential system so long as the legislature is controlled by the party of the president and the presidential and parliamentary wings of the party are united.[36] As the name implies, legislative democracy is incompatible with presidential government. A single individual cannot represent a series of different coalitions; the same is true of a collectively responsible cabinet. Legislative democracy requires instead individual responsibility on the part of executives each responsible for a different policy and to a different coalition. Similarly, legislative democracy cannot exist with only two cohesive parties. In principle, no parties are required; in practice, implementation of legislative democracy ordinarily will call for a multiparty system with each party standing for a different combination of policies across different issue areas.

In general terms, the function of the electoral system in each of these theories is to put into office individuals who are so selected, organized, and motivated that they will put the popular will into practice. Precisely what this means depends on how the popular will is to be defined and found. Taking binary democracy as the norm or starting point, this most straightforward notion of popular sovereignty calls for competition between two cohesive and durable parties, with parties primarily interested in advancing specific policy goals and voters attracted without regard to sociological distinctions on the basis of the policy promises of the parties. Each of the other theories implies the negation of one of these five conditions. In Downsian democracy, parties pursue office rather than policy. In Ostrogorskian democracy, parties are not durable. In legislative democracy, there are more than two parties or the parties are not cohesive. Tory popular sovereignty calls for voters to decide on the basis of confidence rather than policy. Socialist popular sovereignty is predicated on class solidarity.

Finally, before leaving the subject of popular sovereignty, two alternatives to the conflict model implicit in majoritarian decision making deserve brief comment. In fact, each entails problems that lead inevitably back to some variant of majority rule. The concerns they reflect, however, may have a significant bearing on how those majority decisions are made.

Binary democracy clearly pits a coalition of winners against a coalition of losers. The same is true of Ostrogorskian and legislative democracy, although in the former case the membership of the winning coalition is expected to change over time while in the latter it is expected to change from issue to issue. There is no guarantee, or even concern with guaranteeing, that any particular person or group will ever be on the winning side. Downsian democracy guarantees moderation, but from the viewpoint of those not in the middle of the distribution of opinion, this is just another way of saying that they always lose. Would not a better notion of popular sovereignty assure that each individual or group saw its view prevail a fair proportion of the time?

The word "fair" in this formulation presents an immediate and intractable problem. If every citizen wanted something different, and if every citizen were equally dissatisfied when any view other than his own prevailed, fairness would present no problem; it could mean only that each citizen had an equal chance of having his view selected as the social choice (and a lottery would be the only possible social choice mechanism). In the real world where neither of these premises is true, however, a lottery means that those whose views are closely shared by a large number of their fellow citizens will be more satisfied more of the time than others. On the other hand, giving each viewpoint rather than each citizen an equal chance of selection simply encourages trivial differentiation and a return to the same problem.

Deciding everything on the basis of the roll of the dice is a rather perverse notion of the sovereignty of the people, but, unless everything were resolved by lottery, another problem would arise. Assuming one knows how often any individual ought to get his or her way, on which particular issues ought individuals to prevail? Presumably, this could be resolved though compromise, issue trading, and side payments. The objective would be to arrive at an overall package that satisfied everyone, or at least to which everyone would consent. What if there is irreconcilable conflict? In fact, this notion is tantamount to requiring unanimity and will be discussed more fully in the next chapter. Suffice it to say here that it is better adapted to restraining government than to directing it. It encourages citizens to overstate their intransigence as a bargaining tool. Moreover, unless one is prepared to accept the terribly conservative consequences of unanimity as a decision rule—thus allowing those who are most happy with the status quo to prevail most of the time—there must a way of overruling intransigent minorities. But this problem immediately returns one to the conflict model of politics.

The other alternative is utilitarianism. The problems here are well known. How does one define utility? If one person decides, then he or she is effectively a dictator and in any case one still must decide how that person is to be chosen. If more than one person decides, all the old problems of collective choice must be confronted anyway. The obvious solution is to let each individual judge utility personally, but this solution raises the problem of interpersonal comparisons. Further, it gives each individual an incentive to exaggerate intensity of feeling.

One way to deal with this problem would be to decide arbitrarily that the utility of each individual would be counted equally. He or she could then express relative preference among the possibilities from which a choice was to be made. Three devices to accomplish this end have been proposed and illustrate the problems involved. The oldest is the Borda method. If there are n possibilities, each voter gives n points to his or her first preference, $n-1$ points to the second preference, and so forth. The possibility receiving the greatest total number of points is selected. The principal problem is that the choice may depend on irrelevant alternatives. A slightly more flexible method would give each citizen some number of votes that could be distributed among the possibilities in any way he or she chose. While this method might have some use in elections where several representatives were to be chosen at a time, if only one choice can be made, the only intelligent strategy is for a citizen to give all his or her votes to one possibility, in which case the system is just majority rule. Finally, one could insist that each citizen assign all possibilities to one of only two utility categories, good enough or not good enough. The possibility regarded as acceptable by the greatest number of voters is selected. This is the system of approval voting.[37] Again, this system is better suited to liberal democracy than to popular sovereignty. In arbitrarily assigning equal weight to every individual over the possibilities being considered, each of these systems defeats the fundamental purpose of utilitarianism. Moreover, each is just another variant on the conflict model.

Liberal Democracy

In the liberal democratic view, "Democracy is a political *method*, that is to say, a certain type of institutional arrangement for arriving at political—legislative and administrative—decisions and hence incapable of being an end in itself, irrespective of what decisions it will produce under given historical conditions."[1] The value is liberty. Democracy is supported because people believe that it will ensure liberty better than any other political method, but that support is conditional. More than being a liberal theory of democracy, liberal democracy refers to attempts to find a democratic implementation of liberalism.

One can analyze liberal democracy without regard to its historical and sociological origins, but the various liberal democratic theories are easier to understand if one notes two key features of their past. First, liberal democracy and capitalism have been closely connected. They have been the dominant political and economic ideologies, respectively, of the same people, they share a common conception of the nature of man and society, and indeed some people have argued that one is necessary for the other. Second, liberal democracies were liberal before they were democratic.[2] They were created by democratizing already established liberal systems, in particular by expanding the right of suffrage.

Both liberal politics and liberal economics are based on an individualistic conception of society and on an egoistic conception of man. What counts is the welfare of individuals, and each individual seeks to maximize his or her own welfare without regard for the welfare of others. Whereas earlier thinkers regarded such men as depraved or vicious, however, capitalist economists turned their avarice into the force driving economic progress. For the competition of self-interested individuals to produce the maximum aggregate social gain requires that two conditions be satisfied. First, competition must be free; each individual must be able to sell goods or labor and invest capital to maximize the gain for himself or herself; the only standard of value is what someone is willing to pay and the only standard of fairness in a transaction is that all parties entered voluntarily.

Second, each person must be secure in his or her property, or the incentive for work and investment disappears.

Liberal democracy carries much of the capitalist market ideology into the political arena, in particular, its emphasis on rights, including property rights, and faith in competition. On the other hand, there is one crucial difference. Whereas economic avarice, the love of money, could be turned into a social virtue to be exploited and encouraged, political avarice, the love of power, remained a vice to be contained. Although the liberal solution to containing the love of power, pitting ambition against ambition in free competition, is similar to economic competition, its objective is opposite and complementary. Fundamentally, the liberalism of liberal democracy is restraint of government. This emphasis on restraint fits nicely with the liberal economic conclusion that government interference can only undermine the efficiency of the market. It also reflects the perceived economic self-interest of the capitalist class in its political struggle with the mercantilist successors of feudalism. Liberalism developed as the political theory of the "out" class and thus naturally reflects its fear of those in power.

Although liberals characteristically remark, "If men were angels, no government would be necessary,"[3] liberal theory denies the possibility of such angelic humans, from which it follows "that government is necessary to the existence of society and society to [man's] existence."[4] Government must have power if people are to be secure in their life, liberty, or property. Yet government must be restrained because the love of power that makes one person dangerous to another makes government a danger to all. The fundamental dilemma is how to give the state enough power to protect individuals from one another while preventing it from tyrannizing over them. Liberal democracy is that elaboration on liberalism per se that solves the dilemma by making rulers responsible to the people through periodic, freely contested elections.

The defense of rights is the central principle of liberal theory. Three points require elaboration. The first is that the liberal notion of rights is negative. A right is freedom from outside compulsion or restraint, rather than a guarantee of the ability to do something. Thus, liberal freedom of the press means freedom from censorship, not guaranteed access to a press. In general, rights define areas of activity from which the state is excluded.

The second point is that rights cannot be absolute. Transactions in the market are justified by the consent of all parties to them. Political liberalism, however, is a system of government, and government necessarily involves forcing some people some of the time to do what they would not do voluntarily. The state must be able to deprive criminals of their property, their freedom, or even their lives without their consent if others are to be secure in their lives or property. More generally, government must be able to tax and to make a variety of other decisions contrary to the interests (and thus potentially to the rights as they see them) of some people if it is to survive. However, unless restraints are placed on the state's ability to take actions prejudicial to the interests or rights of the people, no right can be secure.

Finally, although not all liberal theorists use the term, one way of expressing their view is to say that they want to minimize the likelihood of tyranny, defined as any unjustified deprivation of rights. In fact, the core notion of tyranny in liberal democratic theory is more restricted, not any unjustified deprivation of rights, but especially any deprivation of rights by the state. Preventing tyranny thus means preventing the state from excessively or unjustifiably restraining an individual.

In contrast to the traditional view of an organic society in which government was an important and directing constituent pursuing the common interest, and in contrast to the later popular sovereignty view of government as a tool of the people in the pursuit of their own or the common interest, liberals see government as necessary for social life but also as set apart from the rest of society and potentially, or even naturally, opposed to its aggregate interest. Two related ways of seeing this reflect two strands of liberal democratic theory. First, in a world made up of opposing interests, the government and the governing class may be seen as forming an interest of their own. Just as the interests of worker and employer, or buyer and seller, are naturally opposed, so are the interests of the governed and governors. Second, even if government itself lacks interests that might lead to exploitation or tyranny, it might be taken over by some combination of interests that would try to use its power tyrannically.

Moreover, the conflict of interest between the state or those who control it and the rest of society is particularly worrisome. In the economy (in theory), for example, the interests of all parties are protected by freedom of contract; anyone dissatisfied with a proposed transaction can opt out. The relationship between government and the governed is different. One cannot opt out of laws as one can opt out of contracts. Moreover, contrary to the implicit assumption of equality among contracting parties, the state and the citizen are vastly unequal partners. Not only is the government a potential enemy of the rights and interest of the governed, it is a particularly dangerous one.

It follows from liberalism's "grand governing principle of human nature [that] every government would be rapacious unless it were made in its own interests not to be so, or impossible for it to be so."[5] Liberal democratic theories deny that government constraint can be accomplished by constitutional prohibitions alone. Instead, primary reliance is placed on the distribution of power in society, and in particular on redressing the imbalance of power between the state and the citizens. Institutionally, this works by having the rulers chosen and periodically removable by the ruled in freely contested elections. The democracy of liberal democracy refers principally to the extension of the right of suffrage to the vast majority of the adult population.[6] The power given to the people by these theories is to be defensive rather than directive. Liberal democracy tends to be more concerned with avoiding potential evils than with achieving potential benefits, more concerned about sins of commission than about sins of omission.

Although at the cost of ignoring many subtle distinctions within categories and of exaggerating the clarity of the distinctions between categories, one can identify three basic types of liberal democratic theory, based primarily on their conceptions of the divisions among groups in society. Within each type, one can distinguish two subtypes. In each case, one subtype stresses the dangers of unrestrained government while assuming a relatively high potential for political understanding among the general public. Although these theories recognize the possibility that government could fall into the hands of some interest or coalition of interests that will oppress the others, all are especially concerned with the danger of tyranny imposed by the class of officials qua officials. The alternative subtypes, derived from twentieth-century empirical research, emphasize the apparent illiberalism and incompetence of the mass electorate. Representative democracy thus is positively superior to direct democracy (which theories of the first subtype reject only on the grounds of impossibility) because it limits the direct influence of ordinary people. Though still concerned with the need to control and limit public officials, these theories take a far more positive view of the role of elites and of their need for independence.

As for the main types, the first assumes an unstructured citizenry. Even though conflicts of interest on particular questions will arise, they will be unrelated across interests. Simple majority rule will be adequate to prevent tyranny since oppressive majorities will not form. Theories that rely simply on popular election to prevent tyranny may be called collectively "majoritarian liberalism." The second and third types perceive society to be made up of many interests, but with a potential for organization and enduring structure. Thus to the danger that the governors will oppress society must be added the possibility that an enduring majority will form and will act through its representatives to oppress the minority. In the second view, "pluralist liberalism," to prevent such a majority from forming or from being effective is possible by a variety of devices while still retaining the basic majority principle. This possibility rests, however, on the assumption that the cleavages among interests are fluid and cross-cutting, rather than fixed and mutually reinforcing. The third type, "veto group liberalism," assumes instead a segmented society. Whatever majority forms will likely endure and oppress the minority. Thus the only guarantee against tyranny is to abandon the majority principle and to require the consent of *every* significant social group for all policies.

Majoritarian Liberalism

Benthamite Radical Liberalism

One of the first liberal democrats was Jeremy Bentham. Like liberal democracy in general, he was a liberal first, and only later became a democrat. Throughout his writing, he was primarily a utilitarian; the basic moral principle for him was to produce the greatest good for the greatest number. Both his liberalism and his commitment to democracy derived from that principle.

Utilitarianism involves two intractable problems. The first is that of measurement with its core dilemma, the noncomparability of the utilities or happinesses of different people. The second is that the principle of the greatest happiness for the greatest number does not tell one how to judge cases in which the greatest aggregate happiness would be achieved by one policy but the greater happiness of a majority would be achieved by another. In effect, Bentham solved both problems by ignoring them. Occasionally recognizing that some people, or even classes of people, might be more sensitive than others, he concluded that each individual must be counted equally since otherwise "it would be impossible to form a single general proposition." As for measurement, although he lists a great variety of pleasures, Bentham tended to identify happiness with money. The equation was by no means direct—Bentham conceded that "the excess of happiness on the part of the most wealthy will not be so great as the excess of his wealth"[7]— but for practical purposes he often ignored the distinction. Allowing money to be the unit of comparison for happiness, and tacitly resolving the dual maximum problem in favor of the greatest aggregate wealth, Bentham could easily arrive at liberal capitalism as the best economic system. Moreover, the tripartite position of wealth as the substance, measure, and producer of happiness and of the capacity for happiness permeates Bentham's political thought as well. In particular, the dangers of "bad rule" that most concerned him were threats to property.

The principle of utility defines what ought to be done; it does not guarantee that it will be done. All liberals presume protecting the weak from the depredations of the strong, as well as protecting everyone from external threats, to be among the central functions of government. Who, however, would protect society from the government? The only solution is to make the selfish interests of the governors coincide with the interests of the governed.

From this principle, Bentham arrived at a definite prescription: "The only species of government which has or can have for its object and effect the greatest happiness of the greatest number is . . . a democracy: and the only species of democracy which can have place in a community numerous enough to defend itself against aggression at the hands of external adversaries, is a representative democracy."[8] The central problem is that "force, intimidation, and remuneration are . . . necessary to all rule," but also give to the government the capacity to oppress the governed. "The problem is,—throughout the whole field of legislation, how to prevent the sinister sacrifice: leaving at the same time unimpaired, both the will and the power to perform whatsoever acts may be in the highest degree conducive to the only right and proper end of government."[9] How can this be done?

One solution would be to give power to public-spirited altruists who independently would pursue the greatest happiness of the greatest number. "If there were any other [than the governed] individual or set of individuals, by whose conduct the only right and proper end of government were likely to be in a greater degree promoted . . . such other individual or individuals would be those in whose hands the greatest-happiness principle would require that the exercise of those same powers should be lodged." But it follows from the basic liberal assumption about human nature that there can be no such individual or set of individuals.[10]

Alternatively, one might rely on the weight of religious or other moral sanctions. These, however, are inadequate except in a democracy. On one hand, given the ability of those in power to control the climate and expression of opinion as well as the institutions of religion, these sanctions might become instruments of oppression in the hands of the rulers, "giving facility instead of applying restriction to misrule." On the other hand, the threat of such sanctions, "of all ideas that are capable of presenting themselves to a ruling mind, the most disagreeable, the most hateful and afflictive" will lead to "a war which, until either the form of government be made to give way to the democratical, or the people reduced to the condition of beasts, . . . can never cease." [11]

Thus the only possible solution is to give the people direct power over their rulers by making the latter removable at frequent intervals in elections. Where each holder of public office "not only was placed, but at a short interval is displaceable by the subject many, what he sees from first to last is, that any considerable and lasting sacrifice of their happiness to his own is impracticable: and that for every attempt to effect it he would be liable to be punished." [12] Elections, thus, are the central linchpin of Benthamite political liberalism.

The most radical reform that Bentham proposed was essentially universal suffrage. [13] In its defense, he argued first that the people had the necessary moral and intellectual aptitude to select their rulers, and moreover that this aptitude would continually increase. Further, each being primarily interested in securing himself against depredation and oppression, no candidate or citizen, "for the gratification of any sinister desire at the expense of the universal interest [could] hope to find co-operation and support from any considerable number of his fellow-citizens." [14] Bentham's reliance on the fitness of the ordinary voters is illustrated by his insistence on a secret ballot to assure that each voter expressed his own genuine opinion. This faith in the virtue and self-restraint of ordinary citizens is one essential feature of the Benthamite theory.

The other reform that requires mention was Bentham's proposal for annual elections. The purpose was to facilitate "divesting of their power all unfit representatives, before they have had time to produce any lasting mischief." [15] Earlier, Bentham argued that "no practical bad *effect* can be produced but by a *lasting majority* of the House." [16] This argument highlights two more essential features of Bentham's majoritarian liberalism. First, organization is dangerous because it leads to the possibility of lasting majorities. Second, the primary concern is preventing bad effects and removing unworthy representatives, rather than producing good effects and choosing the best rulers possible.

Schumpeterian Democracy

In the end, Benthamite democracy can only be defined institutionally; it results when the principal officers of government are chosen in free elections with effectively universal suffrage. On this, modern majoritarian liberals agree. They agree that democracy so defined is desirable, because it will likely produce outcomes broadly satisfactory to the people and prevent tyranny as well. But where Bentham saw representative government as a necessary compromise, modern liberals see it as absolutely superior to direct popular rule. "If results that prove in the long run satisfactory to the people at large are made the test of government *for* the people, then government *by* the people . . . would often fail to meet it." [17]

Bentham and his followers assumed that people could and would think rationally about politics. Modern liberals, based primarily on survey research, assert that voters in actual democracies do not. Voters have ill-formed, poorly informed, unstable, and mutually incompatible opinions on most issues. Their votes are determined largely by nonrational forces. Their belief in liberal democratic values does not extend beyond limited recognition of platitudes; given a concrete situation, ordinary people see nothing wrong with abrogating freedom of speech, press, or religion for those with whom they disagree. Intellectually, "the typical citizen drops down to a lower level of mental performance as soon as he enters the political field."[18]

The general incompetence of the public has two important implications. The first is that the people cannot, do not, and should not rule themselves. At best, they can react to proposals and decisions made elsewhere. Leadership plays a vital role in this theory, and leaders require wide discretion to govern effectively. Indeed, it can be argued, in direct contrast to Bentham's call for annual elections, that elections should not be too frequent, since frequent elections would force political leaders to pay excessive attention to voters' opinions. Voters are competent to judge results, but leaders must be given an adequate term of office with adequate discretion to produce results.

The second implication is that some protection against the appeals of demagogues is necessary.[19] This comes first from the process of elite recruitment; each generation of political leaders is screened by its predecessors through the process of selective advancement. To make a successful political career in a modern democracy requires the support of party leaders, but they will systematically filter out those aspirants who are not "safe." Being safe requires a commitment to liberal democratic values, which research has shown to be more prevalent among the elite than among ordinary citizens. (In contrast to the Benthamite view that favored popular involvement in the selection of candidates, this view is consistent with nominations by party caucus.) Further, the oligarchic control over the channels of political recruitment exercised by the democratically committed elite is reinforced by the inertia of the electorate, particularly as manifested by party identification. This situation reduces the intensity of political conflict, gives established elites room to maneuver, and makes the rapid swings of opinion that might allow a demagogic outsider to come to power unlikely. Thus, ironically, precisely the vices said to make direct democracy impossible become virtues.[20]

Some critics claim that this conception of democracy is so elitist as to make it a sham democracy. The Schumpeterians respond that they are merely being realistic. Moreover, they claim that while they envision a limited role for the people as a whole, the political activity and influence of each person is limited not by the system but by his or her own choice. The crucial condition is not that everyone participates, but that everyone who wishes to participate is afforded the opportunity. "[D]emocracy is 'the power of the active demos,' which amounts to saying that power resides in those who avail themselves of it."[21] As for "the iron law of oligarchy," Schumpeterians claim it is irrelevant, for "democracy on a large scale is not the sum of many little democracies."[22] Competition for votes forces teams of elites to be attentive to the needs and interests of the public and thus is sufficient, and indeed superior to more direct popular involvement. "Precisely in the best instances, the people are presented with results they never thought of and would not have approved of in advance."[23]

Both Benthamite and Schumpeterian liberalism look to the electoral process to prevent tyranny, but because they see the principal threat and the principal bulwark in different locations, their detailed prescriptions differ. For the Benthamite, all leaders are potential tyrants, and all voters, seeing every threat to liberty as potentially inimical to their own interests, are guardians against tyranny. Voters are able to judge the worth of candidates and the likely consequences of their proposals. Hence Bentham called for annual elections in which the voters would make prospective judgments. Organizations of candidates (i.e., parties) and loyalties to parties are all suspect as potentially sinister combinations. Thus, while the Radicals did form a party, they were never prepared to accept party discipline as appropriate.[24] In contrast, the Schumpeterians call for comparatively infrequent elections, reflecting their belief that the mass poses at least as much of a threat to liberty as the elite. The decision of the voters should be based only on what they are competent to judge—results—and thus should be primarily retrospective. Parties must be organized both to facilitate the recruitment-by-cooptation by means of which the continuing democratic commitment of elites is assured and to enable leaders to govern effectively.

At this level, Schumpeterian liberalism appears quite similar to Tory popular sovereignty. There is an important difference, however. Schumpeterian liberalism perceives real conflicts of interest, not, as for the Tory, a manifest national interest. Thus, although Tory popular sovereignty does not propose that parties should compete on the basis of policy promises, it does assume that parties are, in Edmund Burke's terms, groups who intend to promote the public interest "upon some principle on which they are all agreed." For the Schumpeterian, although promises and issues may be tools in a campaign, a party itself is simply "a group whose members propose to act in concert in the competitive struggle for political power."[25]

Pluralist Liberalism

The starting point for pluralist liberals, in contrast to the homogenized society of the majoritarians, is that each citizen actually is part of a complex pattern of groups based on affinity, proximity, ascription, or interest. Society is composed of groups, not just individuals. Thus the possibility of a majority combination forming and becoming tyrannical must be considered along with the problem of tyranny by a minority.

Madisonian Democracy

One early version of pluralist liberalism was the argument made principally by James Madison in the debate over the proposed Constitution of the United States. Its starting point is the same as that of Benthamite liberalism. If unrestrained, any individual or group will maximize its own wealth and power unjustly at the expense of others; that is, it will be tyrannical.[26] One of the primary functions of government is to protect citizens against exploitation by others. Therefore, the principal danger is that the government itself will become tyrannical. The problem is to devise a political system strong enough to protect against foreign threats and domestic insurrection, able to protect individuals and to promote the general welfare, yet unable to tyrannize over its citizens. From the liberal perspective, primary concern must be directed toward the limitations on, not the powers of, the government.

Analogous to Bentham's concern with sinister interests is the central Madisonian concern with the evils of faction. In the case of factions consisting of less than a majority, the Madisonians shared Bentham's belief that popular election provided an adequate check. The great problem is to control the effects of a majority faction.

The Madisonian argument involves three ways of limiting the danger from a majority faction. The first is representative government. By passing public views "through the medium of a chosen body of citizens . . . it may well happen that the public voice, pronounced by the representatives of the people, will be more consonant to the public good than if pronounced by the people themselves." But Madison recognized the possibility that "the effect may be inverted. Men of factious tempers, of local prejudices, or of sinister designs, may, by intrigue, by corruption, or by other means, first obtain the suffrages, and then betray the interests, of the people." [27]

The second limitation on the danger of majority tyranny derives from a large republic. In the first place, Madison makes the dubious claim that "as each representative will be chosen by a greater number of citizens in the large than in the small republic, it will be more difficult for unworthy candidates to practise with success the vicious arts by which elections are too often carried." [28] Far more crucial to the pluralist position, however, is his second claim. "Extend the sphere and you take in a greater variety of parties and interests; you make it less probable that a majority of the whole will have a common motive to invade the rights of other citizens; or if such a common motive exists, it will be more difficult for all who feel it to discover their own strength, and to act in unison with each other." [29] Although factions may be able to control local majorities, they will be unable to extend their influence throughout a large, diverse country.

Finally, even should a national majority faction develop, its influence can be contained by restricting the scope of the elective principle. While accepting that government must "[derive] all its powers . . . from the great body of the people" and that "the persons administering it [must] be appointed either directly or indirectly by the people," [30] most of the appointments to office in the original Madisonian system were to be indirect. In the Constitution for which Madison was arguing, only one house of the legislature would be elected directly. The other legislative chamber would be chosen by the state governments; the president would be chosen by an electoral college; popular selection of judges would be even more remote, as they were to be appointed by the indirectly elected president and confirmed by the indirectly elected Senate. Thus a national faction would have to maintain its majority for some time before it could capture control of the entire government, a feat Madison implied would be impossible.

Assuming that the system just outlined would be able to "guard one part of the society against the injustice of the other part," it is still of "great importance in a republic . . . to guard the society against the oppression of its rulers." [31] This, the Madisonians argue, can be done only if power is divided. "The accumulation of all powers, legislative, executive, and judiciary, in the same hands, whether of one, a few, or many, whether hereditary, self-appointed, or elective, may justly be pronounced the very definition of tyranny." Presumably this follows from the natural inclination of people to be oppressive. To concentrate all power in the same hands would give the rulers the capacity to be tyrannical. Inclination plus capacity inevitably would lead to action.

Although this syllogism precisely follows an analogous argument of Bentham, one major premise is diametrically opposed. Bentham claimed that elections were sufficient to prevent rulers from behaving tyrannically, but Madison denied this argument. He accepted a number of arguments Bentham dismissed about the undesirability of frequent elections.[32] More important, he allowed for the possibility of a majority faction that could control elections. Appeals to the electorate could not be depended upon to prevent the legislature from dominating all other branches of government nor from becoming an instrument of tyrannical rule. Hence, where Bentham supported an omnipotent legislature, the Madisonians perceived the greatest danger precisely from a too powerful legislature.

If frequent elections are insufficient in themselves to restrain leaders, so too are constitutional limitations. Rather, "the great security against a gradual concentration of the several powers in the same department, consists in giving to those who administer each department the necessary constitutional means and personal motives to resist encroachments of the others. . . . Ambition must be made to counteract ambition. The interest of the man must be connected with the constitutional rights of the place."[33]

What exactly does this mean? One possibility, suggested by Dahl, is that "individuals in one department can invoke the threat of rewards and penalties against tyrannical individuals in another department."[34] Having ruled out moral sanctions and such factors as loss of status, respect, prestige, and friendship, whose utility as checks Madison specifically denied, and the power of money, whose use as a check the Constitution strictly limited from fear of an overpowerful legislature, Dahl turns to the question of physical coercion. This too he dismisses as implying that the republic would always be on the verge of violence and civil war and especially as leaving unanswered the question of why any group, whether a majority or a minority, with control over the means of coercion would refrain from tyrannizing over the rest. Dahl's conclusion, then, is that "the Madisonian argument is inadequate."[35]

However, another interpretation is possible. Notwithstanding talk about separation of powers, the Madisonian scheme in fact calls for the sharing of powers. Rather than being independent within its own sphere, each branch requires the cooperation of the others. The check each branch was given over the others was the power to prevent an encroacher from *legitimately* exceeding his authority. The pitting of ambition against ambition and the tying of personal interest to the "constitutional rights of the place" were to give each branch the incentive to protect itself.

As seen, liberals in general and Madison in particular are not overly impressed with legitimacy per se as a restraint on human rapaciousness. Given a choice between a low-cost but illegitimate way of achieving one's aims and one that is legitimate but more costly, the liberal presumes choice of the former. Separation of powers, however, is intended not only to determine the legitimacy of actions but also their costs. Each branch has the power to force the others to respect its authority and to cooperate and compromise with the interests it represents because it is cheaper for the others to achieve their own aims with its consent than without. While the threat of force may linger in the background, it need not intrude on ordinary politics.

It is unclear whether the "accumulation of all powers . . . in the same hands" refers to the officials themselves or to the interests they represent. Both the context and the attention to private motives suggest the first. If so, then an important problem has been overlooked. Although officials in different departments may have conflicting interests in some respects, they will also have a significant common interest in their shared capacity as government officials. Moreover, they are relatively few and communicate regularly, just the conditions that Madison suggests will allow the members of a faction to recognize their common interest and to act in concert. There is ample evidence that, for example, incumbent legislators do act as a faction to provide themselves with generous perquisites,[36] but Madisonian theory sidesteps this possibility.

What of the role of elections? Most obviously, they must allow the majority to prevent a minority from winning control of the government. This majority veto, however, is a far cry from giving the majority positive control. Indeed, once the problem of minority tyranny has been solved by having one organ of government directly reflect the will of the majority, elections should contribute to the control of potential majority tyranny. This implies different modes of election and different bases of representation for different departments of government in order to prevent any one transient majority from gaining control of the whole.

All the supposed benefits of separation and division of powers and a large and diverse republic could easily be overridden by organization. In particular, parties could bridge the divisions within government and organize stable majorities in the electorate. The original Madisonians were positively hostile to the idea of political parties, which represented to them the political embodiment of faction.[37] Before many years had passed, parties came to be recognized as necessary, inevitable, and legitimate, but only as loose affiliations of primarily local groups. Whereas policy-oriented prospective campaigns by individual candidates are compatible with Madisonian democracy, disciplined parties are not. Instead, the system requires that each official represent the interests of his or her own, unique, electorate.

Polyarchal Democracy

The twentieth-century revision of Madisonian democracy may reasonably be called polyarchal democracy, using Robert Dahl's term for those real-world systems that approach the democratic ideal.[38] I propose to use the term in more restrictive terms than his, referring to a particular theory about *how* systems come to approximate that ideal, but conforming closely to his treatment of the United

States as a polyarchy. The only serious discrepancy is that I regard consociational democracy (the modern version of veto group liberalism, discussed later) as an alternative to polyarchal democracy, but Dahl regards it as an alternative form of polyarchy.

Polyarchal democracy differs from Madisonian democracy in at least three crucial respects. First, and most centrally, it differs in its attitude toward special interest groups. For Madison, these were the very essence of faction and therefore to be deplored and controlled. For the modern pluralist, such groups are not only legitimate but necessary for polyarchy to exist. Thus the first institutional guarantee listed by Dahl for *each* of the three defining opportunities of polyarchy (to formulate preferences, to express preferences, to have preferences weighed equally) is "freedom to form and join organizations."[39] In particular, whereas the early Madisonians were hostile to political parties, polyarchy would be unthinkable without them. Second, polyarchal theorists see the interest structure of society as far more complex than did the Madisonians. It is not much of an exaggeration to suggest that the Madisonian system recognizes only two classes of interests, those related to wealth and those related to locality; the limited use of direct popular election was intended to protect the rich from the poor while the various territorially relevant provisions of the Constitution (e.g., equal representation of the states in the Senate and the limitations on the power of the national government) were to protect minority areas. Even though modern pluralists recognize these interests as important, they do not accord them preeminent status. Especially the recognition of interests not tied to local communities has suggested that selection of representatives from territorially defined constituencies *cannot* be sufficient to ensure articulation, let alone protection, of all interests. Finally, while continuing to accept the importance of political institutions, including those to which Madison gave primary attention, the theory of polyarchy is far more concerned with the sociological preconditions of continuing liberal democracy. Polyarchal theorists are most concerned with how social forces shape the operation of institutions, whereas Madison looked to institutions to control social forces. Nonetheless, although modern pluralists have less faith in the power of institutional arrangements, a fundamental similarity remains. Madison assumed institutions to be important because they would affect the self-interested calculations of the rulers. Similarly, rational calculations by leaders play a key role in the theory of polyarchy, but the costs, benefits, and possibilities are influenced more importantly by social than by institutional forces.

The concerns of the theory of polyarchy mirror the twin concerns of Madisonian liberalism about the exploitation of society by its rulers and of one group in society by another. One central question is the relationship between government and opposition. What conditions favor or impede the development and maintenance of a regime in which opponents of the government can openly and legally form parties to oppose the government in fair elections?[40] When will opposition be tolerated, and when will it be suppressed? The other central question is the ability of any group, whether nominally a supporter or an opponent of the particular politicians in office, to assure that its interests are taken into account in the formulation of public policy. Here the toleration of opposition is assumed, and the ideal is summarized by Parenti's "school room" version of American democracy. "The role of government is to act as a mediator of [different groups'] conflicting demands, formulating policies that benefit the public. Although most decisions are compromises that seldom satisfy all interested parties, they usually allow for a working consensus; hence, every group has a say and no one chronically dominates."[41]

Not being suppressed is different from having one's interests taken into account, but the theory of polyarchy argues that the first inevitably will lead to the second. The reasoning by which this conclusion is reached within the framework of contested elections and majority rule requires additional assumptions about the nature of social cleavages. Indeed, precisely these assumptions distinguish polyarchal democracy as a subclass of pluralist liberalism, as the terms have been used here, from consociational democracy.

The polyarchal theory assumes that the likelihood that opposition will be tolerated increases with the cost of suppression and decreases with the cost of toleration. Hence, "[t]he more the costs of suppression exceed the costs of toleration, the greater the chance for a competitive regime."[42] What conditions assure that the expected costs of suppression are likely to exceed the expected costs of toleration?

Suppression is costly when those to be suppressed have the means to resist. The resistance may be active, as in strikes, riots, or rebellion, or it may be passive; in some cases, mere failure to exert oneself will be a costly sanction. From the other side, suppression is less costly when government has effective use of the means of coercion, primarily violence and socioeconomic repression. Thus polyarchy is more likely when the military is removed from politics[43] and when control over the economy is diffuse rather than centralized. In general, diffusion of political resources among many groups will increase their capacity to resist while decreasing the government's capacity to suppress.

As well as providing the ultimate guarantee of liberty by making suppression too costly to attempt, a pluralist social order also provides the basis for peaceful competition. The institutional guarantees that define polyarchies are empty unless the negative freedom from restraint, for example in organizing groups, is coupled with the positive capacity to make use of these opportunities. In this vein industrial society is said to be conducive to polyarchy; industrialization leads to high levels of literacy, reduces the extremity of economic inequalities, increases the variety of resources relevant to politics, and leads generally to greater social pluralism. One likely consequence is a system of dispersed inequalities. Groups that are relatively poorly endowed with one resource will be better supplied with another; labor, although lacking money, has the resource of numbers, while for the capitalist class just the reverse is true.

Of course, the capacity to resist suppression is also the capacity to resist other policies. Likewise, the resources used to compete also could be used to rebel. The theory so far is a recipe for permanent strife, moderated, however, by two additional factors. The first is a social system in which the cleavages defining social groupings crosscut one another. In Lipset's view, "the chances for stable democracy are enhanced to the extent that groups and individuals have a number of crosscutting, politically relevant affiliations. To the degree that a significant portion of the population is pulled among conflicting forces, its members have an interest in reducing the intensity of political conflict."[44]

Conflict also is moderated by elites' adherence both in government and in opposition to the norms of the polyarchal system. Among these is acceptance of government decisions by the losers of any particular conflict and, conversely, restraint by the winners in pressing their advantage. Similarly, belief in the legitimacy and value of compromise, in the basic trustworthiness of one's political opponents, and in the effectiveness of the polyarchal system in dealing with the problems of society and of one's particular group within it all should increase the range in which government is prepared to tolerate opposition and opponents are prepared to accept their status.

Even if the officials in effective control of the government are selected in free and fair elections, and even if opponents of the regime have the necessary resources to contest those elections, it is possible that some groups will suffer regular and severe losses. That they are allowed to continue protesting these deprivations means that they are not suppressed, but it does not mean that they are not tyrannized over in the broader sense in which liberals have understood tyranny. If the same groups lose all the time, the fact that they were allowed to compete will afford small comfort. Majority rule gives little protection to those who are, and will be in the future, in the minority.

One guarantee against excessive costs being imposed on minorities is the possibility of revolution. Even if the revolution could be defeated, the expected costs of suppression may exceed not only the costs of toleration but the costs of compromise as well. What could be called the distributional theory of polyarchy, however, suggests that the threat of revolution can be avoided altogether under appropriate institutional, socioeconomic, and attitudinal circumstances.

The first of these conditions is the imposition of limitations on the power of national majorities by placing constitutional restrictions on the national government and expecting they will be observed in the interests of maintaining the legitimacy of the government, itself a valuable political resource for those in control. Additionally, some policy areas may be assigned to local governments, where different majorities may be found, or to semipublic or private entities. More important than giving responsibility for different policies to different agencies is the sharing of responsibility for individual activities among several agencies. This sharing creates multiple points of access to the decision process, giving potentially affected groups many opportunities to press their claims and voice their protests. In particular, it creates many points at which policy proposals can be killed. For example, in the United States, a proposed law must be approved by committees and the full chambers of both houses of Congress, probably clear a joint conference committee and then both chambers again, be approved by the president or else be repassed by extraordinary majorities in Congress, be implemented by effective administrative action (which may require state or local actions or separately approved appropriations), and be validated by the courts if challenged. Failure at any one of these stages can derail the proposal. Moreover, and one key to the polyarchal system regardless of its precise institutional forms, different groups are expected to have privileged access to, or to be especially well endowed with the resources relevant for, different decision agencies. Consequently, many groups can veto proposals that they vehemently oppose. Furthermore, because their proposals may be so easily defeated, every group, including a national majority, has an incentive to bargain and compromise with its opponents.

The second condition concerns the nature of cleavages in society, in particular those that define the party system. Political parties inevitably develop in a competitive system, but the possibility that a disciplined party will become a faction in the Madisonian sense, transcending and nullifying the effects of the system of multiple decision points, remains. The polyarchal solution is for the parties to crosscut the major ideological and social cleavages of society. This does not mean that the social bases of all parties must be the same, but that ideally no party should be able to ignore any group completely. For example, while black Americans overwhelmingly are Democrats, there are enough black Republicans that the Republican Party must be attentive to black interests as well; even though the British Labour Party was founded as *the* party of the working class, it cannot survive without middle-class support. Thus parties are compelled in their own interests to broker compromise. The other key feature of distributional polyarchy is that, while parties may form the nuclei for coalition formation, there are no permanent winning coalitions because of the crosscutting nature of political and social cleavages. Instead, decisions are made by ever shifting alliances, each restrained by recognition that allies on one issue may be opponents on the next.

All this depends on a congenial system of attitudes and beliefs, especially at the elite level, that also reflects the presumption of crosscutting cleavages. Both mass and elite members of each group will perceive that they have interests in common with the members of groups that oppose them on any particular issue. Because they have been allied on other issues and have many characteristics in common, opponents can recognize each other as trustworthy, the kind of people with whom one can do business.

Elections serve three functions in the polyarchal system. First, they provide an arena for peaceful competition among interests and a forum for the expression of opposition. For elections to do so implies the guaranteeing of such rights as freedom of speech, press, and association, as well as an electoral system perceived to be fair. Second, elections provide for representation of minorities in the decision-making agencies of government. Moreover, elections themselves represent one of the points of access to the decision process and thus give political power to groups that control electorally relevant resources such as numbers, money, and organization. In this sense, they further the system of minorities rule. Third, elections allow the majority to rule in the sense that "politicians subject to elections must operate within the limits set . . . by their expectations about what policies they can adopt and still be reelected."[45] As with all liberal systems, the objective is to set bounds beyond which the government may not go, rather than to provide it with positive directions.

Finally, two objections to the theory just outlined must be observed. The first is that the system is biased against government action. All the checks designed to protect minorities against exploitation by the majority can be used equally by exploitive minorities to prevent the government from taking action to protect their victims. American political history is replete with examples of groups—employers of child labor, racists, industrial polluters—that for long periods could impose severe costs on others while using their differential access to one or more stages of the decision process to prevent the government from stopping them.

One reason for this bias, and the basis of the other objection, is that to fully justify a regime the theory must assume that all groups are at least adequately, if not equally, endowed with political resources. The general proposition that political activity is a correlate of intensity of feeling has been carried to its logical extreme, applied to groups, and reversed. Lack of vehement protest thus becomes evidence of acceptance, or at least indifference. In fact, this presumption often has proven false; passive acquiescence has meant inability to organize protest, not satisfaction with the status quo. Of course, this need not be taken as a condemnation of the theory of polyarchy, which asserts only that each group *ought* to have the resources and access necessary to protect its vital interests. Nonetheless, given what is now known about the difficulties of organizing collective action,[46] a valid question asks whether any theory can be adequate that assumes all groups will be able to stick up for themselves if only they are not positively restrained.

Veto Group Liberalism

Like majoritarian liberalism, pluralist liberalism cannot guarantee society against the tyranny of a durable majority without sacrificing commitment to majority rule. Instead, it proposes conditions to minimize the likelihood of a tyrannical majority forming. Madisonian liberalism divides power among different levels of government and sets, at each level, one branch of government against another, based primarily on their different electorates. Polyarchal liberalism adds the assumption of crosscutting political and socioeconomic cleavages, ameliorating the intensity of conflict, encouraging intergroup compromise and accommodation, and minimizing the chance that some organization, such as a party, will dominate all the various power centers and establish hegemonic control. What if these guarantees are thought inadequate? In this case, the only guarantee that a group will not be exploited is to abandon the majority principle altogether and to give each significant group a veto over every decision. This thinking leads to theories of veto group liberalism, two of which are John C. Calhoun's theory of concurrent majorities and the model of consociational democracy.

Concurrent Majorities

At one level, Calhoun's theory is just a case of special pleading for the southern interest in antebellum America. At the same time, it, like *The Federalist*, is argued at a level of abstraction and with an analytic rigor that allow it to be interpreted as a legitimate political theory. Moreover, as a direct reaction to the Madisonian system in action, it highlights at least one limitation of that theory.

The basic argument is the same for Calhoun and Madison. People are social by nature, but if unrestrained, each person's egocentrism would lead to attempts to dominate others, if only from fear that they would attempt to dominate; the result would be universal discord and confusion. Just as people need society in order to be fully human, society requires government. "But government, although intended to protect and preserve society, has itself a strong tendency to disorder and abuse of its powers."[47] Hence government, or more particularly the people in whom are vested the powers of government, must also be restrained. The central problem is to develop a constitution that will embody the necessary limitations while still allowing government sufficient powers to perform its necessary functions. The first requirement for such a constitution is that officials be elected, but election is not sufficient because it "can do no more than give complete control to those who elect, over the conduct of those they have elected. . . . [B]ut in doing so, it only changes the seat of authority, without counteracting, in the least, the tendency of the government to oppression and abuse of its powers."[48] Thus one arrives at Madison's central problem, tyranny by the majority.

Madison suggests that majority tyranny will be less of a problem in a large, diverse country than in a small, homogeneous one. Calhoun argues just the reverse.

> [N]othing [is] more easy than to pervert [government's] powers into instruments to aggrandize and enrich one or more interests by oppressing and impoverishing the others. . . . Nor is this the case in some particular communities only. It is so in all . . . with, however, this difference, that the more extensive and populous the country, the more diversified the condition and pursuits of its population, and the richer, more luxurious, and dissimilar the people . . . the more easy for one portion of the community to pervert its powers to oppress, and plunder the other.[49]

Where Madison suggests that diversity will prevent a majority coalition from forming, Calhoun asserts that a majority inevitably will form. Similarly, Calhoun dismisses Madison's reliance on division of government powers. "[A]s each and all the departments,—and, of course, the entire government,—would be under the control of the numerical majority, it is too clear to require explanation, that a mere distribution of its powers among its agents or representatives, could do little or nothing to counteract its tendency to oppression and abuse of power."[50]

Overall, Calhoun offers two criticisms of majority rule. The first claims that a majority will form, by the definition of majority rule it will assume the full powers of government, and from the nature of man it will oppress the minority, leaving it no better off than the subject population of an aristocracy or monarchy. While it is true that the minority might hope to become the majority at a subsequent election, however, "the very uncertainty of the tenure, combined with the violent party warfare which must ever precede a change of parties under such governments, would rather tend to increase than diminish the tendency to oppression."[51] This thought leads to Calhoun's second objection. Majority rule must promote social conflict and discord, and ultimately rule by force. Moreover, it will lead to disciplined parties, each controlled by its own majority, so that majority rule becomes in fact minority rule and the offices and honors of government are converted to rewards for partisan service.[52]

Calhoun's solution was the system of concurrent majorities, "that is, by taking the sense of each interest or portion of the community, which may be unequally and injuriously affected by the action of the government, separately, through its own majority, or in some other way by which its voice may be fairly expressed; and to require the consent of each interest, either to put or to keep the government in action."[53] This requirement, he claimed, would have several advantages. Most obviously, it would prevent a majority from using the instruments of government to oppress the minority since each minority could exercise a veto. It would encourage compromise, since each group would know that it could not achieve its objectives without the consent of all the others; thus, it would tend to unite rather than to divide the community. Where majority rule ultimately would lead to demagoguery and the oppression of the rich by the poor unless the right of suffrage were restricted, in governments of concurrent majorities "the wealthy and intelligent being identified in interest with the poor and ignorant of their respective portions or interests of the community, become their leaders and protectors. And hence . . . the right of suffrage, under such a government, may be safely enlarged."[54]

Elections perform two functions in a government of concurrent majorities. First, they make public officials the servants rather than the masters of the citizenry. Second, they provide representatives of each of the constituent interests of society. In this respect, they are analogous to parliamentary elections in pre-reform Britain. Conspicuously absent is any major concern with representation of the true national majority. As Calhoun put it, "The numerical majority, perhaps, should usually be one of the elements of a constitutional democracy; but to make it the sole element, in order to perfect the constitution and make the government more popular, is one of the greatest and most fatal of political errors."[55]

This theory has two obvious problems, only one of which Calhoun appears to have recognized—the question of how unanimous consent is to be obtained. Every policy is likely to be redistributive in some degree. Moreover, even if different policies favor different interests, Calhoun admits that the result never can be a perfect balance. Why should the interests that fare relatively badly consent? The answer, in modern terms, is that government is a positive sum game. Those who fare relatively badly are still better off than they would be without government; thus, they will consent to decisions that adversely affect them so long as the net balance is positive. And recognizing that they would suffer even more were the government to be rendered ineffective by constant interposition of minority vetoes, the majority is restrained from attempting to enact policies that the minority could not accept.

The other problem concerns the definition of the groups whose consent must be obtained. If groups are to exercise a veto power, they must be organized. Moreover, Calhoun's argument assumes that each person is a member of only one interest; in fact, it is clear from the context that the groups Calhoun has in mind are the states. This definition, however, leaves some obvious interests without a veto. Calhoun did not regard the poor as a group requiring the protection of a veto. He certainly did not regard blacks as such a group. The system of concurrent majorities assumes a society divided into relatively few groups united by a common interest, identity, and understanding. If some significant groups are not accorded veto power, the danger that the system of concurrent majorities will preserve private oppression rather than prevent public oppression becomes particularly acute.

Consociational Democracy

Suppose one has a society characterized by segmentation into a small number of cohesive and mutually suspicious groups. Does this mean, as the pluralist argument would seem to suggest, that liberal democracy is impossible? Evidently not, as the examples of Switzerland and the Netherlands attest. Consociational democracy has been proposed as an alternative to the majoritarian competitive model of pluralist polyarchy in order to account for these cases.

The basic principle of the consociational model is that "overarching cooperation at the elite level can be a substitute for crosscutting affiliations at the mass level."[56] It is a government by elite cartel characterized by four conditions: "government by a grand coalition of the political leaders of all significant segments of a plural society"; operation of a system of mutual vetoes by the leaders of all significant segments of society; proportionality as the standard for allocation of all or most political "goods"; and a high degree of internal autonomy for each group.[57] Fundamentally, it is the theory of concurrent majorities updated to reflect modern research concerning elites and modified to apply where the significant social groups are not necessarily coterminous with the local units of a federal system.

One central difference between consociational democracy and Calhoun's system concerns the position of elites. For Calhoun, they were to be the agents of the ordinary citizens in each social group; in the consociational system they are, and must be, largely independent. Certainly, so long as they depend on votes for their positions, leaders will be subject to pressures and limitations imposed by their followers. But, as Arend Lijphart observes, "the extent of pressures on the elite must not be exaggerated. In Dutch politics, the elites have usually enjoyed great freedom to act independently without constant demands from their followers—a freedom vital to the success of the system of overarching cooperation among the blocs."[58] In a segmented society, stable democracy requires that leaders have the freedom to make compromises that their followers would not make themselves.

The principle of segmental autonomy is basically the same as "states' rights" in Calhoun's system. Indeed, federalism is usually seen as an institutional device favoring consociational democracy precisely because it allows contentious issues to be removed from the arena of intersegmental conflict and to be turned over to each segment to manage according to its own preferences. It is more far-reaching, however, especially when coupled with the principle of proportionality. Moreover, in its general form it allows resolution of conflicts among groups that cut across local government boundaries.

In cutting the system of mutual veto, proportionality, and segmental autonomy free from territorial constraints, consociational democracy expands the function of elections and solves the problem of defining significant segments. A group is entitled to be included in the consociational system to the extent that it is successful at the polls. While proportionate distribution of public largess in individual policy areas is likely to be based on numbers participating in the relevant activities,[59] distribution of particularly governmental rewards, such as cabinet ministries, will be based on parliamentary election results. Thus, in contrast to the system of concurrent majorities, which is fundamentally indifferent on the subject, consociationalism requires that elections fairly register each social group's strength, in addition to confirming their leaders and imposing some restraint on them.

Given the universal expectation that contested elections inevitably will produce some kind of competitive party system, one way of recapitulating these theories' expectations about elections is to examine the kind of party systems they envision, or which would be most appropriate to them. The first two questions are the number of parties and their degree of internal cohesion. The majoritarian theories require two parties so that one or the other will achieve a majority. In Schumpeterian democracy, it would appear that these parties should be cohesive at the national level so that the electorate can, in fact, choose a government, although the theory does allow for coalition governments chosen by a parliament chosen by the people. Moreover, the models Schumpeterians hold up as good examples include the United States with its very low levels of party unity. In spirit, Benthamite radicalism is opposed to political organization, and the Radical party was never characterized by high cohesion. However, many of the institutions Bentham suggests, in particular his demand for equal constituency populations, seem designed to produce a reflection of the national majority in the legislature and are certainly compatible with cohesive parties. Both cases are, thus, best assigned to a category of indifference on this question.

For the pluralist theories, the indifference appears on the question of party number. The polyarchists are overtly indifferent except as they suggest that too many parties (usually meaning more than five or six) are harmful to democratic stability. The indifference of Madisonians stems from an ambivalence on the question of having parties at all. Both theories, however, are opposed to high levels of disciplined uniformity among parties. Finally, the position of the veto group theories is clear on both questions; there must be at least one cohesive party for each relevant social segment to defend segmental interests.

The third question concerns the ties between party and social groupings. Majoritarian theories deny the relevance of social categories to political organization, while pluralist theories are based on the crosscutting of political and social cleavages. On the other hand, this is precisely the basis for partisanship in the veto group view.

The fourth question concerns the degree to which leaders are to be constrained by their supporters. In each case, the twentieth-century theories call for a high degree of elite autonomy. Although they are less clear on the subject, a reasonable inference is that each of the nineteenth-century theories envisioned leaders more clearly as agents of their supporters. (In fact, both Bentham and Calhoun are reasonably explicit on this point.)

Finally, the fifth question concerns the nature of the competitive system. All these theories regard elections as a time of choice. By their nature, these choices must be competitive in the most direct sense; whatever one party or group wins must be lost by the others. They differ significantly, however, about what happens next. For the majoritarians, competition continues; the process of governing is a continuing struggle for a majority, and whoever achieves a majority makes the decisions as they see fit. For the veto group liberals, competition stops after the election, to be replaced by a process of consensus formation and government by compromise, accommodation, and unanimous consent. The pluralists take a middle position. While accepting the basic logic of majority rule for final decision making, they assume that the social and political structures they envision will lead at least to a moderation of the positions of all participants, if not to an explicit consensus.

Participationist Democracy

Both popular sovereignty and liberal theorists of democracy focus primarily on the content of government decisions. Participationist theorists focus instead on the consequences of the *process* by which decisions are reached. For these theorists, democracy means that the great mass of the people are regularly, actively, and intimately involved in the making and implementation of public policies. In contrast to theories that either accept or positively value limited popular involvement and assign the immediate task of governing to a small elite, participationist theories attempt to maximize democracy as government by the people in the literal sense.

Implementing the will of the people or avoiding tyranny has a prima facie desirability that direct popular rule does not; Will Rogers' dictum that democracy ensures that the people are "governed no better than they deserve" is hardly adequate justification for maximizing direct popular participation. Those who value participation point to four basic objectives to be achieved. Two are already familiar. First, popular participation is the best way both for leaders and for the people themselves to discover what the people want. Second, widespread participation will ensure that all relevant interests are considered.[1] These objectives, instrumental to the achievement of popular sovereignty and liberal democracy, are reasons for advocates of these theories to value at least some popular participation.

Third, participation may increase the legitimacy, acceptance, and enforceability of policies, in part because decisions made in light of popular participation should be more in keeping with the desires of the people. Additionally, however, people are more prone to accept decisions they help to make, even if they do not like the decisions reached. Participation contributes to integration into society and thus to cooperation in achieving its aims. In this regard, participation becomes as much a strategy of manipulation and control as a way for the people to govern themselves and again is congenial with the elitist popular sovereignty or liberal democratic approaches. Moreover, if the first two objectives could be achieved with limited participation, achievement of this objective appears to require only the perception of participation.

The fourth objective, however, requires substantial real participation and clearly distinguishes participationist democracy from the other varieties of democratic theory. Democracy, with mass participation in political life, is supported primarily because "such involvement is an essential means to the full development of individual capacities,"[2] which is held to be the central aim of government and society. Consider the position each theory would take regarding an enlightened and benevolent despot to clarify the distinction. Liberals object only that a benevolent despot is impossible. Collectivist popular sovereignty theories, particularly the Tory version, come close to identifying "the party" as an enlightened despot, while individualist theories see popular voting as valuable because it defines the popular will. If an enlightened despot who "knew" the popular will were available, there would be no inherent need to involve the mass of the people at all.

For a participationist democrat, however, an enlightened despot would be unacceptable because the primary value of democracy is not reflected in policy, but in its effect on the moral and intellectual character of the citizens. Imagine that a virtuous ruler could be found.

> What should we then have? . . . What sort of human beings can be formed under such a regime? What development can either their thinking or their active faculties attain under it? . . . If they have any knowledge . . . it is but a *dilettante* knowledge, like that which people have of the mechanical arts who have never handled a tool. Nor is it only in their intelligence that they suffer. Their moral capacities are equally stunted.[3]

It is the process rather than the decision that leads to the desired outcome, and hence there can be no substitute for direct involvement by the people.

Popular sovereignty and liberal democratic theories take people and society basically as they find them. If people frequently attempt to exploit one another, the problem is to control their exploitative nature. If they disagree about principles and policies, the problem is to reach a collective choice in situations of conflict. In contrast, participationist theories assume that people are shaped by the system of rule under which they live. Introducing a participatory system, they assert, will alter these characteristics. Problems of decision making under conflict and protection of minorities are to be solved by eliminating the cause rather than controlling the symptoms. Participationists seek to reform people, not just government. What precisely is participation expected to do?

The goal of participationist democracy is the development of human potential, of a more complete human being, and of a more humane society. One aspect is the development of each person's intellectual capacities, which should be promoted in two ways. On one side, in a participatory society, people would seek out information and would have the opportunity and the incentive to test and improve their ideas, knowing that they ultimately would have to reach decisions and live with the consequences. On the other side, because the people decide policy, those who wish to influence outcomes will seek constantly to inform them.

Second, participation will increase the virtue of the citizen. Popular sovereignty and liberal theorists regard people as naturally self-regarding, and indeed in the elaboration of their theories have tended to make this a virtue. For participationists, regard for others and public involvement are virtues to be furthered by participation.

> It is not sufficiently considered how little there is in most men's ordinary life to give any largeness either to their conceptions or to their sentiments. . . . Giving [a man] something to do for the public, supplies, in a measure, all these deficiencies. . . . He is called upon, while so engaged, to weigh interests not his own; to be guided, in cases of conflicting claims, by another rule than his private partialities; to apply, at every turn, principles and maxims which have for their reason of existence the general good. . . . He is made to feel himself one of the public, and whatever is their interest to be his interest.[4]

And both the obligation and the inclination to be public-spirited should extend even to the act of voting.

Third, participation is essential to "true" democratic equality. Most modern participationists argue their position in the form of a critique of twentieth-century "elitist" theories of popular sovereignty, and especially liberal democracy.[5] Participationists do not argue against the inevitability of leadership; naturally some people will be better qualified by talent or interest to advise the general public. But leadership will be manifested as advice, which the people may weigh against other advice before deciding, rather than as direction. Where the people rule themselves, the whole authority pattern of society is altered and the distinction between rulers and ruled eliminated.

From the participationist perspective, real freedom is not avoidance of external restraints, but mastery of one's self. For government explicitly, "We must never see the government as something other than ourselves, for then automatically we become children; and not real honest children, but adults dwarfed to childhood again in weakness and ineffectiveness."[6] True freedom requires that one takes charge of one's own life by participating in the major decisions affecting it. Participation also should lead to an increased sense of personal effectiveness.[7]

Finally, many have argued that participationist democracy will increase the sense of community citizens feel. Some allusion to this has already been made, but full discussion will be deferred to the next chapter.

Broadly speaking, one can distinguish two dimensions to describe the level of popular participation. The simplest concerns the frequency of participation. Frequency of participation is limited by citizens' other needs, but if participation is to have an impact on the character of the citizens, it must be more frequent than the periodic national elections envisioned by the elitist theories of democracy. As Mill put it, "[a] political act, to be done only once in a few years, and for which nothing in the daily habits of the citizen has prepared him, leaves his intellect and his moral dispositions very much as it found them."[8]

The other dimension concerns the intensity of participation. Following Pateman's discussion of participation in the workplace, one can suggest three exemplary levels.[9] The lowest is "pseudo-participation." In the industrial example, a supervisor might allow questions and discussion of a decision rather than merely announcing it; the decision, however, remains entirely the supervisor's. There is not so much participation as there is a feeling of participation.[10] The second level, "partial participation," gives workers (citizens) more power, but still leaves them in a fundamentally subordinate role. The main decisions are made elsewhere, but they may be able to determine how they will be implemented or to impose some sanctions on the principal decision-makers that allow them to influence the outcome. This form is the most popular participation envisioned by any of the popular sovereignty or liberal democratic theories. Finally, with "full participation" all workers or citizens have an equal share in the making and implementation of all decisions.

The ideal for participationists would be regular full participation at all levels of government, as well as, for many, in all other authoritative decision-making bodies in society, most notably in the workplace. Obviously this end is not possible and no participationist claims that it is. Rather, it represents a normative goal toward which society should be striving.

The limits on possible participation are most clear at the level of the national government. This is the primary focus of the elitist theories, so it is little wonder that they conclude that participation must be limited. The scale of mass societies is too large to allow intensive participation by all citizens. Further, most of the business of national governments is beyond the direct knowledge or concern of ordinary citizens; most of its actions have little direct impact on most of them. As Giovanni Sartori observes but as even the most ardent advocates of participation admit, "the only matters we understand are those with which we have personal experience,"[11] and the vast majority cannot have personal experience of national politics. Apparently, to increase the scope of participation, one must sacrifice its intensity.

Whereas the reaction of elitist theorists to this fact has been to propose more "realistic" theories of democracy, participationists point to other spheres in which more intensive and more frequent participation is possible. Foremost among these is local government. The scale is smaller so that one citizen's participation may have a noticeable impact and the problems are closer to the citizen's daily experience. In Alexis de Tocqueville's words, "[T]own meetings are to liberty what primary schools are to science: they bring it within the people's reach, they teach men how to use and how to enjoy it."[12] Even without town meetings, "local government may act as a training ground for political competence. Where local government allows participation, it may foster a sense of competence that then spreads to the national level."[13]

In contrast to Sartori's assertion that "democracy on a large scale is not the sum of many little democracies,"[14] the participationist position is that "a democratic constitution, not supported by democratic institutions in detail, but confined to the central government, not only is not political freedom, but often creates a spirit precisely the reverse."[15] Democratic local governments certainly are required, but can afford only limited opportunities for participation when set against the backdrop of all the social relationships of life. The solution is to democratize these relationships as well.[16]

Central among the organizations that many participationists feel must be democratized are industrial concerns. Many theorists argue that the workplace is not just *a* relevant arena into which popular participation might be introduced, but the *central* arena that must be democratized if people are to control their own lives meaningfully.

Before considering the relevance of participationist theories to the specific problem of electoral systems, one must consider three objections to the entire enterprise. The first is that people lack the necessary qualities for widespread participation to be reconciled with the needs of viable democratic government. They are illiberal, ill-informed, apathetic, and when roused to activity "incapable of action other than a stampede."[17] The answer is that these traits are the result, not the cause, of nonparticipation: "Once the participatory system is established . . . it becomes self-sustaining because the very qualities that are required of individual citizens if the system is to work successfully are those that the process of participation itself develops and fosters; the more the individual citizen participates the better able he is to do so."[18]

A second criticism is that the kind of democracy envisioned by the theory is impossible because of the problem of leadership. Direct democracy is impossible because of the scale of modern society; therefore, organization is necessary. Once there is organization, leadership inevitably develops, and becomes more and more separated from the led. Gradually, the leadership stratum loses its taste for democracy and becomes interested primarily in maintaining its own position. From this argument emerges Michels' "iron law of oligarchy," that organization is inevitable but that it also leads inevitably to the domination of the leaders over their followers.[19]

Elitist theorists have taken this as evidence that their position is the only realistic possibility. But, although Michels certainly is pessimistic regarding the ultimate realization of democracy, this means neither that he denies the possibility of progress toward democracy nor that he approves of elite domination. On the contrary, only the "blind and fanatical" could fail "to see that the democratic current daily makes undeniable advance."[20] Moreover, "[s]ometimes . . . the democratic principle carries with it, if not a cure, at least a palliative, for the disease of oligarchy." A democratic movement (or society), "in virtue of the theoretical postulates it proclaims, is apt to bring into existence (in opposition to the will of the leaders) a certain number of free spirits who . . . desire to revise the base upon which authority is established."[21] If a tendency to oligarchy is inevitable, it is only the participationist principle that keeps it in check.

Finally, perhaps people will not, in fact, participate no matter how many opportunities they are given. The usual evidence is the low turnout in elections, especially at the local level where participationist theory might lead one to expect involvement would be greatest. Perhaps most damning, however, is the evidence of industrial nonparticipation, even in a firm deliberately organized along participatory lines.[22]

While admitting that this evidence suggests "that it is over-optimistic to expect the ordinary worker to avail himself of opportunities for higher level partial participation," Carole Pateman suggests that "for the ordinary worker, who has been socialised into the existing system of industrial authority structures and who still has no opportunity to participate every day at the lower level," opportunities for participation are not as real as they may appear to academic observers.[23] Although there may be some truth to this, one still wonders what evidence Pateman would accept to prove genuine lack of interest in participation, or even a conscious choice, whether in government or in the workplace, to value good government over self-government.

A second response to the apparent indifference of people to participation is that the principal benefits accruing from participation flow from involvement in the process rather than impact on the outcome, and one cannot expect those who have not had the experience of participation in the past to anticipate those rewards. In this case, disinterest in participation may be the result, not the cause, of nonparticipation.[24] Even if a participatory system would be self-sustaining, it might not be self-initiating.

A third response denies the relevance of the question altogether. The benefits of participation are public as well as private. While it is good for Jones to participate in governing herself, development of her full potential requires that she interact with other fully developing human beings. If Smith fails to participate, not only is he worse off, so is Jones. Moreover, even if Smith fails to participate, he benefits from interaction with Jones. From this perspective, self-government is less an opportunity than a duty.[25] As with any public good, one legitimately may be compelled to contribute. Once a social preference for democracy is established, individual disinclination to participate is no more relevant than individual disinclination to pay taxes. Once opportunities for participation are provided, people may be forced to use them.

The simplest response, however, is that the original premise, that people do not participate at present, is factually mistaken. The basis of this premise has been the small numbers in surveys who report such activities as party membership or contacts with public officials and the similarly small numbers who report interest or demonstrate knowledge in public issues. The elitist conclusion—because few citizens engage in each activity and few are interested in each issue, there are few participatory citizens—is wrong. While few are interested in any particular issue, the vast majority report they are concerned with at least one issue.[26] Similarly, political activity is more common than the figures for any one action imply.[27] Participationist democracy does not require that everyone participate in every decision, merely that everyone participate regularly in some area and that all people can participate fully in any area in making decisions that affect themselves and their community.

The participationist ideal is admittedly unrealizable. There can never be enough participation; one only can have as much participation as possible at any moment while constantly attempting to expand the realm of possibility. Even so, no participationist regards the opportunity to vote in quadrennial or quintennial national elections by itself as adequate for a true democracy. The involvement of the national electorate in the process of governing is too remote and the occasion of that involvement is too infrequent for the educational, personal developmental, spiritual, and psychic benefits of participation to be realized. Conversely, no participationist claims that elections are impermissible and must be replaced by direct involvement of all citizens in every decision. Some governing functions must be performed by representatives, not the people.

Within these broad limits, participationists have expressed a variety of opinions concerning the adequacy of electoral participation in a democratic scheme, stemming generally from differences over three questions. First, are elections the most effective practical avenues for participation in particular circumstances, or alternatively, is the kind of participation afforded by elections adequate to achieve the benefits ascribed to democracy? Second, can elections, over the long term, remain avenues of meaningful citizen participation rather than degenerating into instruments of elite cooptation and control? Third, once chosen, are the officials elected capable of controlling both the government apparatus and the other organs of society making decisions that fundamentally affect people's lives? Naturally, those who answer these questions affirmatively are more favorably disposed toward elections and the conventional definition of politics.

Overall, one can distinguish three basic positions. The first is that elections are effective means of achieving the benefits of participation, particularly at the local level. While greater participation than the periodic casting of a ballot is required, conventional electoral politics can stimulate and provide channels for the additional involvement in public life needed. The second position is that elections are necessary, but that they are fundamentally inadequate for democratic advancement. As much as possible of the decision making and administration of government should be transferred to the most local level, where citizens can participate directly as private citizens, not only as elected local officials. Moreover, the range of activities to which the principle of democratic participation is applied must be expanded beyond the formally governmental. These two positions are optimistic in as much as they can propose practical measures to increase democratic participation. The third position, although participationist in its perspective, is pessimistic. Elections are necessary, and indeed superior to other means of selecting leaders, but they are at best a mixed blessing. Elections give the illusion, rather than the substance, of control to the people, but lessen the likelihood they will try to participate in more effective ways. To the extent that people believe they should participate, elections become national expiations of guilt. Moreover, the limited and illusory participation entailed by elections helps to legitimize the very hierarchical system that participationists seek to replace.

John Stuart Mill represents the first of these positions, although his proposals really are an attempted compromise between participationist and liberal premises. He believed in the moral improvability of people and in their ultimate ability to rule themselves in a public-spirited way that extended to all classes of individuals. Yet he also believed that the most enlightened members of society should exercise a predominant influence in the direction of its affairs. On one side, the aim of democracy is to transform the citizens, making them more active, educated, virtuous, and efficient. On the other side, however, "[g]overnments must be made for human beings as they are, or as they are capable of speedily becoming."[28]

The resulting tension led to a number of curious compromises and contradictions. Mill simultaneously called for virtually universal suffrage and a system of plural voting. The standard for plural voting ideally was to be intelligence or knowledge, but for a provisional surrogate, Mill was prepared to accept an occupation, or even a property qualification. Moreover, in addition to arguing that plural voting was right in principle, Mill also suggested it was valuable because it would prevent the uneducated (poor), by virtue of their numbers, from dominating the enlightened (middle class). In this respect, his argument recalls Cicero's comments on the Severian constitution.

A similar apparent inconsistency concerns the relationship between representative and represented. In arguing against indirect election, Mill complains that when the voter only chooses the choosers, "he will not occupy his thoughts with political opinions and measures, or political men, but will be guided by his personal respect for some private individual, to whom he will give a general power of attorney to act for him."[29] Yet in discussing the question of requiring pledges from members of parliament, Mill appears to argue the reverse. "[I]f it be an object to possess representatives in any intellectual respect superior to average electors, it must be counted upon that the representative will sometimes differ in opinion from the majority of his constituents, and that when he does, his opinion will be the oftenest right of the two. It follows, that the electors will not do wisely if they insist on absolute conformity to their opinions."[30] But does this not call precisely for a representative with "a general power of attorney"?

Although the parliament would exercise the ultimate controlling power, Mill recognized "a radical distinction between controlling the business of government, and actually doing it." Notwithstanding his criticism of indirect election, he argued that "[t]he proper duty of a representative assembly in regard to matters of administration, is not to decide them by its own vote, but to take care that the persons who have to decide them shall be the proper persons."[31] The direct power of the parliament was to be only the right to accept, reject, or return for revision the proposals of an expert commission.

Nonetheless, the representativeness of the parliament was extremely important to Mill. To this end, he proposed adoption of the single transferable vote electoral system (STV), which would have a number of advantages. It would ensure representation of minorities, in proportion to their strength and by representatives they themselves had selected. Here he denied the adequacy of "virtual representation" of groups that were in a minority in one area by members elected in other places where people of that general opinion were a majority. STV also would ensure that each member represented a constituency that was, in effect, unanimous; members need not worry about representing a divided constituency. Moreover, the problem of wasted votes would be eliminated, and virtually every vote would make a difference.

Mill's discussion of electoral systems elucidates the apparent contradictions just cited. C. B. Macpherson, for example, complains that there is little reason to suppose the working class would participate and thus become more developed since the system was stacked by plural voting to prevent their will from prevailing.[32] Clearly, nothing can eliminate the inegalitarian nature of the plural voting proposal, but Macpherson overstates its significance. STV would ensure that working-class votes contributed to the election of members who would otherwise have been defeated. Moreover, because the parliament would be composed of independently minded people, not disciplined party hacks, each representative would make a difference. Even if the working class were denied a permanent majority, it was not denied effective influence.

While Mill opposed the instructed delegate model of representation, he did not suppose that the opinions of candidates could or should be irrelevant to electors' evaluation of their competence. Thus there should be a basic congruence between the opinions of member and constituents. Under the majority system, with a diversity of opinions in each district, this could be little more than a platitude. STV, however, would assure a much closer agreement so that, while the member would use his own judgment, he would act less as an outsider with power of attorney than as the leader of a cooperative enterprise.

The fundamental point is that Mill saw democracy as an educational exercise. The primary value was the development of the critical and evaluative faculties and of a social rather than individualistic outlook on public affairs. Knowing that they would cast meaningful votes in reasonably frequent elections would inspire people to pay attention to politics, and politicians to pay attention to the people, on a continuing basis. Direct participation in the "doing" of governing was not necessary to achieve the aims of democracy. Indeed, Mill talks about direct participation in local government in terms appropriate to a school laboratory; the student learns about science, but does not "do" science in the way a professional scientist does. Democracy would teach people to judge merit and to increase their own merit, but at the same time the "doing" of government would be in the hands of the most meritorious.

The second position, that representation and elections are necessary but that simply increasing participation in the electoral process as currently organized is inadequate, is the most common among modern participationist democrats. Although no one theorist is sufficiently prominent to be taken as exemplary, common themes are sufficient for a composite summary. While not everyone would agree with every point, three main assertions characterize most of these theories. First, citizens must have opportunities to participate in the actual management of affairs, not just in the choice of those who will manage them. Second, if the aims of self-rule are to be achieved, the sphere to which the democratic principle is applied must be expanded, especially to include the industrial workplace. Third, the basis of representation must be changed from anonymous aggregations of individuals to some kind of meaningful social units. Moreover, according to a fairly general consensus, all this must be predicated on a far-reaching reformation of society, in particular sweeping away the class conflict and hierarchical authority patterns that these theorists see as central to industrial capitalism.

Actual self-government at the level of the modern nation-state is patently impossible. Several conclusions follow about the organization of government. The first is that, whenever possible, power should be devolved on local governments which afford more opportunities for direct participation simply because there are more posts to be filled. They also reduce problems to a scale comprehensible by ordinary citizens and are likely to make the connection between decisions and tangible results considerably clearer. Still, even local governments deal with a wide variety of problems, the connection between decisions and daily life is often remote, and, except in small towns, even here the scale may be too large for effective mass participation.

A second conclusion is that positive efforts should be made to involve citizens in decision making, perhaps through the appointment of lay advisory boards. In this regard, participationists frequently cite approvingly the "maximum feasible participation" principle of the Office of Economic Opportunity.[33] This device is still inadequate, however, if it maintains the view of citizens primarily as consumers of public services produced by someone else.

Third, even though participation at the national, or local, level is necessarily inadequate, it can be improved. Access to information can be increased. More important, the people must begin to see themselves as competent to make decisions and as equal to the erstwhile political elites. There must be "a change in people's consciousness (or unconsciousness), from seeing themselves and acting as essentially consumers to seeing themselves and acting as exerters and enjoyers of the exertion and development of their own capacities."[34]

At this point, two problems converge. On one hand, many participationists believe the current system of economic management impedes this reorientation because it creates tremendous disparities of power and because its hierarchical system of management accustoms workers to accept authority. On the other hand, limiting the democratic principle to government as currently constituted strips citizens of control over many of the most important and immediate influences on their lives. A solution commonly proposed for both these problems is some form of industrial democracy—extend the principle of participation to the management of industry.

The most commonly proposed mode for full worker self-management involves direct democracy on the shop floor coupled with pyramidal representation. Those workers cooperating in the performance of a single task—the primary work group—would decide directly. Where coordination of several groups was necessary, each primary group would elect representatives to a joint committee. This committee, in turn, might elect representatives to a committee coordinating several factories, and so forth. In each case, the representative would really be one with the represented—in close contact with them and engaged in the same task.

These same proposals can also be adapted to the more general political arena. Macpherson, for example, suggests adapting the pyramidal structure of representation to political parties. The primary function of the current party systems of capitalist countries, he suggests, "has been . . . to moderate and smooth over a conflict of class interests so as to save the existing property institutions and the market system from effective attack"[35] by protecting representatives from their constituents. If, however, the potential for class conflict were reduced, genuinely participatory parties would become possible.

Implicit in this notion is the assumption of a community of interests so that compromise will be unnecessary. For many participationists, the creation of such a community is one of the aims of democracy, but to assume its existence is questionable. G.D.H. Cole approached the problem from a different direction. To have such a community spanning all issues is impossible, but without it, representation can only be gross *mis*representation. True social association, however, is not general purpose; it is functional. In contrast to most geographic constituencies that have no existential basis and no continuing basis from which to advise, admonish, and if necessary recall their representatives, functional groups have a shared purpose and sense of identity. This characteristic, which they share preeminently with the primary work group, made them, for Cole, the proper basis for representation. Functional representation would assure that "not only will the representative be chosen to do a job about which he knows something, but he will be chosen by persons who know something of it too."[36]

The final position, that elections are positively pernicious, is relevant here primarily because of the dangers it points up, although some theorists who take this position do argue that elections, though dangerous, are nonetheless superior to government without elections in large-scale societies; the conclusion, simply, is that real democracy is only possible in an isolated city-state. Many of the basic concerns of these theorists duplicate those of theorists taking the more optimistic positions; theorists who find elections dangerous, however, doubt that these problems can be overcome and also warn that the illusion of democracy will lend oligarchic governments undeserved legitimacy and power.

In particular, they point to the potential that schemes allowing only limited participation could be used as instruments of control from above, rather than control over those who are above. Many schemes of low-level worker participation, for example, have been introduced by management in order to defuse worker unrest and secure more ready compliance with executive decisions.[37] Many suffrage-expanding reforms of the nineteenth century also were introduced for this reason. Moreover, when people believe that they can control government, they appear far more willing to consent to expansions of its powers.[38]

Again, within the context of the modern nation-state, none of these theorists would advocate abolishing elections, although some might be reluctant to call the system that remains a democracy. They do, however, suggest a dark side of elections that must be considered.

Communitarian Democracy

Each of the varieties of democratic theory discussed so far assumes a basic community of interest or feeling among citizens, or at least would work more smoothly if one could be assumed. Nonetheless, each proposes mechanisms by which decisions may be made, or undesirable consequences avoided, given whatever the current level of community feeling. Especially popular sovereignty and liberal democracy are directly concerned with resolving or containing conflict to serve, not improve, the people.

Although collectivist popular sovereignty theories posit a single community interest, in "real life" they assume an ineluctable conflict between at least two communities, one right and the other wrong in a fundamental sense. Competitive democracy is justified, notwithstanding the possibility that the wrong party may win, because of the daunting prospect of the alternative. Still, the relinquishing of office by a defeated party only seems logical if communal feeling moderates the behavior of the winners and leads them voluntarily to relinquish office in their turn. For individualist popular sovereignty theories, conflicting interests and opinions are the natural state of affairs. Even they, however, must assume enough commonality of interest that the losers perceive themselves better off than they would be if they rebelled instead.

Although liberal democratic theories are most directly predicated on conflict among unconnected individuals or groups (where the focus is on groups, the fundamental point is that they are unconnected to each other, notwithstanding the possibly high level of solidarity or community within each group), they too require that conflict be mitigated by a common interest or common understanding. Only then will the rulers exercise self-restraint, and the policies of the ruling group be accepted voluntarily by the losers. Without the requisite levels of elite and social restraint and solidarity, stable democracy is impossible.

In the participationist argument, men and women are not taken as is, but rather their improvement is the objective of democracy. The primary concern is the development of the citizen as an autonomous human being. So long as the independent and self-motivated exercise of a person's faculties is the principal means by which a fully human existence is achieved, there is no ambiguity, and one can imagine the personal development valued by participationists achieved even in a situation wherein there is little sympathy between citizens. Although many participationists argue that one of the consequences of political participation will be to eliminate fundamental conflicts, this is a "side" benefit, rather than a first-order objective or defining characteristic.

Many communitarian democrats also claim that participation is valuable, but the basis for their argument is fundamentally different. From their perspective, integration into a community is a basic requirement of humanity. In contrast to the autonomous, but potentially isolated, individual of participationist democracy, the communitarian view is that life is meaningfully human only when lived, and felt to be lived, as part of an organic community. Indeed, in contrast to the liberal counterposing of community and autonomy, some communitarians assert community to be a necessary condition of meaningful autonomy.

In fact, many participationists should be counted as communitarian democrats as well. Nonetheless, there are two logically distinguishable sets of objectives; one could be a participationist and value the goals of individual human development yet accept the radical individualist conception of man, and thus reject the communitarian goal as impossible, irrelevant, or even fundamentally undesirable.

By communitarian theories of democracy, I refer to those that particularly stress the creation, maintenance, or expression of the reality of community. Within this generalization, one must distinguish two very different categories of communitarian democratic theories. First, some theories define democracy on the basis of the community of citizens. Given the existence of a community, any political system that gives it expression is by definition democratic with respect to that community, no matter how illiberal or authoritarian it may be. Because the appeal to community in these theories is so often emotional rather than rational, I refer to them as "emotive" communitarian theories. Second, some theories see community as a necessary condition for or a product of political arrangements that would be recognized as democratic on other grounds, especially some form of public participation in or control over the process of ruling. With their emphasis on the continuous creation and recreation of community as a goal to be pursued but never fully achieved, these theories may appropriately be called "developmental."

In some respects, the emotive theories of communitarian democracy are simply collectivist popular sovereignty revisited. Thus one could argue that with their ideological roots in the struggle between the proletariat and the bourgeoisie, the "people's democracies" were no more than the logical fulfillment of socialist popular sovereignty. In the same way, one could argue that the "guided democracies" of some Third World countries, with their roots in the struggle for national independence and development, are close cousins of Tory popular sovereignty, or perhaps that Tory popular sovereignty carried to its logical extreme is simply authoritarian nationalism. However, important differences between collectivist popular sovereignty and emotive communitarianism make these claims misleading; a socialist democrat is not simply a prudent or timid communist nor is a Tory simply a prudent or timid authoritarian.

Although both collectivist popular sovereignty and emotive communitarianism can be traced to medieval ideas of an organically integrated society, they adapted this idea to the rigors of the modern world in radically different ways. Collectivist popular sovereignty combines the ideal of community with concerns for individual autonomy or liberty and for legitimacy through free and temporally limited choice. In theory, a party remains the authentic voice of the community whatever its fate at the polls, but it must periodically convince the people that it is right before converting that voice into action. The insistence on authorization through free choice then requires that a panoply of political liberties be respected and always defers to the autonomous will of the individual citizens.

The emotive communitarian, on the other hand, simply reemphasizes the central existence of community that necessarily defines the political being of the citizen. The ties that bind the community together are far tighter and more intimate than those in collectivist popular sovereignty. The individual is totally identified with the community and in fact ceases to exist as an autonomous political personality: "The government embodies the unitary community . . . —the citizen is the community, which is the state—and thus functions directly in the name of the citizenry."[1] Thus, opposition to the government as the community's voice is possible only from someone outside the community, so that dissent becomes indistinguishable from apostasy, indistinguishable in turn from treason.

The distinction between the two varieties of communitarian theory can be characterized in a number of ways. One already has been suggested. For the emotive theories, the community has a natural and prior existence; it needs neither to be created nor to be maintained; the problem is only to give it an institutional and powerful expression. However, for the developmental theories, the bringing into being and nurturing of the community is precisely the task of political organization.

A second distinction lies in the nature of the community. For the emotive theories, community represents an identity of fundamental interests and "real" wills to do particular things. Individuality is transcended and submerged in a single corporate or general will. For the developmental theories, however, the general will is not a will to do particular things, but rather a will to take common action, to reconcile and compromise opposing interests and opinions. Community lies in the bonds of sympathetic understanding among individuals who, while deriving their identities from their social context, remain autonomous agents.

Finally, a third distinction concerns the nature of citizenship. In the emotive theories, citizenship is essentially ascriptive; one is a citizen by virtue of being part of the community defined by social or ethnic position or characteristics. From the developmental perspective, however, citizenship is an achieved status, based on voluntary will. "Citizens are neighbors bound together neither by blood nor by contract but by their common concerns and common participation in the search for common solutions to common conflicts."[2] Whereas in the emotive view, citizenship is "a function of *what or who we are* and thus a matter of identity," in the developmental view "it is a function of *what we do* and thus a matter of activity."[3]

Emotive Communitarian Democracy

People's Democracy

Before I discuss "people's democracy" of the former Communist bloc as the first example of emotive communitarian democracy, three points must be made. First, I will not consider whether people's democracy ought to be called democracy at all. On one hand, it illuminates a strain of democratic theory that resonates in contexts even the most fervent opponents of communism would call democratic; in this sense, whatever perversion of the theory may have been committed in practice is irrelevant. On the other hand, one of the central themes of this book is that there is no single true definition of democracy; from this perspective, the question of whether the theory is "entitled" to be called democratic is unimportant. Instead, I am examining a theory that emphasizes one of the range of values identified with democracy and considering the place of elections in attempts to achieve that value.

The second point is that people's democracy, as the political system of a regime in transition between capitalism and communism, is not regarded as "complete" democracy even by its adherents.[4] Nonetheless, I will address this transitional democracy because, as Lenin says, "the more complete [this democracy] is the more quickly will it become unnecessary and wither away of itself."[5] While a true communist society presumably would have some mechanisms for reaching collective decisions, they are beyond the scope of this study.

Finally, as with other democratic theories, people's democracy has several subtypes—at the very least, one can distinguish Soviet and Maoist variants. In this section I primarily treat the Soviet elaboration.

The starting place for any discussion of people's democracy must be Marx, although the concept owes far more to the elaborations and "corrections" made by Lenin and his successors. The most elementary Marxian theory can be summarized relatively briefly. People have the capacity to be free and creative beings, but to date this capacity has been suppressed by economic scarcity, which has forced the vast majority to engage in compulsive labor simply to survive. In order to organize this labor, a ruling class, distinguished by its control over the means of production, has been necessary; thus, humanity has been divided fundamentally into two classes, an oppressing class who control the means of production and live off the surplus value extracted from an oppressed class who must sell their labor. The exigencies of production are pervasive, shaping both the society and the character and aspirations of its people. As the social pressures engendered by advances in productive technology increase, the ruling class, using the state as its instrument, becomes more repressive. "At a certain stage of their development the material productive forces of society come into contradiction with the existing production-relations, or, what is merely a juridical expression for the same thing, the property relationships within which they have operated before. From being forms of development of the productive forces, these relations turn into fetters upon their development. Then comes an epoch of social revolution. With the change in the economic foundation the whole immense superstructure is slowly or rapidly transformed."[6] Thus "the history of all hitherto existing society is the history of class struggles,"[7] and the agent of human progress is revolution by the oppressed class.

The latest step in this dialectic process is the triumph of capitalism. As before, the new economic system created a new class system, with the capitalist or bourgeois class oppressing the proletarian class. As before, a political transformation accompanied the economic transformation and institutionalized the political power of the bourgeoisie. As before, technological developments will lead to increasingly severe contradictions between "material productive forces" and "existing productive relationships," with the state becoming progressively more repressive until a revolutionary situation is achieved. This revolution, however, will be fundamentally different. First, the productive technology of capitalism has created for the first time a society of abundance. Thus compulsive labor and an oppressive class to organize it are no longer necessary. Second, capitalism has changed the nature of men; "it collectivizes them, teaches them that their life is not individual spontaneity but membership in a collective. . . . [D]ialectical history produces a society of universalist men. . . . "[8] After the final, communist, revolution, society could be "completely democratic," organized by voluntary cooperation among men who are by nature cooperative; there would be only one class, and hence no class struggle; and the state as the instrument of class oppression could wither away.

The bourgeois class and interests, of course, cannot be expected to give up without a struggle. Intermediate between the capitalist/bourgeois system and the communist system, therefore, must be one final class state, the dictatorship of the proletariat. During the period of proletarian class rule, the capitalist organization of production will be replaced by socialism, and the last vestiges of the bourgeois class will be eliminated. But, "[i]f the proletariat during its contest with the bourgeoisie is compelled, by the force of circumstances, to organize itself as a class, if, by means of a revolution, it makes itself the ruling class, and, as such, sweeps away by force the old conditions of production, then it will, along with these conditions, have swept away the conditions for the existence of class antagonisms and of classes generally, and will thereby have abolished its own supremacy as a class."[9]

Marx's expectation was that the inevitable revolution would be brought about by industrial workers suffering under and shaped by the economy and society of late capitalism. In fact, as the working classes of western Europe and the United States organized, they used their apparent political power to improve their wages and working conditions within capitalism rather than to make a revolution, and the capitalist class apparently expanded the range of political rights to include workers rather than becoming more repressive.[10] Moreover, Lenin, who became the successor of Marx if only because his revolution was the first to succeed, was struggling to create a communist revolution in a backward society barely emerging from feudalism. The conjunction of these facts led to the theoretical elaborations that transform the spontaneous and direct dictatorship of the proletariat into "people's democracy."

According to Lenin, the universalist man of Marx's theory could not be produced spontaneously because of the pervasive corrupting influence of capitalism. Lenin saw workers failing to recognize their true interest in eliminating rather than merely ameliorating "wage slavery." His prescription was that the communist revolution be led, and the dictatorship of the proletariat managed, by a "vanguard" whose tasks would include not only eliminating the bourgeois system and class, but also fostering the development of the new universalist man. After the revolution and during the dictatorship of the proletariat, there is a true community of the proletarian class, which, by virtue of the exclusion of the bourgeoisie from the category, embraces all citizens. Although the people can recognize this fact, their consciousness is not sufficiently developed for them to comprehend its implications and imperatives in full elaboration. Consequently they turn to and require a group of "minds trained in the art of dialectical thinking, realistic but constructive, in terms of the future that is potential in the present rather than in terms of a mere static worship of present facts." [11]

Like all intermediate stages in the dialectic process, the dictatorship of the proletariat is founded on a contradiction, in this case the problem of a state whose purpose is its own eventual abolition. One danger is that those people in control of the state will become a "new class," perverting the state from a proletarian dictatorship to a bureaucratic dictatorship. Lenin apparently recognized this problem and prescribed popular participation as its cure. This prescription leads to a restatement of the same contradiction in even starker form. On one hand, the Leninist theory calls for widespread participation in soviets at every level of organization, in effect a true participationist democracy of the working class and their allies. But on the other hand, it assumes that the actual citizen has not achieved an adequate level of political consciousness for that degree of self-management, and therefore requires the leadership of the vanguard of the proletariat in the form of the Communist Party. The central problem in people's democracy is to reconcile the call for active mass initiative and participation and for the turning over of "all power to the soviets" elected by universal suffrage with the "leading role" of the Communist Party. In considering both these claims, it is important to bear in mind the primary goal of community.

This emphasis on community, in turn, has two important implications. First, the theory of people's democracy draws a tight connection between rights and duties, a characteristic it shares with many other democratic theories, but the argument is carried to a greater extreme here. "Only those who contribute to the common cause in accordance with their abilities and who observe discipline and public order have the right to make demands upon society. . . . As Marx pointed out, ' . . . no rights without duties, no duties without rights.' " [12]

The second implication is that people's democracy "rejects individualism. It rejects the counterposing of the individual to the collective." [13] Not only is the collective good superior to the sum of individually perceived private goods, but each individual ought to identify his or her own good with the good of the whole and to affirm not private desires, but the good of the collectivity. If this ideal were real, the condition for the withering away of the state would have been achieved,[14] but its acceptance as an ideal is crucial to the theory of people's democracy. From the failure of the ideal to be realized flow the legitimacy and the necessity of centralism and discipline. Although there may be, and indeed ought to be, discussion and criticism before a decision is reached, once the true collective interest has been determined, all are obliged to accept that determination as embodying their own wills as well. Not to accept it is to place oneself outside the political community, and therefore to become not only a dissident but indeed a traitor.

Within this framework, the proper nature of the mass participation can be understood. In the first place, the intermittent and limited mass participation of the western electoral process is rejected. Instead, a high value is placed on mass mobilization in a wide range of organizations.[15] Given the goal of the eventual withering away of the state, and the general proposition that all states (including proletarian people's democracy) exist to be instruments of class oppression,[16] responsibilities that in the west are assumed by government ought in this view to be assumed instead by "spontaneously formed" associations of neighbors or coworkers.

One of the recurring themes in Marxist-Leninist writings is the oppressiveness of the petty officials of the bourgeois state. When workers themselves assume administrative roles, the oppressive nature of being "administered" is transformed into the self-administration of the proletarian class. Moreover, participation of all citizens in the administration of the state and in the management of economic and cultural development is an important step in the evolution to complete democracy and communism, both in leading the citizen to fuller involvement with the collectivity and in training him or her to the role of citizen/member of the collectivity in place of his or her role as object/subject.

The constant use of the word "administration" is, however, significant in precisely the terms of the often criticized distinction between politics and administration. On one hand, true freedom in the Marxist conception consists of acceptance of and submission to the "objective" laws of history. In this respect, the script is already written by a higher authority, and all that is left is administration. From the same perspective, once a classless society is built, the basis for politics, as the warfare of classes, disappears, and again all that is left is administration. On the other hand, to the extent that choices still must be made, the emphasis on mass participation in administration reaffirms the party's central role in the making of *political* decisions.

These themes are continued at higher levels of government through the treatment of representative institutions. One of the major complaints about bourgeois "parliamentarism" throughout the writings of Marx, Lenin, and Mao is that, even when the workers ostensibly have political rights, in practice these rights are shams. What good is it to elect a government if the only choice is between factions of the oppressor class? Since the soviets represent the mechanism by which the workers seize and operate the state apparatus, it is essential that the members of the soviets themselves be workers. Thus, Soviet writers stress the sociological make-up of the membership of the soviets. Further, many Soviet deputies would retain their regular employment in order to retain their ties to the proletariat.

Counterbalancing the emphasis on direct participation and on the authority of the soviets, however, is the leading role assigned to the Communist Party. The struggle for communism is a collective struggle, and as the organization of the "most active and politically conscious citizens" and "the highest form of working class political organization,"[17] the party serves the function of director and guide of the collectivity. Moreover, the leading role of the party is essential to the main-tenance, consolidation, and expansion of the dictatorship of the proletariat.[18] Thus anything that interferes with the leading role of the party is counterrevolu-tionary (the communist equivalent of heretical), opposed to historical necessity and the true interests of the working class, and anathema.

The leading role of the party is reconciled with notions of freedom through two devices. The first is the idea of democratic centralism and the need for disci-pline. Although eventual victory is assured by the laws of history, in the short run, the proletariat is locked in a life or death struggle with the forces of capitalism. In ideological terms, it must be "[e]ither bourgeois or Socialist ideology. There is no middle course. . . . Hence, to belittle the socialist ideology *in any way, to turn aside from it in the slightest degree* means to strengthen bourgeois ideology."[19] But the party is the articulator of socialist ideology. Moreover, democratic centralism implies a sharp distinction between the articulation of interests and the making of decisions. Debate and discussion by the mass are legitimate, but once a deci-sion has been reached by the party, any further contest of opinion must cease, and discipline takes over. To do otherwise is to yield to the temptation of egotistical individualism and oppose the true interest of the community.

The second way in which freedom and party control are reconciled is by the assumption that the party has widespread mass support. As Lenin wrote, "the dictatorship of the proletariat is . . . a domination that . . . enjoys the sympathy and support of the toiling and exploited masses."[20] This could be taken as a requirement for party rule, implying that defeat of party candidates in elections, demonstrations or strikes against party/government policy, or other evidence of opposition indicates that the party must correct its course. In fact, however, the support of the proletariat was taken as an article of faith, with everything else reinterpreted to coincide with that fundamental premise. Since the revolutionary working class and their allies unanimously support the leading role of the party, opposition is possible only from counterrevolutionaries, who neither have nor deserve political rights.[21]

Elections play an important role in people's democracy, but a significantly different role from that played by elections in the democratic theories discussed so far. Elections neither create nor limit political authority. Nor are they a time of popular choice among alternative courses of action. Rather, they are a time of coming together to express consent and loyalty to the party as the vanguard of the proletariat and ultimate guarantor of democracy. Virtually 100% turnout and vir-tually unanimous approval of the single slate of candidates presented are im-portant because they embody the presumed unanimity of the working class and their allies. While warning that the party should not assume that a 99% vote for party candidates meant that 99% of the population were "class-conscious Marx-Leninist internationalists," the leader of the Czech party nonetheless suggested that the result of the 1971 election in his country showed that "the great majority of the working people support the policies of the Communist Party of Czechoslovakia out of inner conviction."[22] The presumption of popular support was so strong that apparent evidence to the contrary had to be reinterpreted. Thus rejection of an officially endorsed candidate (as happened regularly in a small percentage of the cases, especially at the local level) was taken to reflect poor preparation or candidate choice by local officials, not rejection of or protest against the system as a whole.[23]

Elections also serve important educational functions. The electoral machinery was designed so as to involve large numbers of people as candidates for minor offices, as members of administrative boards managing the conduct of the elections, and as participants in organizational and mass meetings to propose and discuss prospective candidates. Elections also provide a focus for mass mobilization and an occasion for the party to explain its program to the people. Nomination of only one candidate for each position was not taken to indicate the suppression of opposition, but rather the success of the party in leading the workers to achieve consensus.[24] Given the supposed widespread popular involvement in the process of nomination, the formal election as a confirmation rather than a choice would not detract from the democraticness of the overall process, and the absence of opposition parties became a virtue rather than a vice.[25]

As subsequent events amply demonstrate, opponents of reforms to allow serious electoral competition were right to fear that the formation of opposition groups would lead workers to desert the leadership of the Communist Party and to the "restoration of the old order" (if by that phrase one means a capitalist market economy). Whether the states of the former Soviet bloc will persist in this path, and whether they will maintain political institutions more in keeping with western ideas of democracy, is unclear. It also remains possible to ask whether the collapse of Marxism-Leninism as the ruling ideology of eastern Europe and the Soviet Union indicates the bankruptcy of the theory in the abstract, or merely the failure of the Communist Parties to adhere to it adequately—and if the latter, whether that failure, including the obvious venality and corruption of many party officials, was inevitable.

Guided Democracy

"Guided democracy" as discussed here is a synthesis of theories and propaganda statements from several of the newer nations of Africa and Asia. Although I have adopted Sukarno's phrase, the discussion draws at least as heavily on Ayub Khan's "basic democracies" and Sékou Touré's "national democracy." Guided democracy often is seen merely as a variant of people's democracy, and it does share some of its underlying assumptions and rhetoric, especially the notions of a "vanguard" party or group and "democratic centralism," a frequent reference to "revolution," and a labeling of the west as "imperialist" or "neoimperialist." Nonetheless, in other assumptions, and in many conclusions and prescriptions, it stands in virtually diametric opposition to the communist position.[26]

Guided democracy, unlike the other theories discussed in this book, including people's democracy, does not purport to be universally applicable. Rather, it is developed from the experiences of the former colonies of Africa and Asia and intended to be applied as a model only in countries that share their historical, social, and economic situation.

The basic elements of this situation immediately after independence can be grouped under three headings. First, the social structure, and the general condition of the majority of the people, was traditional rather than modern. Grafted onto this traditional society, however, was a stratum of colonial people "who had been introduced into these Western mysteries and who also had traditional claims to a ruling position [who] inevitably felt they could and should take the Europeans' place."[27] Second, elite attitudes toward the institutions of parliamentary democracy were strongly shaped by the struggle for independence. Rather than being a device for popular rule, these institutions often appeared primarily to divide the native population and so make colonial domination easier to maintain.[28] Third, once independence was achieved, the new states faced two major problems. For one, the states themselves were largely artificial creations of the colonial powers, encompassing many peoples who often had deep-seated historical animosities toward one another, and who certainly felt no particular attachment to their new country. And second, the economic underdevelopment of the new states severely limited their real, as opposed to their legal, independence. The raising of capital and modernizing of their economies without simply replacing formal political domination with informal economic domination were principal objectives of the originators of guided democracy.

As in Rousseau, the central focus of guided democracy is the general will, and the ultimate sovereign is the people.[29] Many of the difficulties in Rousseau's use of the general will are relevant for guided democracy. On one side, there is the confusion of will and interest. While one can assume that the "real" will of each individual affirms that which is in his or her own interest, one cannot assume that the individual *knows* that ultimate interest. Thus the individual's articulated will may not be the real one. On the other side, the general will is not simply the sum of the individual wills of the people, even if these were known. The general will, instead, is the collective will of the community or nation, which has its own personality. "[R]eflecting this collective personality, we find a collective consciousness forming, collective faculties which, we must point out, *are not the sum of the consciousness and faculties of the individuals involved, but the synthesis of their wills and transcendental aspirations.*"[30] The synthesis of these two problems is the core difficulty with the concept of the general will as a guide for real-world democracy—the people cannot be expected to express it spontaneously.

Rousseau solved this problem with an individual able to articulate the general will, even if the body of the citizens cannot. Where Rousseau stops here, indeed leaving the likelihood that such an individual could be found seriously in doubt, the advocates of guided democracy continue, identifying themselves or their single party with that role and resolving the interest versus preference problem in favor of interest. Moreover, they continue beyond Rousseau to specify the content of that interest, namely national independence and economic development. This paramount common interest then defines the nature of the political community and underlies the great stress placed on unity.

The a priori specification of the public interest reflects the ambivalence with which the originators of guided democracy have viewed the mass of citizens of their countries. Guided democracy claims to implement the popular will while at the same time one of its objectives is to educate the people to close the gap between what the people *do* desire and what they *should* desire.[31] The originators of guided democracy were also ambivalent about the traditions of their societies. Although guided democracy is an ideology of modernization, its originators have stressed its roots in their own cultures. In particular, they have likened the nation to a traditional village or family and emphasized decision making by discussion and consensus, rather than by conflict and majority rule. This analogy supports as well a further tenet of guided democracy, that citizens should "regard themselves as 'men of the community' who will constantly put the general welfare ahead of everything else."[32] Although in some contexts this is presented as a revolutionary change, in others it is presented as a return to the values of traditional society. The synthesis of old and new is captured by Sékou Touré when he writes, "In creating a régime of 'National Democracy', the P.D.G. [Parti Démocratique de Guinée] chose, not class struggles and rival factions, but instead unitary action of the people, which brought back, in the terms of its democratic and progressive aims, all the old values and hierarchies."[33]

This confounding of tradition and modernity bolsters the legitimacy of the new regime by portraying it as a return to precolonial values.[34] Moreover, the particular features of this mysticized traditional culture were also useful in terms of their content. In particular, association of democracy with consensus justifies rejection of the western identification of democracy with elections among several parties.

The theory of guided democracy, then, calls for and justifies a one-party state. (Guided democracy in Indonesia formally was identified with a no-party state, but in fact the National Front functioned as a single party.) In the first place, a single party represents the continuation of the unity of the independence movements and reflects the unity of the people in the pursuit of the goals of national and economic independence and modernity. Given no real conflicts of interest and no social classes, there is no social basis for competing parties.[35] If there are vertical cleavages, the problem is to mitigate these differences, but a multiparty system that, in the absence of ideological differences, could only be based on religious or ethnic groups would instead aggravate and perpetuate them.[36]

Arguably, the general will is better expressed by a single party than by competing parties, each of which represents only the selfish interests of one section of the population. As Kwame Nkrumah put it, reflecting the general rejection of liberal democracy by leaders of the Third World, "[a] people's parliamentary democracy with a one-party system is better able to express and satisfy the common aspirations of a nation as a whole, than a multiple-party parliamentary system, which is in fact only a ruse for perpetuating, and covers up, the inherent struggle between the 'haves' and the 'have-nots.' "[37] In this view, the general will is found through discussion and recognized through consensus.

Finally, the weakness of the new states, and the dangerous situation in which their leaders felt themselves to be, called for stability. A single party, in which differences can be resolved informally, is supposed to ensure stable government, even if the actual individuals in office change periodically. "It is necessary to create a single party to be efficient . . . and not to give aid to the anonymous adversary, colonialism, which up to the present has been instrumental to the division of our country. We must have the unified party in order to limit the possibilities of corruption and to attempt to destroy opportunism."[38]

If guided democracy differs from western democracy in having only a single party, it differs from people's democracy in its assessment of what that party should be like. For people's democracy, the party is an elite, originally a conspiratorial elite and after the revolution a visible vanguard elite. For guided democracy, however, the party has the character of a mass movement. Rather than using the principle of centralism to purge the party of dissenters and fellow travelers, leaving a coherent and united core, all of the leaders of guided democracy have stressed inclusiveness, looking to the party to achieve unity, at least at the top of the hierarchy, among the many linguistic, ethnic, religious, cultural, and economic groups in their societies.[39] As with the people's democracies, the party is seen as locked in a struggle against an enemy, but whereas for the communists the enemy, at least initially, was internal, for guided democracy the enemy from the beginning has been external. In principle, this makes it easier for the advocates of guided democracy to recognize that "in a one-party system, party membership must be open to everybody and freedom of expression allowed to every individual."[40]

Elections are not intended to be choices of government in guided democracies any more than they are in people's democracies. Neither, however, are they merely reaffirmations of loyalty to the party elite. Rather, they are to provide substantial local choice of representatives, often extending to the opportunity to reject junior and even senior ministers. In this respect, they can provide important avenues of elite renewal, although not necessarily of elite circulation in Mosca's terms.[41] The situation is structured, however, not as a contest between competing opinions, but as a choice of the most confidence-inspiring party loyalist. Although subtle, this distinction between contest and choice is crucial to understanding the place of elections in guided democracy.[42] Moreover, the choice may be made within the party either in primary elections or party conventions, with the formal institution largely restricted to ratifying a decision previously made elsewhere.[43]

In addition to this difference, and to the rejection of the class conflict model in favor of a model of communal national unity and the rejection of the elitist party in favor of the party as mass movement, one final difference between guided democracy and people's democracy requires mention. Theorists of people's democracy argue that the people have made an irrevocable decision for communism, and hence are irrevocably committed to the Communist Party. While the leaders of guided democracies also assume that without a clear demonstration to the contrary (a demonstration they have made virtually impossible) they have the confidence of the people, they make no such claims of irrevocable support for their parties. As even Sékou Touré admits, *"it is the people, in the last resort, who have the final word. It is the people who must, if necessary, triumph over their Party, if the Party should no longer merit the people's confidence."* [44]

As expounded by their advocates, both people's democracy and guided democracy seem extremely appealing. This appeal, however, requires two assumptions, at least one of which might better be characterized as an article of faith. People's democracy is based on the belief that in an industrialized and socialized society, the state and problems of political power will wither away. Guided democracy is based on belief in a common will for national independence and economic development that transcends all other conflicts, including conflicts about how the costs and benefits of independence and development will be distributed.

These beliefs serve the same function as a definition of good and evil. Each theory has its own equivalent of the "forces of darkness" as well. For people's democracy it is the bourgeois/imperialist camp; for guided democracy it is neocolonialism. If one accepts these beliefs, failure to support the party of good is obviously tantamount to giving aid and comfort to the enemy of the community. If one lacks faith, however, it is difficult to see belief in a constant struggle against a counterrevolutionary conspiracy, whether from within or without, as other than paranoia or an excuse to suppress dissent, or to see either theory as anything but a rationalization for dictatorship.

Even if one accepts the basic moral premises of the emotive communitarian theories, a further assumption would be required: the single party will continue to represent the true popular will rather than degenerating into a self-serving clique. It is the possibility of such continuing virtue that liberal and popular sovereignty theories of democracy deny. Certainly, even the most devoted advocates of emotive communitarian theories recognize that private greed may triumph in individual cases. [45] Such problems infect all regimes, however. The question is whether the single-party states of emotive communitarian theory are as able as others to deal with them, or whether, in the words of a third world critic of the single-party state, "[t]he single party means an unusual concentration of power in the hands of one man, aided and influenced by a group. . . . What in the long run is fatal is that even in their own consciences they identify what is good for them with what is good for the country. . . . Once the single party is established in power, it is the last to perceive the need for change or for its own disappearance." [46] As the experience of the Soviet Union demonstrates, however, this kind of self-delusion can persist only so long before reality manifests itself.

Developmental Communitarian Democracy

The final variety of democratic theory to be discussed is the modern western form of communitarian democracy. As such, its point of departure is the society, political institutions and practices, and public philosophy of those countries that we would commonly call "democratic." Advocates of developmental communitarian democracy find them all fundamentally deficient, however, amounting at best to what they call "thin democracy."[47] What is lacking, they argue, is community, both as a central element of democratic theory and as an existential phenomenon fostered by existing institutions and practices.

Of the democratic theories discussed here, developmental communitarianism is the most difficult to characterize for at least three reasons. First, its advocates have devoted far more attention to articulating their opposition to the "poverty of liberalism"[48] than to the richness of their alternative. Second, when its advocates have made concrete proposals, their proposals have tended either to be too timid to justify claims of fundamental distinctiveness or to depend too heavily on technological "quick fixes" to be taken seriously. Third, the argument is fundamentally circular, assuming, despite frequent denials, the prior existence of the community it purports to be creating and thus appears to work only in the "easy" cases. Rather than delineating subtheories within this general type, I simply address each point in turn.

Communitarian complaints about liberalism can be divided roughly into two types, "logical" and "political." Both ultimately stem from dissatisfaction with the atomistic nature of society that communitarians see as the keystone of liberalism, and from which, communitarians claim, follow liberal democratic theory's "characteristic suspicion of politics," its denial of "the possibility of a public good that was more than an aggregation of individual and particular goods," its denigration of intensive popular participation in government, and its corresponding emphasis on representation.[49]

The most philosophical of the logical arguments against liberalism is exemplified by Michael J. Sandel's critique of John Rawls. The basic question, to which Sandel offers a negative answer, is whether the "unencumbered self" to be found behind Rawls' "veil of ignorance" has sufficient substance to support the weight of the central liberal premise, that the rights and liberties of the individual should have priority over the good. Rawls' derivation of the priority of rights is an attempt to reconstruct Kant's deontological argument for justice without the transcendentalism of the original by means of the metaphor of the "veil of ignorance." Behind this veil, persons know that they will have rational life plans, but they do not know what those plans will be. Thus, when they choose Rawls' principles of justice, this choice "does not depend on any particular values or ends."[50]

There are, however, in Sandel's view two problems. First, to get not just the priority of liberty but also the "well-ordered society" that Rawls wants requires a theory of community that goes beyond either the individualistic notion of community as an instrument of individual aims, or Rawls' more extensive (Sandel calls it "sentimental") community in which benevolent as well as selfish motivations may underlie cooperation, to a theory "that could penetrate the self even more profoundly than even the sentimental view permits."[51] But, if community is "constitutive of the shared self-understandings of the participants . . . , not simply an attribute of certain of the participants' plans of life,"[52] the deontological argument collapses, for the self is no longer defined independently of its motivations and community precedes justice. Second, the primacy of liberalism cannot be established in this deontological way, which requires that "[n]o transformation of my aims, or attachments could call into question the person I am, for no such allegiances, however deeply held, could possible engage my identity to begin with," "for we cannot coherently regard ourselves as the sort of beings the deontological ethic requires us to be." Moreover, even if we could think of ourselves in this way, it would not be desirable to do so, for "[t]o imagine a person incapable of constitutive attachments . . . is not to conceive an ideally free and rational agent, but to imagine a person wholly without character, without moral depth."[53] Thus, on one hand, community is necessary to our understanding of what it is to be human, while on the other hand some implicit assumption of community is necessary to establish "justice as the first virtue of social institutions."[54] And thus from both directions the liberal argument fails, for the first undermines its fundamental individualism while the second means that liberty cannot always have priority over the good that defines the community.

Also in the logical vein, Benjamin R. Barber attacks what he calls the "inertial frame of liberal democracy" made up of the major axiom of materialism and several corollaries dealing with "atomism, indivisibility, commensurability, mutual exclusivity, and sensationalism (as a psychology)," as a result of which "liberal theory cannot be expected to give an adequate account of human interdependency, mutualism, cooperation, fellowship, fraternity, community, and citizenship."[55] Here the argument is not so much that the theory of liberalism is logically invalid as that its validity is logically irrelevant because it is based on a counterfactual premise, and wonderfully evocative language portrays the liberal conception of man as not only false but distasteful as well.

From the political perspective, communitarians level three major complaints against liberal democracy: that it formulates the problem so as to deny the possibility of meaningful citizenship or public interest and thus denigrates politics; that it is hostile to participation, yet without direct participation it cannot justify obligation; and that it takes as immutable characteristics of man that are in fact liberal democracy's consequences rather than its justification. In the last respect, the communitarian critique of liberalism is basically the same as that of the participationists: people behave selfishly because they are in a system that destroys community; they do not develop the skills required for meaningful participation because they are denied the opportunity for effective participation; and they appear irresponsible because the system denies them any responsibility.

For the liberal, justice and freedom are necessary for politics; for the communitarian, politics is what makes justice and freedom possible.[56] This difference stems both from a different interpretation of justice and freedom and from a different interpretation of politics. For the developmental communitarian, justice can be defined only within the framework of a community and in terms of the shared values that define the community. The essence of politics is the discovery and development of the common or public interest, and the transformation rather than the resolution of conflict.[57] Similarly, liberty, equality, and fraternity are only hopeless abstractions without community. Rather than the negative freedom of the liberal, which is only the absence of external restraints, "[l]iberty is that secure release and fulfillment of personal potentialities which takes place only in rich and manifold association with others: the power to be an individualized self making a distinctive contribution and enjoying in its own way the fruits of association." [58]

For liberals, citizenship occupies the murky ground between a legal concept—citizens are those who have the right of entry and residence in, and to participate in the elections of, a particular state—and a moral imperative—citizens are those who, by virtue of being affected by a decision, ought to have the right to protect their interests by participating in its making. In either case, citizenship is an individual right with an individual purpose. For the communitarian, however, citizenship is an achieved, rather than an ascribed, status. "The citizen is the individual who has learned how to make civic judgments and who can evaluate goods in public terms." [59] Politics, thus, is not an unavoidable (because humans are not angels) process in which citizens engage, but the very process by which citizens are created, sustained, and reproduced. This process requires intensive participation from the people, so developmental communitarians decry the degree to which liberals tolerate, encourage indirectly through the institutional arrangements they propose, justify, and even glorify popular passivity.

This passivity, however, raises questions about the obligation of people to obey the laws of the state. Carole Pateman addresses these questions from the communitarian perspective.[60] She argues that in the absence of the prior value of community, obedience to the state cannot be given the voluntaristic cast that the liberal argument requires. But the prior value of community is precisely what the liberal view of the world cannot allow. Thus liberals are forced to argue that voting in elections implies consent. This argument Pateman effectively demolishes[61] and argues that the solution is direct and intensive participation in "a political association of a multiplicity of political associations . . . which are bound together through horizontal and multifaceted ties of self-assumed political obligation." [62]

Representative democracy, at least in the liberal mold, is inadequate. Echoing Rousseau, Barber claims that "[t]o exercise the franchise is unhappily also to renounce it. . . . Representation is incompatible with freedom because it delegates and thus alienates political will at the cost of genuine self-government and autonomy." [63] Representative government begins by allowing, and finishes by encouraging, ordinary people to leave politics and government to the elites.[64] It is, thus, incompatible with equality. It focuses attention on electoral competition, thus emphasizing what divides the citizens rather than what unites them. It leads citizens to be primarily concerned with their own interests in a defensive way, rather than with the public interest in an active way. The hostility to elections implicit in this critique of representation appears, however, to apply only to elections held in a "liberal democratic frame of mind"; the institutional prescriptions of developmental communitarians all seem to leave a substantial role for the election of individuals who can be described only as representatives.

Turning to the communitarian alternative to liberal democracy, the striking feature is the paucity of detail and the timidity of the actual suggestions. This is less true of Barber's "strong democracy" than of many other proposals, so it will be the principal focus of this discussion. Strong democracy shares several central features with other developmental communitarian definitions, however. Listing these common points will both locate Barber's argument in its wider context and give an overview of the main points of the argument.

First, developmental communitarians see politics as embedded in a rich network of social interactions. They argue that it is futile to talk about democratic politics without considering the democraticness of social life as a whole. As John Dewey put it, "[t]he idea of democracy is a wider and fuller idea than can be exemplified in the state even at its best. To be realized it must affect all modes of human association, the family, the school, industry, religion."[65]

Second, developmental communitarians stress the publicness, and especially popular awareness of the publicness, of politics. Again quoting Dewey, this means the "perception of the consequences of a joint activity and of the distinctive share of each element in producing it. Such perception creates a common interest; that is concern on the part of each in the joint action and in the contribution of each . . . to it."[66] Thus, in contrast to the liberal ideal, the question for each citizen "is not What do I fancy? but What do I think *we* should do?"[67]

Third, to the extent that they are concerned with majority rule, developmental communitarians regard the process of majority formation as more important than the outcome of voting. The constantly recurring concern is with "political talk," which is expected to create a bond of common understanding and a sensitivity to the common interest. Through political talk community is to be developed and maintained, the public interest discovered, and the interests of minorities taken into account.

Barber defines strong democracy as "politics in the participatory mode where conflict is resolved in the absence of an independent ground through a participatory process of ongoing, proximate self-legislation and the creation of a political community capable of transforming dependent, private individuals into free citizens and partial and private interests into public goods."[68] Echoing the first of the common themes of developmental communitarian theory, this definition appears for the first time in a chapter entitled, "Strong Democracy: Politics as a Way of Living."

The argument for strong democracy begins, as do liberal theories, with citizens whose interests and values are partially in conflict. But where the liberal is concerned merely that these citizens find a way to contain conflict so that they can live together peacefully, Barber is concerned that they "transform" conflict, so as "to live together *communally* not only to their mutual advantage but also to the advantage of their mutuality."[69] Further, while Barber claims that liberals regard human nature as immutable, the theory of strong democracy assumes that human nature is malleable and that participation in a politics of mutuality will transform not only conflict among citizens but the citizens themselves.

The central concerns of Barber's theory—politics, citizenship, and community—are intimately connected. Politics arises when people have to make a decision with public consequences, wish to be reasonable, and yet do not agree about means or ends.[70] For Barber, "[t]he citizen is the individual who has learned how to make civic judgments and who can evaluate goods in public terms."[71] The central point is not the public consequences of action, but the willingness to evaluate and decide upon action in public rather than private terms, the desire to be mutually reasonable rather than individually rational. In other words, citizens are fully participating members of a political community, and given a definition of the political that excludes "[a]ction that is impulsive, arbitrary, or unconsidered," it makes sense to say that "[o]nly a citizen can be a *political* actor."[72] The medium through which politics takes place, and the mechanism by means of which citizens and community are forged, is political talk and its obverse, empathetic listening. "Listening . . . by its very practice enhances equality" and bridges the gap between individuals, leading to mutual understanding. "[O]ngoing talk . . . is a dynamic act of imagination that requires participants to change how they see the world."[73]

The vision of strong democracy is that of a community of engaged citizens, each actively pursuing their joint interest. The task is to devise institutions that will foster and maintain such a community. Barber divides his recommendations under three major headings, with four specific suggestions under each, dealing respectively with strong democratic talk, strong democratic decision making, and strong democratic action.[74] A look at these sheds further light on the meaning and limitations of developmental communitarianism.

Under the heading of strong democratic talk, Barber's most important reform is for the institution of a national system of neighborhood assemblies. Initially, these assemblies would be concerned only with the development of neighborhood consciousness, rather than autonomy and self-rule, although later they are to become the constituencies for regional and national referenda. As Barber observes, however, neighborhood assemblies "reach only local constituencies and can divide and parochialize both regions and the nation as a whole. . . . What strong democracy requires is a form of town meeting in which participation is direct yet communication is regional or even national." To achieve this, he proposes a kind of television town meeting incorporating two-way communication capabilities and supplemented by a vastly expanded system of public access channels on cable systems. Barber's third concern is information. He proposes a national videotext service and subsidized postage for "all legitimate publishers of newspapers, journals, magazines, and books." Finally, under the heading of "supplementary institutions," Barber proposes representative town meetings with members chosen by lot; selection of local officials like members of planning, zoning, and education boards by the same principle; and local lay mediation and justice for petty misdemeanors, family quarrels, and so forth.[75]

The cornerstone of Barber's proposals for strong democratic decision making is a national initiative and referendum process requiring votes separated by at least six months as a "check on public mercurialness" and a multichoice format allowing voters to express reservations and intensity of feeling (although the aggregate numbers of yeas and nays would continue to determine the outcome). Perhaps the most important feature of these referenda would be the use of electronic voting in the neighborhood assemblies to allow proposals to be modified in the light of intermediate votes, and to return voting to the public arena, in which citizens, in addition to making choices, must justify those choices to each other.[76] Barber's third suggestion is selection of petty officials by lot with per diem payment and rotation in office. Finally, and with nearly overwhelming reservations, he proposes a voucher system to allow the market to replace collective choice in many policy areas.[77]

Under the heading of strong democratic action, Barber calls first for universal national (not necessarily military) service to restore some balance between rights and duties of citizenship. Along with compulsory service, he calls for furtherance of neighborhood citizenship through local programs of voluntary action. Because democracy is a way of life, not just a form of government, its reach should be extended to include workplace democracy. Lastly, there should be a new architecture of civic and public space, drawing people together rather than isolating them from one another.

These proposals can be taken as suggestions for marginal improvements in the existing structure of liberal democratic government in the United States. Given the vigor with which Barber denounces that system and the theory he sees underlying it, this seems a strange perspective to take, but it is justified by the remarkable timidity of many of his concrete proposals. At this level, finding fault with Barber's proposals is difficult, and indeed many of them have also been advocated by the liberals about whose theories he complains, except that they see them as improvements, not alternatives, to liberal democracy.[78] The proposals for "civic education and equal access to information," for example, amount to little more than cheap postage and access to existing public databases.

Alternatively, Barber's proposals can be taken as a serious blueprint not just marginally to improve liberal, thin democracy, but to replace it with strong democracy. In this case, the question is not whether his proposals are too radical, but whether they are radical enough, and practical enough, to work. Studying them in detail, one might, with good reason, doubt both their empirical adequacy and their theoretical consistency.

Many of Barber's proposals betray an alarmingly naive faith in technology. Television, for example, may make instantaneous communication possible to millions of people spread over a vast area, but it cannot add hours to the day. Assuming citizens would sit eight hours a day for a five-day week, Barber's television town meetings could hear from only 2,400 citizens, assuming only one minute each (hardly adequate time for a rational argument to be expressed) and no time wasted on switching or introductions. In purely practical terms, the vast majority of citizens could not speak, and access to the floor would inevitably be limited to a small class of professional politicians—exactly what the participationists and developmental communitarians decry.

Barber attempts to counter two arguments that he suspects liberals might raise against his proposed neighborhood assemblies. The first is that people will not participate, either because they are too busy or too apathetic. Barber's response, like Pateman's claim noted in the previous chapter, is that "people refuse to participate only where politics does not count. . . . They are apathetic because they are powerless, not powerless because they are apathetic." But he says this having just argued that the neighborhood assemblies would have no decision-making power! The second anticipated complaint is that the assemblies would "fall prey to peer pressure, eloquence, social conformity, and various forms of sub-rosa manipulation and persuasion." In response, he quotes Douglas Yates' finding that "[w]idespread internal conflict was the dominant characteristic of neighborhood governance."[79] But if so, does it not undermine the claim that neighborhood participation will build community?

A similar problem afflicts Barber's proposal to select local officials by lot. Anticipating the charge that ordinary citizens lack the competence to fill most public offices, Barber limits this proposal to local positions that do not require any special expertise, suggests that officials chosen by lot might only be a minority of board members, and offers them training and advice by a body of permanent officials. This process might be an effective way of transmitting citizen complaints to political decision-makers, but it is not self-rule in anything like the sense of the rhetoric that preceded it. Barber simply ignores the evidence that boards of private citizens selected as a cross-section of the population and assisted by permanent officials very quickly become the captives of those officials.[80] And again, if those selected have no real power, why should selection fundamentally transform their thinking, let alone the thinking of those not selected? And why assume that citizens selected by lot will be any less prone to self- or group-interested conflict than the officials we have now?

This question then points to a more fundamental problem with strong democracy; it is a politics of friends—individuals who are prepared not so much to compromise for their mutual advantage as to redefine their own advantage as that they hold in common, prepared not so much to sacrifice or restrain their own opinions in exchange for similar sacrifice or restraint by others as to change their opinions on the basis of empathetic understanding of others' arguments. This is the familiar claim that all problems can be solved if only "people of good will" can be brought together to discuss their differences. It ignores the fact, brought home almost daily from around the world, that often greater knowledge and understanding lead to greater, not lesser, hostility. It ignores the fact that one of the most difficult, but also most fundamental, problems of politics is that not everyone agrees what a "person of good will" is, or what it is that such a person would will.

As liberals themselves recognize, peaceful democracy is impossible in a country in which two or more groups would prefer to fight, and are able to fight, rather than compromise. Even in less extreme forms, the problem remains that individuals do not have infinitely malleable private standards of evaluation. In the end, a remaining minority is forced, as Elaine Spitz admits, to rely on the charity of the majority for the protection of its rights and interests.[81] All the discussion of participation leading to legitimacy, to a willingness to say, "I am part of the community, I participated in the talk and deliberation leading to the decision, and so I regard myself as bound; but let it be known that I do not think we have made the right decision,"[82] makes sense only if the matter in question does not touch on fundamental differences, that is, if community is more important to the dissenter than the value on which he or she dissents.

Thus we face the most fundamental questions of all about developmental communitarian democracy. Are the people and society it envisions in fact attractive? On what kind of majority would a minority rely? And is it an admirable trait to value community over other moral and political principles? Addressing these

questions brings one to the problem of elections. In their specific recommendations, the developmental communitarians discussed here take a rather ambiguous
attitude toward elections, and again one must distinguish between strong and
weak forms of the theories. First, in the strong form, the principal contrast is
between the basic antipathy of developmental communitarianism toward representative government, and hence also toward elections, and the view that representative democracy is positively superior to direct popular rule, with the electoral
system being the most important democratic political institution. Examining this
contrast will address the desirability of the communitarian ideal. I will then return
to the weaker form, which, although not so clearly supportable as an alternative
to liberal democracy nonetheless leads to implications for the conduct of elections that distinguish even this form of communitarianism from liberal democracy
tout court.

In its strong form, developmental communitarian democracy must be hostile
to elections because it is hostile to representative democracy and because it is
opposed to majoritarian, as opposed to consensual, decision making. In Barber's
words, "[m]ajoritarianism is a tribute to the failure of democracy: to our inability
to create a politics of mutualism that can overcome private interests. It is thus
finally the democracy of desperation, an attempt to salvage decision-making from
the anarchy of adversary politics."[83] It is precisely this politics of mutualism and
denigration of adversary politics that George Kateb, among others, finds alarming.

Simply put, Kateb's argument is that representative democracy fosters commendable moral phenomena in the life of society, whereas communitarian democracy, precisely because of the existence of the community it seeks, "spells the
absence of commendable moral phenomena and the presence of noxious ones[,
some of which] . . . grow out of the very nature of community."[84] The commendable traits Kateb sees as furthered by representative democracy appear much like
those Barber claims for strong democracy. The problems arise when disagreements occur. For the strong democrat, the Rousseauian connection of ruler and
ruled (the citizen as both author and subject of government action) is a virtue;
for Kateb, it is a defect because "[t]he lack of distance between citizens and
political authority may also render authority much more psychologically oppressive by making any impulse to dissent into an act of shameful rebellion against
oneself, of shameful inconsistency. A chastened but separate authority may be
more morally advantageous than one which nobody can sever his identity
from."[85]

A second concern is the emphasis placed by the advocates of direct democracy on citizenship, which they regard as "continuous and all absorbing, and laid
as an obligation on all, not freely chosen by a random few."[86] Barber, at least,
does not go this far; one can choose to cease being a citizen (in the sense of
being a member of the self-governing community, as opposed to the sense of
being its legal subject) by choosing not to participate. Presumably, those who
find themselves in a permanent minority or who disagree with the majority over
fundamental values would be the most likely to opt out. Although abstention
might free them of the problem of self-imposed psychological repression, it only
furthers the possibility of old-fashioned physical repression, since those who have

chosen to opt out of citizenship will not be the beneficiaries of any of the sympathy-building products of political talk. Amy Gutmann's complaint that the communitarians "want us to live in Salem, but not to believe in witches" relates directly to the strong theory of developmental communitarian democracy. A perfectly settled community would not be repressive, but only "because perfect settlement would leave no dissent to repress,"[87] leading to a democratic tyranny every bit as repressive as the tyrannies of the one-party-guided or people's democracies.

This incompatibility of the freedom and justice of liberal democracy with the equality, community, and direct self-rule of developmental communitarian democracy exemplifies the fundamental theme underlying this entire half of the book. Taking one step back, however, one can still ask what the implications of developmental communitarian thought might be for the conduct of basically liberal democratic elections.

One conclusion is that the process of majority formation, rather than the existence of a majority decision, is the central point. Lively and informed discussions are important, and we may apply Barber's prescription for the expression and dissemination of a wide variety of political ideas to the particular context of electoral campaigns, and even more to the processes by which candidates are selected and alternatives for choice defined. In this case, the communitarian clearly must oppose strong and disciplined party organizations that would tend to foreclose these preliminaries.

At the same time, the communitarian desire for direct popular decision precludes support of multiparty proportional politics, in which the determinative majority is formed and the final decision taken only by professional politicians. Proportional systems encourage politicians to appeal to that which divides the citizens; simple majority may allow them to appeal to citizens' common interests. Indeed, it is not clear that developmental communitarianism wants any parties beyond the skeletal organizations required to conduct elections, preferring instead a continuous process of majority building.

Finally, if there are to be elections, clearly they should be based on constituencies that, while hopefully nearly equal in population, above all reflect real communities. Unfortunately, while this concept makes the choice of a single representative from a single district conform well to the ideal of direct popular decision making, with the plausible argument that the process of majority formation will strengthen and preserve the already existing political community of that constituency, it says nothing about how to forge a community that spans districts or how to overcome the well-recognized deficiencies of single-member plurality election.[88]

The Roles of Elections

The central questions of the last four chapters—What desiderata is democracy supposed to foster? What are elections supposed to do?[1]—in the broadest terms have already been answered. Elections are to prevent tyranny (ancient Athens and modern liberal democracy), confirm authority (the Roman Republic but reflected in several modern views, especially Tory popular sovereignty democracy), articulate externally determined truth (the medieval church as well as modern emotive communitarianism), select and empower representatives (pre-reform Britain, popular sovereignty democracy, liberal democracy), allow the will of the people to be articulated and carried into effect (popular sovereignty), prevent selfish interests from using control of the government to exploit others (liberalism), promote the flowering of human potential (personal development), and foster the development and maintenance of viable communities (communitarianism).

Yet these responses are rather remote from the actual operation of electoral systems. This gap was partially closed by drawing a connection between varieties of democratic theory and the types of competition and political party systems for which they call; one could say that the production and maintenance of an appropriate party system are also functions of an electoral system. All this discussion took for granted, however, the performance of some functions, such as the simple filling of offices, to which attention must be devoted in the real world of politics. One purpose of this chapter is to delineate these additional concerns. First, however, one democratic value not yet discussed requires brief attention: equality.

Democracy and Equality

Equality is as complex a concept as democracy, with its own vast literature.[2] It is also intimately connected to democracy, and no theory can be said to be democratic without a significant element of equality. Both the nature and centrality of that connection vary, however, as does the sense in which equality is understood, from one democratic theory to another.

Referring specifically to political influence, equality in the sense of "anonymity" is a defining condition of the individualist theories of popular sovereignty.[3] The equality that anonymity presumes, however, leads generally to insistence on majoritarianism, which many consider dangerous. For these theories, a balance of influence among groups, rather than equality among individuals, is the goal; the individual-level equality that, within limits, they consider as a precondition of democracy is equality of rights and opportunities, what Giovanni Sartori described as "equal opportunities to become unequal."[4] Rousseau, as well as Aristotle, argued, however, that substantial equality of condition is a necessary precondition for viable democracy. Finally, from the perspective of developmental communitarianism, both equality of influence and equality of rights are too narrowly drawn to encompass true democratic equality, which assumes an almost spiritual quality, but this kind of equality is clearly a goal, rather than a defining characteristic or precondition.

At the other extreme, some democratic theories appear on the surface very inegalitarian, even from the point of view of equality of opportunity. Tory popular sovereignty, for example, explicitly argues for inequality of opportunity to the extent that it favors entrusting power to a class essentially bred from birth to rule, as well as for inequality of influence and inequality of condition. Even here, however, commitment to equality of worth —that every citizen is equally entitled to be considered part of the national community whose will the political elite articulates— is central to this theory's claim to be democratic. With the exception of those people excluded from true citizenship, roughly the same argument applies to the emotive communitarian theories, with the vanguard party in lieu of the Tory ruling class.

Of course, the real problems are more complicated than these paragraphs indicate. To have influence often is one of the rights liberals debate. Some equality of rights is likely necessary to make equality of worth or equality of influence effective. The lowest common denominator among these democratic theories is equality at the ballot box. Even Tory popular sovereignty, although not requiring "one man, one vote, one value," still requires the equality of influence implicit in universal suffrage; by extending the right to vote to all citizens, the principle that each citizen is entitled to be counted as a part of the whole is given substance. The promotion of equality is not generally a function of elections, but the reflection of a democratic commitment to equality, at least in this minimal sense, is.

The Functions of Elections

Legitimation

On this note, we can return to the opening sentence of the book and observe that a central function of elections is to make a political system democratic, at least in the negative sense that no modern system without elections (or some other form of popular decision making) conducted under effectively universal suffrage would be considered democratic by advocates of any of the democratic theories discussed.[5] Because democracy is taken virtually universally to be the only acceptable form of government, this becomes a general argument about the legitmacy of a political system, which is legitimate because it is democratic, and democratic because it holds elections.

Simply to hold some form of elections is not adequate either to confer or to confirm legitimacy, however. To confer legitimacy, the elections held must be consistent with the view of democracy adopted by those who are to accept the legitimacy of the system. The requirement that the elections conform to their more general standards of fairness is implicit. That one function of elections is to confer legitimacy means at least that they should enjoy widespread acceptance.

To confer legitimacy is to lead people to think in a certain way; to confirm legitimacy is to produce a visible sign that they do think in that way. In systems that claim to be democratic, the relevant signs are turnout in elections and vote for parties or candidates that publicly reject the legitimacy of the system. At a minimum, very low turnout or a very high vote for antisystem candidates call into question the legitimacy of the system. There is no similar agreement that very high turnout indicates high legitimacy. For participationists and communitarians, everyone ought to want to vote. Thus low turnout must indicate that something is wrong. From the more defensive perspective of the liberals, however, excessively high turnout would be the danger sign; that many people do not vote indicates that they are sufficiently satisfied with the status quo.[6] In either case, as well as indicating legitimacy, its confirmation can also contribute to its conferral; most citizens' acceptance of the system as legitimate may lead to its acceptance by others.

On the other hand, satisfactory turnout and a low level of antisystem party voting prove legitimacy only if citizens have alternatives; if voting is compulsory or if antisystem parties are barred, a turnout or a prosystem percentage of "only" 95% may be a sign of serious disaffection. And, of course, if elections can provide evidence of the system's legitimacy, the mirror image is true as well; elections also can provide citizens with an opportunity to demonstrate that they do not accept the system by refusing to participate, spoiling or defacing their ballots, or, when possible, voting for antisystem candidates or parties.

Installation of Officials

The most elementary function of elections is to fill offices with people. Regardless of the conception of democracy, an electoral system that left unfilled vacancies would be a failure. Thus electoral laws may provide for the drawing of lots to resolve ties, not as an appeal to God, but as a way to ensure that someone fills the office. As an evaluative criterion, this is a nonstarter; all electoral systems are successful.

At the level of government formation, however, the success of electoral systems in installing a government is more variable, as the long inability of the Israeli Knesset in 1990 (March 15–June 8), the Belgian Parliament in 1991–1992 (November 24–March 7), or the Dutch Tweede Kamer in 1989 (September 6–November 2) to install prime ministers and governments all illustrate. A supposed inability to install a government sometimes is raised as an argument against an electoral system.

Aside from the question of whether some electoral systems contribute to the likelihood of government crises, a problem of definition bears directly on how the function of government installation is translated into an evaluative standard for elections. If the choice of a cabinet by a parliament is counted as part of the electoral system—that is, if election of a government by parliament is interpreted as being part of a two-stage, indirect electoral system—then the examples cited above merely reflect protracted, not unsuccessful, elections. If, however, a direct and immediate connection between votes cast and governments installed is required, a strong case could be made that those elections were failures.

Selection and Choice

As ecclesiastical elections illustrate, the function of installation is separable from the function of selection. Any democratic theory must allow some element of choice by the citizens, if only whether to continue supporting the only party. For participationist democrats, elections as occasions for choice lead to the personal development of the citizens. More generally, without a real opportunity to choose, the institutions of any democratic theory become mere window dressing for authoritarianism. Beyond this element of commonality, however, there is considerable disagreement about the desirable range, type, and basis of choice.

With regard to the range of choice, three basic positions emerge from the democratic theories considered. The most restrictive is the "yes or no" choice of emotive communitarianism, combining, but otherwise reflecting directly, the two questions that Rousseau insisted must regularly be put to the people: "Does it please the Sovereign to preserve the present form of government [?] [and] . . . Does it please the people to leave the administration with those who are at present charged with it?"[7] The second possibility is the "either/or" choice of two-party politics, explicitly prescribed by five of the six popular sovereignty theories and by the majoritarian liberal theories, and at least potentially compatible with pluralist liberalism, some varieties of participationist democracy, and, if one assumes the alternatives are chosen through an adequately participatory process and counts only the number of choices when the final decision is made, developmental communitarianism as well. The third possibility, many available choices, is required by legislative popular sovereignty and veto group liberalism. Moreover, if one takes a view of elections that encompasses more than what happens on election day, developmental communitarianism, with its insistence that the alternatives between which the people finally decide must have sprung from the people as well, is also committed to a multiplicity of choice.

Analyzing the type of choice, one can distinguish two broad emphases—elections as choices among persons and elections as choices among policies. These are not entirely distinct, of course, since persons may be chosen on the basis of policy promises or performance while the person espousing a particular policy may influence the degree to which it is accepted. Moreover, each of these broad positions may be further elaborated or refined. Choice of individual can refer to choice of local representative, or party as national representative, or choice of party as potential government. Choice of policy can be based on personal/group interest or on the community interest, which in turn can be defined locally or nationally.

Representation

A fourth general function of elections is to create or foster representation in the twin senses of establishing a normative expectation and facilitating a recruitment or reward structure for the elected to represent the electors. As with equality, the meaning of representation is the subject of a vast and nuanced literature that cannot be replicated here.[8] Instead, I want only to highlight three particularly significant senses in which an elected body or individual can be called representative of the people.

The first of these senses traces its descent directly from medieval representative institutions and is the representative as a person empowered *by* the represented to act *for them, or in their place.* Unless officials are representative in this minimal sense, the resulting government can make no claim to be democratic. Elections are the institutions by which the represented authorize their representatives to act for them, so no system can be democratic without elections. Two questions remain under this heading, however. First, how much choice must the electors have before the elected can claim true authorization to act for their constituents? Second, how broad is the grant of authority? In extreme terms, is the representative empowered to act as he or she judges necessary on whatever questions arise, or to act only on the specific subjects raised in his or her campaign?

The second sense suggests that the elected represent the electors to the extent that they are like them in some significant way. Historically, two types of likeness have been significant. One refers to the sociological characteristics of the elected and electors and is concerned, for example, with the degree to which the distribution of social classes, genders, races, or linguistic groups in a representative body numerically duplicates the corresponding distribution among the population as a whole. Sometimes this distribution is valued for symbolic reasons as a reflection of the ideal that members of all groups are equal, but at other times it is valued as a presumed prerequisite for the second type of representative likeness, that referring to opinions or interests. In this case it might be argued that no one except a manual worker can truly understand the perspective and interests of a manual worker; thus, no one can represent a manual worker except another manual worker. Without necessary reference to sociology, the point would be that representation requires the representative to share the interests or opinions of the represented, and again one could look either at the relationship between a single representative and his or her constituents or at the aggregate distributions of opinions in society and in the representative body.

Finally, representation can mean acting as an agent for the represented, as, for example, in petitioning for redress of grievances. In this case, full representation would mean only that each citizen could find someone who would faithfully present the citizen's case or point of view. Proportionality would be significant only as it correlated with the effectiveness with which the citizen's interests could be represented, and diversity might well be valued above proportionality.

Popular Involvement

Elections are expected to provide an occasion for popular involvement in politics and for popular education about politics. Election campaigns provide a setting for candidates and other involved citizens to present alternative views to the wider electorate, and an occasion when ordinary citizens are expected, and expect, to devote more attention than usual to listening to that debate. As some participationists argue, knowing that a decision will be required can stimulate a person to gather the information required to make it intelligently. Even if the voters have no real choice, during campaigns rulers are expected at least to act as if they had to convince average citizens of their fitness to rule.

In addition to encouraging ordinary citizens to become informed about politics, elections provide opportunities for more direct involvement. Voting itself is an act of direct participation in public decision making. At a slightly higher level, citizens can discuss the issues in addition to listening to the discussions carried on by others, or they can contribute to causes or candidates they support. Elections also provide an opportunity for the citizen to take an even more public role, ultimately perhaps making speeches or even standing for office.

Finally, elections either allow or force the people to take responsibility, at least indirectly, for their own government. On the positive side (allowing the people to take responsibility), to take responsibility for public affairs is an essential component of mature human existence. Opportunities for expressing demands and proposing solutions to problems cannot transform subjects into citizens so long as responsibility lies elsewhere. On the negative side (forcing citizens to take responsibility), however, especially referenda, but also elections, can be used as the "Pontius Pilate" of representative government,[9] allowing officials to wash their hands of responsibility for particularly difficult, dangerous, or divisive questions.

Democratic Theories and the Roles of Elections

This discussion not only provides an alternative structure for considering the expectations about, and evaluative standards for, elections raised by democratic theories, but also underlines the fundamental theme of everything said so far. Although elections play a central role in all theories of democracy, the specific functions of elections vary tremendously from one conception of democracy to another.

This point assumes central importance as one moves to explain and evaluate the operation of real electoral systems. On one hand, electoral systems are purposively designed, so an appreciation of the objectives of their designers is essential to understanding those systems. Of course, the achievement of democratic values is not the only purpose for which electoral systems are adopted. Moreover, in the realm of political engineering, to have a purpose does not guarantee knowing how it can be achieved. Thus, though necessary, an understanding of the role elections are expected to play in different democratic theories is not sufficient to explain the differences among actual electoral systems.

On the other hand, in trying to assess the degree to which various electoral systems promote democracy, it is similarly crucial to remember that democracy assumes different meanings for different people and that the evaluative standards vary accordingly. An institution that epitomizes democratic practice from one perspective may impede democratization from another. The democraticness of an institution can be judged only on the basis of a particular conception of democracy.

At the same time, both explanation and evaluation call for empirical knowledge as well as philosophical understanding. A valid connection between electoral institutions and democratic values must be based on an accurate picture of the options available in the design of those institutions and of the consequences of choosing one option rather than another. To this task the second part of this book is devoted.

The Description of Electoral Systems

In a narrow sense, terms like "election," "electoral law," and "electoral system" refer to what happens on and immediately after "election day" and concern little more than the mechanics of casting and counting votes and the declaring of winners. Thus the seminal work of Douglas Rae defines "[e]lectoral laws [as] those which govern the processes by which electoral preferences are articulated as votes and by which these votes are translated into distributions of governmental authority (typically parliamentary seats) among the competing political parties."[1] Rae's work is an outstanding example of a large literature that has focused especially on electoral formula supplemented only, if at all, by concern over suffrage.[2] A continuing political issue in many countries, the relationship between seats and votes has also been one of the major points at issue in academic discussions of the democratic fairness of electoral systems[3] and of the possibility that some electoral systems facilitate the longevity of democratic regimes more than others.[4]

In the broadest sense, electoral system includes everything that bears on the conduct or outcome of elections. While it is important to be aware of the range of factors that influence elections, this approach includes too much—not just legal restrictions on campaign spending, but the economic system as it bears on the distribution of financial resources, the communications system as it bears on the need for or possibility of paid advertising, and the culture as it bears on the social acceptability of various ways in which money might be spent; not just legal provisions concerning the use of party labels on the ballot, but the degree and nature of partisan attachment in the electorate, the internal structure and coherence of the parties, and the legal, cultural, and economic impediments to the formation of new parties.

My approach, like all intermediate positions, has a certain fuzziness of definition. Here, the term electoral system refers to both more and less than the formal content of electoral law. It means less than electoral law in that I do not address, except in passing, such matters as the composition of electoral commissions, forms for reporting and certifying results, the mechanics of financial reporting if required, and so on, notwithstanding that the majority of electoral law, at least in bulk, concerns precisely matters of this kind and that where the honesty of elections is in question, these matters may be crucial to securing general acceptance of the results. On the other hand, my definition means more than electoral law in that some aspects of the economy, culture, and social structure of a society bear *directly* on the real meaning of formal electoral provisions and so must be included in any complete description of its electoral system. To cite just one example, although the allocation of time for broadcast campaigning to political parties in Britain is made by informal agreement, it is as much a part of the electoral system as the limits on broadcast campaign expenditures imposed by American law.[5]

The discussion here, and in the following chapters, gives a privileged position to elections of national parliaments. The vast majority of the literature on electoral systems treats such elections, and this study will be no exception. The vocabulary used is generally that of parliamentary elections, most questions are posed from that perspective and in that context, and the majority of the empirical data considered come from such elections. In some respects, however, the focus on legislative elections is more semantic than substantive. For example, the term "legislature" can be taken to mean any body of officials, including school boards, city councils, or electoral colleges as well as parliaments, whether they make laws or not. Further, even the choice of a single president or governor can be regarded as a legislative election—it is simply the degenerate case in which the size of the legislature is equal to one.

Dimensions of Electoral Systems

The rest of this chapter presents the main questions pertaining to an electoral system. The remaining chapters of this section then examine the arguments for and against various answers to these questions and the consequences of those answers for politics, and thus also for the nature of democracy and the achievement of democratic values.

These topics can be divided roughly into four categories. The first covers how the distribution of votes cast is translated into a distribution of seats, both at the district and national levels. The second category discusses the format of the choice confronting the elector. The questions encompassed in these two categories basically take the electorate, parties, and candidates as given, at least within the context of a single election. (Among the possible consequences of an electoral system over a longer period are, of course, changes in the nature of the party system, the kind or number of candidates, and the levels of electoral participation.) The other two categories more directly focus on these concerns. The third concerns the electorate, while the fourth treats the selection, control, and support of candidates.

Translation of Votes into Seats

The selection and installation of officials is the central and defining focus of elections. Beginning with how winners are determined focuses attention on two major aspects of the electoral system—the electoral formula and the nature of the constituencies in which it is applied.

Electoral formula An electoral formula is a rule by which a given distribution of votes determines who won an election. Chapter 9 discusses the consequences of the wide variety of electoral formulas. The task here is to specify the criteria along which electoral formulas may be compared systematically.

While there is widespread agreement that the major distinction among electoral formulas is between the single-member plurality formula used in most of the English-speaking world and the variety of list proportional representation formulas used in most of continental Europe, the "intermediate" cases have led to debate about precisely how electoral formulas should be classified. In general, there have been two approaches, one based on the outcome of a system combined with an interpretation of its designers' intentions and the other based more strictly on its formal operation.

The first approach leads to a threefold classification of single-member systems (further subdivided between plurality and majority formulas), semiproportional systems (e.g., limited vote, single nontransferable vote, cumulative voting), and proportional representation (including both list PR and the single transferable vote). Multimember plurality systems that do not involve a limited vote are ordinarily assigned to the single-member category under the rubric of the "blocked vote." But this approach is both circular and self-contradictory—circular in that if the defining characteristic of an electoral formula is its actual degree of proportionality in the distribution of seats, then electoral formula cannot explain that distribution; self-contradictory in that, as will be seen in chapter 9, single-member systems are not uniformly less proportional than all semiproportional systems, which in turn are not uniformly less proportional than all systems using proportional representation.

The alternative approach employed here initially divides electoral formulas between candidate-centered and list systems on the basis of two related characteristics. On one side, candidate-centered electoral formulas are all based on individuals and theoretically could be employed in the absence of parties or any other kind of intercandidate organization; list systems can work only on the basis of groups of candidates or parties. On the other side, list formulas require the totaling of votes received by all the candidates of a party and aim to allocate seats among parties in proportion to the party totals; plurality systems never require the totaling of votes for groups of candidates and allocate seats to *individuals* on the basis of the order of their voting strength.

Once this basic distinction is made, each of the gross categories can be further subdivided on the basis of a number of criteria. For candidate-centered systems, the questions are how the number of rounds of voting is determined, the number of votes each voter may cast, and the number of votes the voter may give to any single candidate; these are adequate to distinguish among single- and multimember plurality, majority, single transferable vote, cumulative voting, approval voting, and limited-vote formulas. For list systems, the first distinction is among largest-remainder, automatic, and highest-average formulas (with each of these further subdivided on the basis of the particular quotas or series of divisors employed); additional variations concern the possibility of alliances among parties, provisions to increase proportionality like a national or regional distribution of remainders or allocation of supplementary seats, and the imposition of thresholds or bonuses.

Constituencies   With relatively few exceptions, votes are counted and electoral formulas are applied in constituencies smaller than the whole political system.[6] Because both the size and the specific boundaries of constituencies play a vital role in determining how an electoral formula works, and especially in determining the proportionality with which it allocates seats among parties, I have included the delineation of constituencies under the general heading of translating votes into seats. The impact of districting on democracy extends beyond its effects on the direct relationship between votes and seats, however, and some of the characteristics of electoral systems introduced in this section relate primarily to other aspects of democratic practice.

The constituency variable that bears most directly on the translation of votes into seats is the number of seats per district, conventionally called the district magnitude, although it is only one of a number of related variables that describe the size of constituencies. More generally, one might also consider the number of districts (in particular distinguishing those systems in which all members are elected at-large, naturally including those in which only a single person is elected, from those for which there is more than one district), the number of voters per district, and the number of voters per member. Moreover, one could also measure district size in geographic terms, a possibility occasionally relevant to districting decisions.

Given that supporters of various political positions are never distributed uniformly throughout a territory, the actual location of the district boundaries—that is, what areas are combined into the same district and what areas are separated into different districts—is essential to the description of a constituency system. To anticipate the conclusions of later chapters, three points need to be emphasized here. First, the way the district lines are drawn can have a significant impact on the outcome of the election. Second, although decisions regarding district magnitude and boundary location make a difference to who wins, there may be no intrinsically fair decisions. Third, although any set of districting decisions likely has unintended consequences, it also likely has major intended consequences; once districting decisions' effect on electoral outcomes is understood, they can be made to produce desired (by the decision-makers) biases in the outcome. Several aspects of the district drawing process need to be considered in any adequate explanation of the relationship between votes and seats, or of electoral outcomes more generally.

The first is the degree and nature of gerrymandering. The term "gerrymander" most often is applied to manipulation of district boundaries in single-member districts, but it may be extended to include the purposive manipulation of any district system. At this level, one can distinguish three genuses of gerrymander. The simplest, malapportionment, has unequal numbers of voters per member; if one's opponents are packed into high-ratio districts and one's supporters are put in low-ratio districts, the effect will be distortion in one's own favor. The second sense of gerrymander refers to drawing district lines so that a favored party wins its seats by small margins, while a disadvantaged party wins its seats with overwhelming majorities, thus wasting its votes. Finally, the third form of gerrymander is based on the fact that the vote thresholds that determine whether a party wins one more or one fewer seat depend on the number of seats assigned to a particular constituency. Instead of manipulating the distribution of party percentages among districts, as is the case with the second form, this form of gerrymander manipulates the number of members returned from each district.

Gerrymandering assumes that election districts are defined geographically, which is usually the case, but not invariably or necessarily so, as the categoric representation in the Irish Senate and the university seats in the pre-1948 British House of Commons illustrate. A second and even more fundamental question about the delineation of districts thus is their basis—geographic, ethnic, occupational, or whatever.

A related way to approach districting decisions is to examine the formal criteria upon which these decisions are *supposedly* based. Four major criteria appear important both historically and in contemporary discussions of apportionment. The oldest is that district lines should follow the boundaries of previously existing communities. A second criterion emphasizes the representation of minorities. The third concern is equality of population. Fourth, as with a partisan gerrymander, evaluations of districting plans can be based on their partisan outcome, but here using a standard of fairness rather than one of partisan advantage. To these political criteria, one may add a variety of more technical standards, such as contiguity, compactness, or manageable size.

The last question about districting is how and by whom the decisions are made. In practice, there are basically one negative and three positive answers to this question, with one additional suggestion worthy of mention. The negative answer is that existing districts remain fixed even if substantial demographic change has altered their relative populations or partisan or social makeups. Although no one overtly makes districting decisions, the failure to alter district lines is itself in effect a decision, indicating that the analysis of active gerrymanders needs to be supplemented by a sensitivity to "passive gerrymanders." If district lines are redrawn, the three commonly chosen decision-making bodies are the legislature, a nonpartisan boundary commission, and the courts. An alternative suggested, but never implemented, is to eliminate all freedom of choice among specific districting plans by adopting a single standard by which all plans could be compared. Under this scheme, anyone could submit a reapportionment plan, but a boundary commission or similar body would be obligated simply to select that plan from among those submitted that best fit the standard.

Nature of Choice

The second major category of distinctions among electoral systems concerns the nature of the choice voters make. The questions under this heading form three clusters. The first revolves around the distinction between choice of party lists or parties as organizations on one hand and choice of individuals on the other, and thus is concerned with the object of voters' choices. The second cluster is about the type and number of voters' choices and raises questions such as what and how many offices are filled by election, or how often and when elections are held. Finally, the third cluster concerns the form in which choices are solicited, focusing in particular on the format of the ballot.

Object of choice   The most fundamental distinction about the object of choice is between systems in which one votes for a person and those in which one votes for a party. As with electoral formula, one can best introduce this subject by comparing the polar opposites of single-member plurality and strict list PR. In both cases, the voter has one simple vote, but in the case of single-member plurality it is given to an individual person, perhaps with no mention of party, while with strict list PR it is given to a party, perhaps with no mention of its candidates. While voters in plurality elections must choose persons, however, the identity between PR and choice of parties is not complete; in some PR systems, votes are cast for individuals who are treated as members of groups or alliances. These are distinguished from candidate-centered systems in that the initial distribution of seats is to alliances rather than individuals and is made on the basis of the total number of votes cast for all members of the alliance.

A second distinction concerns the possibility of splitting one's support among several parties. In some cases, once a voter chooses to support one party, his or her vote is totally lost to all others. This unipartisan choice is a characteristic of the single-member plurality and single nontransferable vote formulas as well as simple list PR. The alternative is a multipartisan choice. Candidate-centered systems involving transferable votes and majority formulas in which voters may change party from one round of voting to another are examples of multipartisan choice. Multipartisan choice also exists in any candidate-centered system in which the voter has more than one vote, since they could be given to candidates of more than one party. Multipartisan choice is achieved in PR systems through panachage; instead of one vote, each voter is given as many votes as there are members to be elected from the constituency, and these votes may be cast for individuals who are not all members of the same party group. However, as in PR systems in which a single vote is cast for a single candidate, the total number of votes cast for all the candidates in each group is computed and becomes the basis for the initial distribution of seats, which is again made among groups rather than individuals. In each case, the key factor is that a voter may split his or her vote among several parties or have it transferred from one party to another, and so is not necessarily making an either/or choice. (The related possibility that a voter might support one party in the election for one office but a different party for the simultaneous election for another office will be dealt with below.)

The final distinction concerns the degree of choice or influence exercised by voters *within* a party. In some cases voters can choose a party, but the party chooses which individuals will be elected to those seats it wins. This is most clearly the case in those PR systems in which parties submit ordered lists of candidates under the condition that the seats won by each party will go to its candidates in the order in which they appear on the list. It is also, in effect, the case whenever a party nominates only one candidate in a district, so that the voter has no alternative to supporting its candidate except to vote for another party altogether.

In many systems, however, voters can influence not only the distribution of seats among parties, but the choice of particular individuals from among a party's candidates as well. In addition, the direct primary, although intermediate between the nomination and the general election processes, performs a sufficiently similar function that it will also be considered in part under this rubric as well as under the heading of selection and control of candidates.

Intraparty preference voting is inherently possible in any candidate-centered system in which a party nominates more than one candidate, if only because a voter could support one of its candidates and not another. From the point of view of candidates, intraparty preference voting must determine which candidates are elected in any candidate-centered election in which a party with at least one seat has more candidates than seats. Looking instead from the perspective of the voter, one can distinguish three possibilities jointly determined by the interaction of the electoral system and the nomination strategies of the parties. First, it may be impossible for the voter to express an intraparty preference when the party has exactly one nominee in the voter's district. Second, it may be possible, but not necessary, for the voter to express an intraparty preference, true in multimember districts in which the number of nominees of the party and the number of votes given to the voter mean that he or she can support all candidates of the party chosen equally. Finally, the expression of an intraparty preference may be an inescapable part of voting as, for example, with STV. Similarly, whenever a party has more candidates than the voter has votes, the voter must choose among them.

With PR formulas, one again has the distinction among systems in which one cannot, in which one may, and in which one must express an intraparty preference. The more significant distinction, however, while retaining the category of systems in which no intraparty preference voting is possible (the order in which candidates are elected is completely determined by their party's original list order), divides those systems in which it is possible to cast an intraparty preference vote between those in which only explicitly cast preference votes determine the order in which candidates are elected and those in which the party can give some institutional advantage to some candidates that will allow them to be elected ahead of other candidates who receive more numerous preference votes. Although other devices are occasionally used, this last possibility is generally achieved by somehow counting those ballots that do not include explicit preference votes as if they were preference votes for the favored candidate(s) or for the entire list in the order presented.

In all of these systems the expression of an intraparty preference is still directly tied to interparty choice, whether a necessary part of casting a party vote or not. Multiround voting systems represent a partial exception in the sense that one could support one candidate of a party over another in the first round but then desert the party altogether in the second; nonetheless, the possibility remains that a candidate could be elected in the first round, so that the initial preference vote is a party vote as well. A more substantial exception is the American direct primary wherein the choice of party nominee is made in a public election held before the general election; thus, a voter can vote in the primary of one party but support the candidate of another in the general election. Primaries can be classified on the basis of the conditions under which they are held or on the basis of how many voters can take part. I discuss the latter distinction in connection with nominations. With regard to the former, the distinction is between those systems in which a primary election is held whenever there is more than one candidate for a party's nomination and those systems with a "challenge primary," in which a party nominating convention is held, but candidates who receive a specified level of support in the convention may force a primary election to challenge its decision.[7]

Type and number of choices   All the questions discussed so far could be addressed within the context of a single election to a single type of office. Another set of questions that bears generally on the nature of electoral choice broadens the focus both temporally and substantively.

The first of these questions concerns the frequency with which elections are held, on one hand asking what is the maximum term for a particular office and whether elections can be called even more frequently and on the other hand asking the same questions for several offices as well as whether elections for all these offices coincide, in consequence determining how often elections of one sort or another are held.

A related question, which can be posed in several contexts, concerns the scope of the electoral principle and asks what offices are filled by direct election. Although it is essentially a defining characteristic of modern democracy that one chamber of the national legislature be directly elected, the second chamber of a bicameral legislature may be elected indirectly or not at all. For the executive branch, the major distinction is between "presidential" systems in which the chief executive is elected directly and "parliamentary" systems in which the chief executive is chosen indirectly by the legislature.[8] The subsidiary question within the presidential category is whether the chief executive can name the other executive officers or whether many of them are elected individually, either directly or indirectly. Similarly, one could also ask whether and how judges are chosen.

Ballot form   The last set of questions about the nature of electoral choice concerns the ballot itself. One question is whether voting is public or secret. One tends to assume a secret ballot in modern elections, but this has not always been the case; nor is it necessarily the case today if one considers such phenomena as the Iowa presidential caucuses as examples of primary elections.

A second question is whether voters can alter the ballot they are given, or whether they must choose among the alternatives formally on the ballot or not vote at all. The possibility of "write-in" voting arises: can people vote for individuals who have not been officially nominated? Moreover, is it possible to cast a deliberately spoilt or defaced ballot, and is the number of such ballots reported?

Third, one can ask several questions about the physical design of the ballot. In candidate-centered elections, are party affiliations listed along with candidates' names (partisan ballot) or not (nonpartisan ballot) or correspondingly for proportional representation elections, are candidates' names listed or only party names or symbols? How are the choices available to voters arranged? There are several common possibilities for listing: in alphabetical order; in the order in which nominating papers are filed; in order of party strength at a previous election; and random or rotating order (meaning that not all ballots are the same). When several offices are to be filled at the same time, there is the additional distinction between a party column ballot and an office block ballot.

Access to the Ballot Box

The third large set of distinctions among electoral systems revolves around access to the ballot box, in particular who is allowed to vote, but also voting ease or difficulty and optional or compulsory voting.

Suffrage Looking first at the right to vote, one might say (simply but inaccurately) that universal adult suffrage is a necessary condition of democratic government. In fact, no democracy allows all adults to vote, and systems that until very recently had severe restrictions on this right were nonetheless regarded as democratic.[9] Even in contemporary elections, who will be allowed to vote is an important question in the design of an electoral system.

Most significant restrictions of the right to vote can be organized into three categories. The first addresses the would-be voter's membership in the political community and personal stake in the outcome, and encompasses such common standards as citizenship and residency, as well as tax-paying or property ownership requirements, religious tests, and disqualifications of members of a former ruling class or officials of a previous regime. The second category is based on the would-be voter's presumed competence. Age as an objective, if not necessarily accurate, indicator of maturity fits under this heading, as do literacy tests, the disqualification of the insane, and the disqualification of women from voting because nature had not fitted them for such masculine duties.[10] Third is the criterion of autonomy. Historically, this was one of the principal justifications for property qualifications, which were intended "to exclude such persons as are in so mean a situation as to be esteemed to have no will of their own,"[11] as well as for restricting the right to vote to heads of households or heads of families, or excluding those in custodial care or dependent on public relief.

Registration of voters Except in communities so small and stable that everyone knows everyone else, a system of voter registration to allow for the correct assignment of voters to polling places (and hence to appropriate ballots) and the timely resolution of disputes about eligibility is one of the prerequisites of efficient electoral administration. At the same time, however, registration itself becomes an additional requirement for voting, raising the possibility that the system by which voters are registered might affect the ultimate character of the electorate.

In this respect, the crucial question is whether the state or the would-be voter takes the initiative to get that person enrolled, with the answers falling into three categories. First, the state may be responsible for producing a list of eligible voters, either as a byproduct of its regular administrative procedures or as a separate function performed periodically or in response to the calling of an election. Alternatively, the voter may have to initiate the process of registration. In the third variety of registration system, the voter must take the initiative to register, but does so with the state-supplied incentive of criminal or civil sanctions.

If the voter must take the initiative, a host of questions about the inconvenience and timing of registration arise. Most important, is registration periodic, so that the voter must register perhaps before every election, or permanent, so that he or she need register only once so long as he or she votes with some regularity? Second, how much in advance of an election must, or may, he or she register? Are the locations and hours for registration convenient? Must registration be done in person or can it be done by post? Can party workers or other citizens become registrars and conduct a door-to-door canvass or set up in well-frequented locations?

Ease of voting   Many of these same questions can be asked about voting itself. Are polling places conveniently located and open for an adequate time period? Are elections held at a time of year when travel is convenient, on working days or weekends, or is election day a holiday? What provisions are made for those who are away from home on election day or for members of linguistic minorities? Finally, is voting made "easier" by being required by law?

Control of Candidacy

The last major category of electoral system variables concerns the candidates and their parties. Here, there are three main questions. First, how does a candidate or a party obtain a place on the ballot? Second, what legal or cultural restrictions limit the campaign activities of candidates, parties, and their supporters? Third, what forms of support are candidates given, and on what basis is the level of support set?

Qualification and nomination   In general terms, limitations on the right of candidacy fall into two groups: those based on suitability and those based on seriousness. The former are designed to screen out those who *should not* be elected, while the latter aim to simplify the situation and, especially where subsidies are involved, limit costs by screening out those who *will not* be elected.

Qualifications of individual candidates based on suitability parallel those for admission to suffrage, although they are frequently more (but occasionally less) restrictive. For candidates, however, culturally defined prejudices must be considered in addition to legally prescribed requirements. Simply to cite an example, neither candidates for the British House of Commons nor candidates for the American House of Representatives are legally required to reside in their constituencies (the American candidates are required to reside in the states from which they are elected), but district residency is far more important in the United States than in Britain. Other restrictions based on suitability may be applied to parties as well as to individuals. Typically, these are tests of loyalty to the regime, illustrated at the individual level by the 1982 Turkish ban on candidacies by leaders, members of the central committees, and 1977 parliamentary representatives of the pre-1980 political parties, and at the level of parties by the banning in the Federal Republic of Germany of "antidemocratic organizations."

Qualifications based on seriousness generally fall into two categories, sometimes with an additional provision guaranteeing candidates of parties that polled a minimum percentage of the vote in the previous election a place on the ballot without further proof of seriousness. On one hand, candidates or parties may be required to show that they have significant public support by submitting nominating petitions signed by a nontrivial number of voters. Alternatively, a smaller number of sponsors selected from a more restricted group, such as members of parliament or other officeholders, may be required. On the other hand, candidates may be required to post a substantial monetary deposit, which is forfeited if they do not obtain a minimum percentage of the vote in the ensuing election.

Satisfying requirements such as these are necessary conditions of legal candidacy, but they are not sufficient conditions for meaningful candidacy. With the exception of nonpartisan elections, only party-endorsed candidates are likely to have any real chance of election. And with the further exception of offices for which party nominations for a general election are determined by success in a primary election, this means going beyond the realm of formal electoral law to look at the practice of political parties as organizations, recognizing, of course, that party practice in some measure may be prescribed by law.[12]

Campaign activity   Once candidates are selected, the next question is what can they do to advance their candidacies? Restrictions on campaign activity can be imposed legally or set by cultural expectation or party practice and rules. The most significant legal restrictions tend to focus on the permissibility of raising and spending money in particular ways or amounts, while cultural or party restrictions relate instead to the practical possibility and effectiveness of various ways of raising and spending money (as well as the acceptability and effectiveness of other campaign techniques, such as polling) and to such questions as how, where an intraparty choice is allowed, candidates may campaign for personal support.

Another side to the question of campaign activity bears on the content and organization of campaigning. What is the relative importance of issues, personalities, partisanship? Are issues selected and positions defined nationally, or does each candidate have significant flexibility? More generally, are campaign resources raised and strategic decisions made centrally, or does each candidate run a more or less autonomous campaign?

Public subsidy   The last set of electoral system variables concerns the provision of public support to candidates and parties. Common types of direct support include provision of broadcasting time, printing and distribution of election addresses, free use of public halls and other spaces, and, of course, cash. In addition, parties or candidates may be supported indirectly, either through subsidies (or salaries) given to officeholders or through incentives for private support such as tax deductions or credits.

Beyond the total amounts of each of these resources given, programs of public subsidy differ in at least four important respects. First, how is the total divided? Here the major dichotomy is between equal shares and proportionality, with subsidiary questions concerning thresholds for inclusion and the criterion for proportionality. Second, is the support given to parties as organizations or to candidates as individuals? Third, is the subsidy given before or after the election? Finally, are there "strings attached" to accepting public support? For example, must a candidate who takes public money accept spending limits that would not otherwise have been imposed?

The Practice and Theory of Elections

Each of the many variables, questions, and distinctions listed above is interesting because of its potential impact on the results—both practical and theoretical—of the electoral process. Practically, an electoral system's construction may contribute to determining who wins, not only in the limited sense of being elected, but in the more general sense of wielding enhanced political influence even in opposition. Theoretically, an electoral system embodies many of a society's understandings about the meaning of democracy and the legitimate bases of political power.

Correspondingly, the data and arguments to be addressed in the following chapters are also practical (empirical) and theoretical. Much of the debate surrounding the design, evaluation, and reform of electoral systems is explicitly normative—this or that reform ought to be made because it will make the system more democratic. From this perspective, the task is to link the values discussed in chapters 2 through 7 more directly to specific electoral institutions. These normative claims frequently are based on empirical assertions—the system will be more democratic because, for example, the nature of the party system will be changed. Here the task is to assess the validity of those assertions. Overall, the twin objectives are to understand the practical consequences of different electoral arrangements and thus also to understand how choices among electoral arrangements are inextricably connected to choices among democratic theories.

Representation: The Relationship between Seats and Votes

The best place to begin an analysis of the consequences of electoral arrangements is with the process by which distributions of votes translate into distributions of mandates among competing parties or candidates, even though this is the last step in the election procedure. The basic independent variables were described in the last chapter. In this chapter, I consider the consequences of electoral formulas as revealed in practice.

The dependent variables considered in this chapter indicate the degree to which the outcomes of elections are representative, measured in two ways. The first is rooted in the idea that a legislature is a deliberative body looking for a universally recognizable national interest or correct solution to problems so that simple representation of a group, interest, or opinion is more important than the quantity of its representation. Equating parties with "groups, interests, and opinions," this sense of representation is measured (inversely) by the proportion of the votes received by parties that win no seats.

The second approach addresses numerical "fairness" and the idea that each group's representation should be proportional to its support in the electorate. Again with parties as the objects to be represented, the question here is the relationship between vote shares and seat shares.

Data

In contrast to the usual practice of looking only at established democracies, the data to be analyzed here include the results of more than 800 national elections held through 1985 in 70 countries. In some cases, the series of elections dates back to the nineteenth century, while in others data could be collected only for elections held since 1945. Aside from increasing the variety of electoral systems included (see table 9.1), this minimizes the need to collapse categories and allows use of more sensitive analytic techniques.

TABLE 9.1 Weighted and (unweighted) numbers of elections by electoral formula and use of electoral thresholds.

First-stage formula	Second-stage formula – no threshold					Second-stage formula – with threshold						
	None	d'Hondt	Ste.-Laguë	Hare	Other	None	d'Hondt	Mod. Ste.-Laguë	Ste.-Laguë	Hare	Direct	Other
Parliamentary elections												
d'Hondt highest average	106 (117)	1 (1)	9 (14)	7 (6)		25 (26)	4 (8)					
Modified Ste.-Laguë highest average	9 (15)							3 (6)	1 (1)	5 (12)		
Hare largest remainder	33 (23)	7 (7)		7 (1)		5 (7)	19 (27)					
Droop largest remainder	9 (5)	4 (3)				5 (9)	5 (8)			2 (3)		
Imperiali largest remainder					1 (1)					6 (9)		
Direct PR											6 (8)	
STV	42 (65)											
SNTV	17 (28)											

Single-member plurality	309 (223)		7 (8)	7 (10)		
Single-member majority	36 (41)					
Multimember plurality	35 (24)		7 (3)			
Multimember majority	15 (40)					
Block vote	5 (13)					
Reinforced PR						5 (9)
Mixed systems	14 (9)	1 (1)			6 (9)	
Indirect election	4 (8)					
Electoral colleges						
d'Hondt highest average	7 (6)					
Block vote	21 (40)					

Use of these techniques require a rule for counting cases. The simplest rule is to count each election as one unit. This rule, adopted by Douglas Rae in his classic study,[1] has been criticized by Arend Lijphart,[2] who argues that the real unit of analysis is the electoral system, so that Rae's rule gives too much weight to systems that hold elections more frequently. While Lijphart's argument that multiple elections held under a single electoral system are not really independent observations has merit, it can be extended to say that serial modifications of a single country's electoral system also are not independent. Thus Lijphart, in counting, for example, three Danish electoral systems but only one Finnish, is weighting his data in an equally arbitrary way. The (also arbitrary) solution adopted here has been to divide the time covered into three periods—pre-World War I (through 1918), the interwar years (1919–1944), and post-World War II—and to count the body of elections for each office (parliamentary chamber or presidential electoral college) within each country and time period equally.[3] The result can then be multiplied by a fraction that leaves the total effective number of elections unchanged, or alternatively each group can be counted as one unit. After deletion of cases for which one or more of the crucial variables was missing, this leaves a weighted N of 832 elections, as shown in table 9.1, or 119 groups of elections.

Unrepresented Voters

Especially from the perspective of liberal democratic theories, the most obvious question is whether interests are represented in the first place, or, reversing the question, how large a proportion of the electorate votes for parties that receive no representation. This question is answered in table 9.2, which shows the single election minimum and maximum plus the average vote totals for parties winning no seats for each of the combinations of first- and second-stage electoral formulas.

As the table shows, most voters are represented most of the time, albeit often in the virtual sense when another district elects a representative of their party. For no cell in the table is the *average* percentage of unrepresented voters higher than 6.54. On the other hand, from time to time very large percentages of the electorate are left unrepresented, and proportional representation (PR) systems apparently are not immune. While 20 of the 29 elections in which at least 10% of the voters chose parties that won no seats were held under plurality (14), majority (3), or single-member alternative vote (3) systems, the other nine were held under PR formulas.

Although the meaning of a large number of unrepresented voters is clear, the meaning of the contrary situation is not. Voters can choose only among parties that present candidates, but parties with no chance of winning likely present few candidates. For example, the French ecologists were unrepresented after the 1978 parliamentary election in which they won 2.2% of the vote, but with candidates in only a minority of constituencies; in 1981, they won only 1.1% of the vote (and were again unrepresented), but their number of candidates had fallen as well. One can only speculate about the number of unrepresented ecologist voters if all Frenchmen had the chance to vote ecologist. Few votes for parties that win no seats only weakly guarantees that most interests are represented.

Payoff Functions

One approach to the relationship between seats and votes is to ask, at the level of individual constituencies, what is the smallest share of the vote a party can win under the *most favorable* possible conditions and still receive one seat (the threshold of representation), and what is the largest share of the vote a party can win under the *least favorable* conditions and still fail to receive a seat (the threshold of exclusion).[4] As Lijphart and Gibberd showed, this analysis can be extended to compute the minimum and maximum vote shares corresponding to any particular number of a district's seats, generating what they call payoff functions.[5] The results indicate formal rather than behavioral properties of electoral formulas, but they also indicate some of the variables that interact with formulas to produce actual results. Table 9.3 shows the payoff functions for a range of party-oriented formulas.

As the payoff functions show, the relationship between votes and seats is influenced not only by electoral formula, but also by district magnitude and by the number of parties competing. The smaller the number of parties and the larger the district magnitude, the smaller the range of vote shares potentially associated with a given number of seats. At the same time, there is considerable room for variation in the relationship between votes and seats left unexplained by the formal factors of formula, magnitude, and number of parties. In particular, the payoff a party receives depends not only on its own vote, but also on the way the other parties divide the remaining vote.

Looking at thresholds of representation (the lower bound of the payoff function for $s = 1$), there is a consistent ordering of formulas within the two categories of PR systems. Among highest-average formulas, the d'Hondt threshold is always greater than the Modified Sainte-Laguë threshold, which is always greater than or equal to (when $p = 2$) the pure Sainte-Laguë threshold, while among the largest-remainder formulas, the Hare threshold is smaller than the Droop threshold, which is smaller than the Imperiali threshold.[6] With a relatively large number of parties, all of the largest remainder formulas have lower thresholds of representation than any of the highest-average formulas. With small numbers of parties, however, this is no longer the case.

The payoff functions relate to the relationship between votes and seats in a single electoral district. Similar, albeit slightly more complex, aggregate payoff functions could be constructed for systems with many districts. Unfortunately, this depends on the fact that the district level minimum (and maximum) vote share functions are based on best- (and worst-) case scenarios; the aggregation simply maps the results of best- (or worst-) case situations happening simultaneously in every district. The actual relationship between votes and seats for one party depends not only on the aggregate distribution of the votes won by the other parties, but also on the geographic distribution both of its votes and of the votes of its competitors.

This discussion has been limited to list systems of proportional representation. It may be extended to candidate-centered systems, although in large measure

TABLE 9.2 Minimum (row 1), average (row 2), and maximum (row 3) vote percentage received by parties winning no seats. (Only one figure cited for unique elections.)

Values in each cell are given as minimum / average / maximum (single figure cited for unique elections).

First-stage formula	Second-stage formula—no threshold					Second-stage formula—with threshold						
	None	d'Hondt	Ste.-Laguë	Hare	Other	None	d'Hondt	Mod. Ste.-Laguë	Ste.-Laguë	Hare	Direct	Other
d'Hondt highest average	0.0 / 1.7 / 26.3	2.2	0.0 / 1.0 / 2.6	0.0 / 3.0 / 11.0		0.0 / 2.5 / 29.7	0.0 / 1.7 / 5.5					
Mod. Ste. Laguë highest average	0.0 / 3.7 / 9.0			2.7				1.8 / 2.4 / 3.8	2.7	0.9 / 2.9 / 7.0		
Hare largest remainder	0.0 / 1.8 / 7.4	0.0 / 0.5 / 1.6				0.6 / 1.8 / 3.1	0.3 / 2.2 / 4.2					
Droop largest remainder	0.0 / 0.7 / 1.2	2.6 / 3.3 / 4.3					0.1 / 1.6 / 3.7					
Imperiali largest remainder				0.0		0.0 / 3.0 / 10.1				0.0 / 2.5 / 5.0		
Direct PR										0.0 / 1.4 / 3.6	0.1 / 0.8 / 2.0	
STV	0.0 / 2.4 / 12.3											

Electoral system				
SNTV	0.0 0.1 2.5			
Single-member plurality	0.0 2.8 25.6	0.3 1.6 5.8	0.0 3.3 7.0	
Single-member majority	0.0 0.9 5.8			
Multimember plurality	0.0 6.5 27.6		1.8 3.5 6.7	
Multimember majority	0.0 3.1 29.7			
Block vote	0.0 2.0 10.2			
Reinforced PR				0.2 1.7 5.1
Mixed systems	0.0 1.2 7.5	0.0	0.0 2.3 6.0	
Indirect election	0.0 1.1 5.2			

TABLE 9.3 Payoff functions for party-oriented electoral systems.

	Minimum vote share for S seats	Maximum vote share for S seats if:		
		$p - 1 \geq M - s$	$M - s \leq p - 1 \leq M - s \over 2$	$p - 1 \leq \dfrac{M - s}{2}$
Highest-average formulas				
d'Hondt	$\dfrac{s}{M+p-1}$	$\dfrac{s+1}{M+1}$	$\dfrac{s+1}{M+1}$	$\dfrac{s+1}{M+1}$
Ste.-Laguë	$\dfrac{2s-1}{2M+p-2}$	$\dfrac{2s+1}{M+s+1}$	$\dfrac{2s+1}{2M-p+2}$	$\dfrac{2s+1}{2M-p+2}$
Modified Ste.-Laguë	$\dfrac{2s-1^a}{2M+1.4p-2.8}$	$\dfrac{2s+1^b}{1.4M+.6s+1}$	$\dfrac{2s+1^c}{1.6M-2p+.4s+1.2}$	$\dfrac{2s+1^d}{2M-p+2}$
Danish	$\dfrac{3s-2}{3M+p-3}$	$\dfrac{3s+1}{M+2s+1}$	$\dfrac{3s+1}{3M-2p+3}$	$\dfrac{3s+1}{3M-2p+3}$
Largest-remainder formulas				
Hare quota	$\dfrac{s}{M} - \dfrac{p-1}{Mp}$	$\dfrac{s}{M} + \dfrac{1-s/M}{M-s+1}$	$\dfrac{s}{M} + \dfrac{p-1}{Mp}$	$\dfrac{s}{M} + \dfrac{p-1}{Mp}$
Droop quota	$\dfrac{s}{M+1} - \dfrac{p-2}{(M+1)p}$	$\dfrac{s+1}{M+1}$	$\dfrac{s+1}{M+1}$	$\dfrac{s+1}{M+1}$
Imperiali quota	$\dfrac{s}{M+2} - \dfrac{p-3}{(M+2)p}$	$\dfrac{s+1}{M+2}$	$\dfrac{s+1}{M+2}$	$\dfrac{s+1}{M+2}$

Table adapted in part from Arend Lijphart and Robert W. Gibberd, "Thresholds and Payoffs in List Systems of Proportional Representation," *European Journal of Political Research* 5 (1977), 219–244; Michael Gallagher, "Comparing Proportional Representation Systems: Quotas, Thresholds, Paradoxes and Majorities," *British Journal of Political Science* 22 (October 1992).

Key: s = number of seats in question. M = total number of seats to be filled. p = number of parties competing.

[a] For s = 1, $\dfrac{1.4}{2M+1.4p-2.4}$; for s = M, $\dfrac{2s-1}{2M+1.4p-2.4}$

[b] For s = 0, 1/(M+1).

[c] For s = 0, 1.4/(1.6M − .2p+1.6).

[d] For s = 0, 1.4/(2M − p + 2.4).

the result shows that the payoff functions themselves are of little interest. The results are shown in table 9.4. Candidate-centered systems in which each citizen has more than one vote also present a technical problem in moving from numbers of votes to numbers of voters; here that problem is sidestepped by assuming that each voter casts all the votes to which he or she is entitled. Given the variable number of votes allowed under some candidate-centered systems, it is convenient to express the payoff functions in terms of numbers, rather than shares, of votes.

In comparison to the functions for party-centered formulas, the most striking feature of table 9.4 is the very low minima for all of the candidate-centered payoff functions in the range $1 \leq s < M$ with the exception of cumulative voting, this continues up to $s = M$. Given that the maxima for all of the candidate-centered payoff functions are the same as for Droop quota largest-remainder PR, this means that the distances between maxima and minima are very much greater for candidate-centered than for list PR formulas. And when one remembers that the maxima of these functions are based on the assumption of optimal distribution of the subject party's vote, so that in a truly worst-case scenario far more votes still might be insufficient to win a given number of seats, clearly the logically necessary constraints on the relationship between votes and seats are, for candidate-centered systems, very weak indeed.

TABLE 9.4 Payoff functions for candidate-oriented electoral systems.

	Minimum	Maximum
Single-member plurality	$\dfrac{sV}{C}$	$\dfrac{(s + 1)V}{M + 1}$
Multimember plurality	$\dfrac{s(V/M)}{s + C - M}$	$\dfrac{(s + 1)V}{M + 1}$
Single-member majority, 1st round[a]	$\dfrac{sV}{2(C - 1)}$	$\dfrac{(s + 1)V}{M + 1}$
Limited vote	$\dfrac{V(q + s - M)}{s + C - M}, s > M - q$ $1, S \leq M - q$	$\dfrac{(s + 1)V}{M + 1}$
Cumulative voting	$s, s < M$ $\dfrac{sV}{(s + 1)}, s = M$	$\dfrac{(s + 1)\,V}{M + 1}$
STV[b]	$0, s < M$ $M\dfrac{VM}{(M + 1)(C - 1)}, s = M$	$\dfrac{(s + 1)V}{M + 1}$

Key: s = number of seats in question. M = total number of seats to be filled. C = number of candidates competing. V = number of votes. q = number of votes per voter.
 [a] Assuming top two candidates proceed to the second round.
 [b] Based on first preference votes and assuming cross-party transfers may occur.

Proportionality

The alternative to the deductive strategy of computing the theoretical limits on the relationship between votes and seats is the inductive strategy of observing the joint distributions of votes and seats in actual electoral systems. The most frequently studied aspect of the relationship between votes and seats is the degree to which the proportion of the votes won by a party is rewarded by an equal share of the legislative seats, or electors in an electoral college. The desirability of strict proportionality is sometimes seen as a logical consequence of commitment to the equality of citizens, and proportionality is sometimes taken to be virtually synonymous with fairness,[7] although as was seen earlier, strict attention to equality and to the representation of interests (parties) in a way that mirrors the distribution of their support among the citizenry is required only by one democratic theory—legislative democracy.

For a single party in a single election, proportionality can be defined as the absolute value of the difference between the party's share of the votes and its share of the seats, both measured at the national level. Summing across parties and dividing by 2 gives a measure of the (dis)proportionality (D) of outcomes for a single election that runs from a minimum of 0 when vote and seat shares are equal for all parties to a theoretical maximum of 1 if all the seats were awarded to parties with no votes. Averaging D across elections yields an overall measure of the disproportionality of a set of elections.[8]

Obviously, disproportionality will be strongly affected by the electoral system. The exact effects have been the subject of much research. Among the most recent, for example, is Arend Lijphart's revision and update of Rae's work. Dividing electoral formulas into three categories (d'Hondt; Droop and Imperiali quota largest remainder, Modified Sainte-Laguë, and single transferable vote (STV); and pure Sainte-Laguë and Hare largest remainder) in place of Rae's two (highest-average and largest remainder), Lijphart concludes that

> we found a very strong effect of district magnitude on proportionality—confirming Rae's conclusion. We also found that this effect remains strong, albeit not as strong, when we hold the electoral formula constant —a control that Rae fails to apply. And we found—contrary to Rae—that effective complex districting tends to make the election result considerably more proportional.[9]

He also found that electoral formula continues to have an impact controlling for magnitudes, with the three categories ordered above in decreasing average value of D.

Lijphart only analyzes postwar elections in the western democracies, collapsing cases into unfortunately heterogeneous categories. For example, examination of the payoff functions leads one to expect that for small magnitudes, significant differences in proportionality will be associated with small changes in magnitude. But the average magnitudes within categories of magnitude are not constant across Lijphart's electoral formula categories. Additionally, Lijphart's analysis ignores the number of parties as an input to disproportionality, treating it instead only as a consequence. The effects of electoral formula, district magnitude, and prior disproportionality on party number will be considered in chapter 10, but the role of number of parties in the payoff functions suggests that it should be included as a predictive variable as well. Thus it is worth revisiting this question with a wider range of data and with tools that treat fewer of the independent variables as categories rather than continua.

Table 9.5 shows the mean value of disproportionality for each electoral formula. In the "total" column, which summarizes the disproportionality observed for each first-stage formula, wide differences are clear; indeed, between 37% and 41% of the variance in the disproportionalities observed for individual elections is "explained" by the first-stage formula. In gross terms, the differences observed with regard to D are what a naive observer would expect: all of the PR formulas are more proportional than any of the non-PR formulas; STV and single nontransferable vote (SNTV) (the two "semiproportional" systems) are the most proportional of the nonlist formulas; reinforced-PR, a list system that does not really aim at proportionality, is barely more proportional than simple plurality or majority systems, while the block vote is the least proportional of all. Slightly less self-evident, majority formulas are more proportional than plurality, and within each category, single-member district systems have more proportional outcomes than those with multimember districts. On the other hand, at least at the aggregate level, the expectation derived from Lijphart that Hare quota largest-remainder PR would be the most proportional and d'Hondt highest-average the least, with the other PR systems in between, is not confirmed by the larger data base.

Finally, within each category defined by first-stage formulas, it is somewhat surprising to find that, although those systems that use a second-stage distribution either of supplementary seats or of remainders are generally more proportional than those that do not, they are not uniformly so. (One explanation, as will be seen later, is that the number of second-stage seats, and not just their existence, plays a significant role in determining the overall level of disproportionality.) The most obvious case of the leveling influence of second-stage seats is for single-member plurality combined with d'Hondt distribution of supplementary seats; these cases come from the German Federal Republic in which the supplementary seats amount to 40% (1949) or 50% (since 1953) of the whole, in effect making the system one of "personalized" PR, rather than supplemented plurality. Again somewhat surprisingly, the use of an electoral threshold apparently does not necessarily mean that the system will be less proportional than the same system without a threshold, but as with the percentage of voters unrepresented, this measure does not take account of the possibility that a threshold discouraged some parties from presenting candidates in the first place.

Simple Formulas

The obvious interaction among first-stage and second-stage formulas and the use of electoral thresholds suggest an analytic strategy of first examining the relationship between votes and seats for those systems that do not have a second-stage distribution of seats or legal threshold, and then considering the difference these

TABLE 9.5 Overall disproportionality.

First-stage formula	Total	Second-stage formula—no threshold					Second-stage formula—with threshold						
		None	d'Hondt	Ste.-Laguë	Hare	Other	None	d'Hondt	Mod. Ste.-Laguë	Ste.-Laguë	Hare	Direct	Other
d'Hondt highest average	.063	.061	.064	.019	.077		.091	.039					
Mod. Ste.-Laguë highest average	.051	.074					.036	.050	.024	.028	.030		
Hare largest remainder	.052	.064	.014		.052		.046	.050			.117		
Droop largest remainder	.047				.029						.049		
Imperiali largest remainder	.024											.024	
Direct PR	.080	.080											
STV	.061	.061											
SNTV	.160	.161						.042					
Single-member plurality	.130	.130				.206							
Single-member majority	.186	.193				.152							
Multimember plurality	.132	.132											
Multimember majority	.240	.240											
Block vote	.119												
Reinforced PR	.147	.174			.046			.098					
Mixed systems													.119

may make in comparison to the resulting baseline. (One modification to this strategy, based on preliminary analysis and desirable because it increases the variance in the independent variables, was to include systems without thresholds but with second-stage distributions based on national totals amounting to at least 20% of the total seats in the parameter estimations *as if the second stage were the whole election.*)

The discussion so far suggests two independent variables that may affect the proportionality of electoral results *within* each category of electoral formula: average district magnitude (M) and number of parties (p). In addition, since overall disproportionality is, in effect, the weighted sum of the disproportionalities of the various electoral districts, some of which may be expected to "average out," the number of districts (d) also may have an impact on D. Of these three variables, M and d are purely institutional and may be understood as being causes but not effects of D; p, however, is the result of decisions by politicians that may be the consequence as well as the cause of D. For this reason, and because institutional variables have been the primary focus of previous research, the analysis that follows initially considers both the relationship between D and all three variables and the relationship between D and only the two purely institutional variables.

For the payoff functions for PR systems, the model of the relationship between D and M, p, and d ought to satisfy the following conditions:

1. For PR systems, holding p and d constant, as M increases, the predicted value of D should decrease at a rate that decreases as M increases (e.g., the decrease in the expected value of D as M goes from 4 to 5 should be more than the decrease in the expected value of D as M goes from 14 to 15);
2. Holding M and d constant, as p increases, the predicted value of D should increase at a rate that decreases as p increases;
3. Holding M and p constant, the expected value of D should decrease as d increases at a rate that decreases as d increases;
4. The magnitude of the errors in prediction of D should decrease as the predicted value decreases.

Conditions 1 and 2 are based directly on the payoff functions for the various electoral formulas, while condition 3 is based on the expectation that inequities in the allocation of seats will tend to "average out" over a large number of districts. Condition 4 follows from the bounded nature of D.

With one exception, the same conditions should apply to candidate-oriented systems. That exception, suggested by the comparison in table 9.5 between single- and multimember systems but especially reflecting the fact that all the seats in a multimember plurality district tend to be won by candidates of the same party, is this:

5. For plurality systems, holding p and d constant, as M increases, the predicted value of D should increase.

There are no strong theoretical grounds to form an expectation for the relationship between M and D for majority or SNTV systems.

Although many functional forms will satisfy these conditions, a relatively simple form is:

$$D = (e^{\beta_0}) (M^{\beta_1}) (p^{\beta_2}) (d^{\beta_3}) (u).$$

This is a model of constant elasticity, with condition 1 corresponding to the expectation $\beta_1 < 0$, condition 5 to the expectation $\beta_1 > 0$, condition 2 to the expectation $0 < \beta_2 < 1$, and condition 3 to the expectation $\beta_3 < 0$; condition 4 can be satisfied regardless of the values of the parameters. Here is the analogous model for the purely institutional variables:

$$D = (e^{\alpha_0}) (M^{\alpha_1})(d^{\alpha_3}) (u).$$

By taking the logarithms of both sides, the equations are transformed so that ln(D) appears as a linear function of the logarithms of the righthand variables plus an additive error term (ln(u)), allowing the parameters to be estimated with ordinary least squares regression.

Parameters were estimated for both models for each formula (excluding mixed and indirect systems) for which data from "simple" elections (no second-stage and no electoral threshold) were included in the data set. The results reported in table 9.6, however, reflect the collapsing of these 11 categories into seven. The three collapsed categories are Modified Sainte-Laguë, Droop largest-remainder, and STV (Lijphart's intermediate category); multimember plurality and block vote; and majority (single-member majority and multimember majority).[10] In each case, the estimation of separate sets of parameters for the systems within the collapsed category did not significantly improve the prediction of ln(D) over the estimation of a common set of parameters. Because the R^2 reported in this table refers to the logarithm of D, additional columns report the proportion of the variance in D itself explained by each equation.

In table 9.6, all but five of the 30 parameter estimates for which particular ranges of values are predicted by conditions 1–5 are within those ranges. Of these five, only two are significantly (more than two standard errors) outside of the predicted range, and both of these, plus one of the insignificant deviations, come from the SNTV elections. Indeed, although the parameters estimated for the SNTV give quite accurate postdictions of D within the very limited range for which there are data (given that all the SNTV elections come from Japan), they are so far outside of the range of reason that there is no alternative but to conclude that the disproportionality of SNTV systems simply cannot be explained within the framework used for the other systems. Accordingly, SNTV is omitted from the remainder of this discussion. Overall, the two and three independent variable models, respectively, explain 42.2% and 49.1% of the variance in disproportionality with the SNTV elections included and 41.2% and 48.2% with them excluded.

Looking more closely at the estimates for the other formulas, one sees several theoretically significant differences among the equations. First, the addition of p as a predictor often results in a large (and in four of the six remaining categories, including those that are most common, a statistically significant) increase in the ability of the model to account for D. Moreover, addition of p also generally

TABLE 9.6 Disproportionality parameter estimates for simple electoral systems.

Electoral system	α_0 constant	α_1 magnitude	α_3 districts	R^2	Explained variance	β_0 constant	β_1 magnitude	β_2 parties	β_3 districts	R^2	Explained variance
d'Hondt highest average (N = 112)	−2.157 (.412)	−.344 (.096)	−.007 (.074)	.221	.093	−3.216 (.466)	−.354 (.090)	.585 (.144)	−.077 (.071)	.318	.161
Modified Ste.-Laguë Droop largest remainder STV (N = 60)	−2.319 (.444)	−.454 (.119)	.045 (.093)	.493	.435	−3.043 (.374)	−.801 (.112)	1.266 (.216)	−.280 (.092)	.686	.535
Hare largest remainder (N = 33)	−1.249 (.679)	−.377 (.169)	−.332 (.167)	.156	.104	−1.493 (.729)	−.486 (.206)	.240 (.258)	−.326 (.167)	.180	.126
SNTV (N = 17)	−28.727 (6.753)	4.517 (1.135)	4.148 (1.104)	.524	.532	−30.645 (10.645)	4.927 (1.960)	−.204 (.782)	4.508 (1.790)	.527	.530
Single-member plurality (N = 308)	−1.383 (.145)		−.131 (.031)	.055	.059	−1.788 (.144)		.568 (.077)	−.237 (.032)	.199	.218
Multimember plurality Block vote (N = 58)	−1.141 (.280)	.258 (.081)	−.264 (.065)	.347	.194	−1.315 (.302)	.234 (.082)	.246 (.171)	−.316 (.074)	.370	.183
Single-member majority Multimember majority (N = 51)	−1.103 (.885)	−.534 (.341)	−.177 (.150)	.050	.083	−1.674 (.854)	−.470 (.320)	.623 (.225)	−.297 (.147)	.184	.154

Numbers in parentheses are standard errors.

results in a large change in the parameter corresponding to at least one of the other variables, indicating that estimates of the impact of the institutional variables that do not take account of this more political contributor to disproportionality will be misleading. For this reason, the rest of the analysis will focus on the model with all three independent variables.

The estimates reported suggest that the variables important to the explanation of disproportionality differ between PR and the candidate-oriented systems. While M is a significant predictor of D for each of the three categories of PR formulas, as well as for multimember plurality (although in the opposite direction—higher values of M predict greater disproportionality for these systems), it is not significant for majority formulas (nor, of course, for single-member plurality, for which it has no variance). On the other hand, while the number of districts is a significant predictor of proportionality for all categories of electoral formula except Hare largest remainder, it is especially significant for plurality elections.

Bearing in mind that these results are observed regularities, not logical necessities, the estimated equations suggest that no one of the three sets of PR formulas is the most proportional under all circumstances. On the other hand, one can conclude that although there is no unequivocally *most* proportional formula, there is for all practical purposes a *least* proportional formula—multimember plurality election, with single-member plurality firmly in second place. Additionally:

1. Electoral formula makes a significant difference to the proportionality of electoral outcomes, and moreover the relationship between proportionality and other variables that contribute to it differs among electoral formulas;
2. For all major electoral formulas, expected proportionality increases as the number of districts (of constant magnitude) increases and as the number of parties competing decreases;
3. For all major electoral formulas except multimember plurality election, expected proportionality increases as average district magnitude increases;
4. PR formulas are more proportional ("fairer") than candidate-oriented formulas, with simple plurality formulas (both single- and multimember) less proportional than majority;
5. The relative proportionality of different PR formulas is not invariant, but depends on the particular combination of M, d, and p considered.

Thresholds and Multistage Formulas

In general, multistage formulas are implemented to increase the proportionality of the outcome without radically increasing the size of constituencies, while thresholds are introduced so that the desired increase in proportionality with regard to "significant" parties is not accompanied by an unreasonable proliferation of splinter parties. (An exception is the Greek system of "reinforced proportional representation," under which second-stage distribution of bonus seats was combined with an extraordinarily high threshold—in some cases as high as 30%—particularly to increase the representation of the plurality party, and thereby to *decrease* overall proportionality.) Careful inspection of table 9.5, however, suggests a far more ambiguous situation. For some first-stage formulas (e.g., Hare PR), the expectation that systems with second-stage distributions will be more proportional is apparently borne out by the data; for others (e.g., d'Hondt and Droop), it is not. Similarly, while single-stage Droop quota systems with a threshold are, on average, more proportional in their treatment of "significant" parties than those without, for single-stage d'Hondt systems the data suggest just the reverse.

Part of the problem is that the systems within each category are not all the same, and that differences in district magnitude, number of parties, and number of districts often coincide with differences in the use of second-stage distributions or an electoral threshold. The true hypothesis is that systems with second-stage distributions will be more proportional than the same systems would have been without, and that systems with thresholds analogously will be less proportional than they would have been without. For those elections using a first-stage formula for which parameter estimates could be estimated from simple systems, those estimates can be used to compute predicted values of D under the assumption of no second stage and no threshold, even for those systems that in fact used these devices. The difference between the observed and predicted values then indicates whether the actual election was more or less proportional than would have been expected without second-stage or threshold provisions.

As a first indication of the impact of these provisions, table 9.7 shows the average difference (computed so that a positive value indicates greater proportionality) for six combinations of provisions: use or nonuse of a threshold at either the district or the national level crossed with no second-stage distribution versus a second-stage distribution based on vote remainders versus a second-stage distribution based on the national or regional vote totals. With the effect of the "base" electoral system controlled, expectations about second-stage distributions are strongly supported by the data; for each category of threshold use, systems with second-stage distributions based on vote totals tend to be more proportional than those with distributions based on remainders, which in turn tend to be more proportional than systems with no second-stage distribution at all. The impact of thresholds, however, appears to be more complicated. For systems without a second-stage distribution or with one based on remainders, use of a threshold apparently decreases proportionality, but for second-stage distributions based on total votes received, systems with thresholds tend to be *more* proportional than analogous systems without thresholds. This anomaly, however, stems entirely from the single case of West Germany, which is the only case in which a particularly disproportional first-stage formula (single-member plurality) is combined with both a proportional second-stage formula *and* a threshold, and would disappear if the Federal Republic's two-stage system were treated, as it effectively is, as a single-stage PR system.

Although it is interesting to observe that thresholds and second-stage distributions make a difference, it would be more useful to quantify that difference. Assuming that the threshold and second-stage distribution effects are additive and that they are independent of the particular first-stage system involved, quantification can be accomplished using multistage regression.[11] The results are presented

TABLE 9.7 Average difference between predicted and observed values of D.

Use of electoral threshold	Second-stage distribution of seats		
	None	Based on vote remainders	Based on vote totals
Yes	−.0318	−.0035	.0236
No	−.0139	.0098	.0170

in table 9.8, which gives the formula for predicted disproportionality for each combination of threshold use and second-stage distribution.

These procedures allow expected disproportionalities to be computed for 753 of the original 818 weighted cases (767 of 844 unweighted). Of the remaining cases, six (all of which, except Austria 1945, are from before 1930) were eliminated because one of the necessary variables was missing, while the others were elections using a formula at one stage for which there was not sufficient variance in the relevant independent variables to compute meaningful parameter estimates. In these 753 elections, the predicted values account for just over 50% of the variance in observed disproportionality. Although some of this "explanatory" power stems from the great difference in proportionality between PR and other systems, even restricting attention to PR systems alone, these procedures still account for over 43% of the variance. In contrast, generalizing Lijphart's procedures to the full set of elections and using the averages he computed for European elections between 1945 and 1985 as predicted values for the whole set actually is *worse* than simply using the mean disproportionality for all PR systems as the

TABLE 9.8 Predicted disproportionality.

Second-stage distribution	Threshold	Predicted disproportionality
None	None	$F1$
	District level	$F1 + 2.26dt - 12.18dt^2$
Based on remainder votes	None	$sh*F2 + (1 - sh)*F1*(1.87 - .07*mag1)$
	District level	$sh*F2 + (1 - sh)*F1*(1.87 - .07*mag1) + 2.26dt - 12.18dt^2$
	Second level or both levels	$sh*F2 + (1 - sh)*F1*(1.87 - .07*mag1) + .79nt - 1.84nt^2$
Based on vote totals	None	$F2$, for $sh > .20$
		$(sh/.2)F2 + ((.2 - sh)/.20)F1$, for $sh < .20$
	Second level	$F2 + .79nt - 1.84nt^2$, for $sh > .20$
		$(sh/.2)F2 + ((.2 - sh)/.20)F1, + .79nt - 1.84nt^2$, for $sh < .20$

In these formulas, $F1$ and $F2$ refer to the functions whose parameters are in table 9.5 applied respectively to the first- and second-stage formulas. In each case, the number of districts is counted at the corresponding distribution; for second-stage distributions based on vote totals, magnitude is total seats divided by the number of second-stage districts, while for distributions of remainders, it is the number of remainder seats divided by the number of second-stage districts. Key: sh = share of the seats awarded at the second- or higher stage of distribution. dt = threshold applied at the first-stage district level. nt = threshold applied at the second- or higher level. mag1 = average magnitude of first-stage districts.

predicted value for each; using instead the observed means (i.e., simply performing an analysis of variance) explains only 12% of the variance.

These predictions are based on four classes of variables: district magnitude, number of parties, number of districts, and electoral formula. The relative importance of each can be assessed by comparing the predictive power of a model in which it is included to that of a model from which it is excluded, as in table 9.9.[12] Since much of the explanatory power attributed to electoral formula merely reflects the difference between PR and non-PR systems (and since much of the debate over the significance of electoral formula is restricted to differences among PR formulas), this analysis is done for the full data set, and then again only for systems using a PR formula in their final-stage distribution. The impact of formula is assessed in three ways: by allowing the constant term to vary among systems but holding the parameters of the other terms constant across systems, by fixing the constant term but allowing the other parameters to vary, and by eliminating all differences among formulas. For each model, explained variance is computed both taking account of, and ignoring, the effects of electoral thresholds.

Table 9.9 clearly indicates that electoral formula, and particularly difference in the constant terms, is the most important determinant of proportionality when all systems are considered together. When PR systems are considered alone, however, differences among formulas are nearly irrelevant, and, moreover, to the extent that formula makes a difference, the differences in parameters of M, p, and d, rather than the constant term, are significant. Within the context of the full data, taking account of thresholds makes very little difference to explanatory power; for PR systems it does. Number of districts is of some importance in the full data, but of virtually none when attention is restricted to PR systems; number of parties is of some importance, especially for PR systems when threshold effects are ignored. The big determinant of proportionality among PR systems, however, is district magnitude; indeed, controlling only for threshold, M by itself accounts for 26.4% of the variance in D for PR systems.

Finally, although the data from elections using the "missing" formulas (direct PR, pure Sainte-Laguë, and reinforced PR) do not allow estimation of parameters analogous to those computed for more common formulas, some indication of

TABLE 9.9 Explained variance in D of full and restricted models.

	All systems: threshold effect		PR systems only: threshold effect	
	Controlled	Ignored	Controlled	Ignored
Full unrestricted models	.534	.526	.432	.317
Magnitude eliminated	.503	.500	.280	.208
Number of districts eliminated	.470	.462	.414	.303
Number of parties eliminated	.472	.462	.336	.202
Electoral formula				
Constant terms fixed as equal	.315	.314	.432	.303
Parameters fixed as equal	.369	.366	.407	.297
Formula totally eliminated	.258	.257	.407	.297

their expected proportionalities can be obtained by comparing the mean observed values of D to the expected values computed from the formulas for each of the "known" systems. These comparisons are shown in table 9.10. The results for direct and reinforced PR are as one would expect; the former is clearly the most proportional system, while the latter shows a level of disproportionality nearly as high as the average for plurality systems. Pure Sainte-Laguë highest average, however, deviates from the expectation that it would be the most proportional system, with the observed D lying between the predicted values for Modified Sainte-Laguë and d'Hondt highest-average systems.

Again, conclusions can be listed briefly:

1. Electoral formulas differ significantly in their degree of expected disproportionality, but this is principally a difference between PR and non-PR systems. The differences among PR systems are overwhelmingly the result of differences in district magnitude, the use of electoral thresholds, and the number of parties competing.
2. Thresholds applied at national and district levels have different effects, with the impact of district level thresholds being greater (within the range of real thresholds) at each "height" of barrier.
3. Second stage distributions are effective in increasing proportionality because they have higher effective district magnitudes. Their impact is a function of the number of seats actually distributed.

Bias and Responsiveness

Some of the disproportionality of electoral results is the inevitable result of the fact that seats must be awarded in larger quanta than those in which votes are won. This fact would remain even if the resulting advantages and disadvantages experienced by parties were randomly distributed. Often, however, they are not. Whether because of their (relative) size, ideological position, geographic distribution, intentional bias, or for some other reason, some parties may be systematically advantaged and others systematically disadvantaged in the translation of votes into seats.

One of the earliest systematic descriptions of this phenomenon was the so-called "cube law."[13] Following on work by Tufte[14] and Theil,[15] Gary King has

TABLE 9.10 Observed disproportionality and comparison to expected disproportionality for direct PR, pure Sainte-Laguë, and reinforced PR.

	Direct PR	Pure Ste.-Laguë	Reinforced PR
Mean observed disproportionality	.024	.019	.119
Mean expected disproportionality treating formula as:			
d'Hondt highest average	.033	.025	.050
Modified Ste.-Laguë highest average, Droop quota, or STV	.026	.014	.047
Hare quota	.042	.034	.045

suggested that this law may be generalized to the following relationship, which allows both for multiparty competition and for the possibility of systematic bias in favor of particular parties.[16]

$$m_i = \frac{e^{k_i v_i{}^q}}{\sum_j e^{k_j v_j{}^q}}$$

In King's vocabulary, the k's are measures of bias, while q is a measure of responsiveness. Since the predicted value of m_i is unchanged by subtracting a constant from all of the k's, the results do not depend on the particular party for which k is constrained to be 0 and can be standardized in a variety of ways. In the analysis that follows, the estimated k for the party with the highest average vote was subtracted from all the others, yielding a set of parameters indicating bias relative to the largest party.

The same data as used in the analysis of proportionality were used to estimate k's and q's for each combination of electoral system (except indirect election, mixed systems, and reinforced PR) and period, provided it included at least three elections. Altogether, 93 q's (one for each combination of country, system, and period) and 885 k's (one for each party with country, system, and period, but including 93 set equal to 0 by construction) were estimated.

These data show responsiveness to differ significantly with category of electoral formula. As the first block of table 9.11 shows, formulas effectively fall into three categories with respect to q: PR plus STV, SNTV, and majority, for all of which q averages a bit over 1 with a variance no greater than .21; single-member plurality, for which q averages a bit over 2 with a variance of over 1.6; and multimember plurality, for which q averages over 3.6 with a variance of 5.38. With the possible exceptions of the result for SNTV and majority formulas, this is entirely unsurprising. The simple categorization (either into three or the full five categories) accounts for roughly 35% of the variance in q. More detailed investigation shows no significant (or consistent) difference among the various PR formulas.

Aspects of electoral system other than formula also contribute to the explanation of q. Here, all of the variables examined in the analysis of disproportionality were considered. In addition, the nature of the curve being estimated makes it reasonable to suppose that estimates of q might be sensitive to the part of the curve for which there are actual data, and hence to the distribution of votes among parties. Thus, the mean and standard deviation of this distribution were also considered as potential explanatory variables. The second block of table 9.11 reports regression analyses based on those variables that were found to have a significant impact on q for any of the three categories of electoral formula. As this block shows, district magnitude (broken down into its two components, number of districts and number of seats) and the distribution of votes are significant predictors of q for all three categories, but the way they combine to predict q differs markedly from one formula to another. In general, however, these results lead to the expectation of a positive relationship between q and D, and this is indeed the case ($r = 0.56$).

TABLE 9.11 Responsiveness (q) and bias (k) by electoral formula.

	PR	SNTV	Majority	SMP	MMP	Overall
Responsiveness (q)						
Minimum	.38	1.01	.69	.56	.53	.38
Mean	1.19	1.24	1.07	2.03	3.61	1.59
Maximum	2.37	1.44	2.09	5.31	6.67	6.67
Variance	.13	.05	.21	1.61	5.38	1.36
Number of observations	48	3	9	26	7	93
Regression parameters predicting						
responsiveness (standard errors in paren.)						
If single-member plurality (dummy)						1.64
						(.336)
If multimember plurality (dummy)						2.28
						(.438)
Number of districts	.0075			−.0020	−.014	−.0054
	(.0019)			(.0010)	(.0021)	(.0012)
Number of seats	−.00033				.0051	.0030
	(.00037)				(.00086)	(.00086)
Mean vote	−1.10			2.86	−8.79	1.71
	(.495)			(1.69)	(2.01)	(.995)
Standard deviation of vote	1.21			−6.18	12.54	−2.95
	(.97)			(2.62)	(5.20)	(1.69)
Constant	1.09			2.60	3.06	.87
	(.67)			(.92)	(1.56)	(.38)
R^2	.373			.531	.993	.521
Bias (k)						
Minimum	−2.90			−3.51	−74.60	
Mean	.10			.40	.56	
Maximum	4.35			6.76	21.78	
Variance	.42			2.63	178.47	
Number of observations	543			193	39	

SMP = single-member plurality.   MMP = multimember plurality.

Turning to the k's, as the third block of table 9.11 shows, the primary difference among electoral formulas is not in the mean bias, which quite naturally tends to be about o for all formulas, but in the range and variance of the biases observed. Even discounting the extreme values by looking at the interquartile range confirms the basic finding. The ranges for PR, single-member plurality, and multimember plurality are, respectively, .34, 1.57, and 3.96.

Within each category of formula the greatest biases, both positive and negative, as well as the greatest variance among biases, are associated with the smallest parties. Very small parties (those with average vote less than one tenth of that of the largest party) appear particularly likely to benefit from a positive bias. Even here, however, for many small parties the bias is negative. Moreover, one should remember that given the "S" shape of the curves being estimated, a small party could have a positive k and still expect to receive a proportion of seats substantially smaller than its proportion of votes.

The q is a property of the electoral system as a whole (i.e., it is constant within the system), and as such tells only part of the story. Although a higher value of q indicates a steep slope, and therefore a higher responsiveness (in the sense that small vote shifts will be associated with large seat shifts) at some points on the votes-seats curve, the general shape of the "S" curve means that this steeper slope must be compensated by shallower slopes (i.e., lower responsiveness) at other points. A fuller picture of the responsiveness of electoral systems can be obtained by examining the slope of the curve predicting seats from votes computed for each party at its own average vote.

As table 9.12 shows, there is a considerable range in the degree to which parties can expect to be rewarded or punished for marginal changes in their vote. Again, the principal difference is between the plurality systems (for which the range is dramatically larger and highly skewed, for which reason the median is shown as well as the mean) and all the rest. In general, single-member plurality and especially multimember plurality tend to magnify shifts in votes in translating them into shifts in seats, while PR (and the other systems) tend to dampen them. Nonetheless, for each system, some parties can expect their share of the seats to swing more widely than their share of the votes, while for others relatively small vote swings would be expected to have no appreciable consequence at all.

This analysis suggests the following generalizations about responsiveness and bias:

1. Aggregate responsiveness and aggregate proportionality are influenced by much the same factors, but are inversely related.
2. Multimember plurality systems, and to a lesser degree single-member plurality systems, tend to have higher aggregate responsiveness than do PR systems.
3. The range of biases for and against particular parties is higher for multimember plurality than for single-member plurality, and the range for single-member plurality is higher than for PR.
4. Electoral systems tend to be biased in terms of k in favor of small parties, but this bias is not enough to overcome the bias against small parties inherent in the "S" shape of the curve relating votes and seats. Consequently, small parties tend to be underrepresented, and large parties overrepresented.
5. Marginal responsiveness tends to be highest for parties in multimember plurality, followed by single-member plurality, followed by PR systems.

Votes, Seats, and Democracy

What does this analysis say about the choice of the "most democratic" electoral system? Only a partial answer can be attempted at this point, and even this answer will be subject to revision once other aspects of electoral systems have been considered more fully. Nonetheless, the evidence presented here bears directly on

TABLE 9.12 Marginal responsiveness by electoral formula.

	PR	SNTV	Majority	SMP	MMP
Marginal responsiveness					
Number of observations	543	33	77	193	39
Minimum	.09	.21	.08	.05	.00
Mean	.79	.64	.75	1.31	2.53
Median	.73	.56	.67	.95	1.12
Maximum	3.85	1.09	2.18	16.75	19.22

SMP = single-member plurality.   MMP = multimember plurality.

the relationship between the choice of electoral formula and the relative priority given the values of liberalism and popular sovereignty. In this regard, the principal trade-off is between proportionality, on one hand, and responsiveness (both aggregate and marginal) coupled with a greater likelihood of bias, on the other.

For this evaluation, popular sovereignty theories can be divided into two categories: legislative democracy, for which a multiparty system and true proportionality are required, and all the others, which call for a two-party system. For the latter, the important concern is that a single party receive both a majority of the votes and a majority of the seats, or at least that no coalition with less than a majority of the votes receive a majority of the seats. (In the case of Tory democracy, the concern is simply that a single party with substantial, even if less than majority, electoral support win a majority of the seats.) The impact of electoral systems on party systems and the likelihood of majority government formation are the subjects of a later chapter, so real consideration of what system is most appropriate to these visions of democracy must be left until then. One can observe, however, that the demand that a party with a majority of votes receive a majority of seats would apparently require that the system be unbiased with regard to the larger parties. From this limited perspective, the data analyzed here would suggest a slight advantage to PR over plurality formulas.

Turning particularly to legislative democracy, the choice is clearly for large-district PR. Although one might suppose that popular sovereignty would be furthered by having the people's voice pass through the amplifier of high responsiveness (which would suggest an advantage for plurality systems), this is incompatible with the more important goal of proportionality. Liberal theories, however, are less concerned with the proportionality of the aggregate outcome, and more concerned with restraining those in power through the structure of rewards and punishments. Thus the amplification of changes in support implicit in a highly responsive system is quite compatible with this school of thought.

The expected political influence of minorities is particularly important for majoritarian and pluralist liberalism. This influence can be seen in two ways. If one refers only to the chance of minority parties electing representatives, then it appears that minorities will be more influential with large-district PR, although an exception must be made for locally concentrated minorities that may be better off under a plurality system. If, however, one refers to the expected impact of votes cast for minorities on the distribution of seats among the larger parties, and so to the attention that those larger parties must pay to the interests of those who *might* vote for the minority parties, then it appears that minorities are given the greatest weight under multimember plurality and single-member plurality formulas. This gives rise to the phenomenon of the "blackmail party," a short-lived party created, or threatened, not to win elections but to cause the party the blackmailers would normally support to lose an election as punishment for paying inadequate deference to their demands.

Finally, notwithstanding the usual association of consociational democracy and PR, neither proportionality nor responsiveness need be of major concern to advocates of veto group liberalism. Instead, the most important criterion is the direct representation of each significant interest. Given some geographic separation of group members, so that each group will be dominant in some areas, representation may be achieved by plurality election as well as by PR.

Overall, the preliminary conclusion is that large-district PR is most appropriate for those views of democracy that require the direct representation of minorities or a high degree of proportionality in the distribution of seats among parties, while plurality systems are most appropriate for views that value indirect representation of minorities. At this point, and with strong qualifications as just noted, this suggests that plurality election is most appropriate to liberal democracy, while PR is most appropriate to legislative popular sovereignty.

Parties and Governments

An election takes place, and an electoral system has its effect, at a particular time and within the context of a particular party system. Over time, however, an electoral system may influence the characters of the parties as well as the party system as a whole. This potential impact of electoral systems is the first subject of this chapter, in particular, the relationship between electoral formula and the number of parties. The relationship between electoral system and the range of options available for electoral choice, and especially the presence of extreme or ideological politics, receives briefer attention, on the basis of less comprehensive data. Another subject, the relationship between electoral system and party factionalism, is left to chapter 12.

The other major subject of this chapter is the formation of cabinets in parliamentary systems. Here there are two major concerns. First, to what extent can one say that the votes cast in an election determined the subsequent government, and how does this determination differ among electoral systems? Second, how does the character of governments in parliamentary systems—especially their longevity and majority or minority status—vary among electoral systems?

Parties and Party Systems

Number of Parties

The seminal theoretical statement (hypothesis) concerning the relationship between electoral system and the number of parties is Duverger's Law:

> (1) Proportional representation tends to lead to the formation of many independent parties, . . . (2) the two-ballot majority system tends to lead to the formation of many parties that are allied with each other, . . . (3) the plurality rule tends to produce a two-party system.[1]

Although Duverger introduced it with the strong language of "sociological law," he quickly tempered his position, emphasizing that "tends to lead" is far weaker than "causes" and in fact implies no *necessary* relationship.[2] Moreover, if "tends to lead" has any causal import at all, he virtually abandons the first clause of the law on the next page, observing that "[o]n the whole, PR maintains virtually without change the party system existing at the time of its adoption."[3]

In the strongest sense of "law" (a set of necessary and sufficient conditions with no exceptions), Duverger's Law as originally stated clearly is false—Canada and India combine single-member plurality with multiparty systems while Austria appeared at least through the 1970s to combine PR with a two-party system. This qualification has led to a series of attempts to rescue the law either in terms of tendencies rather than conditions, or with various qualifications and exceptions.[4] Whether approached from the perspective of necessary and sufficient conditions or as a question of tendencies, however, the first condition for either test or analysis is a rule for the counting of parties. Six rules representing the range of rules used in the past were explored initially: three based on simple counts of parties, two on the "effective" number of parties,[5] and one based on Sartori's notion of significant parties.

The most obvious rule is to count all the parties that present candidates in an election (N.RUN), the rule (with the result identified as "p") used in predicting disproportionality in chapter 9. In talking about party systems however, N.RUN vastly inflates the number of parties by counting, for example, the Communist Party of the United States as equivalent to the Democrats or Republicans. A somewhat more restrictive rule counts only those parties that win at least one seat (N.ONE). The problem here is that the definition of party then depends on the electoral system—the higher the threshold of representation, the stronger a party must be before it "counts." Alternatively, an arbitrary vote threshold for significance can be imposed by the analyst; in this research, the threshold chosen was 5% of the vote (N.5%).

Although N.ONE and N.5% limit the number of weak parties counted, they still count every party that meets their conditions equally. Taagepera and Shugart propose instead weighting each party's contribution to the count by its size, thus defining the "effective" number of parties. This equals the raw number of parties only if they are of exactly equal size; otherwise, it is smaller. Since the calculation can be based either on vote shares or on seat shares, it gives rise to two "effective number of parties" measures, EFF.V and EFF.S, respectively.

Finally, Sartori suggests that a party ought to be counted as significant if it has governing experience or potential, or blackmail potential, over a significant period of time. In my implementation of this rule, I dropped the last criterion and calculated the number of parties (N.COAL) on an election-by-election basis. As a result, N.COAL here may be somewhat larger than strict adherence to Sartori's rule would allow. On the other hand, governing potential was operationalized by counting any party with sufficient seats to be included in *some* potential minimum winning coalition in the legislature. As a result, N.COAL may exclude parties that actually have been in government if their contribution to the government's majority was numerically unnecessary or if it was a minority government. The greatest problem, however, is that if a single party wins a majority, there is only one possible minimum winning coalition, and (by virtue of considering the largest opposition party as also significant) the result is counted automatically as a two-party outcome.

Table 10.1 shows the average number of parties per election for each of the major categories of electoral formula; table 10.2 shows the percentage of elections that might be classified as contested by two parties. (For EFF.V and EFF.S, values under 2.5 were regarded as equal to 2; the other four counting rules naturally yield integral values. These tables are based on the full data set; comparison with tables based only on the postwar period shows no substantial differences.) Systems are classified on the basis of their principal formula (e.g., the West German system is classified on the basis of its second stage as an example of PR), with all PR systems, including STV, combined and then divided on the basis of use of a statutory threshold. The tables show a strong, but not overpowering, relationship between formula and both average number of parties and two-partyism, with the most restrictive counting rules showing the strongest relationships.

If one focuses only on list PR and single-member plurality and looks particularly at EFF.V, the number of exceptions to Duverger's Law is far greater than indicated by the usual Eurocentric data. In addition to Austria, eight countries (Colombia, Costa Rica, El Salvador, West Germany, Guyana, Liechtenstein, Uruguay, and Zimbabwe) had at least one postwar election with fewer than 2.5 effective parties, while 16 (Burma, Canada, Fiji, India, Kenya, Lesotho, Malaysia, Nepal, New Zealand, Nigeria, Pakistan, South Africa, St. Vincent, Sri Lanka, Trinidad, and the United Kingdom [UK]) had at least one single-member plurality election with more. While many of these are open to the "inexperience with democracy" argument,[6] many are not.

If one addresses the problem as one of tendencies and concentrates on the average number of parties, single-member majority shows the same tendency toward multipartyism as PR, as the law suggests it should. The alternative vote, however, looks more like single-member plurality, although the logic that leads to the expectation of multipartyism for single-member majority should apply here as well. The various candidate-oriented multimember formulas, including multimember majority, behave like single-member plurality. Turning to propensity to two-partyism, both alternative vote and SNTV occupy an intermediate position, with the block vote showing a tendency toward a two-party system even stronger than that observed for single-member plurality. As indicated by Duverger's logic, the more the allocation of seats is an "all-or-nothing" proposition, the greater the likelihood of two-partyism. But even in the most extreme cases (excluded from the data analyzed here), direct election of a single president, while there may be two predominant parties, there are virtually never exactly two parties, and as the French and recent Finnish experiences suggest, there may be many more.

Duverger's Law makes no specific predictions for PR and majority formulas regarding either the trend in numbers of parties over time or the absolute number of parties (except that it will be greater than two). For single-member plurality, however, clearly if there are not already two parties, then at least the trend should be in that direction. If one omits the period from 1945 through 1949 as a postwar "settling in" and looks at elections held between 1950 and 1985, we see that this

TABLE 10.1 Average numbers of parties per election by electoral formula.

Formula	N	N.RUN	N.ONE	N.5%	EFF.V	EFF.S	N.COAL
					Counting rule		
PR—with threshold	99	10.0	7.5	4.4	3.9	3.7	6.5
PR—without threshold	229	8.9	7.0	4.2	3.9	3.5	5.1
Single-member plurality	309	5.6	4.2	3.0	2.6	2.0	2.3
Alternative vote	21	5.4	3.6	3.3	2.8	2.6	2.7
Single-member majority	36	8.5	7.9	5.1	4.9	4.4	6.7
SNTV	17	5.6	5.6	4.0	3.2	2.8	3.5
Multimember plurality	42	5.5	4.7	3.5	2.8	2.4	3.2
Multimember majority	15	5.0	4.0	3.3	2.8	2.2	2.1
Block vote	26	5.9	2.7	2.3	2.2	1.6	2.0
Eta-squared		.18	.16	.26	.31	.40	.31

often has not been the case. For example, if one examines the values of EFF.V over time for the 10 countries that held at least five single-member plurality elections between 1950 and 1985 the prediction based on Duverger's Law is supported by four of the 10 cases: for the United States and Jamaica EFF.V stayed consistently within a narrow band around 2, while for Botswana and Malaysia it tended toward 2, in the Botswanan case from below and in the Malaysian case from above. In three cases (Canada, India, and Sri Lanka), however, EFF.V stayed consistently above 2, while in three others (New Zealand, South Africa, and the UK) plus Canada, it started above 2 and then *increased*, so that by the end of the period Canada, New Zealand, and the UK all would be more accurately described as three-party, rather than two-party, systems. The evident conclusion is that as one moves beyond the general observation that candidate-oriented systems (other than single-member majority) are more likely to be associated with two-party systems and PR and single-member majority with multiparty systems, Duverger's Law either has very little to say (e.g., it allows no predictions about which PR systems will have more parties and which less) or else is not generally true

TABLE 10.2 Percentage of elections with two-party systems.

Formula	N	N.RUN	N.ONE	N.5%	EFF.V	EFF.S	N.COAL
					Counting rule		
PR—with threshold	99	4.1	7.1	7.2	14.3	23.5	18.9
PR—without threshold	229	0.0	1.7	3.8	10.9	17.1	26.0
Single-member plurality	309	3.5	28.1	37.6	55.0	81.2	86.8
Alternative vote	21	0.0	11.1	22.2	29.5	42.0	49.3
Single-member majority	36	0.0	0.0	3.3	16.3	28.8	28.8
SNTV	17	0.0	0.0	5.7	22.5	36.2	47.8
Multimember plurality	42	13.5	44.1	45.4	53.6	68.6	60.8
Multimember majority	15	16.6	33.2	33.2	33.2	82.3	93.5
Block vote	26	0.0	54.4	77.2	93.9	100.0	100.0
Eta-squared		.05	.17	.21	.23	.37	.38

(e.g., most major single-member plurality systems do not have and are not moving toward two parties). The logic that underlies the law—that the number of parties will decrease in response to systemic characteristics that reduce the likelihood of small parties receiving some reward for contesting the election—may still be valid, however.

Again, with a focus on EFF.V, and looking within the PR category, previous theorizing has suggested that d'Hondt PR systems would have fewer parties than Modified Ste.-Lague, Droop quota or STV systems, which would have fewer parties than Hare and Ste.-Lague systems—all based on the presumption that this is also the order of increasing proportionality. As was seen in chapter 9, this presumption is not supported by the data, but one might expect a relationship between EFF.V and district magnitude, which might interact with PR formula. A first glance at the data (not shown here) indicates that district magnitude is indeed related to EFF.V, but that other institutional factors, notably the use of an electoral threshold and presidentialism, also play a role.

All of this discussion may be combined in a regression model, as reported in table 10.3. In this model, both the constant and the parameter associated with district magnitude (in keeping with the expectation that magnitude will have a declining marginal impact, the logarithm of magnitude was used) are allowed to vary among formulas. For these, the first line of the table shows the values estimated for d'Hondt and Imperiali PR,[7] while subsequent lines show the *difference* between those values and the values that would be estimated for the other formulas. Presidentialism and the use of statutory thresholds, however, are modeled as having a constant effect across formulas. Because elections from Uruguay and Guyana appeared to be extreme outliers in preliminary analyses, they were excluded.

The regression explains nearly half of the variance in the effective number of parties and confirms the strong association of number of parties with district magnitude. With magnitude controlled, however, the effects of PR formulas appear to be precisely the opposite of those conventionally expected. One possible explanation is that supposedly less proportional systems are adopted in the first place to counteract observed or anticipated fissiparousness in the party system, although they are only partially successful in doing so.[8] Additionally, the effects of electoral formula may be balanced by other provisions in the electoral law. For example, Sweden (1952) changed from "less proportional" d'Hondt allocation to "more proportional" Modified Ste.- Lague to replace the advantage to small parties offered by apparentement.[9] The effective number of parties then decreased, but does this example really contradict the original hypothesis? Similarly, the positive association of thresholds with EFF.V, while contrary to expectation, may reflect the inability of these provisions to control entirely the effects of the larger district magnitudes with which they are generally associated. Finally, the increase in party number associated with presidentialism may indicate that presidentialism changes the nature of a parliamentary election by emphasizing the legislature's role as representative, rather than as elector of the executive. On one hand, this increases the incentive for distinct opinions to try to secure independent representation rather than be folded into a larger coalition, while on the other hand it lessens

TABLE 10.3 Regression predictions of EFF.V.

	Regression coefficients			
	Constant	ln(Magnitude)	Presidential	Statutory threshold
Base equation (d'Hondt, Imperiali)	3.513	.105	.458	.298
Modified Ste.-Lague, STV Droop	−1.238	.242		
Hare, Ste.-Lague	−3.093	.759		
Direct PR	.947	.312		
Single-member plurality	−1.011			
Alternative vote	−.741			
Single-member majority	1.254			
Single nontransferable vote	−.113	− .289		
Multimember plurality, block vote	−.013	−.914		
Multimember majority	.167	−1.159		
$R^2 = .456$				

the negative consequences of failing to secure parliamentary seats, since the supporters of parties that win no seats still can participate in the separate election of the president.

The regression approach suggests, however, that these effects are not simply the result of differing levels of disproportionality. Lagged disproportionality is, by itself, a statistically significant ($p < .001$) but substantively trivial ($R^2 = .04$) predictor of EFF.V; with the variables in Table 10.3 controlled, the marginal increase in R^2 accompanying the inclusion of lagged disproportionality is only .003, and the associated coefficient is not significantly different from 0. If one restricts attention to PR systems, the relationship is weaker still. Even if one considers disproportionality in the current election (for which any observed correlation might well be dismissed as tautological), in neither case is as much as 4% of the variance in EFF.V accounted for by disproportionality.

Proportionality Reconsidered

Although EFF.V is, in general, the more interesting definition of number of parties, N.RUN is the most relevant for predicting disproportionality. One problem with this variable was that it is political, while the other variables considered in chapter 9 are institutional, but as the preceding analysis has shown, number of parties is itself strongly influenced by institutional factors. This problem can be eliminated by replacing p (observed N.RUN) in the predictive model with the value of N.RUN predicted from institutional variables.

Predicting N.RUN from institutional variables gives results substantially the same as those reported in table 10.3, and so the details are not reproduced here. The overall R^2 is .376. When predicted values are substituted for p, the basic structure of the model also remains unchanged. Although the value of R^2 is reduced, it is still possible to account for over 42% of the variance in disproportionality, now on the basis of purely institutional variables.

Range of Choice, Extremism, and Ideology

One of the charges frequently leveled against PR is that it encourages both the fractionalization of the party system and the growth of extreme parties, both said to be undesirable because they lead to unstable and ineffective governments, and ultimately to the collapse of democracy itself.[10] However, PR often is defended with the claim that it allows a broader range of opinions to be represented in the electoral arena, and thereby provides a kind of "safety valve" that reduces the chance that discontents will be expressed in extralegal actions or violence. This chapter has already shown that there is a tendency toward a more fractionalized party system associated with PR. In this section, I present evidence addressing the questions of whether PR also is associated with party systems offering the electorate a broader range of choice at the polls and in which the electoral strength of extreme parties or parties embodying an "ideological style" of politics is greater.

Unlike the relatively objective question of party number, range of choice, extremism, and ideology can only be addressed subjectively. Especially at the level of empirical indicators, there are several competing definitions of ideology. Often one person's reasonable position is another person's extremism. Alternatives that appear to differ significantly from one standpoint may appear virtually indistinguishable from another.

At the least, one can distinguish three senses of the term "ideology" relevant to the discussion of elections and democracy. The first simply equates ideology and extremism. Hence, by definition, there can be no moderate or center ideology. Implicit is the expectation that extremism will result in intransigence, so that ideological parties will be unwilling to moderate their demands or to compromise with less extreme parties. This notion of ideology was central to the "end of ideology" literature of the 1960s, in which the electoral decline of extreme (particularly Communist) parties was taken to indicate the dawn of an era of consensus politics.[11] If one assumes moderation and pragmatism are preferred to extremism and dogmatism and observes that extremism frequently has been associated with questionable loyalty to the democratic system, ideology by this standard usually is considered a bad thing.

The second sense of ideology focuses on consistency, either across time or issues, and is related to the concept of "constraint" prominent in research on political attitudes in the mass public.[12] Under the same rubric, ideology is identified with the use of overarching principles, such as a left-right conceptualization of politics. Here the contrast is between principle and opportunism; ideologues may be willing to make informed compromises, and moderates can be as ideological as extremists.

Finally, ideology may be evidenced by the use of symbols that refer to particular worldviews, even if those views are not reflected in consistent or coherent policy positions. This sense of ideology refers to a style of political discourse rather than to its specific content. When the symbols involved are sociological (social class, ethnic group, religion), ideological parties in this sense are likely to approximate "parties of integration" rather than "catch-all parties."[13] Although moderation does not qualify as an ideology in this sense, liberalism or Christianity do, and hence again parties generally regarded as "responsible" may also be ideological. I do not address being ideological in this sense, but one should remember that it often colors thinking on this subject.

I have drawn on several previous studies to derive a variety of indicators of the range of choice available to voters as well as of the extremism, and in that sense the extent to which parties are ideological. This approach has advantages: the studies drawn upon are fully documented, cover a range of times and countries, have been based on a variety of methodologies, and so have the potential to serve as cross-checks on one another. At the same time, however, there is considerable overlap in the countries included in these studies; especially to the extent they measure a kind of "professional consensus," they are not really independent of one another.

The first source is a "reputational" study by Castles and Mair.[14] They asked 115 "leading political scientists" in 1982 to place the major political parties from their own countries on an 11-point, left-right, scale. Each of 119 parties was scored by three to 12 "experts." The second source is a similar, but more detailed, study conducted by Michael Laver of 162 parties or political tendencies in 24 countries.[15] Whereas the Castles and Mair experts were asked to rate the parties as wholes, Laver's respondents were asked to rate the parties' leaders and voters separately. The third source is the *International Comparative Political Parties Project* of Kenneth Janda.[16] This study attempted to score a worldwide sample of parties on a variety of dimensions for each of two time periods, 1950–1956 and 1957–1962. In this case, scores were based on "library-type sources," including party and government documents, as interpreted by a team of coders. For purposes of this analysis, only parties from countries for which electoral data for the appropriate period were collected have been considered, reducing the sample to 74 parties from 22 countries (from Janda's full sample of 158 parties in 53 countries).

Range of Choice

As an approximate measure of the range of choice offered to voters, table 10.4 shows the average by electoral system of the national range of scores on a variety of left-right or policy-position measures from the three studies. Because of the limited number of cases, all list systems are grouped together, and it must be underscored that, as shown in the table, there is generally only one case for each of the formulas other than single-member plurality and PR.

The results are striking. The average party system in countries with list PR spans nearly all of Castles and Mair's 11-point left-right scale; the average party system in single-member plurality countries covers just a bit more than half of it. If attention is restricted to those parties receiving at least 5% of the vote in the general election closest to the Castles and Mair study, the difference is reduced but remains quite large. In specific policy areas, Laver's data also show a consistently and substantially larger range for PR party systems than for single-member plurality party systems. Janda's data generally support the same conclusion, with the sole exceptions being policies regarding redistribution of wealth and social welfare, for which the average range is slightly smaller in the PR systems. In both

TABLE 10.4 Mean interparty issue range

	SMP	PR	STV	Alternative vote	SMM	SNTV	MMP
Castles and Mair, placement of parties on 11-point left/right scale (N)	4	10	1	1	1		
All parties in study	5.5	9.2	7.0	5.5	9.0	15.0	
Parties with over 5% of vote	5.3	7.4	5.2	5.5	7.5	11.3	
Laver, placement of party leadership on 20 point issue scale (N)	4	15	2	1	1	1	
Increase services vs cut taxes	8.4	12.5	8.7	7.6	15.9	15.0	
Pro-friendly relations with USSR vs anti-	4.9	10.6	6.9	6.0	17.7	11.3	
Pro-public ownership vs anti-	6.8	13.3	6.9	6.7	17.0	16.9	
Pro-permissive social policy vs anti-	8.5	15.0	11.3	11.8	15.5	6.0	
Anticlerical vs proclerical	3.8	14.5	11.2	6.5	13.6	14.2	
Pro-urban interests vs anti-	6.4	11.0	4.8	11.9	7.9	12.9	
Pro-decentralization of decisions vs anti-	6.8	10.9	7.0	5.4	9.9	10.2	
Environment over growth vs growth over environment	6.4	12.3	2.9	13.3	14.3	12.4	

Comparative political parties, 11-point issue scales, 1950–1956/1957–1962 (N)	4/6	11/10	1/1	1/1	0/1	1/1
Government ownership of means of production	4.3/3.0	5.8/5.5	4.0/4.0	5.0/3.0	–/6.0	4.0/4.0
Government role in economic planning	3.8/3.2	4.6/4.2	0.0/0.0	1.0/1.0	–/5.0	1.0/1.0
Redistribution of wealth	3.5/3.2	3.5/2.7	2.0/2.0	2.0/2.0	–/6.0	0.0/0.0
Social welfare	3.7/4.0	3.6/3.6	4.0/4.0	3.0/3.0	–/6.0	0.0/0.0
Secularization of society	1.0/2.2	2.6/2.9	4.0/4.0	0.0/0.0	–/6.0	5.0/5.0
Support of the military	0.5/1.3	3.7/3.2	2.0/2.0	3.0/3.0	–/8.0	4.0/4.0
Alignment with East-West blocs	0.0/1.3	5.0/3.1	2.0/2.0	4.0/4.0	–/10.0	0.0/0.0
Anticolonialism	1.5/1.3	2.1/2.1	2.0/2.0	0.0/0.0	–/6.0	0.0/0.0
Supranational integration	1.0/1.8	3.7/3.0[a]	0.0/0.0	0.0/0.0	–/6.0	0.0/0.0
National integration	2.0/2.5	2.3/1.5	2.0/2.0	3.0/3.0	–/4.0	0.0/0.0

SMP = single-member plurality.
ΣM = single-member majority.
MMP = multimember plurality.
These abbreviations apply in succeeding tables.
[a] Ns = 10/9.

cases, the reversal can be explained by ranges of o observed for two PR systems (Uruguay and Venezuela for redistribution of wealth; Denmark and Iceland for social welfare policies). This apparent consensus in turn reflects Janda's decision to restrict attention to parties that won at least 5% of the parliamentary seats, which, as the Castles and Mair data suggest, has the effect of limiting the range of views included. Thus, although the data strongly support the conclusion that voters will have a wider range of choice in PR than in single-member plurality systems, this conclusion must be tempered by the observation that the increased range may be partly the result of the greater likelihood under PR that fringe parties with little practical significance will continue to exist.

Extremism

Castles and Mair define as extreme ("ultra-left" and "ultra-right") parties that scored below 1.25 or above 8.75 on their 11-point scale. A roughly equivalent definition of extremism for the Laver data would be scores below 3.5 or over 17.5, and for the Janda data, a coding in the two extreme categories (± 5). What is the relationship between electoral formula and the frequency and strength of extreme parties?

Table 10.5 reports the relevant data, showing for each study the number of systems with at least one extreme party as well as the average proportions of votes and seats won by such parties.[17] Countries using some form of PR for parliamentary elections are more likely to have at least one extreme party, and extreme parties are likely to receive more votes and more seats than in countries using single-member plurality. Moreover, the principal exceptions underscore the observation that extremism is a highly subjective characterization. In the Laver data, the average strength of parties coded as extreme with regard to public ownership is higher for single-member plurality than for PR systems because both the British Conservative and American Republican parties were coded as *extremely* opposed. It should be noted that the UK, United States, and Belgium (PR) were the only countries in which all of the parties coded as extreme on this dimension were on the right. Right "extremism" among British, American, Canadian, and New Zealand parties also accounts for the "exceptional" results for alignment with east-west blocs in the Janda data.

Clearly, PR is associated with more small parties and with more extreme and ideological parties, while single-member plurality and other barriers to the representation of small parties are associated with fewer parties and a tendency toward an abbreviated political spectrum. The key question, however, is whether electoral arrangements reflect or shape the party system. On one hand, single-member plurality and related electoral systems may have squeezed out minor parties and parties with extreme ideologies, so that over time the thinking of voters in their natural constituencies has been conditioned and ultimately the base of their support has disappeared. On the other hand, electoral systems that are apparently hostile to a multiplicity of parties and to extreme parties may have been adopted and survived precisely in those countries in which the support for such movements initially was less significant.

Unfortunately, cross-sectional data cannot resolve this question, and the longitudinal evidence is too slim both quantitatively (too few major changes in electoral formula) and qualitatively (no reliable public opinion data from before the 1960s) to be more than suggestive. As in much of social reality, the suggestion is that causation runs both ways. The reform of the French electoral system with the advent of the Fifth Republic, both the shift to single-member majority and the introduction of a strong, directly elected president, played an obvious role in bringing a kind of bipolar order to the French party system and in sapping the strength of the ideological extremes, especially on the left.[18] At the same time, these changes have not prevented the rise, if not to power then at least to electoral significance, of the National Front on the extreme right, nor have they prevented the revival of the center.

Left-Right Self-Placement and Constraint

An alternative approach to the question of ideology is to look at the electorate rather than the parties. While the need for cross-nationally comparable data must limit this analysis to only a few countries, the pioneering work of Philip Converse suggests two ways in which the extent to which electorates are ideological may be assessed.[19] First, one can look at willingness to use terms like "liberal" and "conservative" or "left" and "right," or operationally at willingness to place oneself on a left-right scale. Table 10.6 shows the percentages of respondents coded as "missing data" with regard to left-right self-placement in four cross-national surveys—the 1973–1976 "Political Action" study with data from Great Britain, Germany, the Netherlands, Austria, Italy, Switzerland, Finland, and the United States; Eurobarometer 19 (1983), with data from the then 10 members of the European Community; Eurobarometer 29 (1988) with data from the same countries, Spain, and Portugal; and the 1981–1983 World Values survey data from 18 countries—plus similar data from the 1976 Center for Political Studies (CPS) American election study and the 1965 Canadian election study.[20] The conclusions indicated by these data are somewhat ambiguous, both across countries within a single survey, and within countries across time. The finding that Americans are singularly reluctant to use the simplifying abstractions of ideological discourse (or at least the particular abstraction of a left-right dimension) is confirmed by the Political Action and CPS data, but contradicted by the World Values data. The more general form of this hypothesis—that single-member plurality is associated with lower levels of ideological abstraction—is supported by the data, but this support is far from overwhelming. Interpreting these survey results as a random sample of possible surveys, the mean percentage of missing data is 22.0 for single-member plurality systems and only 14.0 for PR, a difference statistically significant at the level of $p < .02$. If the outlying South African case is removed, however, the single-member plurality average drops to 18.8%, which, given the broad overlap of the distributions and the small number of cases, is no longer statistically significant.

A second sense of how ideological populations are that is suggested by Converse's analysis is constraint among opinions on diverse issues, as indicated by the

TABLE 10.5 Number, vote share, and seats share of extreme parties.

	SMP	PR	STV	Alternative vote	SMM	SNTV	MMP
Castles and Mair, placement of parties on 11-point left/right scale (N)	4	10	1	1	1		1
All parties in study	0[a] 0 0	8 4.9 4.2	0 0 0	0 0 0	1 0 0	1	
Laver, placement of party leadership on 20-point issue scale (N)	4	14	2	1	1	1	
Increase services vs cut taxes	0 0 0	9 6.4 5.6	0 0 0	0 0 0	1 21.0 4.5	1 8.8 5.1	
Pro-friendly relations with USSR vs anti-	0 0 0	9 4.7 3.7	1 2.5 2.1	0 0 0	1 21.0 4.5	1 17.2 16.6	
Pro-public ownership vs anti-	2 21.9 24.5	12 6.9 5.5	1 2.5 2.1	0 0 0	1 21.0 4.5	1 58.2 63.7	
Pro-permissive social policy vs anti-	0 0 0	13 11.6 11.0	0 0 0	0 0 0	1 9.8 0.2	0 0 0	
Anticlerical vs proclerical	0 0 0	11 8.5 7.8	0 0 0	0 0 0	1 11.2 4.3	1 18.2 16.0	
Pro-urban interests vs anti-	0 0 0	7 5.4 5.2	1 2.5 2.1	1 11.5 12.8	0 0 0	0 0 0	
Pro-decentralization of decisions vs anti-	0 0 0	1 2.7 2.4	0 0 0	0 0 0	0 0 0	1 0.8 0.8	
Environment over growth vs growth over environment	0 0 0	14 4.6 3.6	0 0 0	1 6.0 0	1 0.4 0	0 0 0	

	SMP		PR		STV		Alternative vote		SMM		SNTV		MMP	
	1950–56	1957–62	1950–56	1957–62	1950–56	1957–62	1950–56	1957–62	1950–56	1957–62	1950–56	1957–62	1950–56	1957–62
Comparative political parties, 11-point issue scales	4	5	11	10	1	1	1	1	0	1	1	1	1	1
Government ownership of means of production	1 / 2.8 / 1.8	0 / 0	7 / 13.3 / 12.0	6 / 8.3 / 7.8	0 / 0	0 / 0	0 / 0	0 / 0		1 / 34.0 / 12.0	0 / 0	0 / 0	0 / 0	0 / 0
Government role in economic planning	1 / 0 / 0	2 / 0 / 0	7 / 14.6 / 15.9	7 / 12.3 / 13.8	0 / 0	0 / 0	0 / 0	0 / 0		1 / 20.0 / 3.0	0 / 0	0 / 0	0 / 0	0 / 0
Redistribution of wealth	1 / 0 / 0	2 / 0 / 0	2 / 4.0 / 2.8	1 / 1.0 / 0.6	0 / 0	0 / 0	0 / 0	0 / 0		1 / 20.0 / 3.0	0 / 0	0 / 0	0 / 0	0 / 0
Social welfare	3 / 25.8 / 24.8	4 / 20.0 / 18.6	8 / 28.4 / 28.1	7 / 26.7 / 26.9	1 / 56.0 / 57.0	1 / 56.0 / 61.0	1 / 48.0 / 42.0	1 / 45.0 / 41.0		1 / 34.0 / 12.0			1 / 92.0 / 97.0	1 / 88.0 / 97.0
Secularization of society	0 / 0	1 / 4.2 / 1.8	3 / 4.5 / 3.3	2 / 0.8 / 0.8	0 / 0	0 / 0	0 / 0	0 / 0		0 / 0	0 / 0		0 / 0	0 / 0
Support of the military	1 / 24.5 / 25.0	1 / 19.8 / 20.0	7 / 26.7 / 26.7	6 / 24.3 / 24.6	0 / 0	0 / 0	0 / 0	0 / 0		1 / 25.0 / 40.0	0 / 0		0 / 0	0 / 0
Alignment with East-West blocs	4 / 95.5 / 99.0	4 / 74.6 / 79.0	7 / 34.5 / 34.5	6 / 40.3 / 41.2	0 / 0	0 / 0	1 / 49.0 / 58.0	1 / 44.0 / 59.0		1 / 40.0 / 20.0			1 / 92.0 / 97.0	1 / 88.0 / 97.0
Anticolonialism	0 / 0	1 / 14.2 / 14.2	5 / 12.7 / 11.6	3 / 11.8 / 11.5	1 / 43.0 / 46.0	1 / 46.0 / 52.0	0 / 0	0 / 0		1 / 25.0 / 40.0	0 / 0		0 / 0	0 / 0
Supranational integration	0 / 0	1 / 7.4 / 5.8	3 / 8.9 / 8.2	2 / 5.1 / 5.0	0 / 0	0 / 0	0 / 0	0 / 0		0 / 0	0 / 0		0 / 0	0 / 0
National integration	0 / 0	1 / 4.2 / 1.8	5 / 13.6 / 12.2	3 / 7.1 / 6.8	1 / 74.0 / 76.0	1 / 76.0 / 81.0	0 / 0	0 / 0		1 / 25.0 / 40.0	0 / 0		0 / 0	0 / 0

[a]The three vertical numbers in a row represent, respectively, number, vote share, and seats share.

TABLE 10.6 Percentage missing data on left-right self-placement

	Canadian 1965 study	Political Action (1973–1976)	CPS 1976 study	World Values (1981–1983)	Baro-19 (1983)	Baro-29 (1988)
SMP						
Great Britain		18.3		14.9	6.7	11.0
United States		32.4	24.6	8.4		
Canada	7.4			26.4		
South Africa				50.4		
SMM						
France				18.7	10.7	11.6
STV						
Ireland				20.5	12.9	15.9
SNTV						
Japan				41.8		
Alternative vote						
Australia				9.2		
List PR						
Norway				8.3		
Sweden				7.7		
Iceland				5.8		
Belgium				16.2	25.2	25.3
Netherlands		9.7		9.3	3.7	7.9
Germany				7.6	11.9	9.8
Italy		26.1		9.2	15.5	15.7
Luxembourg					8.7	12.3
Denmark		7.9		8.7	11.1	6.7
Greece					19.6	16.2
Spain				12.4		27.5
Portugal						31.5
Austria		24.9				
Switzerland		21.2				
Finland		7.5		15.7		

correlations among them. Rather than reproduce 10 full correlation matrices, table 10.7 simply reports the percentage of the overall variance accounted for by the first, and also by both the first and second, principal components of national-level factor analyses of responses to 11 policy questions in Eurobarometer 19 and of two sets of responses to nine policy questions in the Political Action Study;[21] the more variance explained, the more responses to those questions tend to cluster, the higher the correlations among them, and thus presumably the more ideological the populations. Again the primary question is where the British and American respondents rank relative to respondents from countries using list-PR.

These data suggest the British electorate to be relatively nonideological, this time in the sense of having relatively unconstrained preferences across issues, although only with regard to the first principal component in the Eurobarometer data are they the least constrained of the electorates surveyed. But just as the British data undermined the hypothesis that use of single-member plurality is

TABLE 10.7 Percentage of variance in issue opinions accounted for by principal components factor analysis

	Eurobarometer 19		Political Action: importance of problem		Political Action: government responsibility	
	First principal component	First and second principal components	First principal component	First and second principal components	First principal component	First and second principal components
SMP						
United States			28.2	40.6	34.0	45.2
Great Britain	16.8	32.0	25.9	38.0	31.1	43.1
SMM						
France	20.6	35.3				
STV						
Ireland	20.6	33.3				
List PR						
Belgium	17.9	32.5				
Netherlands	20.3	32.6	25.1	37.1	26.7	39.1
Germany	18.9	34.7	32.6	44.8	33.0	44.7
Italy	17.1	30.8	25.8	40.3	34.1	46.5
Luxembourg	19.5	34.0				
Denmark	22.3	37.9				
Austria			29.8	41.8	32.8	44.3
Switzerland			27.9	39.4	32.7	43.0
Finland			27.6	40.5	33.1	45.3

related to failure or inability to use ideological labels, so the American data undermine the hypothesis that single-member plurality is associated with unusually low levels of cross-policy constraint.

It is important to realize that these findings regarding the range of choice and extremism are not simply the logical consequences of differences in party number. Single-member plurality elections, for example, could be characterized by the competition of two strongly differentiated parties, as is the demand of the socialist or binary democracy versions of popular sovereignty theory, with the additional parties expected to be found under PR positioning themselves between the two poles. In this case, neither the range nor the incidence of extreme parties would be any larger in PR systems than in those using single-member plurality.

In fact, the data show the range of parties competing, the incidence of extreme parties, and the correspondence between the positions of parties and those of their average voters all to be higher under PR than under single-member plurality. The different competitive situations faced by parties in PR versus single-member plurality systems explains why. Parties competing in single-member plurality elections have an incentive to move towards the center of the distribution of voters. Since parties arising on their flanks should simply result in the easy victory of the other side, it is unlikely that such more extreme parties will arise in the first place, or survive if they do. Thus the primary voters for which the remaining (large) parties must compete are those in the center. Under PR, on the other hand, flanking parties can expect to win a proportionate share of the seats and hence are more likely to pose a countervailing pressure, discouraging convergence. One additional bit of evidence supporting this view comes from the Laver data looking at the direction of the divergence between leaders and voters. Taking the weighted (by vote percentage) average of the positions ascribed to parties' voters as indicating the center of the voter distribution,[22] the tendency for the leaders' position to be closer to the system center than is the voters' position is stronger for parties in single-member plurality systems than for parties in PR systems. Single-member plurality appears to exercise a centripetal influence, whereas the influence of PR appears to be centrifugal.

Governments and Governmental Stability

Discussion of fairness as indicated by disproportionality generally starts from the presumption that the aim of an election is the representation of opinions, interests, or groups in the legislature. There is, however, an alternative position—that the aim of an election is the installation of a government meeting at least minimal standards of popular choice or sufferance. These standards are related—great disproportionality may allow a party with the support of far less than half the voters to form a "majority" government, as for example the British Labour Party did in October 1974 (39.2% of the vote) or the Conservatives did in 1979 (43.9%), 1983 (42.3%), and 1987 (42.4%)—but they are different. Indeed, in each of these cases, the party that formed a majority government had a plurality of the votes and could be said to have "won" the election. Certainly, by the standard of popular choice of a stable government, for a party or coalition with just over one half the vote to be awarded a substantial majority in the parliament must be counted a plus, even though it is clearly disproportional.

Although proportionality often has been an explicit criterion in the design and defense of electoral systems, in other cases, majority formation has played this role, especially with regard to single-member plurality in Britain and the electoral college in the United States, whose advocates often turn disproportionality into an asset because it virtually guarantees one party or candidate a parliamentary/electoral college majority—regardless of whether third parties keep the winner from achieving an electoral majority.[23] Easing the problems of majority formation has also been a justification for limiting the proportionality of PR systems—for example by restricting district magnitude or imposing statutory thresholds.[24] Carried to even greater lengths, it has been used to justify such "distortions" as Greek reinforced proportional representation or the Italian *legge truffa*.

At least four characteristics of government formation and maintenance must be considered in an assessment of the relationship between electoral systems and governments. For the most part, these are unproblematic for presidential systems, although the use of an electoral college can make a presidential election similar in some respects to the process of cabinet formation in a parliamentary regime. As a result, with appropriate references to presidential regimes when required, these characteristics will be discussed with particular reference to parliamentary systems.

The first characteristic is the government's coalitional status. Is it a single-party government, or must it rely on a coalition of parties for its continued existence? For presidential systems, the analog is whether a president and his or her party are able to govern alone, or whether they must form a formal coalition in order to win legislative support for their program, or for any other reason. Because coalition formation inevitably involves compromise, the general expectation is that single-party governments will be both more effective and more true to the principles on which they campaigned than coalitions, as well as better able to respond to changing circumstances and issues. These criteria suggest that single-party governments would be preferred from the "activist" perspective of popular sovereignty theories; from the more conservative liberal perspective, on the other hand, the constraint imposed by coalition governments make them at least as desirable.

The second characteristic is the government's majority status, which for parliamentary systems usually refers to the proportion of the parliamentary seats held by parties represented in the cabinet, with the principal distinction being between majority and minority governments. Occasionally an intermediate category is added for cabinets receiving regular support, either in the form of votes or guaranteed abstentions, from parties whose members do not themselves hold ministerial posts; these generally are considered minority governments, and are so classified here. It is possible, however, to consider the majority status of a government from the electoral perspective and to ask whether the parties represented in the government received the support of a majority of the voters in the last election. For all democratic theories, majority governments—especially in the electoral sense—are preferred to minority governments. For some however, in particular Tory popular sovereignty, a parliamentary majority is a more acceptable substitute than for others.

The third characteristic is the government's durability. One of the charges commonly leveled against "hyperproportional" PR is that it leads to frequent cabinet crises. To the extent that instability diminishes government effectiveness or transfers effective power from elected officials to their permanent civil servants, it is undesirable from any democratic perspective. Yet, barring these ills, the Ostrogorski model prescribes frequent changes in coalitions.

Finally, there is the degree to which election results directly determine the choice of government. In particular, is the government that forms after an election the only government that could have formed, or is it only one of several numerically possible governments? If one includes both minority and supermajority governments (both of which do, in fact, form with some regularity in many systems), many governments are possible,[25] but it is reasonable to count only the number of potential minimum winning coalitions. When there is only one, the voters may be said to have chosen the government. The greater the number of potential coalitions, however, the more the actual choice of government has devolved on the politicians in parliament and the leaders of their extraparliamentary party organizations. Moreover, one can return to the question of majority status and ask how many of the potential coalitions that satisfy the minimum winning criterion at the parliamentary level would be coalitions with majority electoral support.

The connection between elections and governments also may be addressed by looking at changes. While not every change in electoral results need be reflected in a change in government, a simple reading of democratic theory would appear at least to require nonperversity—that a party whose vote goes up be no less likely to be in government, and conversely. Although there are too many variables to be taken into account relative to the number of cases to estimate such likelihoods, one can look at changes in governments that occur immediately after elections and ask whether these changes are consistent with the changes in vote distributions.

Data

Two basic types of data illuminate the relationship between electoral system and government formation. One concerns the cabinets that might have formed given the actual outcomes of the elections; for each of the parliamentary elections included in the analysis in chapter 9, the number of possible minimum winning coalitions was computed.[26] The other type is the beginning and ending dates and the partisan compositions of 571 cabinets formed between 1946 and 1985 in 44 of the countries for which electoral data were available. In compiling these data, I assumed any change in the parties included in the cabinet or a change of prime minister or the intervention of a general election to indicate the termination of one government and the inauguration of another. I also counted "major reshuffles" generally reported in the press as indicating a change of government, but not minor reshuffles.

Coalitional Status

Whether single-party governments are desirable per se is open to debate. That they are far more likely to form under single-member plurality electoral systems than under PR is not. As table 10.8 shows, over 90% of cabinets formed under single-member plurality contain representatives of only one party, whereas over 70% of cabinets formed under PR (including single transferable vote) contain more than one party.[27]

Majority Status

In one sense, all cabinets in parliamentary systems must have majority support, because without it they would lose a vote of confidence and fall. Nonetheless, there is generally thought to be a significant difference between a cabinet that includes parties collectively commanding a majority of the parliamentary seats and one that survives only because of the support or abstention of a group of parties outside of the government. In the former case, the government presum-

TABLE 10.8 Coalitional status by electoral formula.

	Single-party cabinet	Multiparty cabinet	N
PR without threshold	21.2	78.8	212
PR with threshold	41.6	58.4	149
SMP	91.7	8.3	133
Alternative vote	22.7	77.3	22
SMM	0	100.0	17
SNTV	66.7	33.3	30
MMP	87.5	12.5	8

ably is free to pursue any policy and so can be held accountable for it. In the latter case, the distinction between government and opposition begins to blur significantly, with the government able to plead the constraints of its minority position while its external supporters cannot entirely escape responsibility for allowing to survive a government that they could have dispatched. This blurring is especially so in the intermediate case, in which a minority government is formed on the basis of the negotiated and stable sufferance of one or more parties that nonetheless choose, or are forced, to remain outside the cabinet. While it is not possible to distinguish these from other minority cabinets, both the minority and majority categories can be subdivided usefully on the basis of their parliamentary support. On one hand, some countries (e.g., Finland) have a tradition of occasional, usually short-lived, governments of nonpolitical or technical experts that make no pretense of parliamentary origin or support and should be distinguished from other minority governments. On the other hand, oversized cabinets can be distinguished from those based on minimum winning coalitions.

Table 10.9 shows the distribution of these four types of cabinets on the basis of electoral formula. The expectation that majority governments will be more common in single-member plurality rather than PR systems is strongly confirmed. Within these categories, PR systems with legal thresholds were slightly more likely to have majority governments than those without, and PR systems were more likely to have oversized majorities, while single-member plurality cabinets tended overwhelmingly to be of minimum winning size. This last difference is, however, in a sense artifactual, since single-member plurality systems have a far greater

TABLE 10.9 Parliamentary majority status by electoral formula.

	Nonparliamentary	Minority	Minimum winning majority	Oversized majority	N
PR without threshold	0.5	31.1	37.7	30.7	212
PR with threshold	8.7	29.5	45.0	16.8	149
SMP		10.9	82.7	6.0	133
Alternative vote		4.5	86.4	9.1	22
SMM		41.2	35.3	23.5	17
SNTV		16.7	66.7	16.7	30
MMP	12.5		87.5		8

likelihood of single-party majorities, which count as minimum winning coalitions, no matter how large they are. If attention is restricted to cabinets comprised of more than one party, then those formed under single-member plurality are the *most* likely to be oversized. Looking at the less common formulas, the (French) cabinets formed under single-member majority were the most likely to be formal minorities; this, however, is probably the result of the French semipresidential executive rather than the parliamentary electoral formula.

The apparent ability of single-member plurality (as well as the alternative vote, SNTV, and multimember plurality) to produce majority cabinets disappears if the attention is shifted from the parliament to the electorate. If a majority cabinet is defined as one including parties that collectively garnered a majority of the popular vote, then PR formulas are most likely to yield majority governments. As table 10.10 shows, over half (51.7%) of the single-member plurality majority cabinets in fact received a majority of the vote. In contrast, while minority cabinets were far more common in PR systems, nearly 80% of the majority cabinets that formed in those systems had been supported by a majority of the voters as well as by a majority of the members of parliament. Apparently, the price one pays for the electoral simplification engendered by single-member plurality and its resulting high likelihood of single-party legislative majorities is a correspondingly high likelihood that those legislative majorities will not be based on electoral majorities.

Duration

One of the reasons why both single-party cabinets and majority coalitions are considered desirable is that they are more likely to last. The experience of the cabinets considered here confirms both of these assumptions. The average duration of single-party cabinets in these data was 881.5 days and for multiparty cabinets, only 618.1 days; the average duration of cabinets including parties with a majority of the legislative seats was 849.0 days, nearly twice the average of 436.8 days recorded by minority cabinets.

These effects partially, but only partially, explain the data in table 10.11, which show that the average duration of cabinets under the single-member plural-

TABLE 10.10 Percentage of cabinets including parties with a majority of the votes by parliamentary majority status and electoral formula.

	Minority	Minimum winning majority	Oversized majority
PR without threshold	0 (66)	82.5 (80)	93.8 (65)
PR with threshold	0 (44)	53.7 (67)	96.0 (25)
SMP	0 (15)	52.7 (110)	37.5 (8)
Alternative vote	0 (1)	10.5 (19)	50.0 (2)
SMM	0 (4)	0 (6)	25.0 (4)
SNTV	0 (5)	40.0 (20)	100.0 (5)
MMP		28.6 (7)	

TABLE 10.11 Mean duration (days) of cabinets by electoral formula.

	Full data set	Less nonparliamentary cabinets	First cabinets
PR without threshold	634.6 (212)	637.5 (211)	868.7 (110)
PR with threshold	610.9 (149)	647.3 (136)	892.6 (73)
SMP	1,121.3 (133)	1,121.3 (133)	1,289.0 (94)
Alternative vote	735.2 (22)	735.2 (22)	829.4 (16)
SMM	545.6 (17)	545.6 (17)	759.2 (6)
SNTV	467.7 (30)	467.7 (30)	539.9 (15)
MMP	938.5 (8)	1,065.7 (7)	1,227.3 (6)

ity electoral formula is substantially greater than that of cabinets formed under any of the other electoral formulas considered. In the first column, data from all 571 cabinets are included. In the second (virtually identical) column, the 18 nonparliamentary cabinets have been eliminated. Finally, because these averages may be said to overcount the systems with unstable governments, and hence to exaggerate the differences between categories, the third column is based only on the first cabinet formed after each election. In this last case, the difference between PR and single-member plurality is greatly reduced, but not eliminated.

The difference in longevity between PR and single-member plurality cabinets interacts with the electoral cycle to produce quite different relationships between the birth and death of cabinets and elections. Just under 71% of the single-member plurality cabinets were formed in the immediate aftermath of a general election, whereas only 51% of the PR cabinets were. Of those "first-born" cabinets under single-member plurality, 54% survived to the next general election, as opposed to only 21% of the first-born PR cabinets. Moreover, of those single-member plurality cabinets that did not last to the next election, nearly half were terminated by a change of prime minister without a change in the party composition of the cabinet; this was the case for under 18% of the PR cabinets, which were instead most often (over 68% of the time) terminated by a change in partisan composition, resignation, or the loss of a vote of confidence. Thus, while the formation and demise of cabinets under single-member plurality appears largely to be the direct result of the electoral process, the comings and goings of cabinets under PR are far more often the result of the parliamentary process.

Uniqueness and Transparency

Cabinets formed immediately after an election can be said to be the direct result of the election only if there is a transparent connection between the electoral outcome and the cabinet formed. This question is addressed in table 10.12, which shows the average number of *mathematically (but not necessarily politically) possible* minimum winning coalitions (mwcs) based on the outcome of legislative elections. If only one minimum winning coalition were possible, it would appear reasonable to say that the election had determined the choice of government

TABLE 10.12 Number of potential minimum winning coalitions.

	All legislatures			
	Post-World War II legislative elections		All legislative elections	
		N		N
PR with threshold	28.1	121	36.2	143
PR without threshold	76.2	139	50.9	230
SMP	1.9	144	1.8	225
Alternative vote	2.1	18	2.1	33
SMM	4.9	7	67.6	41
SNTV	2.7	15	3.5	28
MMP	1.2	9	2.3	27

(even though minority or oversized majority cabinets might form under such circumstances). If the number exceeds one, however, postelection bargaining likely plays a major role in government formation.

Given the results so far, fewer possible mwcs will be expected under single-member plurality than under PR, and the results are surprising only in the magnitude of the difference found. Whereas the average single-member plurality election produces under two possible mwcs, the average PR election produces well over 40. In both cases, the average is higher for post-1945 elections than for the entire set of elections. Alternative vote and multimember plurality appear to behave like single-member plurality in producing few possible mwcs, although the small number of cases precludes any firm conclusion. Single-member majority appears to be an intermediate case based on post-1945 (French) elections. In the full data, it appears as an extreme case, but this is entirely the result of pre-World War I Germany; if these elections are removed, the average becomes 10.7 based on 28 cases. These differences derive virtually entirely from the impact of formula on the number of parties. Once the number of parties represented is controlled (in a two-way analysis of variance), the impact of electoral formula is statistically insignificant.

Changes in Governments and Electoral Change

Finally, one can ask about the relationship between changes in electoral results and changes in government composition. The literature is replete with examples of parties that suffer serious electoral setbacks and yet move from opposition to government or that are expelled from government on the heels of electoral success, sometime with a regularity that suggests that the best way to assure a place in the cabinet is to lose votes. Thus in 1977 the Dutch Labor Party (PvdA) gained 10 seats, but moved into opposition, only to return to government in 1981 after losing nine seats; between 1985 and 1989, the Norwegian Conservative Party lost over one fourth of its electoral support, yet moved from opposition to the prime ministership. Even more, there appears to be a virtually perfect inverse relationship between the electoral success of the Danish Liberals and their inclusion in government.

The coalition data analyzed here contain 147 cases (from 32 countries) in which a change in the parties included in government occurred immediately following a parliamentary election. In many cases, the changes in government composition were only partial—one or more parties remained in government, with new coalition partners or the loss of old partners. If there is a straightforward connection between electoral outcomes and government membership, those parties newly entering government should have increased votes, while those leaving government should have decreased. No unequivocal expectation can be formed regarding the parties that remain in (or out of) government, except that those whose votes increased should not be expelled from office, and so the analysis here is restricted to those parties that newly entered or left government immediately after elections.[28]

Table 10.13 shows the distribution of parties in the four categories (enters or leaves government crossed with vote increase or decrease) for each of the categories of electoral formula. In this table, the data are weighted so that each country counts as a single case (except that Denmark and France are counted as one unit in each of two categories, Denmark as PR with and without a threshold, and France as single-member majority and PR without a threshold). As usual, the limited numbers of cases mean that the data for alternative vote, single-member majority, SNTV, and multimember plurality are presented for information only. The key figure is the sum of the vote increases/leave government and vote decreases/enters government categories—that is, the average proportion of the changes in government composition that run counter to the changes in vote shares. For each of the categories of PR this is roughly one fourth of the changes, while for single-member plurality it is less than 5%.

Democracy and Electoral Formula

The implications of the these findings for the fit of electoral formulas to democratic theories are summarized in table 10.14, along with the implications of the analysis in chapter 9. Several preliminary observations are necessary. First, because of the paucity of examples from other electoral systems, the table reflects only the choice between single-member plurality and PR. In general terms, it appears reasonable to regard multimember plurality and block vote as extreme examples of single-member plurality, and alternative vote and single-member majority as intermediate cases between very small-district PR and single-member plurality, but whether this appearance reflects a corresponding reality must remain a matter for speculation. SNTV is too different, and its one exemplar too atypical in its nonwesternness for any generalization to be drawn beyond the observation that it does not appear to conform terribly well to the requirements of any of the democratic theories considered here.

Second, with a few exceptions, no account is taken in the table of differences (formula, magnitude, thresholds, and so forth) within the category of PR systems; in general these distinctions are of minor importance when compared to the distinction between PR and single-member plurality.

TABLE 10.13 Changes in vote and changes in government inclusion.

	PR with threshold		PR without threshold		SMP		Alternative vote		SMM		SNTV		MMP	
	Leaves government	Enters government	Leaves government	Enters government	Leaves government	Enters government	Leaves government	Enters government	Leaves government	Enters government	Leaves government	Enters government	Leaves government	Enters government
Vote increased	.11	.41	.08	.33	.01	.38	.22	.33	.67	.33	.25	.37	0	.66
Vote decreased	.35	.13	.41	.19	.57	.03	.33	.11	0	0	.13	.25	.33	0
N	10		9		11		1		1		1		1	

Finally, Ostrogorskian democracy requires a brief comment. Taken at face value, this model of democracy requires the unrealistic rapid rise and fall of parties. Presumably, were the Ostrogorskian model to be realized, it would look like a series of binary democracies, and so would call for the same kind of electoral system. It is shown in this way in the table. Alternatively, Ostrogorskian democracy might be approximated by legislative democracy, with succeeding elections contested by varying coalitions of parties. In this case, the parties would be durable while the coalitions would be formed around specific issues before each election, and the prescription for legislative democracy would be appropriate.

Looking at the content of the table suggests two groups of relatively clear cases and two groups ambiguous for different reasons. On one hand, among the clear cases are Tory democracy, the two majoritarian liberal theories, and the two pluralist liberal theories. At least with regard to the analysis presented so far, each of these is completely consistent with the use of single-member plurality. On the other hand, legislative democracy and the two veto-group liberal theories each are completely consistent with the use of PR. The distinction is between an assumption of two-partyness or bipolarity, coupled with relative indifference about the possibility that electoral and legislative majorities will diverge on the first side, and an assumption of a multiparty system or multiplicity of distinct viewpoints, coupled with great concern for their direct representation on the other.

Participationist and communitarian democracy both appear to be more consistent with single-member plurality, but because these theories are not primarily concerned with the kinds of variables tapped by these data, this assumption is no more than indicative. The other category of ambiguous cases consists of all the remaining popular sovereignty theories. These all want two-party competition, stable majority governments, and transparency of the connection between electoral choice and government formation, all of which are favored by single-member plurality, but they also demand that the government have majority electoral support, which single-member plurality quite frequently fails to provide. This observation suggests an important dilemma with respect to most popular sovereignty theories. It should be noted, however, that this dilemma stems at least in part from the failure of many single-member plurality systems actually to produce two-party systems. If they did, far more single-member plurality governments would enjoy majority electoral support. Yet, given the discrimination of single-member plurality against small parties demonstrated in the last chapter, one must also conclude that the failure of two-party systems to arise in single-member plurality systems suggests that some of the fundamental sociopolitical assumptions (e.g., bipolarity or unidimensionality of political issues) of the two-party popular sovereignty theories simply are false.

Quite aside from the "minor" electoral systems, suggesting a stark dichotomy between PR and single-member plurality ignores significant, albeit secondary, distinctions within each category. For example, as discussed in the next chapter, the direct representation of minorities under single-member plurality can be manipulated by districting decisions, although increased minority representation is likely to be achieved only at the expense of even greater disproportionality or lowered responsiveness. The former is a high price to pay from the perspective of popular

TABLE 10.14 Democratic theory and electoral systems.

	Government majority status (seats)	Number of parties	Coalition v. single-party government	Relationship between electoral and governmental change	Stability/ duration of coalition	Transparency/ uniqueness	Representation of minorities	Responsiveness v. proportionality	Government majority status (votes)	Range of choice	Ideological sophistication	Leader/ follower agreement
Binary	SMP	SMP	SMP		smp	SMP		pr	PR	SMP or small district, high threshold, PR		PR
Downsian	SMP	SMP	SMP		smp	SMP		pr	PR	SMP	PR	
Ostrogorskian	SMP	SMP	SMP		smp	SMP		pr	PR	SMP or small district, high threshold, PR		PR
Legislative	PR	PR	PR		PR		PR	PR	PR	Large District PR	PR	PR
Tory	SMP	SMP	SMP		SMP	SMP				SMP or small district, high threshold, PR	PR	PR
Socialist	SMP	SMP	SMP	SMP	smp	SMP		pr	PR	SMP or small district, high threshold, PR	PR	pr

Benthamite	SMP	SMP		SMP	SMP	SMP	SMP or small district, high threshold, PR
Schumpeterian	SMP	SMP		SMP	SMP	SMP	SMP or small district, high threshold, PR
Madison	SMP	SMP	PR with a president or nonparliamentary government	smp	SMP	SMP	SMP or small district, high threshold, PR
Polyarchal	SMP	SMP	PR with a president or nonparliamentary government	SMP	SMP	SMP	SMP or small district, high threshold, PR
Concurrent majorities	PR	PR			Depends on geographic segregation of groups		Large district PR
Consociational	PR	PR			Depends on geographic segregation of groups		Large district PR
Participationist	SMP		SMP	SMP			
Communitarian			SMP	SMP			PR

sovereignty theories, while the latter is a high price from the perspective of liberal theories.

As seen in chapter 9, the degree of "PR-ness" of PR systems is a function of many variables, but especially district magnitude. Given that policymaking is not restricted to legislation, but includes a range of administrative actions, and that government is not restricted to policymaking, but includes policy implementation and administration, even those theories that suggest relatively short-lived coalition governments require some stability. Given that the difficulties of coalition formation, the costs of acquiring information about electoral contenders, and the problems of assessing responsibility all increase as the number of parties increases, even those theories that suggest a multiplicity of parties require some limits. In institutional terms, this suggests that district magnitude ought to be set high enough to assure reasonable proportionality among all significant interests and parties, but no higher. The definitions of "reasonable" and "significant," of course, must be decided politically rather than scientifically, and on the basis of individual circumstances.

Particularly in balancing the trade-off between proportionality and a manageable party system, such additional questions as electoral thresholds and apparentement become important. The imposition of an electoral threshold allows the greater proportionality of large-district magnitude to be achieved while limiting the concomitant tendency to party system fragmentation. Moreover, an electoral threshold also ensures that parties that enter parliament do so with sufficient people to keep up with the range of parliamentary business.[29]

Apparentement allows the restrictions on the multiplication of parties (and perhaps also the supposed advantages of more personal rather than partisan-anonymous representation) that are associated with small-district magnitudes to be combined with a loophole through which certain kinds of small parties may squeeze. Apparentement allows individual parties to present a variety of faces (as with allied French and German lists in some bilingual Swiss cantons[30]) or for rival factions to separate without going all the way to a rancorous divorce. (In this respect, apparentement can serve the same function as intraparty preference voting; see chapter 12.) From the perspective of voters, apparentement allows a more nuanced set of choices without the danger of wasted votes (and so might be particularly desirable from the perspective of participationist theories). All of this variety applies, however, only within the context of compatible groups of parties or lists. In this way, apparentement allows the more accommodating or "responsible" minor parties to survive an institutional structure that drives out small parties whose behavior or ideological isolation make finding allies impossible.

Districting: Apportionment and Gerrymanders

This chapter begins with a simple but true statement: if one knew how (and whether) each individual would vote, then it would always be possible under single-member plurality with two-party competition to construct contiguous equipopulous districts, *all of which* would be won by a party commanding just over one half the votes, or alternatively to guarantee that a party with just over one quarter the votes would win a majority of the seats. Of course, those who draw district lines do not know how each individual will vote, although they may have a fairly good idea how the votes of various neighborhoods will divide, and this limits their ability to maximize the advantage of a particular party. On the other hand, rather large departures from population equality often are tolerated, potentially allowing a party with less than one quarter of the vote to win a legislative majority nonetheless. And, while the literal truth of the statement might require districts a yard wide and 100 miles long, in fact, not only have extremely contorted districts been adopted but even the basic requirement of contiguity has at times been honored more in the breach than in the observance.[1]

Although single-member plurality provides the most extreme possibilities, and examples, of the impact of district definitions, all electoral systems are sensitive to district drawing, and all for the same basic reason: the distribution of seats, especially at the district level, is a step function, with a party's number of seats making quantum leaps at discrete points corresponding to particular numbers/ shares of the votes. In PR systems, each district has more of these breakpoints, but just as single-member plurality gives a party no extra seats for having 80% of the vote in a district instead of 51%, a quota PR system gives a party with just under two quotas no more seats than a party with just over one. Moreover, under PR the very location of the breakpoints can be altered by changing the district magnitude.

Possibilities, Consequences, and Criteria

Malapportionment

Although many criteria have been advanced for judging districting plans,[2] the standard of equality of population occupies a central position both historically and normatively. In terms of the modern slogan, this is the requirement of "one (wo)man, one vote, one value," which is, at least on the surface, satisfied when single-member districts have nearly equal populations or when the numbers of representatives assigned to multimember PR districts are proportional to the districts' populations. As will be seen shortly, the question of equal representation for equal populations is considerably more murky in the case of multimember plurality systems.

The problem of population equality arose in its starkest form with the rotten boroughs of pre-reform England, in which a few places with no resident population at all were returning MPs—while other major centers were unrepresented because they had not existed when constituencies were being defined. (This example points to the distinction between equality of population and equality of electorates; while a rotten borough may have had no residents, all had at least one qualified elector.) In less extreme form, the same thing happened in the United States before the "reapportionment revolution" of the 1960s. For example, in 1960 the 16th Congressional District in Michigan had a population more than 4.5 times that of the 12th Congressional District; even more, the largest district for the California state senate was more than 44 times as populous as the smallest, while the largest district for the Connecticut state house had more than 420 times the population of the smallest. Before the 1964 reapportionment in Canada, parliamentary constituency populations ranged between 12,479 (Îles-de-la-Madeleine) and 267,252 (York-Scarborough).[3]

Tremendous disparities in representation generally came about through the confluence of three factors. First, equality of population was not a strong criterion in the original drawing of district lines; rather, previously existing towns or counties became the constituencies. This reflects the conflict between the criterion of population equality, rooted in individualism, and the criterion of community representation. The second factor is that, even when the constitution permitted reapportionment, district lines were left alone as population shifts occurred. Third, because population shifts were systematic, any reapportionment would have been detrimental to the interests that held a majority in the legislatures. Thus, while one reason for failure to redistrict was inertia, another was political self-interest.

As observed in chapter 2, representation of communities began at a time when the community rather than the individual was the basic unit of society. In a more individualistic era, support for districts based on existing communities or political subdivisions rests initially on several interconnected arguments. Most centrally, because the winner in a single-member district will not only take all but be expected to represent all, it is important that the constituency have at least some interests shared by all its residents. Commonality is more likely with longstanding units like towns and counties, especially since many political issues revolve around the allocation of resources among precisely those units.[4] Moreover, a sense of community is fostered by the flourishing of a series of institutions all serving the same people. In the narrowly political sphere, people participating in the politics of the same town council district should also be in the same regional district and the same national parliamentary district. More generally, these districts should be coterminous with or wholly include (or be included in) school catchment areas, parishes, and so on.

The basic argument for equality of population is fairness; equal numbers of individuals should have equal representation. And if not exactly an argument for population equality, at least an argument against giving primacy to subdivision boundaries claims that the kind of local particularism and inward-looking local community advanced to support community-based representation are, in fact, bad things. Thus districts that cut across existing boundaries should be valued because they militate against parochialism and encourage identification with a broader general interest.

At least in the case of single-member districts, the fairness argument may be fallacious. If equal power means an equal chance that one's vote will make a difference, then equal representation for equal numbers of citizens does not mean that each citizen has an equal share of political power; instead, each individual voter in a marginal constituency has a far greater chance of making a difference to the outcome than the nominally equal voter in a safe district. Moreover, even considered as groups, the voters of a marginal constituency may be more influential than those in a safe district if parties and candidates pay particular attention to those areas that are "up for grabs."[5] Nonetheless, modern advocates of respect for community boundaries do not dismiss the fairness argument for population equality, but rather suggest that its application should be limited. For one thing, equality of population does not preclude the deliberate exclusion or dramatic underrepresentation of interests by the drawing of district boundaries to their disadvantage. But, advocates of respecting traditional boundaries point out, obsession with equality of population actually makes gerrymandering easier. Another argument for compromising with regard to equality of population is the desire to keep districts in sparsely populated areas to a manageable size. Finally, both the equality of population and the respect for community boundaries arguments may be attacked by suggesting that certain groups—whether because of their particular virtue,[6] their contribution to the nation,[7] their minority status, or in compensation for past or present deprivations—deserve more representation than they would otherwise win.

Beginning with *Baker v. Carr* in 1962, a series of Supreme Court decisions has held that the equal protection clause of the Fourteenth Amendment requires adherence to the standard of "one-(wo)man-one-vote" for virtually every elective office in the United States.[8] In general, the standard of equality has been most strict for the House of Representatives; while the Court has not always insisted on the apportionment plan with the smallest population deviation, it has refused to set a limit to the quest for ever greater equality, so that plans with population deviations of less than 2% have been overturned.[9] On the other hand, the constitutionally mandated distribution of seats in the House of Representatives among the states before they are assigned to particular districts can result in significant deviations from population equality; thus, in 1982 the ratio of populations between the largest and smallest congressional districts in a single state was only 1.1:1, while nationally it was 1.8:1. For other offices, however, the Court has been more flexible; although exceptional, in 1983 the Court allowed Wyoming to give each county its own state representative, even though this resulted in a population deviation of over 89%.[10] For the most part, however, the Court has ruled that respect for subdivision boundaries does not justify deviation from equality of population.

The problem of population equality might also be addressed through multimember districts or weighted voting (each member given a voting weight proportional to the population of his or her district). These raise a further problem concerning the meaning of equality of representation. Since this problem is raised in sharpest relief by weighted voting schemes, it will be elaborated in those terms, but to the extent that party discipline, commonality of interest, or any other factor leads all the representatives of a multimember district to vote in the legislature as a bloc, the same analysis would apply in that case as well.

After the Supreme Court's ruling that the one-(wo)man-one-vote principle had to be applied to local governments, a number of counties in New York State restructured their legislatures so that each town supervisor could cast a number of votes proportional to town population (in place of the traditional one-town-one-vote system). Although this plan was criticized for adopting an unreasonably narrow conception of the legislator's role, when finally adjudicated by New York's highest court, the question was whether votes in proportion to population satisfied the one-(wo)man-one-vote requirement. The court ruled that it did not, noting that if one town had 60% of the population the vote of its supervisor would determine every issue, and so rather than having 60% of the voting power he or she would have all of it. Instead of banning weighted voting, however, the court allowed weighting schemes in which power, as defined by the game-theoretic "Banzhaf power score," rather than raw numbers of votes was proportional to population.[11] While this standard was rejected in the federal courts on the ground that it is based on unrealistic assumptions,[12] the debate highlights the problem that power is not directly proportional to number of votes.

Other countries using single-member plurality election also have come to give greater weight to equality of population in designing their parliamentary constituencies, although none goes to the same extremes as the United States. In Britain, the disparity between the largest and smallest constituency was reduced to approximately 8:1 by the Reform Act of 1885 and to approximately 5:1 by the Representation of the People Act of 1918.[13] The entire system of redistribution of seats then was reformed in 1944. The first requirement, and constraint on population equality, is that Scotland must have at least 71 constituencies, Wales at least 35, Northern Ireland between 16 and 18, and Great Britain as a whole (England, Wales, and Scotland) not substantially more nor less than 613. Within each country, constituencies are to be of as nearly equal population as possible. That this regulation means far less in the UK than it might in the United States is indicated by the repeal of the rule in the 1944 Act that so far as practicable all constituencies should be within 25% of the average because it was too restrictive. Moreover, respect for local government boundaries has been made superior to population equality, at least in England and Wales, by the requirement that constituencies not cross county or London borough lines except to avoid "excessive disparity." As well, these rules may be violated "if special geographical considerations, including in particular the size, shape and accessibility of a constituency, appear . . . to render a departure desirable." [14]

Overall, in 1983 the population of the largest constituency (Isle of Wight) was 4.13 times the population of the smallest (Western Isles). These rules result in the overrepresentation of the "Celtic fringe" of the UK. Had equal standards been applied in 1983, for example, England would have been given 19 more seats at the expense of Scotland (12), Wales (6), and Northern Ireland. In partisan terms, the overrepresentation of Scotland and Wales has helped the Labour party, while the overrepresentation of rural areas that results from attention to the listed "geographical considerations" has aided the Conservatives.

The apportionment system that led to the 21:1 ratio of largest to smallest constituency in Canada cited above has been revised several times so that the situation now is substantially similar to that in the UK. Constituencies are first divided among the provinces and territories in proportion to population, but with each province assured at least as many MPs as its number of senators, thus building in substantial disparities. Within each province, constituency populations are to be "as close as reasonably possible" to the provincial electoral quota, except where

> necessary or desirable to depart therefrom
> (i) in order to respect the community of interest or community of identity in or the historical pattern of an electoral district in the province, or
> (ii) in order to maintain a manageable geographic size for districts in sparsely populated, rural, or northern regions of the province. [15]

But the aim was still to keep all constituencies within 25% of the provincial quota. In 1984 the ratio of largest (York-Scarborough, Ontario, 207,803) to smallest (Hillsborough, Prince Edward Island, 27,532) constituency had been reduced to 7.5:1. Much of the disparity resulted because Prince Edward Island cannot have fewer than four seats; all of its constituencies were about half as populous as the least populous constituency in Ontario (Timiskaming, 55,186). The ratio of largest to smallest constituency within a single province (which was Ontario) was 3.8:1. In partisan terms, all three of these constituencies were held by the Progressive Conservatives. Thus, whether measured nationally or within regions, there is a bit less equality among constituency populations in Canada than in Britain, but neither approaches the level of equality in the United States.

Among other countries whose electoral arrangements derive from the British model, Australia and New Zealand are far stricter regarding equality of population, while India is far less so. The New Zealand Electoral Act of 1956 specifies a maximum departure from equality of population of plus or minus 5% from the island quota.[16] In Australia, the tolerance was reduced from plus or minus 20%, to plus or minus 10% in 1973. Unlike the other countries, in which the objective is to obtain population equality at the time of the reapportionment, the Australian statute calls for an attempt to ensure equality three years and six months (half the maximum allowable period between redistributions) after. In India, on the other hand, although the constitution calls for population equality "so far as practicable," wild disparities in population have been tolerated. In part, this is the result of federalism; in 1980, the smallest number of electors in any district was only 20,117 in the only district in Lakshadweep, with 96,084 electors in the only district for the Andaman and Nicobar Islands, and 118,224 electors in the only district in Sikkim, while the national average was over 670,000 electors per district. On the other hand, the constituency of Ladakh had only 77,833 electors and was one of six constituencies in Jammu and Kashmir, the largest of which had an electorate of 691,358 (a ratio of roughly 1:8.9). Overall, the largest constituency, Bombay North East, had 916,054 electors (over 45 times the number in Lakshadweep), which was 1.6 times the electorate of the smallest constituency in the same state.

In France, although there were periodic adjustments to a few constituencies, the basic boundaries established in 1958 remained unchanged until the temporary replacement of single-member majority election by proportional representation for the 1986 election. In 1958, there was one constituency with a population under 40,000 and three constituencies with populations over 125,000.[17] Between the requirement that each département have at least two deputies and the movement of population, by 1981 there was even greater inequality among constituencies, of which the largest was Salon-de-Provence in Bouches-du-Rhône (189,384 registered voters) while the smallest was Marvéjols in Lozère (26,251), for a ratio of 7.2:1. Within Bouches-du-Rhône, the smallest constituency was part of Marseille (41,463), yielding a ratio of largest to smallest of 4.6:1. When single-member districts were reinstituted after 1986, greater restrictions were placed on their construction. In the first place, except for départements that were islands or themselves not contiguous, each constituency was to be contiguous.[18] With the exceptions of Paris, Lyon, and Marseille, départements with discontiguous cantons, and cantons with populations over 40,000, cantonal boundaries were to be respected. Moreover, no constituency could "stray more than 20% from the mean population of the constituencies of the département," and a provision was added to the law requiring periodic reapportionment.[19] Every département, no matter how small, retained at least two deputies, so that the smallest (Lozère) "had two deputies for 74,284 inhabitants, while Savoie had three deputies for 354,675 inhabitants, a differential ratio of 1:2.9."[20]

In multimember systems in which seats are likely to be divided among parties (PR, STV, limited vote), the problem of population equality can be solved by making the number of representatives proportional to population without giving rise to the problems discussed for multimember plurality systems. In the simplest case (aside from use of a single national constituency), previously existing units like provinces or counties become constituencies, and seats are apportioned among them using some form of PR formula; as with proportional distribution of

seats among parties, the larger the number of members per district, the less difference caused by the choice of formula and the more equitable the allocation of
seats. For example, in Italy in 1979 (apportionment by Hare quota largest remainder) the ratio of most to fewest electors per deputy (excluding the single-member
district of the Val d'Aosta) was 1.2:1. In apportioning seats among extant units,
however, strict equality is mitigated by the requirement that every district, no
matter how small, must have at least one, and in the case of PR, often as many
as three representatives. This contributes to a tendency for rural overrepresentation even in PR systems.

Although the numbers of residents or voters per representative will not be
precisely equal, given the constraints of existing boundaries and a previously
agreed formula for distribution, they can be made as equal as possible. The same
cannot be said as assuredly if ad hoc constituency boundaries are used, since in
this case nothing short of exact equality is "as equal as possible." An example
arose with STV in Ireland. The reapportionment of 1959 (based on the 1956
census) was challenged as violating the Irish Constitution, which requires that
the ratios between populations and numbers of members "shall, so far as it is
practicable, be the same throughout the country." Under the Electoral (Amendment) Act, the largest constituency would have had a population 1.35 times that
of the smallest, a fairly close approximation of equality by the standard of systems
that adhere to existing boundaries, given the relatively small district magnitudes
(between 3 and 5) involved. The High Court, however, found that relatively small
changes in district boundaries would have greatly increased equality of representation and declared the statute in violation of the Constitution, and therefore
void.[21] (In contrast, at the 1981 election, the largest ratio of population to representation was only 1.13 times the smallest.)

Many systems apportion seats among units on the basis of a formula particularly favorable to those with the smallest populations. Rural overrepresentation
also results when the distribution of seats among constituencies is set in the law
or constitution, and so not regularly reassessed, or when there is a constitutionally
mandated minimum or a maximum number of representatives per province or
state. Thus, even after the requirement of twice as many rural as urban seats was
removed from the Norwegian constitution in 1953, and after redistributions of
seats in 1953 and 1973, by 1985, the most underrepresented county (Akershus) had
over 1.6 times as many eligible voters per representative as the most overrepresented (Finnmark). Analogously, the minimum of eight and maximum of 70
deputies per state in Brazil results in gross numerical inequality of representation.[22] Finally, as with single-member districts, those with the power to equalize
representation may, for political or other reasons, choose not to do so. Thus, in
spite of reapportionments in 1967, 1976, and 1986, the number of Japanese voters
per representative was still 4.9 times as great in the third district of Osaka as it
was in the fifth district of Hyogo prefecture.

Some indication of the importance (or unimportance) of reapportionment to
achieve equality of population can be gathered by looking at two measures of
partisan fairness derived from the analysis in chapter 9—disproportionality (D)
and the difference between the observed value of D and that expected on the

basis of the equations estimated (DDIF). In both cases, larger values indicate less "fair" results.

If fair apportionment produces fair representation, one would expect it to lead to a decline in D and even more in DDIF (because it takes possible changes in other factors affecting D into account). Thus, for the United States, one would expect D and DDIF to decline starting in 1962 (the year of *Baker v Carr*), but instead they increase—the average values of D going from .13 for 1962–1970, to .19 for 1972–1980, to .23 for 1982 and 1984, and of DDIF from -.004 to .02 to .07 in the same years. In Britain, a sea change in favor of equipopulous districts occurred before the 1950 election. In this case, there was a marked drop in both measures (from .19 to .06 and from .06 to -.05), but in the face of continuing reapportionments both have crept up to averages for the 1975 to 1985 period higher than they were before 1950. Precisely the same thing happened in Canada following its 1964 "reapportionment revolution;"[23] initially D and DDIF dropped, but they then rebounded to levels higher than ever. Australia followed more closely the American pattern: after the debate on rural overrepresentation and tightening of the standards for population equality, disproportionality rose. The disproportionality of the Norwegian PR system dropped after the reform of 1953 eliminated the radical overrepresentation of rural areas. After a finetuning in the early 1970s, however, it rose. Adherence to tighter standards of equality in Ireland following the *O'Donovan* case led to an ambiguous result: D declined, but DDIF rose until the mid-1970s and then fell.

Although gross malapportionment is associated with a high level of disproportionality, within a quite broad range further increases in population equality do not yield corresponding increases in fairness, except in the most blindly numericist sense. Indeed, evidence suggests that just the reverse happens, suggesting some truth to the speculation by Justice Harlan (concurring in *Whitcomb*) that "a coherent and realistic notion of what is meant by 'voting power' might have restrained some of the extreme lengths to which this Court has gone in pursuit of the will-o'-the-wisp of 'one man, one vote.' "

Equal Population Gerrymandering

Districts can be constructed to bias electoral outcomes in either (or both) of two ways. One can manipulate district boundaries so as to alter the vote distributions within individual districts. Or, in PR or STV systems, one can manipulate the district magnitude, thereby moving the breaks in the step function translating votes into seats. Significantly, either of these devices can be used even within the constraint of perfect population equality.

Although one might dispute which measure of population equality is the "best," for gerrymandering there is no obvious measure; one person's gerrymander may be another's reasonable reapportionment. Reflecting this problem, the analysis of gerrymanders has been approached in two general ways. One is to look for evidence of manipulation, either directly in the records (speeches, memoranda) of the body drawing the district lines, or indirectly in the "otherwise inexplicable" shape of the resulting districts, while the other is to compare the results of actual elections with those expected theoretically for unbiased apportionment.

The advantage of direct evidence of intent is obvious, but it is rarely found, if only because rationalizing self-interested manipulation in public-spirited terms is easy. The indirect evidence of district shape shares with this the advantage that it can be brought to bear before a series of elections with the new districts has taken place but is also subject to the problem of rationalization. Even the most contorted of districts often can be justified, for example, as combining physically separated pockets of voters who share a common interest. For example, the California 28th Congressional District (1961) was justified "as a grouping of independent coastal cities with common interests that warrant special consideration,"[24] as was the New Jersey district that some opponents complained would disappear at high tide.[25]

One solution is the a priori imposition of objective standards against which the shapes of proposed districts may be judged, or desiderata, violation of which at least raises the question of intentional bias. The most obvious of these is contiguity. Although in practice this requirement raises a number of technical questions (e.g., is the district contiguous if the only road connection leaves the district?), it is generally respected even when not formally required. The problem is that really separate areas frequently can be made formally contiguous by the inclusion of a narrow connecting strip.[26]

Respect for existing local political or natural geographic boundaries may help to control this abuse. An analogous result may be achieved by a requirement of compactness. Whether defined in terms of total perimeter (Colorado), rectangular or square shape (Michigan), comparison of length and width, or "the ratio of the dispersion of population about the geographic center of the district to the dispersion of population about the population center of the district" (Iowa), or in some more informal way, irregularly shaped and narrow twisting districts would likely violate a compactness requirement.[27]

Another set of standards looks first at concentration or dispersion of political or other (in the United States, especially racial) groups. Although this appears to be the very definition of a gerrymander, the problem is that differential concentration in residential patterns may produce the same result without conscious manipulation—indeed, only manipulation may be able to *prevent* bias. Imagine a rectangular state with a population of 1,500 and perfectly uniform population density. Imagine further that it is divided into 15 perfectly square counties, each of which has a population of 100, and that the first of two parties wins 90 votes in two counties, 55 votes in five counties, 45 votes in three counties, 35 votes in four counties, and 20 votes in one county. Then with exactly 750 votes to its opponent's 750, that party will win seven of the 15 seats. If it loses six votes in each county, it will win only two seats with 660 votes, while if it gains six votes in each county it will win 10 seats with 840 votes.[28] But, by subtraction, this means that while 660 votes win this party only two seats, they win its opponents five and while 840 votes win it 10 seats, they win its opponents 13. The system appears systematically biased against this party even with equally populous, optimally compact districts that follow local subdivision boundaries.

This example was based on two relatively equal groups. With a smaller minority, single-member plurality is likely to produce no minority representation at all unless the minority voters are concentrated in a few districts. Moreover, especially if fixed political or geographic boundaries can be ignored, it is relatively easy to subdivide an area so that a group that would be a majority in one district becomes a minority in several. Alternatively, a local majority can be submerged in a multimember region where it is again reduced to minority strength.

Instead of concentrating groups of voters, a gerrymander may concentrate or disperse incumbents. An example was the California congressional redistricting after the 1980 census. Notwithstanding that California gained two congressional seats, the Democratic state legislature redrew district lines so that six Republican incumbents were packed into only three districts (while no Democrat was forced to run against an incumbent of either party). Together with other devices, this allowed the Democrats to win 28 of 45 seats (compared to 22 of 43 in 1980) with only 51.6% of the vote.

Although a gerrymander may be partisan, it may also be personal. A Rhode Island Superior Court overturned a plan "designed to oust . . . an independent Democrat and . . . the only Republican Senator [in the] Providence area,"[29] but in general, although American courts have affirmed the right of redistricters to minimize contests between incumbents, they have not recognized any obligation to do so. In another case, Congressman Barney Frank (D-Mass) was redistricted into competition with Republican incumbent Margaret Heckler by the Democratic state legislature. The district seemed calculated to defeat Frank, a result widely attributed to the fact that "in his four terms in the state House, Frank irked the leadership with maverick stands that seemed to be calculated annoyances to party leaders."[30] Frank won, however, suggesting that successful gerrymandering is not a simple exercise. Similarly, in the case of Sam Stratton (D-NY), after two unsuccessful attempts to defeat him by placing him in Republican districts (including one that was seven counties long and only at one point more than one county wide), the Republican state legislature "simply gave up and added Democratic voters to his district in order to help Republican chances elsewhere."[31] Finally, the mirror image of the types of gerrymanders discussed so far is the incumbent protection gerrymander; rather than trying to increase one party's share of the seats or to defeat some particular members, this bipartisan gerrymander aims to protect the seats of incumbents regardless of party.

The same kinds of results may be achieved in PR or STV systems in which district boundaries are not fixed by constitution or tradition. As an example, Peter Mair cites the transfer after the 1973 Irish general election of a heavily Labour area from South Tipperary where their votes would not be needed (because the Labour Speaker of the Dáil would be reelected automatically) to North Tipperary, where in 1977 the additional Labour votes contributed to the narrow victory of a Labour candidate.[32] In addition, however, PR and STV allow what Mair calls a "district-size gerrymander." By manipulating the number of members returned by particular districts, the party in power can try to maximize its own return on its votes. For example, a party with 51% of the votes would expect to win two of three seats (67%), two of four seats (50%), or three of five seats (60%), while with 41% it should win one of three, two of four, or two of five. Given an opportunity to redraw district lines in 1974, the Fine Gael and Labour government attempted to turn this to their advantage by, inter alia, allocating all 27 Dublin seats to three-member constituencies, in place of six four-member and only one three-member constituencies in 1973. Had the coalition maintained its Dublin vote (53.2% in 1973), it could have expected to win 18 of the 27 Dublin seats in 1977. In fact, however, it won 45.2% of the vote and only 12 seats.

This example, as well as the single-member plurality examples, illustrates three important points about gerrymanders. First, in order to gerrymander effectively one must be able to *anticipate* election returns. Second, the more a party attempts to maximize its share of the seats, the more vulnerable it becomes to even minor losses of votes. Third, excessively blatant attempts to gerrymander can lead to a public backlash; in the Irish case, an independent electoral commission was put in charge of devising constituencies for the 1981 election.

Turning to outcomes, the first fact to be noted is that a simple discrepancy between seat shares and vote shares is *not* necessarily evidence of gerrymandering, since all electoral systems tend to overrepresent large parties. Rather, the test must be whether different parties would expect the same numbers of seats had they received the same numbers of votes. One problem with this approach is illustrated by the example cited earlier of the rectangular state with the 15 square counties; that system *is* biased, but because of residential patterns, and not because of gerrymandering. This bias leads Grofman to suggest a distinction between the standards of "No Bias in Favor of a Particular Party" and "No Imposed Bias in Favor of a Particular Party," but in looking for imposed bias, one returns to the problem of inferring motives.

All results-oriented analyses of gerrymandering proceed by estimating a hypothesized "seats-votes" curve, where the underlying model includes one or more parameters that indicate the degrees of responsiveness and bias in the relationship.[33] In addition to the general model discussed in chapter 9, King has proposed a second model particularly suited to the two-party case and has applied it to the question of reapportionment and gerrymandering in the United States.

King's "American" model allows not only for the possibility of partisan bias, but also for the effects of incumbency and uncontested seats. Based on elections of the lower houses of state legislatures in the United States (10 elections in each of 13 states), King estimated the effect of partisan versus bipartisan reapportionment methods on electoral responsiveness and bias. With regard to responsiveness, King's analysis suggests that *both* sides of the scholarly debate—one arguing that bipartisan[34] or partisan[35] redistricting should produce a less responsive electoral system and the other that reapportionment has "no influence at all on the swing ratio"[36]—are wrong, and that both bipartisan and partisan redistricting increases responsiveness. One reason is that incumbency, even more than gerrymandering, appears to fix the partisan outcome in a district, and reapportionment is associated with particularly high rates of retirement—regardless of the nature of the process and regardless of the party of the incumbents themselves.

King's findings about bias are unsurprising, but far more precise than previous work. "Democratic-controlled redistricting biases electoral systems in favor of the Democratic party; Republican redistricting produces Republican bias; and bipartisan plans have little or no effect on partisan bias."[37] Quantitatively, Republican plans produce about four times the bias of Democratic plans, a result that

King attributes in part to the strength of the Democratic Party—because there were far more Democratic incumbents, the tactic of shoehorning two or more incumbents into a single district was more available to the Republicans.

Although King's analysis, as well as the conventional wisdom of politicians, suggests that districters can substantially manipulate the partisan balance of a legislature, evidence also suggests that gerrymanders may backfire, as gerrymanderers often give themselves too little margin of error. There is a clear tradeoff between seat maximization and security—additional seats can be won with a constant vote percentage only by making the party's base seats more marginal. While this result increases responsiveness, and can thus alter the partisan balance, it is hardly the effect the districters hoped to achieve.

Even more, most gerrymandering, and many analyses and challenges to redistricting plans, assume that the partisan vote distribution will be constant across different districting plans, with only the way in which voters are aggregated into constituency totals altered by the location of the district boundaries. An innovative analysis by Mark Rush disagrees. Looking at the voting behavior of Massachusetts and Connecticut towns that were moved from one congressional district to another, Rush found dramatic shifts in voting behavior. Whether these changes were the result of the personalities of particular candidates, the general advantages of incumbency, the strength of party organizations, or something else, they certainly suggest strong limits to the ability of redistricters to alter electoral outcomes simply by changing the allocation of voters to constituencies.[38]

Affirmative Gerrymanders and the Representation of Minorities

Given the bias against small groups inherent in all electoral systems, the representation of minorities can become a significant problem. Especially in single-member systems, even substantial minorities may receive very little or no representation (in the 1983 British parliamentary election, the Liberal-Social Democratic Alliance won only 23 of 650 seats with over 25% of the vote), but imposition of thresholds in PR systems may similarly shut out sizable groups. When the minorities are purely partisan, this problem generally is ignored, or even turned into a virtue (prevention of fragmentation; facilitation of majority formation) by all except its victims. Where the minorities are racial or ethnic and can (or should) cut across party lines, however, the question often becomes exclusion from full and equal citizenship.

Even if one accepts the principle that representation of ethnic groups should be treated differently from representation of parties, the selection of groups deserving special consideration is inevitably arbitrary. Rather than pursuing this unanswerable question, this section is devoted to the analysis of methods by which minority representation may be protected or enhanced. I begin with the problems of the "dilution" of black voting strength and its reverse, affirmative gerrymandering, in the United States, and then survey some of the devices used elsewhere to promote or assure ethnic representation.

The general question of racial gerrymanders in the United States arose with regard to the representation of blacks in the south and continues to focus on those groups specially protected under the Voting Rights Act, that is, primarily blacks, Native Americans, and Hispanics. The initial thrust was to outlaw blatant forms of discrimination. One target has been vote dilution through the use of multimember districts. In *White v. Regester*[39] the Supreme Court overturned use of multimember districts in two Texas counties on the grounds that it effectively and, inferring from historical experience, intentionally excluded blacks and Hispanics from effective participation. Subsequent debate focused on the questions of whether racial intent or merely effect was required for a challenge and what evidence would be required to prove racial effect. On the basis of an amended Voting Rights Act, *Thornburg v. Gingles* (1986) laid down a three-pronged test for challenging use of multimember districts.

> First, the minority group must be able to demonstrate that it is sufficiently large and geographically compact to constitute a majority in a single-member district. . . . Second, the minority group must be able to show that it is politically cohesive. . . . Third, the minority group must be able to demonstrate that the white majority votes sufficiently as a bloc to enable it—in the absence of special circumstances . . . —usually to defeat the minority's preferred candidate.[40]

In proving polarized voting, it is necessary only to address the question of effect, not of intent.

The same general analysis has been applied especially by the Fifth Circuit to single-member districts, with the conclusion that if it is impermissible to submerge a cohesive minority in a multimember district, "slicing up [among single-member districts] a cohesive minority vote area in a community where there is bloc voting" is also impermissible.[41] Again, only the effect of continuing past discrimination, rather than racial intent, need be proven.

If gerrymanders can be used to magnify the advantages of the strong, they can also be used to compensate the weak for their disadvantages. This is the idea of the "affirmative gerrymander" that has developed in the United States in response to Sections 2 and 5 of the Voting Rights Act. While the law specifically states that "nothing in this section establishes a right to have members of a protected class elected in numbers equal to their proportion in the population,"[42] in a case made particularly contentious by the fact that it pitted the representation of one minority (nonwhites) against another (Hasidic Jews), the Supreme Court ruled that the preclearance (by the Justice Department) requirement of Section 5 might be used not only to justify (or effectively to compel) the intentional creation of minority districts, but also the further step of ensuring minority control by taking into account lower turnout rates by minority groups.[43] This whole question was reopened with initially successful challenges to the drawing of majority-minority districts with particularly contorted shapes in response to the 1990 census.[44]

One logical problem with affirmative gerrymanders stems from the question of whether the right to ethnic representation is a right of the group or a right of its individual members. If it is an individual right, can one decide that only some (and which) group members will be able to exercise this right? Moreover, just as minority group members who do not live in the favored districts are denied their right to ethnic representation, so too are the members of the majority who do live in those districts. The problem of a class of voters denied meaningful participation is "solved" only by integrating the class of victims. On the other hand, if ethnic representation is a group right, the creation of racial boroughs is justifiable, but many group members (those who live in the wrong districts) are denied participation in the selection of "their" representatives. These problems can be solved by adopting the position of virtual representation, but this: (a) requires a trustee rather than a delegate conception of representation and a conception of politics as the pursuit of a common interest rather than the clash of private or group interests; and (b) is fundamentally incompatible with a prior concern for equality of population.

Moreover, while minority representation may be justified in terms of integration into majority society, there is at least the question of whether the creation of racial boroughs favors this goal. By segregating minority voters into one set of districts, in which candidates appeal to their "minorityness," leaving other districts in which candidates have few or no minority voters about whom to be concerned, one may simply increase polarization.[45] Further, if the polarized voting patterns that are part of the justification for affirmative gerrymanders continue in the legislature (and the removal of minority voters from majority districts should make this more, rather than less, likely), the minority will still be without an effective political voice, in effect "trading real influence for a few black faces around the table."[46]

An alternative to affirmative gerrymandering is use of cumulative voting. Abandoned by Illinois for its state legislative elections in 1980, since 1987 cumulative voting has been employed in several jurisdictions in order to comply with the Voting Rights Act while retaining multimember or at-large election. Cumulative voting allows a minority to assure itself of representation, even against the concerted opposition of the majority—with the size of minority needed to secure representation declining as district magnitude increases. As a result, blacks were able to secure representation on four local councils in Alabama, even though they were significantly less than 15% of the population.[47]

Finally, no discussion of affirmative gerrymandering would be complete without at least a brief reference to the representation of women—the other "protected group" within the general context of affirmative action. With no separate geographic concentrations analogous to those of blacks or Hispanics, the construction of "women's" districts is impossible. Nonetheless, research has shown that districting decisions can play a significant role in furthering the entry of women into elective office. Perhaps ironically, that research shows that women are aided by precisely those arrangements—multimember districts and at-large election—that are said to dilute the votes of blacks and Hispanics.[48]

Alternative Devices for Assuring Minority Representation

The United States is not the only country in which the problem of racial or ethnic representation has arisen. Where ethnic groups are relatively separate geographically, it has been solved relatively easily: Scots are represented by MPs elected from virtually exclusively Scots constituencies in Scotland, and there is no claim that Scots resident in England need special representation; Francophone Canadians are represented by districts in Quebec; Flemish and Walloon Belgians by districts in Flanders and Wallonia. Where the groups are intermixed, the problem has been more complicated and often is accompanied by the prior problem of acceptably classifying voters among groups. Both for its own sake, and because it helps locate the American problem in a broader context, a brief review of the variety of not always successful devices tried in other countries to assure a reasonable balance between or among groups is worthwhile.[49]

Concern for minority representation arises most frequently under plurality electoral systems; presumably with PR a minority that wants its own representation can have it. Under some circumstances, however, PR alone is not enough. The first such circumstance is when the minority is large enough to be entitled to representation on purely proportional grounds, but is excluded by virtue of an electoral threshold. Such would be the case of the Danish minority in north German Land elections. In order to accommodate such groups, the normal 5% threshold "does not apply to parties representing national minorities."[50]

The second circumstance occurs when district magnitude is too small to allow adequate proportionality. The two major language groups in Belgium basically live apart, with the country divided into two "linguistically pure" regions. Brussels, however, is a bilingual exception. This is easily accommodated in national elections, since the 34 deputies and 17 senators assigned to Brussels are enough for both Flemish and Walloon parties to compete with fairly proportional success. Elections of the European Parliament, in which Belgium has only 24 members altogether, presented a problem. The solution was to assign them to two districts (Flanders and Wallonia) in proportion to their populations, but to give to each voter in Brussels a ballot with both the Flemish and Walloon ballots side by side and then count it in the constituency appropriate to the party chosen. In this way, the problem of assigning voters, or requiring public self-assignment, to one of the ethnic groups was avoided.

The third circumstance occurs when the constitutional settlement that allows a government to be formed requires a particular division among groups regardless of relative populations or the wishes of the voters. This situation arose in Zimbabwe in 1980, with whites guaranteed 20 of the 100 legislative seats. In effect, two (nearly) simultaneous elections were held, one using PR in eight 10–member districts for blacks to elect their 80 members and the other using single-member plurality for the whites to elect their members.

Other non-American attempts to provide assured minority representation fall basically into four categories. First, and most like affirmative gerrymandering in the United States, is the reservation of a number of seats in the Indian national and state parliaments for members of castes and tribes that traditionally had been victims of discrimination. Originally scheduled to end in 1970, but then extended, 77 of 521 lower house seats were reserved for the election of members of Scheduled Castes and Tribes. Prior to 1961, some were in single-member districts (when the Scheduled Caste or Scheduled Tribe population was over 50%). In these cases, nonscheduled caste members who lived in those districts could vote, but were restricted in their choice to a member of a scheduled caste. Where the Scheduled Caste or Tribe population was too dispersed to form a constituency in which they would be a majority, a two-member district might be formed, with one seat reserved for a Scheduled Caste or Tribe member. In these cases, the first seat would be awarded to the Scheduled Caste or Tribe member with the most votes, and the second to the remaining candidate with the most votes, regardless of caste or tribe.

In the second category, special districts are reserved for minority group members, but as in Zimbabwe, and unlike in the United States or India, the electorates are separated as well—usually with the result that the same physical location is in more than one constituency, depending on the ethnic group of the voter. The simplest example is New Zealand, in which four single-member districts are reserved for Maori voters. Naturally, each Maori constituency covers the same territory as many General roll constituencies. Similarly, in Cyprus in 1960, there were six pairs of districts, one Greek and the other Turkish, in this case with each pair occupying the same territory, but with the Greek districts electing more members than their Turkish mates. Fiji, before the 1987 coups, used a more complex but analogous system. Three groups—Fijian, Indian, and General (residual)—each had its own set of communal single-member districts. In addition, there were three sets of National districts in which all electors could vote, but divided among the three ethnic groups with regard to the ethnicity of the candidates. Thus each citizen had four votes, one in his own communal constituency, and one in each of the National constituencies. Overall parity between Indian and Fijian representation was assured, since Indians (50% of the population) and Fijians (44%) each had 22 (12 communal, 10 National) of the 52 seats. As this implies, with eight seats but only 4% of the population, the General roll was overrepresented. Finally, taking the idea of separate electorates and separate constituencies to its logical extreme and reflecting its policy of apartheid, South Africa in 1984 introduced separate parliamentary chambers for Indian and Coloured voters.

The third solution, represented by Lebanon before the breakdown of civil government, is to have one set of multimember constituencies, but to mandate the ethnic balance of acceptable slates of candidates. Thus, in a few districts, only Greek Orthodox, or only Maronite Christian, or only Shia, or only Sunni Moslems could compete, but in most there would be a required mix. For example, in the five-member Baabda district, only slates composed of three Maronites, one Druze, and one Shia Moslem were permissible.

The fourth set of devices includes various "topping up" schemes to provide minority representation. In the case of Sri Lanka, the Governor-General (on ministerial advice) appointed six members of the House of Representatives (in addition to the 95 elected members) "to represent any important interest in the Island which in his opinion is not represented or is inadequately represented."[51] Even more inventive is the "best loser" system of Mauritius. In addition to 62 members elected in multimember plurality districts, eight otherwise defeated candidates are also declared elected in order "to ensure a fair and adequate representation of each community."[52]

That these devices succeed in their immediate objective of assuring a desired balance of representation of various ethnic minorities or other groups is beyond question. Whether they can be successful in their broader objective of bridging the underlying differences and integrating minorities into a more inclusive political community is quite another matter. With the exceptions of New Zealand, India, and Mauritius—in each of which an overwhelming majority has made what amounts to an ex gratia grant of representation to a minority that remains fundamentally symbolic rather than substantive—what is most notable about the examples cited is their failure. The least discouraging example is Belgium, in which linguistic separation essentially has led to a "two-states-in-one" solution that has, at least, generally been peaceful. In Zimbabwe, the reserved seats for European electors were abolished in the constitutional revision of 1987. Again, peace was maintained, but integration and community have hardly been advanced. The Fijian system was overturned by a coup d'état on behalf of the ethnic Fijians. Sri Lanka has been wracked by separatist terrorism; Cyprus has been partitioned by force of arms; Lebanon descended from civil war into simple anarchy.

In discussing the breakdown of order in Lebanon, Lijphart echoes the criticisms expressed by others suggesting that by allowing all citizens to vote for each groups' representatives, not only was the principle of group representation vitiated, but as a result only compromise candidates could be elected so deputies were not true leaders of their sects.[53] The same criticisms might be voiced regarding the National constituencies in Fiji. But surely this was the point. If ethnic divisions are to be bridged, one must have representatives who are mutually acceptable and who have an incentive to espouse mutually acceptable policies. Where this is impossible, perhaps the lesson is not that the wrong institutions were chosen, but rather that the minimal basic consensus required for a democratic political community is lacking. To expect political institutions to bridge a gap of this depth may be to expect too much.

Districts and Fair Representation

Although gross and systematic inequalities in the populations of single-member districts, or in the numbers of citizens per member for multimember districts, are unfair, once a rough parity is achieved, further efforts to assure absolute equality are at best pointless and at worst likely to lead to greater rather than lesser unfairness. Perfect equality of population does not deny discretion. Instead, by requiring that other constraints, such as respect for previously existing boundaries, be abandoned, it increases discretion. This is particularly the case with single-member districts. First, single-member districts cannot be expected to produce proportional results. Thus they must be unfair in aggregate terms to parties or other groups. Second, because the marginal impact of a vote, and hence the attention politicians are likely to pay to the citizen who casts it, depends on the marginality of the district (and this varies across districts), single-member districts must be unfair to voters as individuals. Moreover, to the extent that district lines are discretionary, single-member districts are unfair from both perspectives in the sense that the losers under one plan can produce equivalent arguments for an alternative plan under which they would fare better.

In discussing single-member (or few-member) districts, then, one must make a distinction between those that are fair (an oxymoron) and those that are accepted as fair. Affirmative gerrymandering and other schemes to assure minority representation may be justifiable if they increase acceptance, but might not that goal be better achieved through proportional representation? Similarly, insistence on reasonable equality of population and overturning of blatant gerrymanders may also increase acceptance, but might not quantitative standards of fairness be better achieved by PR?

Concern for equality of population and attention devoted to vote dilution and partisan gerrymandering raise a numerical logic under which single-member districts are inherently and necessarily unfair. In these terms, single-member districts inevitably appear inferior to PR. Does this simply mean that single-member plurality and majority formulas ought to be rejected?

Three counterarguments can be raised. The first rejects the premise that votes cast for the various candidates of a party are votes for the party per se and thus equivalent wherever they are cast. If, as Rush's research appears to show, votes for a party's candidates are not fungible, then the idea of proportionality dissolves into incoherence. While gerrymandering against individual candidates is possible whenever one can identify concentrations of friends and enemies, to talk about partisan gerrymandering requires that voters' choices depend on party and not on individual candidates. The importance of roughly equal populations remains, but PR need be no better at satisfying this goal than a single-member scheme.

Second, if single-member district schemes encourage two-party systems, this may be valued above fairness. In fact, there are real limits to the capacity of single-member systems to deliver two-party systems. Here, however, one can observe that the two-party model presents some fundamental problems for the representation of minorities. Forcing ethnic representation into the two-party model inevitably must (a) vitiate its real substance by allowing minorities to choose one of their own only so long as she or he fits into one of the majority molds, or (b) destroy the coherence of the two parties, or (c) allow minorities to elect representatives who are guaranteed to be marginalized because they are not in one of the two "real" parties. While the second of these possibilities is precisely what pluralist liberalism supports, both the second and third are incompatible with popular sovereignty theories, while the first is acceptable to popular sovereignty views only if one assumes that the minority does not represent a distinct political position — that is, only if minority representation is seen as important to the "equitable" distribution of the private goods of office, but not to the public goods of policy.

Finally, single-member districts may be supported as the optimal method of representing communities. In this case, minority representation is easily accommodated. But in looking at communities rather than individuals, we reject numerical standards of fairness, except with regard to the question of how many representatives each community should have. This approach, moreover, raises three further problems: defining the communities to be represented, defining constituencies for communities that are not geographically concentrated, and identifying the members of any nongeographic communities. These problems are readily solvable, as in the case of Brussels members of the European Parliament, with PR. A community that deserves representation exists to the extent that citizens identify themselves with it by voting for its list of candidates; thus, communities are defined by vote choice rather than residence and citizens classify themselves in the act of voting. Two further questions arise. First, does "community" refer to a single national community, or is the nation made up of many "communities"? And second, is community membership permanent or not? The PR approach regards community membership as fundamentally transient (reestablished at each election) and divisive. If community is to be integrative and permanent, however, one not only returns to single-member districts, but to a geographic view of community as well. If minority group members form such a community, then they deserve to be represented as a community, and districting plans that divide them are illegitimate. However, the artificial creation of minority constituencies through affirmative gerrymandering is equally illegitimate.

Thus the final conclusion is that single-member districts are justified to the extent that there are real communities to be represented and one conceives of representation in terms of community rather than individuals, to the extent that one values parties that are diverse rather than coherent, to the extent that one conceives of government and elections as choices by and between individuals rather than parties. In the first case, one abandons concern with numerical equality even of populations, while in the second and third one either minimizes or ignores the possibility of partisan gerrymanders.

The Nature of Electoral Choice

Almost all the discussions in the preceding chapters have been based on the (sometimes tacit) assumption that elections are about the distribution of seats among parties, with the parties, their candidates, and the voters taken for granted. This assumption ignores important questions surrounding the conduct and regulation of elections. Many of these may be grouped under three broad headings. The first addresses the nature of the choice afforded to the voters: what they may choose among and how they may express their preferences. The second is concerned with the voters themselves: who has the right to vote and how easy (or hard) it is to exercise that right. The third heading relates to the electoral contestants—both parties and individual candidates: how do they gain access to the ballot and what are they allowed, required, or assisted to do in the pursuit of votes. These three headings summarize the subjects of the next three chapters.

The institutional decisions that define the nature of electoral choice, and are the subject of this chapter, revolve around four interrelated questions. First, how many, and which, offices are to be filled by direct election? Second, how often are elections to be held and how are elections for various offices to be related temporally? Third, how is the actual ballot paper or voting machine to be organized, in particular if more than one office is to be filled at a single time? Finally, to what extent are voters given a choice among various candidates of a single party, rather than being presented with each party's choice of candidate(s) on a "take-it-or-leave-it" basis?

The answers to each of these questions impinge directly on the proper role of political parties in modern democracies, and in particular on the question of whether modern democracy necessarily or properly means party government. Party government means that elections ought to be choices among parties that behave as teams and take collective responsibility for government when they are in office.[1] Contrasted to the party government model, which corresponds more directly to the popular sovereignty view, however, are other views, corresponding roughly to liberal democracy, that stress the individual responsibility of office-holders to their individual electorates. Although a number of other questions will intrude, the degree to which various institutions advance or inhibit the partyness of elections will be the central concern in this chapter.

Who Is Elected and How?

Number of Offices, Participation, and Accountability

Many communitarian and participationist democrats draw a sharp contrast between direct and participatory democracy and representative democracy and conclude that the latter can be at best a pale shadow of "true" democracy because representative institutions will restrict continuous and active participation to a very small minority, with the vast majority involved, if at all, only at election times. But this conclusion assumes that the number of officials in representative democracies will be small relative to the number of citizens who would be active participants in a more direct democracy. That advocates of direct democracy may radically overestimate the latter is indicated by the technical limitations and historical precedents discussed in previous chapters. They may also radically underestimate the former figure.

If attention is restricted to national or first-tier subnational governments, then except in the very smallest microstates the number of elected representatives naturally will be a minuscule fraction of 1% of the population. If one considers more local or specialized offices and councils, however, the fraction can be very much larger. In the United States in 1987, for example, there were only 538 elected officials at the national level, and only 18,171 at the state level, about one elected official for every 9,500 voting-age residents. At the local level, however, there were over 485,690 elected officials, bringing the overall ratio down to one elected official for every 353 voting-age residents.[2]

Unfortunately, the United States is the only country for which official estimates of the numbers of elected officials are readily available, but some estimates can be made for other countries. These are shown in table 12.1, along with data concerning the frequency and timing of elections. For example, in 1986, there were just over 26,100 MPs, MEPs (members of the European Parliament), and local authority councillors in the UK. Adding to that approximately 70,000 parish councillors yields an average of about one elective office for every 440 registered voters.[3] In Norway in the mid 1970s, at the national, county, and municipal levels, there was about one elective office for every 190 eligible voters. For Finland, the comparable figure for parliament, presidential electors, and municipal councils was one elective office for every 266 eligible voters.[4] Finally, although the electorate may have had no real choice, with more than 1,820,000 elected local officials, in the early 1960s elections in the Soviet Union provided opportunities for more than one in every 76 Soviet citizens actually to hold government office. While these Soviet positions clearly were administrative rather than policy making, one should recall that the vast majority of positions in the Athenian democracy were administrative as well.

TABLE 12.1 Numbers and terms of elected officials

Country	National		Region		Local	
	N	Term	N	Term	N	Term
Australia	Senate: 76 House of Rep.: 147	Senate: 6 years, half election every 3 years, not necessarily coincident with House of Representatives; House: 3 years. Governor General can dissolve House on advice of prime minister, or both houses after persistent disagreement on a bill.	State parliaments: 618	Lower house: 4 years (3 in ACT and Queensland) Upper house: 6–8 years with rotation (4 years without rotation in Western Australia)	6,542 (excluding Victoria)	2–4 years
Austria	President Parliament: 183	6 years 4 years. Parliament can dissolve itself or president can dissolve once for any given reason.	Landtag: 448	5 years (6 in Oberösterreich)	Gemeinde: 80,124	
Belgium	Senate: 106[a] Chamber of Representatives: 212	4 years, coterminous. King may dissolve if government loses confidence of parliament.	Province: 716	3 years	Commune: 12,749[b]	6 years
Canada	Parliament: 295	5 years. Governor General may dissolve on advice of prime minister.	Provincial legislature: 759[c]	5 years. May be dissolved early.		
Colombia	President and vice president Senate: 102 House of Rep.: 163	4 years	Governors: 32 Mayor of Bogota Departmental Assemblies: 502	3 years	Con. municipal: 10,929	
Denmark	Parliament: 175	4 years. Monarch may dissolve on advice of prime minister	County: 374	4 years	Municipal: 4,704 Church councils: 3,476	4 years

Finland	President Parliament: 200	4 years. May be dissolved by president under exceptional circumstances.	Municipal: 12,571	4 years	None	
France	President Parliament: 577	7 years 5 years. May be dissolved by president after consultation with prime minister and presidents of both chambers. Cannot be dissolved in the year following elections after a dissolution.			Municipal: 463,408 (1965)	6 years
Germany	Parliament: 672	4 years. President can dissolve if Bundestag fails to elect a federal chancellor or if a government motion of confidence is rejected.	Land Parliament: 1991	4–5 years	Gemeinde: 50,273 (excludes district and regional councils)	5 years (6 years in Bavaria; 4 years in Schleswig-Holstein and Hesse)
Ireland	President Parliament: 166	7 years. 5 years. President can dissolve on advice of prime minister. May refuse to dissolve if prime minister has lost majority support in the Dáil.	County and county borough: 883	5 years, can be extended by ministerial order.	Urban and town councils: 735	5 years
Israel	President Parliament: 120	5 years 4 years. May be dissolved by special law of the Knesset.				
Italy	Senate: 315 (plus life senators) Chamber of Deputies: 630	5 years coterminous. The president of the Republic may dissolve one or both chambers after consultation with their presidents.	Region: 1,058	5 years	Province: 3,311 Communes: 121,431	5 years

(continued)

TABLE 12.1 (continued)

Country	National		Region		Local	
	N	Term	N	Term	N	Term
Jamaica	House of Representatives: 60	5 years, can be dissolved earlier on advice of prime minster	Parish: 275	3 years	None	
Japan	House of Councillors: 252 House of Representatives: 511	House of Councillors, 6 years, half election every 3 years; House of Representatives, 4 years. House of Representatives can be dissolved at request of government or after a vote of no confidence if the government does not resign.	Executive: 47 Legislative: 2,874	4 years	Executive: 3,260 Legislative: 63,885	4 years
Luxembourg	Chamber of Deputies: 60	5 years, may be dissolved early.	Communes: approx. 1,070	6 years	None	
Netherlands	Parliament: 150	4 years. Government can request a dissolution in the event of conflict between the chambers. Automatically dissolved after passage of a bill to alter the constitution.	Province	4 years	Municipal: 12,870	4 years
New Zealand	Parliament: 95	3 years. Can be dissolved by Governor General.	Regions: 214	3 years, elected simultaneously with city and district councils.	Cities and districts: 996	3 years, elected simultaneously with regional councils.
Nigeria	Senate: 95 House of Representatives: 435		Governors: 19 State Assemblies: 1,285			
Norway	Parliament: 155	4 years. Cannot be dissolved early.	County: 1,101	4 years	Municipal: 13,648	4 years

Country	National	Term	Regional/State	Term	Local	Term
Spain	Senate: 208 + 48 by regional assemblies Congress of Deputies: 350	4 years, not necessarily coterminous. Can be dissolved on proposal of prime minister. Cannot be dissolved again within 1 year unless no prime ministerial candidate has won a vote of confidence.	Regional parliaments: 1,150	4 years	Provincial parliaments: 1,521 Municipal councils: 65,666	4 years
Sweden	Parliament: 349	3 years. In case of no confidence, the prime minister may call for new elections instead of resigning.	County: 1,743	3 years	Municipal: 13,564 Church councils: 31,245	3 years (church councils elected one month after national, regional, and communal councils)
United Kingdom	Parliament: 650	5 years; can be dissolved earlier by Queen at request of prime minister.	County: 4,089		District, Metropolitan District, and Borough: 21,280 Parish: approx. 70,000 Local officials: 469,957	Various
United States	President and vice president: 2 House of Representatives: 435 Senate: 100	4 years 2 years 6 years, one third elected every 2 years	State executives: 520 State legislatures: 750	2 to 8 years 2 or 4 years		
Venezuela	President Chamber of Deputies: 201 Senate: 46	5 years	Governors: 22 State assemblies: 370	3 years	Mayors: 330 Municipal councils: 2,404 Neighborhood advisory committees: 3,082	3 years

[a] Plus 77 senators elected indirectly.
[b] 23,935 in 1970.
[c] Includes Yukon (24) and Northwest Territories (9).

In estimating the number of involved and actively participating citizens, one must add defeated candidates to the incumbents of these offices. In the case of nonpartisan elections, this may make less difference to the totals than might be assumed, because many such elections are not contested. Attributing their finding to the absence of party involvement, the Redcliffe-Maud Commission estimated that under 35% of parish and rural district council seats were contested in England. Indeed, in over 20% of the parish council elections, there were not enough candidates to fill all of the vacant seats.

Particularly the latter finding suggests quite a different interpretation of the relationship between elections and popular participation from that generally offered by the participationists. Far from restricting the opportunity to participate, especially at the local level, elections create the expectation that a number of positions must be filled, and thus, particularly when parties actively recruit candidates, representative institutions may result in more rather than less *direct* involvement. By increasing the number of submunicipal councils and special purpose boards and by involving political parties in recruitment for the resulting offices, a country can structure its institutions to encourage popular participation in the actual process of governing.

Moreover, the political parties created in response to electoral competition can increase opportunities for participation in governing even more through the creation of appointed boards with membership allocated in direct reflection of electoral results. Indeed, in what must be close to the limiting case, one estimate suggests that once municipal boards appointed by local councils on a party proportional basis are included in the calculation, roughly one out of every 11 Finnish citizens actually holds at least one governmental post. Although the vast majority of these are unpaid and part-time, they still represent more direct individual involvement in actual governing than could reasonably be expected from direct democracy.

Where party discipline is weak, however, a cost must be paid for the proliferation of levels of government and the division of responsibility among many independently elected individuals or boards, especially when, as in many American states, several executive officers are elected independently. Even if responsibilities are not divided across party lines, there is a substantial danger of disagreement with no one official able to claim *the* popular mandate to resolve differences. In this case, both coherence of policy and public accountability are likely to suffer.

Direct versus Indirect Election

Not all representative officials have been or are chosen directly by the people. In some cases, the voters have elected a special group of intermediate choosers to make the final choice; in others, individuals chosen for some other purpose have had the election of other officials as one of their responsibilities. The American and Finnish electoral colleges are examples of the first mode of indirect election, while the electoral colleges of the early Fifth Republic (consisting of "the members of Parliament, of the General Councils and of the Assemblies of the Overseas Territories, as well as the elected representatives of the municipal councils"[5]), the

Italian Republic (members of both chambers of parliament plus three representatives from each of the regions), and India (all members of the state legislative assemblies plus both houses of the national parliament) are examples of the second.

Most early schemes of indirect election were intended to limit popular involvement and control. Thus Norwegian conservatives believed they could safely allow a very broad franchise for choice of primary electors of the Storting since they would be able to control the smaller second-level electoral assemblies. Similarly, the defenders of the American constitution argued that it was desirable

> that the immediate election [of the president] should be made by men most capable of analyzing the qualities adapted to the station, and acting under circumstances favorable to deliberation, and to a judicious combination of all the reasons and inducements which were proper to govern their choice. A small number of persons, selected by their fellow-citizens from the general mass, will be most likely to possess the information and discernment requisite to such complicated investigations.[6]

As democratic pressures grew, these institutions generally were either abolished or transformed in practice, with the individual electors losing their independence and becoming automatic transmission belts for the partisan views expressed by the primary electors at the polls. Where indirect election has been adopted in the democratic era, the motivation generally has been to limit the legitimacy and authority of those elected. The primary examples are the presidents of countries in which real executive power is vested in a prime minister and cabinet; for the president to be head of state without impinging on the prime minister's role as head of government, the president should *not* have the independent claim to legitimate authority conveyed by direct election.

Although indirect election is one of the devices used to subordinate a "figurehead" president to the prime minister in a parliamentary system, one of the most significant cases of indirect election is the choice of the prime minister himself. Whether this election is indirect in form only, or whether the parliament (often meaning the leaders of the parliamentary parties) has substantial room for maneuver, depends on the nature of the party system and the balance among the parties, but decisively influences the meaning of elections. Given the level of party cohesion implicit in the party government models of democracy, three basic types may be distinguished. The first may be called "bipolar party government." In this case, two parties, or coalitions of parties, compete, each with a previously agreed and announced leader who will become prime minister should his or her party or coalition win. In the second case, "dominant party" party government, there are more than two parties, but one party has sufficient strength and centrality of position that it must be the dominant partner in any stable coalition, while in the third case, "coalitional party government," the multiplicity and positioning of parties means that several alternative coalitions are possible. Although the dynamics of the second and third types differ, the more significant difference is between them and bipolar party government. In the bipolar case, since one party/coalition or the other must have a majority in the parliament, voters in electing members to parliament are also clearly, if indirectly, choosing a head of government. With dominant party or coalitional party government, not only is more than one government possible given a particular distribution of seats, it is not even the case that a party's chances of being included in the government are increased by having more parliamentary seats.[7] As a result, voters cannot be sure that they are increasing their preferred party's chance of achieving office or their preferred policy's chance of being realized when they vote for it.

Range of the Electoral Principle

All democracies vest the legislative power in a directly elected representative assembly, or else in the people themselves—through initiative and referendum, town meeting, and so on. The chief executive officer is similarly either directly elected, or else chosen by or responsible to a representative assembly. In the latter case, the principle of indirect popular election may be said to extend to the entire political executive.

Direct election of a wide range of executive officials is basically an American phenomenon (at the state and local level). The states vary tremendously in the number and range of functions of directly elected executive officers, but in most states far more than just the governor (and possibly the lieutenant governor) are chosen by the people and so able to claim independent authority in their dealings with the governor and the legislature. The United States also stands outside the mainstream of democratic systems with regard to the election of judges. Although partisan politics clearly plays a major role in American federal judicial appointments, federal judges are expected to retire from the partisan fray on taking office. Most state judges, to the contrary, are required to submit to election—in some cases partisan election—in the normal course of events.

The desirability of judicial election rests on three related questions. First, can judges be trusted to act responsibly if they do not face the discipline of the ballot box, or is the danger of arbitrary power as great from the bench as from any other position in government? Second, are courts, like other government institutions in democracies, properly seen as instruments of popular rule, or are they bulwarks against the excesses of popular rule? Third, is "politics" properly a very broad concept, encompassing at one extreme all social relationships (in particular, is the judicial process one of the means through which the dominant system of power relations is maintained), or is it quite narrow, involving at the other extreme only partisan conflict over the policy-making (itself narrowly understood) institutions of government?

These questions can, of course, be applied to other officials as well. Can school superintendents be trusted or not? Should the popular will determine the management and curriculum of the schools, or must standards and minority rights be protected from the people? Is education "politics" or merely a question of technical expertise and administration? In each of these dichotomies, the first choice suggests a broad application of the electoral principle, while the second suggests that many offices should be put beyond the reach of direct and immediate popular pressure.

The Frequency and Timing of Elections

Terms of Office

Electoral decisions are made at particular times, by particular people, and under the influence of particular circumstances. As time passes, the electorate is renewed by death and coming of age, issues that led some to participate are replaced by concerns that arouse other citizens, experience is gained and conditions change so that even those who participated in the last election may come to have different preferences. For all these reasons, one might reasonably say that an electoral mandate decays as the last election becomes more distant. Moreover, if fear of defeat is the motivation for politicians to remain responsive to their electorates, the next election should not be too far in the future, lest those in office become complacent.

From either perspective, elections should be frequent, and thus terms of office short.[8] Historically, this was one of the demands of a variety of early nineteenth-century "democratizers," including the English Chartists and American Jacksonians. The idea was to bring government closer to the people and make it more responsive to their needs and desires. The problem is that this position is based on a view of governing as a task requiring neither special talents nor training and experience—and on a view of election campaigning as a relatively inexpensive activity, both in time and in money.

In fact, the problems modern societies confront are both numerous and complex. The bureaucracies developed to deal with them are often labyrinthine. To develop the skills required to understand problems and control bureaucracies requires time, as does development of the personal relationships and trust among politicians that are essential to collective government. By compelling politicians to devote more of their time to campaigning, frequent elections leave them with less time to accomplish these ends. Moreover, frequent elections encourage politicians to pander to popular passions and prejudices, rather than using their own considered judgment. Only some security of tenure gives politicians the opportunity to try to solve problems rather than merely take positions for public consumption. Moreover, frequent elections may not even increase citizen participation; the two modern democracies in which citizens have the most opportunities to go to the polls, the United States and Switzerland, are among those with the lowest rates of voter turnout (see table 13.2).[9]

Finally, three related questions, the first two of which have been of greatest relevance in the United States and the third of which is relevant in parliamentary systems, deserve brief mention. The first is whether there should be a limit to the number of times a single individual can be reelected. The argument in favor of limitations begins with the observation that incumbents almost always are reelected. For example, in 1988, 98.5% of members of the House of Representatives running for reelection (and 92.4% of the total membership of the House) retained their seats. The reasons are numerous—for example, the ability of incumbents to raise campaign funds, greater name recognition, a backlog of favors done, prior (successful) experience campaigning. The result, it is argued, is complacency and indifference to the needs of the people represented. The answer is to force turn-over in office by limiting tenure, thus both limiting the advantages of incumbency and guaranteeing that representatives will shortly be returning to the people to live as ordinary citizens with the consequences of their decisions. In the case of election of the chief executive (president or governor in the American example), the danger of an entrenched personal machine has appeared even greater, with the result that several state constitutions prohibit governors from standing for re-election, while the federal constitution limits the president of the United States to two terms (plus two years of his predecessor's term if he succeeds to the office) altogether. General dissatisfaction with the performance of incumbents has led to passage of a number of state referenda limiting state legislative terms as well.[10]

Like the argument for short terms of office, the argument for term limits ignores the real complexity of government. In assuming that one- and two-term representatives are as effective as those with many years of experience, advocates of this position ignore the enormous capacity of a modern bureaucracy to conceal information and then selectively, and misleadingly, reveal it. Thus, rather than giving the people greater control over the government by making the legislature more responsive, limiting representatives' tenure is likely to make the bureaucracy more independent. Moreover, it likely means only two kinds of individuals will hold office—those who are so secure financially that they do not need to worry about their next job and those who perforce use their offices to secure their next job. Even more serious from the standpoint of democratic theory is the implicit assumption that somehow the voters have been hoodwinked. Advocates of limited tenure propose to substitute their own judgment for that of the people, telling the electorate whom they may and may not choose to elect. Finally, one of the basic premises of the argument—that the frequency with which incumbents are re-elected makes them complacent—is at best questionable. Even if most incumbents are reelected, they generally act as if they were vulnerable, spurred by memory that they have faced at least one close race.[11] Indeed, just as a representative who cannot be reelected may have nothing to gain by kowtowing to special interests, so that representative may have nothing to lose by ignoring the electorate.[12]

The second question is whether, whatever the nominal term of a public official, the electorate should have some means for cutting it short. Part of the program of the American Progressives to wrest government from the politicians and return it to the people, recall procedures currently allow voters in 15 states to force most elected state officials (the exceptions, in six of the 15 states, are judges) to face the electorate before the expiration of their normal terms. Clearly, if recall elections are easily forced, this provision will introduce all of the paralysis and other problems of very short terms. When, as is most often the case, petition signatures equal in number to 25% of those voting at the last election are required,[13] recall may be a reasonable way of combining the advantages of longer terms with those of frequent elections.

The analogous question for parliamentary systems is whether the legislative term is fixed, or whether elections can be called before the expiration of the parliament's full term. On one hand, when the prime minister has the discretion to call an election, the government (cabinet, or simply the prime minister) can appeal over the heads of the parliament directly to the people. This can be a valuable weapon to hold over the heads both of coalition partners and of recalcitrant members of the prime minister's own party. It also provides a way in which parliamentary deadlocks may be broken by letting the people resolve the issues producing the stalemate. More negatively, one might suggest that the unfettered right to call an election gives an unfair advantage to the government, allowing it to capitalize on transient swings in public opinion. Moreover, by providing an escape from deadlocks, it may make them more likely in the first place.

Timing of Elections

If there were only one office to be filled, the question of timing would be resolved with the term of office. When there are several offices, however, the further question of how their elections should be timed relative to one another also must be addressed. This problem arises both with regard to multiple offices at the same level of government (e.g., president, House of Representatives, and Senate) and with regard to different levels.

For multiple offices at the same level, the obvious danger is divided control producing deadlock. As the frequency of split-ticket voting in the United States indicates, this cannot be entirely eliminated with simultaneous elections. Split control is also encouraged by the use of different electoral systems or representational schemes for the chambers of a bicameral legislature (e.g., Japan's use of different systems for the House of Councillors and the House of Representatives; American, Australian, and Swiss equality of representation for the states/cantons in one chamber but representation based on population for the other), or different electorates (a common phenomenon around the turn of the century). When the different offices are elected at different times, however, the vicissitudes of public opinion make divided control even more likely.

If the government in a parliamentary system is responsible only to one chamber of the legislature, divided control is an inconvenience, but not a disaster. When it is responsible equally to two chambers with different majorities, divided control can be intolerable. This led to a minor constitutional crisis in Australia in 1975, when the Labor government lost its majority in the Senate due to the death of one of its senators. The problem of divided control also has arisen in France, where the president is elected for seven years, but the National Assembly only for five.

While unity of control at a single level of government is, except perhaps in the liberal democratic view, generally regarded as a good thing, and thus justifies holding all elections simultaneously, the same is not so clearly true when cutting across levels. Some have argued that national and local politics ought to be kept separate, or indeed that local politics is not, or ought not to be, politics at all, but rather "administration."[14] Precisely to insulate them from the emotion and excitement (and perhaps also from the higher turnout) of presidential elections, many American states hold their statewide, and even more their local, elections in nonpresidential years. With the effects running the other way, one explanation for the increased national uniformity of Indian electoral swings after 1971 was that they had been delinked from state assembly elections, making "it possible for candidates to run for Parliament as representatives of national parties, with national leaders, national programs, and national campaigns." [15] On the other hand, where party government is firmly entrenched, even such temporal separation is inadequate. Instead, in Europe both subnational and supranational (European Parliament) elections are understood by citizens, politicians, and press alike to be "second-order" national elections, in which voters can express their approval or disapproval of the national government, but with relative freedom to cast protest or other expressive votes because the immediate fate of the national government is not in question. [16]

Ballot Format

In the ideal plane on which much of the discussion about the role of elections in a democracy takes place, the mechanics of casting votes would be irrelevant. In fact, however, substantial evidence suggests that votes are significantly influenced by the form in or on which they are cast.

Secret Ballot

The most important ballot reform was the introduction of a written ballot, printed by the state (or to rigid state specifications) and cast in secret. Introduced in South Australia in 1856/1857, the "Australian ballot" replaced systems of open voting or use of ballots printed by the parties, often in distinctive colors and each listing only one party's candidates. [17]

The major advantages of the secret ballot are minimizing the possibility of threats and reprisals and aiding in the suppression of corruption on the theory that the sale of votes would be far more difficult if the buyer could not be assured that the "goods" were being delivered. The secret ballot is not only a procedural reform, however. It also changes the character of voting in a fundamental way— as was recognized by the participants in the original decisions to introduce a secret ballot, as well as by some contemporary communitarian democrats. [18] With an open ballot, voting is a public act or responsibility and elections are the making of a community choice. Only those who are prepared to be responsible to the community for their acts should vote. Votes should not be cast for private motives, but in the public interest; no vote of which the voter ought to be ashamed should count. The secret ballot, on the other hand, makes voting a private act for which the voter is accountable to no one but himself.

Ballot Layout

The Australian ballot also involves an important change in the relationship of the government to elections. Previously, although there might be legal qualifications for taking office, the state did not have to become involved in certifying the eligibility of candidates; once the state began to prepare official ballots, it generally did. While requirements for access to the ballot are among the subjects of chapter 14, two derivative questions may be addressed here. The first concerns whether party affiliations are to be included on the ballot, and, if they are, what legal regulations will be imposed to control the use of a party's name. Second, if party is officially recognized in the layout of ballots and parties have more than one candidate each (either because of multimember election or because several offices are to be filled), how will a party's candidates be related to one another on the ballot? In particular, will there be some device to facilitate casting a straight party ticket, or will voters wishing to do so have to vote for each of their party's candidates individually? And regardless of whether party labels are included, and even if each party has only one candidate, the introduction of an official ballot forces election officials to order the candidates.

Party labels on ballots connect candidates with one another, whether on PR lists, as candidates in multimember districts, or across offices. They also identify candidates as members of a wider organization with an institutional history and with some connections to a program, ideology, or team of leaders. PR elections are impossible without at least temporary alliances of candidates. Although these need not be identified by party labels on the ballot, parties are such a natural focus for PR elections that the more common question is whether to list the candidates on the ballot, or to list *only* the parties. As their name implies, candidate-oriented electoral systems do not strictly require party labels, and, especially prior to the 1960s, many used ballots that identified candidates only by name plus personal particulars such as address or occupation.

The basic reason for continued complicity in the fiction that elections are fought between individuals rather than parties was a desire to avoid state entanglement in disputes over which candidates legitimately were entitled to a particular label. Britain continues with the traditional fiction that parties are outside of the electoral process, but has, since 1970, allowed a candidate to provide up to six words "sufficient to identify him" for inclusion on the ballot. Other countries, including Ireland, Australia, Canada, and Germany, have established party registries. In these cases, only candidates approved by the appropriate official of a registered party are entitled to party designations, all others being identified as "independent." While this step may eliminate some of the color of elections—for example, M. Mouse, the candidate in 1972 for Palmerston North (New Zealand) of the Mad Hatter's Tea Party, would have been identified only as an independent—it assures that candidates claiming to represent a major political party in fact have its endorsement.

The problem with party registries, or other official lists of recognized parties, is to maintain reasonable freedom of entry. If the barriers are too high, registration becomes a device for the unfair protection of previously existing parties. On the other hand, in Australia, any organization for the promotion of election to parliament of a candidate or candidates endorsed by it is entitled to registration if it has either 500 members or one member already in parliament. In Canada, the requirement is the endorsement of 50 candidates in the forthcoming election. In both cases, registration can be refused if the name chosen is likely to be confused with the name of a previously recognized party.

Especially when only one type of office is to be filled, a second problem is the order of candidates' names on the ballot. Traditionally, ballot order was determined according to one of three rules. Candidates (or parties) might be listed alphabetically; in the order in which their nominating procedures were completed; or in relation to party voting results at an earlier election. Research has shown repeatedly that voters are more likely to choose candidates at the top of the ballot, with a small increase in likelihood of vote at the very bottom of particularly long lists.[19] Obviously, there are no reasonable grounds to suggest that some candidates should be advantaged simply because their names come at the beginning of the alphabet, or indeed because they are particularly prompt in turning in their forms or because their party was popular last time. Recognizing that list order does make a difference, some jurisdictions require that names be rotated on successive ballot papers or among different voting machines or that they be listed in an order determined by lot.

Finally, in the context of multiple elections held simultaneously, there is the distinction between office-block and party-column, or grid, ballot formats. The office-block format minimizes the influence of party and in its most extreme form would become a nonpartisan ballot, although in most cases party designations are specified on the ballot. In effect, the voter is given a collection of individual office ballots that all happen to be printed on the same piece of paper or displayed on the same machine. With the party-column format, candidates are arranged in a grid with the rows defined by office and the columns by party (or conversely). In this case all the candidates of a single party are grouped together, and a voter who wishes to cast a straight party ballot need only go straight down the column in order to do so. In its extreme form the party-column ballot provides a single box or lever for the convenience of straight ticket voters. In some states and at some times, the party lever has applied only to state offices or to offices (including Congress) other than the presidency, while in others it applied to the whole ballot.

Numerous studies have concluded that the grid ballot has two important effects relative to the office-block ballot. First, it appears to increase the level of straight party voting and second, to reduce roll-off (the failure of voters to continue all the way to the end of the ballot where the less important and more local offices are listed).[20] Moreover, once these effects are recognized, they, like district boundaries, are subject to manipulation for partisan or personal advantage. For example, in 1940 Ohio Republicans attempted to limit the effects of Franklin Roosevelt's popularity by separating state and federal ballots; the office block was introduced in 1950 to aid Robert Taft and replaced by the party-column format in 1952 to benefit from Eisenhower's coattails.[21]

Intraparty Electoral Choice

Methods

If a party is cohesive, the only question is how many seats each party wins. With differences of opinion or emphasis among a party's candidates, however, the real outcome of an election is determined not only by how many seats each party wins, but also by which particular candidates are elected to fill those seats.

In some systems, this decision is left entirely to the internal structures of the parties. In single-member plurality elections, each party generally has only one candidate per constituency, so that the voters in each district are presented with a choice among "take-it-or-leave-it" combinations of party and candidate. In list PR systems, the equivalent effect is produced when the seats won by a party automatically go to the appropriate number of candidates from the top of the list as submitted by the party. Just as there is no way in which British voters can get the Conservative Party, but not the candidate it nominated in their district, in closed-list PR elections there is no way voters can have the second candidate from a party's list without also having its first candidate.

In other systems, however, ordinary voters are given some, or decisive, influence over the choice among candidates as well as parties. Indeed, in the most extreme case of the American open primary, even the choice of nominees is left to the voters. The wide variety of ways in which an intraparty vote can be structured is illustrated in table 12.2.

With the exception of the direct primary (which is exceptional only if one regards the primary as a separate election, rather than as a temporally removed but integral part of the general election), a number of party candidates greater than the number (greater than zero) it elects is both a necessary and a sufficient condition for an effective intraparty choice in candidate-oriented systems. The "party vote" is a purely notional concept; what counts is votes for individual candidates, and (with the exception of STV) a vote lost to a copartisan is just as irretrievably lost to a candidate as a vote cast for a candidate of some other party. Particularly in SNTV and cumulative voting systems, for a party to nominate a candidate who is *too* popular actually can be damaging, since surplus votes cast for that candidate are not available to help elect his or her running mates. More generally, the candidates of a single party are in direct competition with one another for votes—indeed, to the extent that party ties within the electorate limit the mobility of votes across party lines, this is the only real competition.

With candidate-oriented systems, one votes for a party by voting for one or more of its candidates, and unless one casts exactly as many votes as the party has candidates, the expression of an intraparty choice is a *necessary* part of voting at all. This condition is also the case in some list PR systems. For example, in Finland or the Netherlands each voter formally chooses an individual candidate, but the first step in determining the result is to total all the personal votes received by candidates of a single party in order to allocate seats among parties. In both cases, officials return to the individual votes to determine the order in which candidates will be declared elected. There is a major difference between the two systems, however. In Finland, the intraparty choice of candidates is simply a limited vote election. In the Netherlands, on the other hand, a Hare quota is computed for each party based on the numbers of votes and seats it won. Whenever a candidate has more personal votes than the quota, his or her surplus is transferred to the next candidate on his or her party's list based on the order established by the party. Since the vast majority of Dutch voters choose the first candi-

TABLE 12.2 Methods of intraparty preference voting

Country	Interparty formula	Method of voting	Determinants of order of election/particular candidates elected	Contribution of simple party votes to intraparty decision
Austria	PR	Voter selects a party list. May change order by placing numbers next to the candidates' names listed on the ballot. May not combine lists.	Candidates within a list are elected according to the number of "points" received. Candidate ranked first by a voter receives as many points as there are candidates on the list, candidate ranked second is awarded one less, etc.	Counted as votes for the list in the order submitted by the party.
Belgium	PR	Voter chooses one list, and optionally one candidate from the list.	Candidates with more personal votes than the quota computed by dividing their lists' total vote by one more than the number of seats won in the district are elected.	Counted as personal votes for the first candidate on the list until he or she reaches the quota, then for the second candidate, etc.
Denmark	PR	Voter chooses one list, and optionally one candidate from the list.	In order of personal votes.	Danish parties have a choice of three ballot arrangements and formulas for determining how party votes will be distributed among its candidates: 1. Party votes are shared among candidates in proportion to explicit personal votes received. (simultaneous ordering) 2. Candidate for the nominating district within the constituency is listed first, and party votes in that nominating district are counted as personal votes for him or her. ("usual" ordering)

			3. Party submits an ordered list, although candidate for each nominating district appears first on the ballot there. A quota (as in Belgium) is computed and all candidates with at least the quota in personal votes are elected. Surplus votes of the elected candidates are transferred to other candidates according to a formula that modestly favors those placed high on the party's list.	Not possible
Finland	PR	Voter chooses a single candidate, with individual votes summed within each party to determine the allocation of seats among parties.	Order of election within party is determined by the number of individual votes received.	Not possible
Greece (prior to 1985)	PR	Voter chooses a list and optionally either one or two individual candidates.	Individual votes determine order of election, except that party leaders and former prime ministers are given priority.	Not counted
Ireland	STV	Voter chooses one candidate or ranks more than one candidate.	Candidates are elected in the order in which they reach the electoral quota after transfers of votes.	Not possible
Italy (prior to 1992)	Voter chooses a list and optionally up to 3 or 4 individual candidates.	Individual preference votes determine order of election. Ties are broken with reference to the party's list order.	Not counted	

(continued)

TABLE 12.2 (continued)

Country	Interparty formula	Method of voting	Determinants of order of election/particular candidates elected	Contribution of simple party votes to intraparty decision
Japan	SNTV	Voter chooses one candidate.	Candidates with the most votes win without respect to party.	Not possible
Luxembourg	PR	Each voter may cast as many votes as there are seats to be filled in his or her district. Two votes may be given to a single candidate and votes may be given to candidates of more than one list. Total of votes cast for candidates on a list determines the allocation of seats among lists.	Candidates are elected in the order of their individual vote totals.	One vote is awarded to each candidate on the list.
Malta	STV	Voter chooses one candidate or ranks more than one candidate.	Candidates are elected in the order in which they reach the electoral quota after transfers of votes.	Not possible
Netherlands	PR	Voter chooses one candidate from a list. Votes are totaled at the national level to allocate seats among parties, and then are allocated among regional lists.	Any candidate with as many votes as the quota computed by dividing the party's total vote by the number of seats won is elected. Any surplus over the quota is transferred to other candidates in the party's list order.	Technically not possible. In practice, party votes are cast by selecting the candidate at the head of the party's list.
Norway	PR	There is no official ballot. The voter may write the names of candidates with numbers indicating order of preference, or write the party's name, or use a preprinted party ballot.	Candidate with the most first place votes is elected first; candidate with the most first and second place votes combined is elected second, etc.	Counted as votes for the list in the order submitted by the party.

Sweden	PR	There is no official ballot. The voter may write the name or motto of a party or may vote only for individuals. If the voter uses a preprinted party ballot, candidates may be deleted, replaced, or reordered so long as one of the party's candidates remains at the top of the list.	Limited by the number of seats won by the party, a candidate placed first by half the party's voters is elected, two candidates placed first or second by two thirds of the party's voters are elected, three candidates placed first, second, or third by three fourths of the party's voters are elected, etc. If at any point the first candidates fail to meet this condition, the candidate with the most votes is elected next, his or her ballots are discounted by one half and the process continued.	Counted as votes for the list in the order submitted by the party.
Switzerland	PR	Each voter may cast as many votes as there are seats to be filled in his or her district. Two votes may be given to a single candidate and votes may be given to candidates of more than one list. Total of votes cast for candidates on a list determines the allocation of seats among lists.	Candidates are elected in the order of their individual vote totals.	Candidates receive one vote for each time their names appear on the party's list. (Parties may submit lists with one or more candidates listed twice.)

date on their party's list—the ballot is structured so as to make this the equivalent of casting a simple party vote—the party's list order determines who is elected in virtually all cases.

In other list systems, intraparty voting is optional. In these cases, the question is how votes are counted when the elector does not state an explicit preference. In pre-1992 elections of the Italian Chamber of Deputies, for example, a voter first selected a party and then could (but did not have to) also select up to three or four of its candidates. Only explicitly cast preference votes counted, and although each party's list had an order, it determined the order of election only in the case of ties. In Norway, at the other extreme, votes that do not explicitly alter the party's list order are counted as votes for the list in that order, so that only if at least half of the party's voters explicitly move a single candidate up on the list will the preference votes make any difference in who wins. In intermediate cases, the party can give some advantage to particular candidates, while still allowing the voters a realistic opportunity to affect which candidates are elected.

Intraparty choice presents special problems in single-member systems, since a party has no incentive to nominate more than one candidate and indeed may suffer severely for doing so if they split the party's vote and allow some other candidate to defeat them both. The alternative vote and, to a lesser extent, single-member majority with a run-off eliminate this problem and so allow intraparty choice within the context of single-member districts. In Louisiana, several Democrats and several Republicans often contest the same seat in the first round of voting.[22] Although it was not uncommon for more than one candidate of the same political complexion to contest a single single-member majority district under the French Third Republic, under the Fifth Republic this is no longer the case. In the Fifth Republic, however, the important choice is among candidates of the same block (left or right), even if they are of different parties, and this the first round of single-member majority elections provides regularly.

With single-member plurality, there is no room for intraparty choice; any party with two candidates in a district is virtually certain to lose. The direct primary allows intraparty choice to be introduced to single-member plurality elections by preceding the final choice in which each party has only one candidate with a prior intraparty election. There is, however, one important difference between primaries and other methods of intraparty preference voting. In all of the other systems, one can only express a preference among the candidates of the party for which one has already voted.[23] With a primary, however, there is no guarantee that those who vote for a candidate in his or her party's primary will later vote for him or her in the general election if he or she wins the primary, let alone a guarantee that they will support his or her party if he or she loses. In this respect, a primary is not necessarily an intraparty choice.

Finally, although most of the concerns of this book are irrelevant to noncompetitive elections, the question of intraparty choice is an exception in two respects. One is the possibility that a single party will more or less tightly control nominations, but that it will give the voters a choice by nominating more candidates than offices to be filled. An example is the 1983 election of the Kenyan House of Representatives. Because opposition parties had been banned in 1982, only life members of KANU could stand for election. Nonetheless, this was a truly contested election, with 734 candidates for 158 seats, and a real chance for turnover—38% of the 150 incumbents standing for reelection were defeated (including 19% of the ministers and 41% of the assistant ministers).[24]

The other possibility is that even if the voters cannot choose among candidates, they may reject those nominated. Such was the case with elections in the Soviet Union and many of the countries of eastern Europe prior to the advent of contested elections in the late 1980s. The significance of the ability to vote "no" was limited, however, by a ballot form that meant that unmarked ballots were counted as votes in approval coupled with a norm against using the voting booth to mark one's ballot. As a result, defeated candidates were extremely rare. By one report, only one candidate out of more than 200,000 failed to be elected in the Czech elections of 1971.[25] Similarly, only 249 of 1.8 million candidates in the 1961 Soviet local elections were defeated. Finally, one might note that the option to reject all candidates might be allowed in truly contested elections as well. In this line, the state of Nevada includes in its presidential ballot an explicit option of "None of these candidates," although only the votes cast for actual candidates contribute to the result.

Consequences

The most obvious potential consequence of intraparty choice is turnover in office. Where a party's candidates compete on a reasonably equal footing, defeats based on preference voting often produce more turnover than partisan defeats. Further, while failure to stand for reelection is generally the primary source of turnover, some decisions not to stand undoubtedly are motivated by the likelihood of defeat—including the possibility of defeat in the intraparty poll. Overall, where a meaningful intraparty vote is allowed, it is reasonable to think that between 7% and 20% of the entire membership of the national parliament will be replaced at each election as a direct result.[26]

This demonstrates to candidates in the clearest possible way that party loyalty alone is not enough to assure reelection. To compete successfully with other candidates of one's own party, independent access to campaign relevant resources and organization are necessary. But once a candidate has his or her own organization and resources, he or she has even less reason to be loyal to the party's leaders. Moreover, one has to distinguish oneself from one's copartisans, and again party loyalty is likely to suffer. Thus a second consequence of intraparty preference voting is to lessen the unity and coherence of parties.[27]

Where each candidate can put together a local organization adequate to his or her own election needs, the result simply may be a fissiparous party.[28] Where party rules (e.g., relating to nomination) or the distribution of available resources require intercandidate cooperation in the intraparty electoral competition, the result is more likely to be factionalism. Thus, for example, the use of SNTV is often cited as one of the major factors contributing to the factionalism of the Japanese Liberal Democratic Party,[29] while the Italian system's use of preference voting was regarded as a contributor to the factionalism of all the major Italian parties. In one respect, however, the possibility of preference voting may help preserve party unity; by allowing intraparty competition to be resolved by the voters rather than party leaders, preference voting may minimize the incentive for dissident factions to leave the party altogether.

These consequences flow from the potential of effective preference voting to influence the immediate outcome of an election. Even where preference voting ostensibly is ineffective, however, it may have a significant impact on politics over time by providing politicians, both in office and hoping to be elected, with an opportunity to demonstrate their personal support among the party's electorate.

The Nature of Choice and Party Government

One thread that connects all of the questions discussed in this chapter is their relation to political parties and in particular to how much an election is seen as a choice among parties as national teams. As suggested earlier, this corresponds roughly to the choice between popular sovereignty and liberal models of democracy.

As Ostrogorski made clear, popular sovereignty becomes problematic if the voice of the people is not clear. Independent direct election of executive and legislative officials, or multiple executive officials, increases the opportunity for the people to make confusing or contradictory choices. While this problem ordinarily can be reduced by having cohesive and disciplined parties impose coordination across offices and levels of government, when officials of different parties are elected, party cohesion becomes an aggravating rather than a mitigating condition. In this respect, popular sovereignty is more compatible with parliamentary than with presidential government and, within the category of presidential systems, with the simultaneous election of executive and legislative branches, with a ballot format that encourages party line voting, and with the direct election of only one executive officer. On the other hand, divided control and conflicting mandates, precisely because they make government more difficult, are most appropriate to liberal theories.

The question of intraparty voting returns one to "the little civil war about intraparty democracy" discussed in chapter 3. However, intraparty preference voting is not the only way in which intraparty democracy can be implemented. Thus the control by members inherent in socialist popular sovereignty, or in the mass party of integration model of party organization, takes place outside of the context of public elections and is, perhaps, better served by the absence of provisions allowing the party's broader electorate to overturn or subvert decisions of the party organization, or allowing party candidates to claim a base of personal support in opposition to official party positions.

Again, the conclusion with regard to liberal democracy is just the reverse. Especially for pluralist liberalism, diffusion of legitimate authority and alternative independent mandates are good options. Veto-group liberal theories expect parties to be cohesive in the protection of group interests, and so might be undermined by intraparty preference voting. At the same time, these theories give party members no privileged position compared to ordinary voters. Given the assumption that society is divided into mutually exclusive and ultimately opposing groups (assuring party unity on all crucial questions of group interest), intraparty voting becomes a reasonable way in which each of the major social groups can select and control its leaders.

The institutional demands of participationist democracy are the same as for liberal democracy, albeit for different reasons. Contrary to the view of many participationists, the data considered here suggest that partisan election can increase the amount of participation. Participation also can be increased by having frequent elections, although American and Swiss experiences suggest that a point may come at which the sense of occasion attendant on elections wanes and turnout falls off. Additionally, as will be shown in chapter 13, turnout tends to be lower when an election is not decisive for government formation, as will be the case with staggered elections. Thus one might face a trade-off between increased intensive participation among those actively campaigning and decreased "passive participation" among those who only watch and vote. If the benefits of participation come from consideration and decision, then the less prepackaged the alternatives the better. Hence, intraparty choice should be encouraged, and blind party-line voting discouraged.

Finally, communitarian democracy again calls for fluidity in the parties, openness of discussion, and a restricted role for elites. The opportunities for political talk attendant on electoral campaigns should be multiplied. Especially when local (rather than national) communities take priority, the importance of nationally cohesive parties declines, and with it grounds for objecting to such party-weakening institutions as office-block ballots, divided powers, and intraparty voting.

The Electorate

The right to vote is usually coterminous with full citizenship in a modern democracy. Suffrage is thus of most direct importance for communitarians, because it defines the community. From other perspectives problems of suffrage might appear to be the province of historians. However, even though much of the raw information presented here is historical, it is of more than historical interest. No country allows all adults to vote, and examination of the expansion of the right of suffrage provides a useful vehicle for understanding the restrictions that remain. More generally, it illuminates many problems about the nature of political participation that are relevant not only to suffrage per se, but also to questions like voter registration and compulsory voting.

Table 13.1 summarizes the evolution of the electoral franchise in a variety of countries, referring specifically to requirements for voting in the lower house of the national parliament. Especially in the nineteenth century, far greater restrictions often were placed on voting for the upper house, while requirements might be less stringent for local elections. For example, women received the vote in municipal elections in Finland, Norway, and Sweden far earlier than in national elections. Although the basic trend over the last 200 years has been to remove one barrier to voting after another, many restrictions remain. Although even quite similar requirements may be justified in a variety of ways, most qualifications for voting, and the justifications underlying them, may be grouped under three major headings: those based on community membership and having a personal stake in the outcome, those based on competence, and those based on autonomy.

Community Membership and Affected Interest

Tying the vote to community membership can be approached in two ways. On one hand, if democracy is the self-government of a community, then this aim is defeated either when members of the community are excluded from participation in the management of its (their) affairs, or when those who are not community members are allowed to share in its governance. However, if democracy entails the ability to contribute to the making of those decisions that importantly affect one's life, then to be affected importantly must be a sufficient condition for voting. If one assumes that an important part of democracy is to live with the consequences of one's decisions, then to be affected becomes a necessary condition as well. Although either standard is both clear and easily defensible in abstract terms, in neither case is the proper demarcation between those to be included and those to be excluded uncontentious in practical detail.

The quintessential symbol of community membership at the national level is formal citizenship. For naturalized citizens, it represents both a choice on the part of the citizen to become a part of the national community and his or her acceptance by the community. For citizens by birth, there is no analogous choice and one might question whether mere accidents of birth assure commitment to a real community. Moreover, formal citizenship is not always required for voting. In nineteenth-century America, as many as 22 states and territories permitted aliens to vote;[1] residence or the expressed intent to become a citizen established membership in the political community. A number of European countries now allow noncitizens to vote in local elections after a relatively lengthy period of residence. For example, foreign citizens who have been registered residents of Sweden for three successive years before the election have been permitted to vote in regional and local elections since 1975. In Latin America, Uruguay allows noncitizens to vote in all elections, but only after 15 years of residence. While legal citizenship may be a useful administrative device for identifying presumed members of the political community, it is neither a necessary nor a sufficient condition for membership in the deeper sense required by communitarian views of democracy, nor is it invariably required by real-world electoral laws.

Although residence may be taken to indicate citizenship in a local political community, it more directly indicates inclusion in the set of people affected by government decisions. The principle is that only those who will be there to live with the results of the decisions should be allowed to participate in their making, but prior residence is taken as a predictor of residence in the future. The questions are the length of residence required to establish a real stake in the community and the practical definition of residence.

The trend nearly everywhere has been to reduce both the length of time and the "intensity" of residence required on the grounds that to do otherwise violates the equality of citizens by disenfranchising the mobile (middle class) or the transient (lower class). In the United States, the Voting Rights Act requires that all citizens be allowed to vote for president on no more than 30 days' residence in a state, and that they be allowed to vote for president in their former state of residence until that requirement is met. Moreover, the definition of residence has been substantially broadened in many states; in some states a park bench now qualifies as a place of legal residence![2]

This trend represents a major turnaround from the days in which the disenfranchisement of "undesirables" often was the intent of long residency requirements. Liberalization presents some problems, however, in those cases in which a very large transient population threatens to swamp a smaller group of permanent

TABLE 13.1 International suffrage requirements.

Country	Age	Women's suffrage	Residence	Income/property/status	Other
Argentina	in 1909: 17 1912: 18	1947: Women equal to men		1912: Abolished	1912: Lunatics, deaf mutes unable to write, priests living in religious communities, persons under arrest, inmates of poor-houses, fraudulent bankrupts, criminals, proprietors and managers of houses of prostitution excluded
Australia (federal parliament since 1901)	1856 and after: 21 1974: 18	1894 (S. Australia): Women equal to men 1902: Women equal to men	1901: 6 months in Australia 1953: Members of defense force serving outside Australia entitled to vote	1842 (S. Australia): £200 freehold or house with rental value of £20 (vote in multiple constituencies allowed) 1856 (S. Australia): property requirement and plural voting abolished	1891: Persons of unsound mind, convicted of treason, or under sentence of 1 year in prison excluded 1967: Aboriginals enfranchised
Austria	1848: 24 1919: 20 1929: 21 1953: 20 1968: 19	1896: Women in curia of large landholders allowed to vote in Landtag elections 1919: Women equal to men	1848: 6 months 1849: Dropped 1897: 5th Curia, 6 months 1907: 1 year 1919: Residence in constituency 1929: 6 months	1901: Plural voting abolished 1873: 10 Gulden taxpayers in urban curia; rural curia indirect 1882: Urban and Rural Curiae, 5 Gulden taxpayers 1897: Urban and Rural Curiae, 4 Gulden taxpayers; may also vote in 5th Curia	1848: Servants, day laborers and dependent persons excluded 1907: Mentally deficient, criminals, persons confined to workhouse, parents who have lost rights over their children excluded
Belgium	1831: 25 1871: 21 1893: 25 1919: 21 1981: 18	1919: Mothers and widows of servicemen killed in WWI or women imprisoned by enemy during the war 1948: Women equal to men	1896: 1 year in constituency 1919: 6 months in constituency	1907: None 1831: Direct taxes of 20–80 florins favoring rural areas 1848: Uniform 20 florin tax-paying requirement 1893: 1 extra vote given to married men over 35 with house taxed at 5 francs; owners of property worth at least 2000 florins; recipients of 1000 florins in rents and dividends to a maximum of 3 votes altogether 1920: Abolished	1893: 2 extra votes given to those with higher education, in certain professions or employed in certain offices to a maximum of 3 votes altogether 1919: Plural voting abolished 1919: Mentally deficient, military offenders, criminals, vagabonds and prostitutes, undischarged bankrupts, parents who have lost rights over children excluded

Country	Age	Women	Residence	Property/economic qualification	Other exclusions
Bolivia	1945: 21 1952: 18 if married, 21 otherwise	1952: Women equal to men		Before 1952 was a property test	1945: Literacy; fraudulent bankrupts, convicted and sentenced to corporal punishment, deaf mutes who cannot write excluded 1952: Exclusion of illiterates dropped
Brazil	1824: 25; 21 if in holy orders, married, or a commissioned officer 1889: 21 1932: 18 1988: 16	1932: Women equal to men		1824: Net income of 100 milreis 1846: Net income of 200 milreis 1889: None	1824: Freedmen, illiterates included; sons living with their fathers excluded except for public employees; servants excluded 1889: Mendicants, illiterates, common soldiers, members of monastic orders excluded 1941: Exclusion of religious orders dropped 1946: Literacy, ability to express self in Portugese; civil incapacity; enlisted soldiers and criminals under sentence excluded. 1985: Literacy requirement dropped
Canada	1867: 21 1970: 18	1916: Women equal to men in Man., Sas., Alb. 1917: Women equal to men in BC, Ont.; sisters, daughters, mothers, wives of service men enfranchised 1918: Women equal to men	1885: None (plural voting allowed) 1897: Plural voting abolished except in Quebec 1920: 12 months in Canada (previously varied by province) 1960: Residence in constituency on enumeration day	1867: Ont. and Que.—own, occupy, or rent real property worth $300 or renting for $30 (towns) or $200 and $20 (rural); NB—own real property worth $100 or real plus personal property worth $400 or have income of $400; NS—own real property worth $150 or real plus personal property worth $300 1885: Various property qualifications, including enfranchising sons of property owners at rate of $300 per son 1897: Reversion to provincial franchise. Property qualifications of 1867 still in force in Quebec and Nova Scotia 1920: Abolished	1874: Judges appointed by governor in Council excluded 1885: Returning officers excluded; Mongolians, Chinese, and Indians west of Ontario excluded 1898: Prison inmates and "every person who is restrained in his liberty of movement or deprived of the management of his property by reason of mental disease" excluded 1900: Guilty of illegal electoral practices excluded 1917: All soldiers enfranchised regardless of other qualifications; conscientious objectors, Mennonites, Doukhobors, subjects born in an enemy country or habitually speaking an enemy language naturalized after Mar. 31, 1902 disenfranchised 1920: Provincial disqualifications on racial grounds continued; chief electoral officer excluded 1922: Restriction on alien-born citizens abolished 1934: Assistant chief electoral officer excluded 1960: Indians and conscientious objectors enfranchised 1988: Exclusion of mentally ill and federal judges overturned

(continued)

TABLE 13.1 (continued)

Country	Age	Women's suffrage	Residence	Income/property/status	Other
Chile	1833: 25 (21 if married) 1877: 21 1970: 18	1949: Women equal to men		1833: Property test set by statute 1885: Property test abolished	1840: Literacy required 1925: Literacy; physically or mentally incapacitated, criminals subject to corporal punishment excluded 1970: Literacy test dropped 1985: Members of armed forces, those deprived of political rights by judicial or senate action, mentally deficient excluded
Colombia	1821: 21 or married 1843: 21 1853: 21 or married 1886: 21 1975: 18	1957: Women equal to men		1821: Real property with unencumbered value of 100 pesos or be engaged in business, profession or useful industry and in possession of house or place of business 1830: Real property worth 300 pesos or be engaged as above with income of 150 pesos 1832: Have assured income other than as day laborer or servant 1843: As in 1830 and be paying direct taxes 1853: None	1821: Servants, day laborers, sentenced to corporal punishment, electoral offenders, mentally deranged, bankrupts, vagabonds excluded 1821: Habitual drunkards excluded 1832: Bar to habitual drunkards dropped 1850: Literacy required for those reaching 21 after this date 1853: None 1858: Criminals and the deranged excluded 1873: Literacy required except for those with income of 500 pesos or property worth 1500 pesos 1886: Lawful occupation or means of support 1936: Abolished
Denmark	1848: 30 1855: 25 1863: 30 1918: 29 1920: 25 1953: 23 1961: 21 1971: 20 1980: 18	1918: Women equal to men	1848: 1 year 1918: Residence in country	1848: Those working as servants and farm helpers not having their own households and those receiving or having received poor relief excluded 1855: 200 taler per year in tax or 1200 taler per year income 1915: None	1915: Servants enfranchised; bankrupts and persons deemed incapable of managing their own affairs, those convicted of dishonorable public conduct excluded

Country	Age	Women	Registration in parish of residence		
Ecuador	1861: 21 1884: 21 unless married 1946: 18	1929: Vote compulsory for men, optional for women 1967: Women equal to men			1869: Limited to Catholics 1878: Religious test abolished 1946: Fraudulent bankrupts, fraud, criminals under sentence excluded 1978: Literacy requirement dropped
Finland	1869: Towns—24; Farmers—21 1906: 24 1944: 21 1969: 20 1972: 18	1906: Women equal to men	1906: Inclusion on census register	1869: Towns—Mayors and aldermen, merchants, master craftsmen, house owners; tax-paying independent farmers. Plural voting in proportion to taxes or income. 1879: Towns—taxpayers except seamen, soldiers, day laborers 1906: Abolished	1906: Votes denied to those a) on active military service, b) under guardianship, c) not on citizen rolls for 3 years, d) who failed to pay taxes for any reason other than impecunity, e) receiving public assistance, f) who have given up their property to satisfy creditors, g) who had been committed to public work for vagrancy (3 years), h) deprived of civil rights by court decision, i) convicted of election offenses (6 years) 1928: (d) and (f) abolished; (e) applied only to those totally dependent on public assistance 1944: (a) abolished 1955: (e) and (b) abolished
France	1848: 21 1870: 25 1875: 21 1974: 18	1944: Women equal to men	1848: 6 months in commune 1870: 3 years except in native commune 1875: 6 months in commune	1875: None	1848: Soldiers enfranchised 1852: Soldiers could vote only if in home communes on polling day 1870: Rights of soldiers restored 1875: Criminals (including petty offenders) disenfranchised; soldiers could vote only in home commune and if off duty 1945: Postal or proxy vote allowed for soldiers
Germany	1848: 24 1918: 20 1949: 21 1970: 18	1918: Women equal to men	1920: 6 months in constituency 1956: 3 months in Germany	1848: Recipients of poor relief excluded 1867: None	1867: Incompetent, financially disabled, soldiers and sailors on active service excluded
Greece	1844: 25 1864: 21 1977: 20 1981: 18	1952: Women equal to men		1844: Own some property in the district of residence or have an "independent" trade. (Apprentices and servants excluded.) 1864: Word "independent" dropped from requirement	1877: Clergy excluded; those unable to manage property, those on active duty, those denied vote by judicial decisions excluded

(continued)

TABLE 13.1 (continued)

Country	Age	Women's suffrage	Residence	Income/property/status	Other
Honduras	1839: Literates over 25, soldiers, heads of household 1894: 21, 18 if married or literate 1957: 18	1955: Vote optional for women, compulsory for men 1960: Women equal to men		1894: None	1894: Soldiers on active service excluded 1924: Ordinary soldiers enfranchised; high officials of army or police, prisoners, vagrants, fraudulent bankrupts excluded 1960: Restrictions abolished
Iceland	1874: 25 1934: 21 1968: 20 1984: 18	1915: Women equal to men		1874: Farmers paying tax; burghers and nonfarming fishermen paying local tax over 8–12 Kr; civil servants and men having university or divinity school degree. Limited to those in charge of own finances and properties, not receiving communal assistance 1903: Farmers paying tax; all men not farmer laborers paying local tax of 4 Kr; civil servants and men having university, medical, or divinity degree. Limited to those in charge of own finances and properties, not receiving communal assistance 1915: In charge of own finances and property, not receiving communal assistance 1934: In charge of own finances and property	
India	1950: 21	1950: Women equal to men	1950: 180 days in constituency		
Ireland	1918: 21 1972: 18	1918: Women over 30 1923: Women equal to men	1923: Habitual residence in constituency on registration day	1923: Residency or property or business worth £10	1950: Those of unsound mind, convicted of electoral offenses excluded 1918: Extra votes for university graduates 1923: University vote abolished

Country	Age	Women's suffrage	Property/Tax qualification	Residence	Exclusions
Italy (Sardinia before 1861)	1848: 25 1882: 21 1912: 30 for all men, 21 for those passing means or education test and ex-servicemen 1919: 21 plus ex-servicemen	1946: Women equal to men	1848: L. 40 in direct taxes and own property 1882: L. 19.80 in direct taxes and owning property, or pay agricultural rent of L. 150, or pay town rent of at least L. 150 to L. 400 1912: Abolished for those over 30 and former servicemen 1919: Abolished		
Jamaica	1975: 18 Colony :21 1972:18	Colony: Women equal to men		Colony: Jamaicans, resident in constituency on registration day; Commonwealth citizens, 12 months	Colony: Criminals under sentence of death or serving a sentence of at least 6 months, convicted of electoral offenses, insane, chief electoral officer and other election officers excluded
Japan	1889: 25 1946: 20	1946: Women equal to men	1889: Direct tax of ¥15 1902: Tax of ¥10 1919: Tax of ¥3 1925: None	1889: 1 year in administrative district 1913: 6 months 1925: 1 year	1889: Lunatics, idiots, criminals, bankrupts, men in active military service 1900: Shinto and Buddhist priests, Christian clergymen, teachers of religion excluded 1950: Only criminals, convicted of electoral offenses continue to be excluded
Liechtenstein	1862: 24 1922: 21 1973: 20	1984: Women equal to men	1862: None	1921: 3 months in Liechtenstein 1922: One month in constituency	1862: Bankrupts, those on poor relief, criminals, those under guardianship, "dienstbaren Gesindeverhältnis" excluded 1925: "Persons who receive because of poverty, for their livelihood, public or private aid or support" excluded
Luxembourg	1841: 25 1919: 21 1972: 18	1919: Women equal to men	1841: 10 gulden 1848: 10 francs 1856: 125 francs in district, 10–125 in cantons 1860: 30 francs 1868: 10–30 francs 1892: 15 francs 1901: 10 francs 1918: Abolished	1924: Domiciled in Luxembourg	Criminals, mentally deficient, judges excluded

(continued)

TABLE 13.1 (continued)

Country	Age	Women's suffrage	Residence	Income/property/status	Other
Mexico	in 1909: 18 in 1932: 18 if married, 21 otherwise 1969: 18	1953: Women equal to men			
Netherlands	1848: 23 1897: 25 1946: 23 1956: 21 1972: 18	1919: Women equal to men	1887: 18 months 1922: Residence in country	1848: Paying direct tax of 20–160 florins 1886: Paying direct tax of 10 florins or renting or owning a house with equivalent rental value 1897: Paying direct tax of 1 florin, or living in house with rental value over .80–2.50 florins per week, or receiving wages or pension over 275–550 florins, or owning savings accounts over 50 florins, or having passed an examination qualifying for any office or employment or giving the right to work in any profession, or owning or leasing a ship of 24 tons burden 1917: Abolished	1917: Persons sentenced to more than 12 months imprisonment excluded for 3 years; persistent vagrants and public drunkards, mentally deficient, parents who have lost rights over children excluded 1983: Only mentally incompetent and those disqualified on being sentenced to at least one year in prison excluded
New Zealand	1852: 21 1969:20 1974:18	1893: Women equal to men	1879: 1 year in N. Zealand, 6 months in district in lieu of property requirement 1893: 6 months residency requirement reduced to 3 months	1852: £10 dwelling in town or £5 dwelling in country or £50 freehold or £10 leasehold; voting in multiple constituencies allowed 1868: Maori constituencies created with no property qualification 1879: Freehold qualification reduced to £25 1889: Plural voting abolished	c.1908: Prisoners, mentally deficient, persons on corrupt practices list excluded

Country	Age	Women	Residence	Property/Income	Other
Nigeria	1922: 21 1976: 18	1954: Eastern and Western regions, women equal to men; Northern region, women excluded 1976: Women equal to men throughout country	1922: 1 year in constituency		1922: Criminals, unsound mind excluded
Norway	1814: 25 1919: 23 1946: 21 1969: 20 1978: 18	1909: Women whose own or husband's income exceeded 400 Kr in towns or 300 Kr in rural areas 1915: Women equal to men	1814: 5 years in Norway	1814: None 1828: High government officials, owners or 5-year leaseholders of tax-registered rural land, burgesses, persons owning town houses or land worth 300 dollars 1884: 600 Kr in property for city dwellers or income of 800 Kr in towns and 500 Kr in rural areas 1898: Abolished, but suffrage suspended for bankrupts and paupers receiving public assistance 1914: Provision for bankrupts abolished 1919: Provision for paupers abolished	1814: Oath of allegiance required 1897: Oath requirement abolished 1912: Persons incapable of managing their own affairs, criminals, convicted of electoral offenses excluded
Peru	1860: 21 unless married 1933: 18	1956: Women equal to men		1860: Illiterates required to be managers of business, hold landed property or make a contribution to the public treasury 1920: Special requirements for illiterates dropped	1920: Literacy required; soldiers on active service and government officials excluded 1933: Prisoners, religious professions, physical or mental incapacity excluded 1980: Literacy requirement dropped
Philippines	1916: 21 1935: 20 1981: 15	1937: Women equal to men	1935: 1 year in country; 6 months in district	1916: Taxpayer 1936: None	1916: Literacy; feeble-minded and criminals excluded

(continued)

TABLE 13.1 (continued)

Country	Age	Women's suffrage	Residence	Income/property/status	Other
Portugal	1826: 25; 21 for clergy, married, service officers, with higher education 1878: 21 if literate or head of household 1933: 20 1974: 18	1933: Literate women paying 200 esc. in taxes or having completed secondary education 1974: Women equal to men		1826: Income over 100 milreis 1838: Income over 80 milreis 1852: Income over 100 milreis or with higher academic degree 1878: None for literates 1895: Paying tax of 500 reis for illiterates 1910: None 1933: 100 esc. in taxes if illiterate 1974: None	1826: Members of religious orders, sons living with their fathers, domestic servants excluded 1911: Restriction to head of family dropped 1913: Literacy required 1917: Literacy requirement dropped 1919: Literacy required (after 1933, unless taxpaying requirement met) 1974: Literacy requirement dropped
South Africa	1909: 21 1946: 18	1930: European women equal to men	1909: Orange River and Transvaal only, 6 months	1909: Cape only, occupy property in constituency worth £75 or have income of £50 provided had resided in last 3 months; Natal only, own immovable property in constituency worth £50, or pay £10 rent, or have resided 3 years in Natal and have monthly income of £8 1931: Abolished for Europeans	1909: Cape only, able to sign name, address, and occupation; Natal only, natives including Coloureds excluded with some exceptions; Orange River and Transvaal, franchise limited to Europeans; Cape only, lunatics excluded; Transvaal and Orange River only, those on public relief excluded; everywhere, criminals excluded but for varying periods 1930: Cape literacy requirement abolished for Europeans 1936: Natives removed from electoral rolls 1946: Indians removed from electoral rolls 1983: Indians and Coloureds enfranchised in separate elections
Spain	1868: 25 1931: 23 1977: 21 1978: 18	1931: Women equal to men	1890: 2 years in district 1978: Spaniards resident abroad to be allowed to vote	1843: 200 reale or proof of steady income or academic degree; high ranking officers and civil servants 1869: None 1878: Pta. 25 in taxes or Pta. 50 for business 1890: None	

Country					
Sri Lanka	1924: 21 1959: 18	1931: Women equal to men	1931: 5 years domicile or permanent settlement in lieu of income requirement 1946: 6 months continuous residence in district in last 18 months 1949: Franchise limited to citizens of Ceylon (disenfranchised permanent settlers)	1924: One of a) income of Rs 600; b) ownership of Rs 1500 in immovable property; c) occupancy of premises with annual value of Rs 200–400 1931: None	1946: Prisoners, mental deficients, convicted of electoral offenses excluded; literacy in English, Sinhalese or Tamil required. 1972: Mental deficients, criminals excluded
Sweden	1866: 25 1909: 24 1921: 23 1945: 21 1970: 19 1975: 18	1921: Women equal to men	1967: Residence in country for some time in last 5 years 1975: Residence in country for some time in last 7 years 1977: Residence in country at some time	1866: Own property worth 1000 riksdaler or lease a farm worth 6000 riksdaler or have an income of 800 riksdaler. Those owing taxes (ended 1921) and who lost civil rights (ended 1937) excluded 1909: Abolished. Bankrupts, those on poor relief, and those who had not completed military service excluded 1922: Exclusion of those not having completed military service ended 1945: Exclusion of bankrupts and those on poor relief ended	1909: Those under guardianship, mentally deficient excluded
Switzerland	1848: 20	1971: Women equal to men in federal elections	1848: Residence in country	1848: None	1848: Those excluded by canton 1975: Criminals and mentally deficient excluded
Turkey	1877: 25 1934: 22 1987: 20	1934: Women equal to men	1924: 1 year in locality	1877: Taxpaying 1924: None	1877: Convicts, bankrupts, notorious bad character, in personal service, deprived by law of control over property excluded 1924: Servants enfranchised; military and police excluded

(continued)

TABLE 13.1 (continued)

Country	Age	Women's suffrage	Residence	Income/property/status	Other
USSR	1925: 18	1917: Women equal to men		1917: Abolished	1925: (RFSSR) criminals deprived of political rights, mentally deficient, persons employing hired labor for profit, persons living on unearned income, traders, ministers of religion and monks, employees of Tsarist police, gendarmes and members of the former dynasty excluded 1936: Criminals deprived of political rights and mental defectives only excluded
United Kingdom	1832: 21 1918: Servicemen and ex-servicemen at 19 1948: 21 uniformly 1969: 18	1918: Women over 30 in occupation of (rather than merely resident in) a dwelling house or in occupation of land or other premises worth £5 yearly, or married to a man entitled to be registered as a local government elector 1928: Women equal to men	1884: 1 year in constituency 1918: 6 months residence or occupation of £10 business premises 1927: 3 months in constituency (1 month for soldiers released within 3 month pre-election period) 1948: Resident in constituency on registration day. 1949: 3-month residency imposed for Northern Ireland	1832: Counties—40s freehold, £10 copyhold or leasehold, £50 tenant at will; boroughs—£10 household. 1867: Counties—40s freehold, £5 copyhold or leasehold, £12 tenant at will; boroughs—occupiers of rated houses, lodgers occupying £10 lodgings. 1884: Uniform household and lodger franchise 1918: Abolished	1782: Revenue officers disenfranchised 1867: Bar to revenue officers removed 1878: Mentally deficient, prisoners, convicted for electoral offenses, peers excluded 1948: Citizens of Republic of Ireland continue eligible to vote 1948: Business and university votes abolished
United States	Originally: 21 1971: 18	1920: Women equal to men	1970: 30 days for presidential elections 1973: Durational residency requirement banned for presidential elections	1964: Taxpayer requirements banned	Colonial: Those of unsound mind excluded under common law 1870: Racial requirements banned 1915: "Grandfather" clauses ruled unconstitutional 1944: "White primary" ruled unconstitutional 1965: Literacy tests more stringent than 6th grade education banned

	Age	Women	Property	Other
Uruguay	1830: 20, 18 if married 1918: 18	1934: Women equal to men	1830: None	1830: Wage servants, day laborers, private soldiers, criminals, habitual drunkards, bankrupts excluded 1840: Literacy required 1918: Prisoners, habitual practice of morally dishonorable activities, participation in proscribed organizations, private soldiers, physical or mental incapacity excluded; literacy requirement dropped
Venezuela[a]	1858: 21 1947: 18	1947: Women equal to men	1858: None	1936: Literacy required 1946: Literacy requirement dropped Criminals under sentence, members of armed forces on active service excluded

[a] Prior to 1946, national parliament and president chosen indirectly. Suffrage requirements are for municipal councillors and members of state legislative assemblies.

residents. The most obvious cases are small towns with universities or military installations. In both cases, the danger is that the temporary, and frequently non-taxpaying, residents will impose large obligations on the localities. Although analogous, these cases generally have been treated differently, with servicemen required to vote (if they are allowed to vote at all) in their original home districts, while students usually are able to vote in the district where their university is located. A similar situation has been recognized regarding temporary workers at mining sites in the Northwest Territories of Canada, where a three-year residency requirement was imposed.[3]

Religious qualifications, once quite common (and surviving well into the twentieth century in some cases), were also tests of community membership. On one hand, religion presumably encompasses the basic values of the community; where those values are deeply held and widely shared, those who fail to embrace them truly are outside the community. On the other hand, when kings claimed to rule "by the grace of God," to reject the common religion was also to reject the basis of the government's claim to sovereignty.

Also primarily in the past, property requirements for voting were justified in terms of the criterion of affected interest. Those who owned real property were presumably tied to place, while those without could always leave the consequences of their decisions behind. Similarly, those who paid taxes would bear the costs of their decisions; for nontaxpayers, voting would be the irresponsible act of deciding how to spend someone else's money. John Stuart Mill's proposal of a small poll tax so that even the poor would have a direct financial stake in the government fits under this heading.

Although property and taxpayer qualifications generally had been dropped for national elections by the end of World War I, they survived rather longer in the United States for local—especially bond-authorizing—elections, where it was "considered a sufficient brake on local spending and indebtedness if the people who pay the tax bill have the power of deciding whether or not the tax is to be levied."[4] Such provisions were ruled unconstitutional in 1969.[5] Conversely, property may be a sufficient, rather than necessary, condition for voting. Here the argument is that property owners are sufficiently affected by government decisions that they should be allowed to participate even if nonresident or otherwise disqualified.[6] This may, of course, mean that some individuals are qualified to vote in the elections of several localities. For example, the property qualifications in Britain, Canada, Australia, and New Zealand originally allowed an individual to vote in each constituency in which the qualification was met; although plural voting in parliamentary elections was abolished in Britain in 1948, a right to vote based on occupancy of business premises continued in British local government elections until 1969. In the Netherlands, the right to vote in the assemblies of the Waterschappen (local authorities that maintain the dikes) often is limited to those owning over a specified amount of land in the Waterschap; charges levied by the Waterschappen similarly fall on those with property in the district.

The problem of an interest-based franchise is illustrated by the case of Alabama cities, which are given various police and licensing powers that extend three miles beyond the city limits. The right to vote in city elections, however, is limited to residents. The Supreme Court rejected a challenge to this arrangement, while agreeing that "[t]he imaginary line defining a city's corporate limits cannot corral the influence of municipal actions." The Court went on to note that other municipal decisions, like the siting of a garbage dump or waste treatment plant, might have even greater impact on surrounding nonresidents than the Alabama police jurisdiction statutes, yet "no one would suggest that nonresidents likely to be affected by this sort of municipal action have a constitutional right to participate in the political processes bringing it about."[7] A franchise based on affected interest requires impossible judgments and arbitrary exclusions, or else a franchise literally universal even for local elections.

The concept of community also may be bent to justify exclusion of individuals, sometimes regardless of citizenship and sometimes accompanied by deprivation of citizenship, particularly on racial or ethnic lines. For example, "adult manhood suffrage" in the United States in the early nineteenth century applied to "whites only because, as a resident of Michigan said, Indians and Negroes were excluded from the 'great American family.' "[8] By the same token, the policy of apartheid in South Africa segregated whites, Asians, "coloureds," and blacks into four separate communities. In even more virulent form, appeal to community was one basis of Nazi policy with regard to Jews, gypsies, and other "non-Aryans."

Competence

A second set of criteria for voting focuses on the competence of the elector. Most prominent here are age requirements. Although the "age of reason" has varied (and generally has been reduced to 18, with a few countries allowing even younger citizens to vote), no country allows young children to vote. Equally unproblematic, if not equally universal, are proscriptions to voting for the mentally deficient. In the past, property holding was often taken to be an indicator of competence.[9] Literacy tests, as well as ability to communicate in the national language, are also defended (and defensible) in these terms, although use of the national language as a qualification for voting is perhaps even more justifiable as a symbol of integration into the national community. In some cases, these qualifications have been fungible (or in the case of Belgium between 1893 and 1920, additive), as with the Italian requirement (1912–1919) that a man be over 30 *or* be literate *or* pass a means test *or* have served in the army.

Two points deserve mention. The first is that although competence requirements are defensible in principle, in practice they, like tests of affected interest or autonomy, often have been thinly veiled excuses to purge the electoral rolls of particular groups on the basis of their (supposed) political preferences. One effect of literacy tests in South America was to prevent most of the Indian population from voting. Given differential mortality rates, even an age requirement can alter the class balance of the electorate significantly. For example, in the 1840s "in the French textile city of Mulhouse average additional life expectancy at age four for a member of the wealthy classes was 46 years, but only 18 additional years for a textile factory worker."[10] Seen in this light, the 1848 decision to raise the French voting age from 21 to 25 introduces an obvious class bias.

The second point is of a different character. Unlike other personal rights of the incompetent, the right to vote cannot be exercised on their behalf by a guardian. A number of reasons might be suggested, including the absence of an externally agreed standard of the ward's political interest and a feeling that the equality of citizens would be violated if the guardian exercised a second vote even as a trustee. A more compelling reason looks to our understanding of the nature of the right to vote. If the vote is an opportunity to *do* something in one's own interests, as it is assumed to be by liberal democrats, then the incompetent should not be denied the right to have that thing done on their behalf. But if instead the vote is an opportunity to *be* something—to be consulted, to be included—then it is, by its nature, nontransferable. The ward cannot be incorporated into a community or developed as a person vicariously. On the other hand, a competent citizen might well instruct a trusted friend to perform the physical act of casting a ballot for him or her without diminishing his or her personal incorporation or development—and in fact this form of proxy voting or voter assistance often has been permitted for soldiers serving overseas or for the physically handicapped (see table 13.2).

Less defensible has been the exclusion of racial groups or women on grounds of genetic or cultural inferiority or naturally ordained proper spheres of activity. Racial exclusion requires only two observations: (1) that a distinction between citizens and slaves is as old as democracy itself and (2) that although racial exclusion was outlawed (even if continued in practice) in the United States in 1870, Canadian Indians living on reserves were not enfranchised until 1960, individuals of Pacific descent (aborigines, Japanese, Polynesians) in Australia until 1967, and blacks in South Africa until 1994. Exclusion of women is of more recent and less complete demise, and the arguments surrounding it do not so obviously reflect the conflict of an in-group trying to maintain a monopoly of power and an out-group struggling for inclusion, as indicated by the fact that sizable numbers of women opposed suffrage expansion (indeed, women were the overwhelming majority of the leaders of the American antisuffrage movement).[11]

Often, the antisuffrage argument was not that women are inferior, but that they are different, and that the two genders are differentially suited to separate spheres of life. In terms not unlike those used by Tory Democrats to describe a functional division of society that justifies popular deference to the judgment of the political elite, opponents of female suffrage argued for two separate spheres, "the domestic life of the family and the public life of society," with women properly in charge of the first, and men of the second.[12] The question of separate spheres has led to a continuing debate in feminist theory.[13] That the idea of women belonging in the private rather than the public sphere is not yet dead also was made abundantly clear by much of the rhetoric surrounding the 1992 Republican presidential campaign.

Autonomy

The final category of qualifications for voting concerns the autonomy of the individual. This category includes many of the qualifications already discussed, but approaches them from a different angle. Children not only may be presumed incompetent, but also dependent; thus, property requirements for voting would prevent even the middle aged sons of wealthy landowners from voting if they had no property of their own.[14] The same principle underlies a householder franchise or a requirement of financial independence and in some cases might also underlie the exclusion of married women (e.g., Portugal 1930–1974).

Especially when applied against religions whose leaders claim the right to dictate the votes of their followers, the criterion of autonomy can justify religious tests for voting even in countries where a majority of the members of the community adhere to the religion in question. For example, the Brazilian constitution of 1891 denied the vote to "[m]embers of monastic orders, companies, congregations, or communities of whatever denomination, subject to a vow of obedience, rule, or statute which involves the renunciation of individual liberty."[15] A similar rationale may underlie the relatively frequent exclusion of private soldiers as being too directly under the influence of their officers.

Suffrage Expansion

Table 13.3 indicates the effects of changes in requirements for voting by showing for a selection of countries, by decade, the percentage of the total population eligible to vote.[16] Together, tables 13.1 and 13.3 illustrate several important points about the history and politics of suffrage expansion.

Examining the demise of property requirements, one can distinguish two basic patterns. The first, illustrated archetypically by the UK, but also by the Netherlands, the United States, Australia, and New Zealand, was for these tests to be reduced in several stages, while the second, typical of France, Finland, Germany, Japan, Italy, and Belgium, was for a highly restrictive franchise to be replaced by universal (manhood) suffrage virtually overnight. Examining particularly the difference between Britain and Italy, authors have suggested that the delay and then precipitate rush in enfranchising industrial workers and peasants that made it "impossible for the established parties to adapt to and absorb the new voters" contributed to the breakdown of Italian democratic institutions three years later.[17] In contrast, the Netherlands developed a fragmented party system even though the working class was granted the suffrage gradually, and while democracy certainly broke down in Germany, it is hard to attribute that to the speed with which the working class had been enfranchised some 50 years earlier.

The greatest increases in the percentage of the population eligible to vote is associated with the enfranchisement of women, which except in those few cases in which it was introduced gradually, effectively doubled the eligible electorate overnight, with no noticeable impact either on party systems or on regime stability. Clearly, women were informally integrated into the politics of their husbands, fathers, and other male associates before they were formally enfranchised. Apparently, rapid expansion alone cannot explain party fragmentation or regime collapse.

Lowering of the voting age generally occurred first in Latin America. In the United States and Europe, the 18-year-old vote generally was not introduced until

TABLE 13.2 Registration and voting provisions and voter turnout.

Country	Registration automatic or by application	Postal voting or other special provisions	Compulsory voting	Number of days polls open	Work day or rest day	Average turnout 1960–1985 (N)
Argentina	Automatic	None	Up to age 70	1	Either	84 (3)[a]
Australia	Application	Postal votes for ill and infirm, constituency transfer for absentees	Yes	1	Rest	95 (11)
Austria	Automatic	Polling stations in hospitals, constituency transfer for absentees	In Styria, Tyrol, Vorarlberg (26% of electorate)	1	Rest	93 (7)
Belgium	Automatic	Postal votes for hospitalized, public officials, and absentees	Yes	1	Rest	93 (9)
Brazil	Application	Polling stations for sick, aged, civil servants, and military outside their constituency	Yes	1	Either	79 (1)
Canada	Automatic	Advance voting for those who will be absent; proxy voting available for students, mariners, and prospectors	No	1	Work	76 (9)
Chile		None	Yes	1	Rest	90 (2)[a]
Colombia	Application		No	1	Rest	48 (6)[a]
Costa Rica		None	Yes	1	Rest	81 (5)
Denmark	Automatic	Advance voting permitted	No	1	Work	87 (11)
Fiji	Application	Postal votes for sick, infirm, and absentees	No	1		74 (1)
Finland	Automatic	Advance voting permitted	No	2[b]	Both	80 (7)
France	Application	Sailors, certain members of armed forces, civil servants, country absentee may vote by proxy; postal votes permitted for certain members of armed forces, civil servants, sick, certain professionals	No	1	Rest	78 (6)
Germany	Automatic	Postal votes for absentees	No	1	Rest	89 (7)
Greece	Application		Yes	1	Rest	
India	Automatic	Postal votes for high officials, armed forces, prisoners	No	5	Both	58 (5)
Ireland	Automatic	Military and police must vote by post	No	1	Work	75 (8)
Israel	Automatic	Special polling stations for soldiers	No	1	Work	81 (7)
Italy	Automatic	Military may vote where stationed	Effectively	2	Both	92 (6)

Country	Registration	Absentee / special voting provisions	Compulsory voting		Day	Turnout
Japan	Automatic	Advance voting for business absentees	No	1	Rest	71 (9)
Liechtenstein	Automatic	None	Yes	2	Both	95 (1)
Malaysia	Application	Absentees, police, those on duty on election day may vote by post	No	1	Either	n.a.
Malta	Application	Polling stations in hospitals	No	1	–1976, Monday; 1976–, Saturday	93 (5)
Netherlands	Automatic	Absentees may vote in a different municipality with written notice and special permission	Through 1967	1	Work	95 (2) pre-67; 84 (4) post-68
New Zealand	Application	Advance voting for absentees, ill and infirm	No	1	Rest	88 (9)
Norway	Automatic	Advance voting for absentees	No	2	Both	82 (7)
Peru	Application		Yes	1	Rest	78 (3)[a]
South Africa	Automatic	Postal vote	No	1	Work	57 (6)
Spain	Automatic	Postal vote		1	Rest	73 (3)
Sweden	Automatic	Postal vote; special polling stations in prisons, hospitals, etc.	No	1	Rest	89 (9)
Switzerland	Automatic	Postal and advance voting possible	In Aargau, Thurgau, Schaffhausen, St. Gallen (17% of electorate)	2	Both	56 (6)
USSR	Automatic	Special polling stations in hospitals, railway stations, long distance trains; constituency transfer	No	1	Rest	99 (5)[c]
United Kingdom	Automatic	Proxy voting for armed forces, Crown servants abroad, those outside UK because of employment; postal votes permitted for sick and infirm, those away for business reasons	No	1	Work	75 (7)
United States	Application	Postal vote permitted under constitutions which vary among the states	No	1	Work	47 (12)[d]
Venezuela	Application		Yes	1	Rest	92 (5)

[a] Presidential elections. Number in parentheses is the number of elections on which the average is based.
[b] Sunday only since 1991.
[c] Voters requesting "absentee certificates" are not counted as non-voters, whether or not they actually vote. One estimate puts the true turnout at 75%–80%. See Stephen White, "Non-competitive Elections and National Politics: The USSR Supreme Soviet Elections of 1964," *Electoral Studies* 4 (1985), 215–29.
[d] Based on voting age population.

TABLE 13.3 Percentage of population eligible to vote by decade.

Country	1810	1820	1830	1840	1850	1860	1870	1880	1890	1900	1910	1920	1930	1940	1950	1960	1970	1980
Argentina[a]										20	'12 13	16	17	18	51	50	56	62
Austria						5.9	5.9	'80 5.9, '85 7.7	'90 7.7, '95 7.2		'10 20, '19 54	59	62	'45 50, '49 64	66	68	67	70
Belgium	1.4	1.4	1.1	'40 1.1, '48 1.8	2.0	2.2	2.2	2.2	'90 2.2, '93 22	22	'10 22, '19 28	30	32	'46 32, '49 65	65	65	65	70
Canada									27	22	25	50	52	58	55	52	61	66
Chile[a]											'15 5, '18 10	12	10	12	'50 14, '52 18	'60 24, '63 33	'70 36, '73 42	
Denmark					15	15	15	16	17	17	'13 17, '18 40	'20 39, '20 49	55	59	61	65	69	74
Finland	(7)	(7)	(7)	(7)	(6)	(5)	(5)	(5)	(5)	'00 4.4, '07 4.5	46	48	51	60	60	61	'70 68, '75 80	67
France	.03	.3	.4	'46 .7, '48 25	25	25	27	27	28	29	29	28	28	62	61	59	'70 58, '78 64	67
Germany							'70 19, '74 20	20	21	21	'12 19, '14 61	62	67	63	65	65	68	71

Country																				
Italy	3.9	3.9	2.1	2.1	*'80* 6.9 *'85* 2.2	*'90* 9.0 *'95* 6.7	7.8	*'13* 27 *'19* 24	30	—	61	64	67	72	77					
Japan						1.1	2.0	2.9	*'20* 5.5 *'28* 20	20	51	55	*'67* 68 *'69* 60	*'71* 61 *'72* 68	70					
Netherlands	3.5	2.5	2.6	3.0	*'80* 3.1 *'88* 3.1	*'94* 6.3 *'97* 12	13	*'13* 23 *'18* 15	47	51	55	56	58	*'71* 61 *'72* 68	72					
New Zealand			7.5		*'82* 6.4 *'85* 5.2	*'90* 34 *'93* 49	52	56	55	59	61	59	54	*'72* 55 *'75* 66	65					
Norway	10	9.5	9.1	8.3	7.8	*'91* 6.9 *'94* 8.9	*'06* 19 *'09* 32	*'12* 44 *'15* 33	52	57	64	66	65	69	74					
South Africa	(9)	(8)	7.7	5.7	5.9	6.3	8.1	5.7	5.9	11	11	10	10	9	9					
Sweden	7.1	6.9	5.8	7.7	5.9	*'90* 23 *'96* 28	8.1	19	*'20* 20 *'21* 56	61	66	67	67	71	74					
Switzerland	22	22	22	22	22	16	26	23	26	28	30	29	27	59	63					
United Kingdom	*'31* 1.8 *'32* 2.6	3.5	3.7	4.0	*'66* 3.5 *'69* 6.4	*'83* 16 *'85* 7.4	16	*'10* 48 *'18* 17	*'24* 63 *'29* 48	66	68	68	67	72	75					

Sources: Italicized data are from Robert Justin Goldstein, "Political Repression and Political Development: The 'Human Rights' Issue in Nineteenth Century Europe," *Comparative Social Research* 4 (1981), 170. Data in parentheses are identified as "estimates . . . [to] be regarded as correct within a 25 percent margin of error." Other data are derived directly from official election records and population estimates. Data for Argentina and Chile are from Ronald H. McDonald and J. Mark Ruhl, *Party Politics and Elections in Latin America* (Boulder: Westview Press, 1989), pp. 192, 160.
[a] Percentage registered.

the 1970s. The American decision to lower the voting age is illustrative. Although the idea had been raised many times in the past, and indeed adopted in four states, the real catalyst for change was the student unrest engendered by the Civil Rights Movement and the war in Vietnam. Supporters raised three major arguments: that mass education had made 18-year-olds competent; that 18 was generally recognized as the age of majority for such things as criminal law, marriage, and military service; and that student unrest reflected a feeling of exclusion from the normal political process.[18] While the linking of the rights of citizenship to military service dates at least to Athens and Rome, the idea that dissenters might be coopted, or at least contained, by extending to them the right to vote mirrors the nineteenth-century argument that workers with votes would be less dangerous than workers without votes. Moreover, extension of the right to vote to students was not one of their primary demands, and in this too the 1970–1971 American reform mirrors earlier reforms both in the United States and in Europe, in which the suffrage was extended to preempt potentially revolutionary agitation and to bind previously marginal citizens more firmly to the system rather than in direct response to irresistible pressure.[19]

Impediments and Incentives to Voting

Having the right to vote is not the same as exercising that right. Some people fail to vote for reasons beyond their control—illness, failure of transportation. Others may make a principled decision not to vote, to protest against all the candidates, for example. Whether citizens *ought* to be given the freedom to make this choice is open to debate, but there is strong evidence that actual rates of voting can be influenced significantly by a number of policy choices that affect the ease of, and incentives for, voting. Most prominent among these are the procedures for registration of voters, the provisions made for voters who will be away from their ordinary polling places on election day, and, from the other direction, provisions making voting legally obligatory. In addition, electoral formula itself may have an important bearing on citizens' decisions whether to vote.

Registration of Voters

An electoral register is one of the prerequisites for fair and efficient administration of elections. As Mackenzie observes, a register is vital for three reasons. First, its preparation allows the timely adjudication of disputes regarding eligibility. Second, it allows the allocation of voters to the proper constituencies. Third, an accurate register is an important resource for party organization.[20]

Registration of voters was introduced in France in 1791 as one of the innovations of the French Revolution and in Britain by the Reform Act of 1832. The first registration law in the United States, enacted in Massachusetts in 1800, required the assessors in every town or plantation to prepare lists of qualified voters.[21] In 1989, voter registration was required in at least part of every state except North Dakota.

Registration often was introduced to control fraud (illustrated in extreme form by the 1876 election in South Carolina, in which 101% of the voting age population turned out), but often merely served as a cloak for it. When personal registration was not required, politicians might "hand in long lists of names to be registered, often of persons who had long since died or moved away, or fictitious names."[22] The introduction of personal registration was intended to curb these abuses, as well as the original problems of personation and repeat voting, but, although elections generally are more honest today, abuses clearly remain.[23]

If registration is a prerequisite to fair elections, however, it is also an impediment to voting. In the United States, the most frequently given reason for failure to vote is failure to be registered.[24] Looking at American registration laws as they existed in 1972, Wolfinger and Rosenstone estimated that turnout would be increased 9.1% if (1) the closing date were eliminated, (2) registration offices were uniformly open during normal business hours, (3) registration offices were open at least some Saturdays or evenings, and (4) absentee registration were permitted.[25] Other estimates, however, suggest that this one is too optimistic. Noting that 1988 turnout in Wisconsin and Minnesota was lower than before the introduction of election day registration and that turnout was only up 0.1% over 1984 in Colorado, although driver's license registration had increased registration by 13%, Curtis Gans estimates that turnout might be increased by six to eight million (at most, 6.3%) "if the remaining registration barriers were removed."[26]

Complicated and time-consuming registration and voting procedures have also depressed participation in Latin America. Even where the law nominally calls for permanent registration, changes in regime or requirements may require reregistration of the entire electorate, as in Mexico in 1952, 1955, and 1958, or Ecuador in 1968. Before 1962, Chilean voters could only register on eight days each month, and that only during a two-hour period.[27]

Roughly 70% to 75% of the otherwise eligible voters in the United States are registered.[28] In Mexico in the 1950s, the figure was between 67% and 85% (with the latter figure predating the enfranchisement of women, and a figure of 80% achieved in 1958 only after a massive registration drive in which the deadline was extended twice).[29] In contrast, estimates for Europe and Canada suggest that between 90% and 99% of eligible voters are registered. One difference is that registration of voters in Europe and Canada generally is the responsibility of the government rather than of the citizens themselves. In Canada, registration takes the form of a door-to-door canvass once the election is called; it is estimated that 95% of the eligible electorate are registered. Britain similarly uses a door-to-door canvass (with forms left if no one is at home), but on an annual schedule; the register is estimated to be 97% accurate when new, but this figure naturally diminishes over the course of the year. Sweden, Finland, Italy, and Germany derive their voter registers from an annual administrative census of all individuals within local government areas. Although not the only administrative difference, it contributes to American presidential turnout—about 50%–55% of the voting age population—that averages between 15% and 32% below turnout (as a proportion of registered voters) in every other major democracy without compulsory voting except

Switzerland and India, and of course even farther below those in which voting is compulsory. Although the French registration system is quite similar to that of the United States, French turnout has been roughly 20% higher (see table 13.2).

Does Voting Make a Difference?

While not a direct impediment or inducement to voting, electoral formula affects the percentage of voters in a position to feel that their votes will make a difference to the outcome. Where turnout is low in Latin America, it often is attributed to belief that fraud rather than popular preferences will determine the result. In an extreme case of rendering elections nearly irrelevant (intraparty voting continued to play a role in determining precisely who was elected) the Liberals and Conservatives in Colombia formed a pact to alternate the presidency while dividing the congress equally; turnout dropped from 68.0% in the first election under the pact (1958) to a low of 33.4% in 1978.[30] Although plurality and majority electoral systems are more responsive than PR in the aggregate sense that smaller changes in marginal vote distributions are associated with larger changes in seat distributions, at the individual level only those voters who live in marginal districts are likely to feel that their votes are effective. Among PR systems, the higher the effective district magnitude, the more each voter is likely to feel effective in influencing the outcome. If people vote in order to influence the result, this potential for feeling efficacious should be positively related to voter turnout. Blais and Carty, for example, found that after a variety of institutional and intervening variables were controlled, turnout in plurality elections averaged 11.2%, in single-member majority elections 5.7%, and in multimember majority elections 3.0%, below the average for PR.[31] They, however, make no distinction among district magnitudes for PR elections.

Compulsory Voting

In extreme form, a country can encourage turnout by making voting compulsory, as in Belgium, Greece, and Liechtenstein, as well as in three provinces of Austria (in the whole country for presidential elections) and four cantons of Switzerland, and in the Netherlands until 1970. For all practical purposes, voting is also compulsory in Italy (although there are no criminal sanctions, the constitution describes voting as "a civic duty" and a nonvoter's identity papers are so stamped). Elsewhere, voting is also compulsory in Australia and much of Latin America.[32] Often, exceptions are made for the very old (e.g., those over 70 in Greece), the very young (e.g., under 18 in the Philippines), those who live a great distance from the polls (e.g., more than 200 km in Greece), and in the early days of women's suffrage in Latin America for women as well. Even though sanctions are rarely imposed, comparison of turnout before and after the introduction (or in the Dutch case, the repeal) of compulsory voting suggests that this provision increases turnout by at least 10%.[33]

A *Quantitative Test*

The question of whether such institutional decisions influence rates of participation is addressed in table 13.4, which reports a regression analysis explaining parliamentary turnout in 460 elections (weighted as described in chapter 9) in 19 countries. Because the decision to cast a vote is likely to be influenced by culture (unlike the more mechanical translation of votes into seats), this analysis was restricted to western democracies (the countries and time period considered by Blais and Carty, with the exclusion of Japan both because of its nonwestern culture and its unique electoral system). The explanatory variables considered are:

- *COMPULS:* Coded 1 for countries with compulsory voting, 0 for those countries without compulsory voting, and as the appropriate fraction where voting is compulsory in only part of the country (i.e., Austria and Switzerland);
- *PLUR, MAJ:* Dummy variables, coded 1 for elections conducted under plurality (PLUR) or majority, including alternative vote, (MAJ) electoral formulas, 0 otherwise;
- *MAG:* Effective district magnitude in PR systems, 0 otherwise;

TABLE 13.4 Explanation of turnout

	Elections through 1918	Elections 1919 through 1944	Elections 1945 through 1985	Full set of elections
COMPULS	.161	.211	.083	.160
	(.056)	(.021)	(.012)	(.012)
PLUR	−.061	.0005	−.083	−.047
	(.039)*	(.023)*	(.013)	(.013)
MAJ	−.026	.005	.031	−.033
	(.032)*	(.027)*	(.016)*	(.012)
MAG	.00068	.00020	.00009	.00015
	(.001)*	(.0001)	(.00003)	(.00004)
NOTGOVT	−.074	−.082	−.124	−.092
	(.024)	(.025)	(.014)	(.012)
PROPERTY	.037			−.0003
	(.027)*			(.018)*
MALSUFF	−.031	−.079		−.064
	(.042)*	(.030)		(.019)
GENDER	−.042	.018	−.054	−.069
	(.050)*	(.013)*	(.024)	(.012)
FEMSUFF	−.069	.013	−.068	−.092
	(.068)*	(.032)*	(.018)	(.017)
NONEXPED	−.096			−.095
	(.042)			(.031)
NZ	.095	.173	.139	.103
	(.051)*	(.038)	(.020)	(.020)
Constant	.698	.738	.790	.735
	(.035)	(.021)	(.024)	(.013)
R^2	.29	.65	.62	.58
N	128	104	228	460

Numbers in parentheses are standard errors.
* Not significantly different from 0 at $p < .05$.

- *NOTGOVT*: Coded 1 for those elections that do not determine government composition, 0 otherwise;
- *PROPERTY, MALSUFF*: These variables allow for the effect of the introduction of manhood suffrage. PROPERTY is a dummy variable coded 1 if there were substantial property qualifications for voting. MALSUFF models drop in turnout following the expansion of the suffrage, followed by a 20-year (for simplicity, linear) reduction in this effect;[34]
- *GENDER, FEMSUFF*: Like PROPERTY and MALSUFF, these variables control for the introduction of female suffrage;
- *NONEXPED*: Coded 1 for Italian elections during the period in which Catholics were ordered by the papacy not to participate in Italian elections;
- *NZ*: Coded 1 for New Zealand, 0 otherwise, reflecting the fact that New Zealand appears as an outlier.[35]

The table presents the results of regressions run separately for three time periods (pre-World War I, interwar years, post-World War II), as well as for the full set of elections. Although there is some stability in the relationships observed over time, the interwar years appear anomalous for both electoral formula and female suffrage.

If one looks first at the variables reflecting the expansion of suffrage, the results regarding property qualifications are about as one would expect given modern survey results showing socioeconomic status positively correlated with voting. When the Vatican dropped its ban on electoral participation by Catholics, expected Italian turnout rose almost 10%. The elimination of substantial property requirements resulted in an immediate drop in predicted turnout percentage of between 6% and 8% compared to similar systems that had not had such requirements for at least 20 years, with this gap gradually being closed, presumably as the new voters were integrated into the political system. A comparable effect was expected for the introduction of female suffrage, and as reflected by FEMSUFF, it was indeed found. The sign of the coefficient for GENDER was the opposite of that expected, on the basis both of survey research (since women have been found to vote less than men, systems in which women were excluded from the electorate should have had higher turnout rates) and of previous analogous research (Blais and Carty report a drop in turnout of 6.4% associated with the introduction of female suffrage). There are two explanations. First, the joint effect of the two female suffrage variables is, in fact, a prediction that the immediate effect of introducing votes for women is to reduce turnout, although far less than the elimination of property requirements. Here one sees some evidence that women were already better connected to electoral politics when they were enfranchised than male members of the working class had been. Second, there is a problem of making causal interpretations on the basis of cross-sectional data. Rather than indicating that the introduction of female suffrage ultimately raises turnout, GENDER may indicate that female suffrage was introduced first into systems that already had high turnout; this is certainly the case in the third period, in which GENDER is based almost exclusively on the low-turnout Swiss case.

Turning to the variables that reflect the likely impact of voting, parliamentary turnout is predicted to be between 7% and 13% lower in systems in which parliamentary elections do not primarily determine government composition. Turnout is lower in systems using majority formulas than in those using PR and lower still in systems using plurality formulas (although the estimated effects are considerably smaller than those reported by Blais and Carty, and depend, as do theirs, on the introduction of a dummy variable to account for the unusually high turnout in New Zealand). Among the PR systems, turnout tends to increase with increases in district magnitude. In each case, the more effective a vote is likely to be, the higher the percentage of potential voters expected to go to the polls.

Turnout and Democracy

All democratic theories regard spontaneously high turnout as desirable. The degree to which turnout should be stimulated by reducing barriers or catering to the disinterested, or even more by compulsion. is another question. There are both normative and political reasons for taking all sorts of measures to increase turnout, but since, with a few exceptions, the arguments pertinent to compulsory voting apply to more voluntaristic policies as well, the discussion can focus on the former.

One argument is that voting is a duty of citizenship. If elections are to discover the will of the people, the overwhelming majority (ideally all) of the citizens must express themselves; no one who withheld his or her opinion before a decision was made should retain the right to grumble about it afterwards. Alternatively, if the purpose of elections is the civic and moral education of the voters, then adult citizens are no more entitled to absent themselves from the polls than their children are to miss school. Like other rituals of community membership, voting is an obligation that can be enforced by social sanctions, but if one accepts the argument that the polity is or ought to be a community, then the distinction between legal and social spheres evaporates, and criminal law can be used to enforce turnout.

Even if compulsory voting is not justified, the removal of disincentives to voting may be. By making voting "cheaper," one lowers the threshold that the damage to an individual must exceed before it becomes cost-effective (the basic calculus of the liberal model) to use the ballot box in self-defense. Since substantial aggregate harm can be done by inflicting small harms on large numbers of people, this need not be a trivial concern. Carried one step farther, and applying the reasoning of Olson's *Logic of Collective Action*,[36] one can develop a liberal argument for compulsory voting. Because the chance that a single vote will alter the outcome of an election is trivial, it is never cost-effective for a single individual to vote. But if no one voted, democracy would collapse and, short of that, many interests would go unprotected because the expected benefit for a single individual would never exceed the cost of voting, and individuals would not be able to organize to protect their aggregate and collective interest through collective action. Therefore, rational liberal individuals might choose to be coerced to vote so long as they were assured that others would be coerced as well in order to achieve the benefits of collective action.[37]

Compulsory voting is to the advantage of those parties and groups whose supporters otherwise would have the lowest turnout rates. From a sociological point of view, it is thus to the advantage of parties representing the urban poor and rural areas. Because it obviates the need for "get-out-the-vote" efforts, compulsory voting is to the advantage of the least well-organized. Finally, given the tendency for turnout to be depressed, especially for the expected losers, when the outcome of an election seems certain, compulsory voting is to the advantage of the less popular—an advantage that is symbolically important when the vote (rather than the seat) totals are interpreted, but that may be practically important as well if factors like ballot access for subsequent elections or state subventions depend on vote shares received.

Compulsory voting also may be introduced to allow unpopular parties or regimes to prevent popular disaffection from being manifested by derisory turnout rates. The danger of this was raised in an early (and unsuccessful) challenge to compulsory voting in Australia.[38] More recently it has been argued that "in Paraguay mandatory voting enable[d] Stroessner to claim that he [was] a popularly elected, legitimate leader."[39] Even when elections are free, both legal and practical barriers to the entry of new candidates may leave some voters perceiving their choice to be only among degrees of evil. Given a choice, many might decide to stay home, confronting the established parties with evidence of their unpopularity. When voting is compulsory, there is no way to tell a coerced choice among evils from a voluntarily expressed positive preference. Where barriers to entry are low, compulsory voting may increase the embarrassment of established but unpopular parties. Thus the abolition of compulsory voting was supported by all the major parties in the Netherlands because of the rise of splinter parties, coupled with the feeling that the voters of the splinter parties were the disaffected who would simply stay home if voting were not obligatory.

Opponents of compulsion see voting as a right or privilege, rather than a duty. While this view is compatible with a desire to lower the barriers to voting (what good is it to give a person a privilege and then make its exercise prohibitively costly?), for one to talk meaningfully about the *right* to vote, one must also allow the right to refrain from voting. Similarly, while the law may compel attendance at the polls, it cannot compel citizens to have preferences or opinions, so that if votes are to be interpreted as expressions of preference, those with no preference must be allowed to remain silent. On logical grounds, this leads to rejection of claims of legitimacy based on high, but coerced, vote totals. Such arguments can also be questioned on practical grounds; it is highly questionable whether regime opponents are, in fact, taken in by the resulting propaganda. If rulers are lulled into a false sense of security, compulsory expressions of support actually may be self-defeating, encouraging or allowing those in power to ignore signs of popular discontent. Finally, one may observe (as did the Australian courts) that citizens are not in fact compelled to vote; they are merely compelled to attend at the polls and in some cases also to take and deposit a ballot. They retain the freedom to protest by defacing or spoiling the ballot or depositing it unmarked, and indeed the percentage of spoiled ballots generally is higher in systems with compulsory voting than it is elsewhere.

If voting is a right, then compulsion would be justified in liberal terms only if failure to vote would impose substantial costs on others. But one could well argue that far from imposing costs, abstainers actually increase the political influence of those who do choose to vote. If electoral decisions were, as advocated by some communitarians, openly made after common deliberation, compelling participation *might* contribute to the wisdom of electoral decisions by assuring the contribution of "all the latent force of discernment and knowledge in the State."[40] When decisions are made instead by individuals who are compelled only to vote privately, but not to share their views publicly, the quality of decisions is unlikely to be enhanced by the random contributions of the ignorant and the uninterested. The same approach also leads opponents of compulsory voting to ask whether discovery of the popular will is, in fact, furthered by the voices of those who have no real opinions.

As for the moral and political education of the citizens or the development of community, the question is whether these aims can be achieved by compulsion. Clearly, the best test would be a comparison of citizens before and after the introduction or abolition of compulsory voting. In practical terms, this means a comparison of pre- and post-1970 Dutch citizens. Based on such a comparison in 66 quarters of Amsterdam that showed significant demographic change among those voting but little aggregate political change, Otto Schmidt concluded:

> The people who voted regularly before 1970 but failed to do so after the abolition of the compulsory vote, were disproportionately uninterested and uninformed about politics. Their party choice (before 1970), therefore, was disproportionately influenced by random factors: e.g. they cast their ballot [for] the party that happened to be on top of the voting-paper, or [for] that candidate whose name resembled the name of a relative, etc. These "voting explanations" may seem far-fetched, but one should remember that a sizable minority of the eligible voters simply do not possess the information which is needed in order to make a reasoned choice. . . . [41]

If this interpretation is correct, one must conclude that compulsory voting when in force did little to contribute to the civic education of Dutch voters.

Candidacy

Regulation of candidacy is forced by the conflict of democratic ideals and reality. The ideal is free and unfettered competition among all comers. The attractions are obvious. Voters are given maximal choice. No restrictions limit the involvement either of ordinary citizens or of would-be candidates. Choices are made by the current citizenry, rather than by government officials or former legislators. The problems, however, are equally obvious. Without some way of identifying candidates, the vote might be meaninglessly fragmented. Unfettered competition, far from being fair, may perpetuate (and magnify) the advantages (like private wealth) that some candidates enjoy, to say nothing of the possibilities of deceit and intimidation.

As this scenario suggests, controls over candidates fall into two main types. The first concerns the requirements to be recognized as a candidate. Whose names (whether of parties or of individual candidates) appear on the ballot? Where the state provides resources to parties or candidates, who is eligible for support and how is the support allocated? The second type are restrictions on the campaign activities of candidates and their supporters and most often concern the raising and spending of money, but they can include prohibitions of a variety of "corrupt practices" as well.

Requirements for Candidacy

Qualifications for Office

One set of requirements for candidacy mirrors the standards of community membership, competence, and autonomy imposed for suffrage. Table 14.1 gives the legal requirements of these types for candidacy or election to the national parliaments of a number of countries. As comparison of this table and table 13.1 shows, while these requirements generally follow those for voting, they frequently have been stricter. Thus, while voters for the U.S. House of Representatives are required only to be citizens over 18, candidates (members) must have been citizens for five years and be over 25. Similarly, while there are no religious tests for voting in Argentina, the president is required to be a member of the Roman Catholic Church (article 76, Constitution). On the other hand, in some cases the requirements for office were *less* strict than those for voting. For example, from 1866 through 1915, the minimum age for election to the Danish Folketing was 25, although voters were required to be at least 30.

Since requirements of this type reflect the same concerns as those underlying restrictions on the right to vote, they need little further discussion here beyond the observation that one might well impose higher standards on those who would manage the affairs of others than on those who are acting for themselves. In particular, the criterion of autonomy assumes heightened importance. On one hand, representatives should not be so autonomous that they may ignore the wishes of the voters, although at the same time they should not be so dependent on their political jobs that they can never afford to take risks or stand up to short-term trends in public opinion. On the other hand, representatives should not be controlled by anyone other than the voters (delegate theory of representation) or their own judgment of the public interest (trustee theory). Thus prejudice against the election of Roman Catholics to office in the United States or Northern Ireland has been justified by claims that their decisions would be dictated by their bishops rather than by the people.

The holding of more than one office or certain combinations of offices is often prohibited. Historically, these limitations were intended to prevent the executive from buying the support of the people's representatives with jobs in the public service. Similar exclusions are also justified by separation of powers. On the other hand, while some combinations of offices are prohibited, others are quite common, such as the cumulation of local and national office in France.

Qualifications for office differ from qualifications for voting in one additional respect: where suffrage qualifications restrict only *who* may decide, qualifications for candidacy restrict the freedom of those deciders with regard to *what* they may decide. Having restricted the electorate to those who are sufficiently involved, competent, autonomous, and responsible, one may ask whether their freedom of choice need be further restricted. One answer is fear that the people will be led astray by a demagogue and so need to be protected from themselves. Another is belief that the people can be trusted to choose their leaders only if that choice is restricted to the "responsible" classes of society. Both arguments are undermined, however, by the frequency with which demagogues and the leaders of subversive movements in fact come from the privileged classes.

Fear that the "wrong" people may be elected leads in the most extreme case to outright bans on the candidacy or election of classes or parties holding or presumed to hold "subversive" views. From the time of the Reformation into the nineteenth century, religious tests—often in the form of an oath that members of the "out" religion would find abhorrent—were the most common. More recently, the idea of "protective democracy" has been embodied in the provision of the German basic law banning antidemocratic parties. Similarly, the electoral laws of nine American states explicitly bar the Communist Party of the United States

TABLE 14.1 Requirements for candidacy or office.

	Age	Residence and citizenship	Disqualifications	Incompatible offices
Argentina	Senate: 30 Chamber of Deputies: 25	Born in constituency or resident at least 2 years Senate: 6 years citizenship Chamber of Deputies: 4 years citizenship	None	Membership in provincial or ministerial assemblies; provincial governors; practicing lawyers; clergymen in Catholic orders
Australia	18	3 years in country; British subject	Insolvency; criminal offenses; allegiance to foreign power	Membership in state legislature; public servants; public contractors
Austria	21	Residence required	Criminal offenses; legal incapacity	Federal president; members of Constitutional Court, Supreme Court, Administrative Court; president and vice president of Court of Audit; executives of corporations, banking, commerce, etc. if so decided by relevant Council committee
Belgium	Senate: 40 Chamber of Representatives: 25	Residence in Belgium; Belgian by birth or full naturalization	Criminal offenses; insanity	Membership in provincial council; salaried government office other than Minister; public officials paid by state; ministers of religious sects subsidized by state; lawyers in public service; agents of state bank; inspectors of limited companies
Bolivia	Deputy: 25 Senator: 35	Bolivian by birth	Must have fulfilled military obligation; insanity; criminal conviction	Minister, diplomatic agent, civil servant or employee, military or police officer on active duty, contractor for public works or services, official of state-related company or enterprise; some church officials

Brazil	21	Nationality and residence within state	Insanity; criminal conviction; illiteracy	Membership in other assemblies; ministers; government or public office; directors of banks or state-owned companies
Canada	18	None		Membership of Senate or provincial assemblies; sheriff; registrar of deeds; clerk of the peace or county or crown attorney; chief electoral officer; assistant chief electoral officer; returning officers of each district; judges appointed by governor in council
Colombia	House of Representatives: 25 Senate: 35	Senate: Colombian by birth and have held high office or undertaken a liberal profession with a university degree	Criminal conviction	
Costa Rica	21	10 years residence, not necessarily in constituency	Under detention; relatives of President of the Republic; illiteracy	Ministers; Supreme Court justices; Supreme Tribunal of Election; president of the Republic; public servant; members of police services; military on active service; director of civil registrar; any other elective office
Denmark	18	Residence in country	Conviction of activities unworthy of a member of the Folketing	None
Ecuador	25	Provincial candidates must be natives of, or have resided 3 years in, province	Loss of civil rights	Government posts and offices connected with public sector, armed forces on active duty, public contractor, banker, clergy, legal representative of foreign company
Finland	18	None	Electoral offenses; under tutelage	Chancellor of justice and deputy; members of Supreme Court; members of armed forces on active service; ombudsman and deputy

(continued)

TABLE 14.1 (continued)

	Age	Residence and citizenship	Disqualifications	Incompatible offices
Fiji	21	None	Insanity; insolvency; criminal conviction	Public servants; electoral offence with previous 3 years; public contractors
France	23	10 years citizenship; no residency requirement	Loss of eligibility by judicial decision; failure to have completed military service	Ministers; ombudsman; prefects, deputy prefects, heads of administrative services of state or department in constituencies where they have exercised their functions; members of armed forces, Constitutional Council, Economic and Social Council, Supreme Broadcasting Authority; holders of public functions under foreign states and officials of international organizations; public servants; executive of state enterprises, state-assisted companies, savings and credit organizations, companies holding government contracts and real estate companies
Germany	18	No residency requirement; German citizenship for at least 1 year	Deprivation of voting rights; mental deficiency; legal incapacity or guardianship	Federal president; judges; public servants; members of armed forces
Greece	25	None	Persons legally disenfranchised	Members of other assemblies (except first 2 members of European Parliament for each party); members of board, directors, or governors of public or semi-public enterprises; members of armed or police forces, certain public officials, notaries, registrars of mortgages

	Age	Residency	Disqualifications	Incompatible offices
Iceland	18			
India	25	5 years in Iceland	Criminal conviction Undischarged bankrupts	Supreme Court judges Members of defense forces, government contractors; offices of profit under government
Ireland	21		Criminal conviction; unsound mind; bankruptcy	President; comptroller and auditor general; judges; members of defense or police force on full pay; public servants; chairman or director of semi-state body
Israel	21		Criminal conviction	President of state, state comptroller; salaried rabbis; judges; senior public servants; army officers must leave positions at least 100 days before election
Italy	Senate: 40 Chamber of Deputy: 25	None	Insanity; criminal conviction; illiteracy	Regional deputies or councillors; presidents of regional commissions; regional governors; government representatives for Sicily and Sardegna; mayors of towns over 20,000; senior police officers; senior public servants; senior officers of armed forces in constituency where they hold office; public contractors or officers of subsidized organizations; office directly or indirectly remunerated by state
Jamaica	21	Commonwealth citizen resident in Jamaica for 12 months	Insanity; bankruptcy; owing allegiance to a foreign state; criminal conviction	Public officers; judges of highest courts; persons linked to government contracts; members of defense forces; election officials

(continued)

TABLE 14.1 (continued)

	Age	Residence and citizenship	Disqualifications	Incompatible offices
Japan	House of Councillors: 30 House of Representatives: 25	None	Criminal conviction; legal incapacity	Public servants; officers of public corporations
Luxembourg	21	In Luxembourg	Criminal conviction; bankruptcy; keepers of disorderly houses	Members of council of state; ministers; district commissioners; receivers of public monies; magistrates of the judicial order; members of audit office; members of armed forces on active service; public servants; primary school teachers; ministers of state-supported religions
Malaysia	21	In Malaysia	Illiteracy; insanity; bankruptcy; criminal conviction; acquired citizenship of another country	Office of profit under government; public office (presiding officers may not exercise a private profession)
Malta	18	In Maltese Islands for 6 of last 18 months	Bankruptcy; insanity; legal incapacity; criminal conviction	Public office; members of armed forces
Mauritius	18	Commonwealth citizen resident in Mauritius 2 years prior to nomination	Undischarged bankrupts; insanity; criminal conviction; ability to read and speak English required	Owing allegiance to state outside the Commonwealth; public or local government officers; undisclosed government contractors
Mexico	Senator: 30 Deputy: 21	6 months in state		Public and parastatal bodies; public or local government officers; contractors to government
Netherlands	21		Criminal conviction; mental disability	Ministers; members of council of state, general board of auditors; judges and prosecutors of Supreme Court; clerk and staff of either chamber; military on active service

Country	Age	Residence	Disqualifications	Incompatible offices
New Zealand	21		Oath of allegiance to or acquisition of citizenship of a foreign state; criminal conviction; mental disability	Public servants; holders of public office; Crown agents for land purchases
Norway	18	10 years residence in Norway, but not necessarily resident at time of election	Insanity; criminal conviction	Ministers; diplomatic post; public office in government depts and at court
Philippines	House of Representatives: 25 Senate: 35	Natural born citizen House of Representatives: 1 year residence in district Senate: 2 years residence in Philippines	Illiteracy; conviction for rebellion, sedition, crimes against national security	Public appointive office except government members; employment in any government-owned instrumentality, including government-controlled corporations. No member of Congress may act as legal counsel or be a government contractor
Portugal	18	No residence requirement; citizens with dual citizenship may not be candidates in constituency adjacent to nation of second citizenship	Insanity; judicial deprivation of political rights	Ministers; ambassadors; ombudsman; head of regional government; magistrates; state public servants; armed forces on active service; director of a public institute; head of minister's office; member of national electoral commission; minister of religion
South Africa	18	5 years in Republic	Unsound mind; insolvency; criminal conviction	Local public office; justice of peace; members of defense force on active service
Spain	18	None		High state administrative office; constitutional court; electoral commission; ombudsman; magistrates, judges, public prosecutors; members of defense, security and police forces
Sri Lanka	18	None	Insanity; bankruptcy; criminal conviction	President of republic; judges; certain state officers; parliamentary staff; commissioner of elections; public service commission; auditor general; armed and police forces

(continued)

TABLE 14.1 (continued)

	Age	Residence and citizenship	Disqualifications	Incompatible offices
Sweden	18	None		Ministers
Switzerland	National Council: 20	None	Insanity or feeble-mindedness; holders of foreign decorations	Ministers; government office in some cantons; federal public servants; federal judges; prosecutors, members of high courts, university professors, public officials, members of armed forces
Turkey	30		Completion of primary education and compulsory military service required; insanity; prisoners	Judges, prosecutors, members of high courts, university professors, public officials, members of armed forces
USSR	21	None	Insanity	None
United Kingdom	21		Insanity; bankruptcy; criminal conviction	Membership of House of Lords or legislature outside the Commonwealth; offices of profit under the Crown
United States	Senate: 30 House of Representatives: 25	Resident in state Senate: 9 years citizenship House of Representatives: 7 years citizenship		Federal government officials (including cabinet); holders of public office
Uruguay	Chamber of Representatives: 25 Senate: 30	Chamber of Representatives: Citizen by birth or naturalized at least 5 years Senate: Citizen by birth or naturalized at least 7 years	Loss of civil rights	Judges, prosecuting attorneys, police officials, military officers in constituencies where hold offices; directors of national enterprises; members of military or university instructors given leave of absence during term in Congress
Zimbabwe	21	Resident in Zimbabwe for 5 of last 20 years	Insanity; mental incapacity; criminal conviction	Public office except ministers and deputy ministers; members of defense forces and reserves of police forces whose services are not wholly in the employ of the state

from presenting candidates, while 11 more bar "subversive" parties or parties advocating the violent overthrow of the government. While a democratic government must be able to defend itself against violent revolution, one may ask whether democracy does not require, as Rousseau asserted, that the people have the option to abolish that system if they so choose. Yet experience in both Germany and Italy clearly demonstrates that antidemocratic forces with far less than a legislative majority can have a corrosive influence much greater than their numbers alone would suggest.

Access to the Ballot

In practical terms, regulations intended to restrict ballot access to "serious" candidates are of three types. The first is demonstration of support by voters in the district that the candidate would like to represent. The second is payment of a filing fee or monetary deposit (the difference is that a deposit is returned to a candidate who polls above a specified share of the vote, while a filing fee simply is part of the cost of contesting the election). The final type is the nomination of a recognized political party. Each may be combined with the others, either as alternatives or to be met jointly.

Table 14.2 summarizes ballot access requirements for a number of countries. The table shows a significant difference between ballot access requirements in candidate-oriented and party-oriented systems, with access far more restricted in the former. At least two reasons may be suggested. On one hand, the "either you win or else you lose" nature of candidate-oriented elections, in contrast to the "fair shares" nature of PR, makes the former more vulnerable to distortion on the basis of votes cast for minor candidates. On the other hand, with their personal orientation, candidate-oriented systems may be more susceptible to "exhibitionist" candidacies.

Among non-American candidate-oriented systems, the primary barrier to "frivolous" candidacies is an electoral deposit. While the deposits required may be substantial for a party attempting to field a full slate of candidates, they are relatively insignificant for a party wishing to nominate candidates only in a few constituencies where it is particularly strong. Even after substantial recent increases in some countries, the deposits required still are insufficient to discourage a large number of candidates whose support is trivial. This point is illustrated in table 14.3, which shows for the UK, a country with one of the highest electoral deposits (nearly $900 U.S. at the then current exchange rate), that 289 candidates (roughly one eighth of the total) failed to achieve the required 5% of the vote and thus forfeited their deposits after the 1987 general election. Many candidates who lost their deposits did not even receive 1% of the vote and can be assumed to have contested the election in the full knowledge that they would lose the deposit as well as the election.

Table 14.3 also shows the numbers of candidates forfeiting their deposits in 1983 when the deposit was lower but the threshold to be crossed for its return was higher, as well as the numbers who would have forfeited their deposits at each election under the threshold rule in force for the other. Although the effects of

TABLE 14.2 Requirements for parliamentary ballot access.

	Requirements for recognition of candidacy	Deposit	Conditions for return
Australia	Petition of eligible voters	House of Representatives: A$250	Receipt of 4% of total 1st preference vote
		Senate: A$500	Membership in group receiving 4% of Senate vote[a]
Austria	Petition of 3 members of the national parliament or 200 voters (Burgenland, Kärnten, Salzburg, Tyrol, Vorarlberg), 400 voters (Oberösterreich, Steiermark), or 500 voters (Niederösterreich, Wien)	ÖS. 6,000	Not returned
Belgium	Signatures of 500 (Brussels), 400 (Antwerp, Ghent, Charleroi, Liege) or 200 (elsewhere) electors or three outgoing members	None	
Canada	Petition of 25 electors in the district. To have the name of a registered party appear on the ballot, written endorsement of the party leader is also required	C$200	Receipt of 15% of the vote
Denmark	Parties: Representation in the outgoing Folketing or petition of a number of voters equal to 1/175 of the total valid vote in the last election	None	
	Candidates: Petition of between 25 and 50 voters. Registered parties may refuse the candidacy of individuals, in which case they are regarded as independents		
Fiji	Nomination of 6 to 8 voters of constituency	F$ 100	Election or receipt of 10% of total votes cast in constituency
Finland	Petition of 100 electors	None	
France	President: Nomination by 500 elected officials from at least 30 departments	Parliament: FF 1,000	Receipt of 5% of the vote cast
	Parliament: Declaration of candidacy		

Country	Nomination requirement	Deposit	Forfeiture
Germany	Independents (single-member districts only): Petition of 200 registered voters	None	
	Candidates of parties represented by at least 5 members in either the Bundestag or relevant Landtag, or representing a national minority: In single-member seats: Signatures of the Land executive committee; for Land lists, signatures of Land executive committee.		
	Candidates of other parties: In single-member districts, signatures of the Land executive committee plus 200 registered voters; for Land lists, signatures of Land executive committee plus one per 1,000 persons entitled to vote at the last election to a maximum of 2,000		
Greece	Petition of 12 voters of the district	Dr. 20,000	Not returned
Guyana	Petition of no less than 200 nor more than 220 qualified voters	None	
India	Nomination by one qualified voter of the constituency other than the candidate	R 500 (R 250 for members of scheduled castes and tribes)	Election or receipt of one sixth of the vote
Ireland	Self-nomination or consent to nomination by any elector of the constituency	IR £ 100	Reaching one third of constituency quota
Israel	Representation in out-going Knesset or petition of 1,500 voters	500,000 shekels required of parties without representation in out-going Knesset	Receipt of 1% of the vote
Italy	Chamber of Deputies: Petition of between 500 and 1,000 electors	None	
Jamaica	Senate: Petition of between 350 and 700 electors; Petition of 10 qualified voters of the constituency	$100	Receipt of one eighth of the valid vote
Japan	Declaration of candidacy	¥2 million	House of Representatives: Receipt of one fifth of the valid vote divided by the number of members to be elected

TABLE 14.2 (continued)

	Requirements for recognition of candidacy	Deposit	Conditions for return
			House of Councillors: Receipt of one eighth of the valid vote divided by the number of members to be elected
Liechtenstein	Petition of 30 electors in constituency	None	
Luxembourg	Petition of 25 electors of the constituency	None	
Malaysia	Proposer and seconder of constituency	M$ 5,000	Receipt of one eighth of votes cast
Malta	Nomination by 4 voters of constituency	Equivalent of US$ 100	Receipt of votes equal to one tenth of total vote divided by number to be elected
Mauritius	Petition of 6 electors of constituency	Equivalent of US$ 25	Receipt of 10% of votes cast
Netherlands	Petition of 25 electors in every kieskring	Dfl 1,000 per election district list	Receipt of three quaters of the electoral quotient
New Zealand	Petition of 2 registered voters of the constituency	NZ$ 100	Receipt of one quarter the votes of the successful candidate
Norway	Lists may be submitted by 500 registered voters or by a registered party	None	
Spain	Nomination by registered party or petition of at least 0.1% (no less than 500) electors of constituency		
Sweden	Registered parties may submit lists of candidates. To register a party for Riksdag elections requires signatures of 1,500 voters. Parties with members are re-registered automatically	None	
Switzerland	Petition of 50 electors	None	
United Kingdom	Signatures of 2 proposers and 8 assentors	£ 500	Receipt of 5% of vote.[b]
Zimbabwe	Signatures of not less than 10 or more than 20 electors of the constituency	Z$100	Receipt of one fifth of vote received by successful candidate

[a] Prior to 1983, the deposit for House of Representatives candidates was $100 returnable on receipt of one fifth of the first preference votes received by the successful candidate and for Senate candidates $200 returnable on receipt of one tenth of the average first preference votes received by successful candidates, or if the group of candidates of which the individual was a member on average received one tenth of the average first preference votes of successful candidates. For both offices, nominating papers required the signatures of six electors of the constituency.

[b] Prior to 1985, the British deposit was £150, recoverable on receipt of 12.5% of the vote.

TABLE 14.3 Numbers of candidates and lost deposits, United Kingdom 1983 and 1987.

	1983 National vote	1983 Candidates	1983 Lost deposits (Under 12.5%)	1983 Lost deposits under post-1985 rule (5%)	1987 National vote	1987 Candidates	1987 Lost deposits	1987 Lost deposits under pre-1985 rule (12.5%)
Conservative	42.4	633	5 (0.8%)	0 (0%)	42.3	633	0 (0%)	12 (1.9%)
Liberal	13.7	322	5 (1.6%)	0 (0%)	12.8	327	1 (0.3%)	21 (6.4%)
Social Democrat	11.6	311	6 (1.9%)	0 (0%)	9.7	306	0 (0%)	30 (9.8%)
[Alliance]	[25.4]	[633]	[11 (1.7%)]	[0 (0%)]	[22.5]	[633]	[1 (0.2%)]	[51 (8.1%)]
Labour	27.6	633	119 (18.8%)	7 (1.1%)	30.8	633	0 (0%)	91 (14.4%)
Communist	0.04	35	35 (100%)	35 (100%)	0.02	19	19 (100%)	19 (100%)
Plaid Cymru	0.4	36	32 (88.9%)	24 (66.7%)	0.4	38	25 (65.8%)	28 (73.4%)
Scottish Nationalist	1.1	72	53 (73.6%)	5 (6.9%)	1.3	71	1 (1.4%)	40 (56.3%)
National Front	0.1	60	60 (100%)	60 (100%)				
Ecology/Green	0.2	108	108 (100%)	108 (100%)	0.3	133	133 (100%)	133 (100%)
Other (Great Britain)	0.6	282	270 (95.7%)	263 (93.3%)	0.1	88	87 (98.9%)	87 (98.9%)
Other (N. Ireland)	3.1	95	46 (48.4%)	30 (31.6%)	2.2	77	23 (29.9%)	35 (45.5%)
Total		2,579	739 (28.7%)	532 (20.6%)		2,325	289 (12.4%)	496 (21.3%)

threshold and amount cannot be separated fully, comparison of the 1983 and 1987 figures offers some insight into the workings of these barriers. Raising the amount of the deposit had a dramatic deterrent effect on candidates of subminor parties and independents, cutting their numbers by more than two thirds. Minor parties like the Communists, Ecologists, and Welsh nationalists, however, were little affected—they presented nearly as many candidates (in fact, somewhat more for the Ecologists/Greens and Plaid Cymru) with the higher deposits, notwithstanding having failed to achieve the 5% mark under the old system. At the same time, the difference in threshold had a significant impact on the number of deposits lost by the major parties, especially Labour, as well as by the Alliance parties and the Scottish Nationalists (SNP). Had the old threshold been in place in 1987, Labour nearly would have repeated its 1983 humiliation of losing over 100 deposits (which conversely would have been only 7 under the new threshold). Over half the SNP candidates would have lost their deposits, costing the party £20,000, instead of only one. In other words, the size of the deposit primarily affects the number of independent and fringe party candidates, while the threshold affects the cost of competition for small (and not-so-small) parties that will present candidates regardless.

The situation in the United States is quite different. Although requirements vary among the states, a number of generalizations are possible. Ballot access requirements generally have been designed on the premise that two-party competition is the ideal, and moreover that those two parties ought to be the two that currently dominate American politics. Thus they are given preferential treatment, while both third-party and independent candidacies actively are discouraged.

Most states make a significant distinction among major parties, minor parties, and new parties, echoing in greatly magnified form the bias in favor of major parties with regard to ballot placement. Although only North Dakota explicitly guarantees the Democratic and Republican parties access to the ballot by name, all states except Mississippi and South Carolina guarantee a place on the ballot to any party with a specified share of voter registration or of the vote at the previous election. In some cases these are nearly trivial, but in 27 states the requirement is at least 5% of the total vote cast, and in 11 of those the requirement is at least 10%. Many small parties cannot meet these requirements, and of course neither can any new party. For these, the only route to the ballot is by petition.

In comparison to other countries in which ballot access is controlled by nominating petitions, American parties and candidates are required to secure many more signatures. Often these must be collected within a narrowly defined time period, an inconsequential requirement when a few hundred names are involved but potentially insurmountable when talking about many thousands. Moreover, American nominating petitions may be subject to a dazzling array of technical requirements that make the number of signatures actually required far greater than that specified by the law. These requirements are particularly difficult for new parties, which have not had the benefit of a campaign in which to win converts in the first place. And when, as in Florida, a verification fee of 10 cents per signature is added to the requirement of petitions signed by 3% of registered voters, it is easy to understand why ballots in the resulting elections rarely include more than the two candidates whose positions are secured by their parties' previous voting strength.

Primary Elections as a Method of Nomination

Virtually all American major party nominations are, or can be, made by primary election. Especially after 1968, primary elections have come to dominate selection of presidential convention delegates, and thus presidential nomination as well. Particularly on the basis of this experience some critics have questioned the democratic desirability of presidential nomination by primary, but the problems raised are not relevant to that office alone.

A first problem is that the nominee chosen by primary may be supported by only a small minority of party activists or voters. One reason is that turnout in primary elections tends to be dismal, even in comparison to the low American general election turnout. Second, in part because of the ease of entry, primary elections frequently have more than two candidates. With four or five contestants, a run-off election offers no promise that the candidate ultimately chosen could defeat all (or any) of the candidates eliminated in the first round in head-to-head contests; without a run-off, the prospect of a candidate supported by only 30% or 35% of the voters emerging victorious is very real.

A second problem is that each of the primary electorates is atypical of the single general election electorate. If voters in the Democratic primary were trying to choose the Democratic candidate most likely to win the general election (and likewise for the Republicans), this might make little difference. But especially given the private nature of voting in mass elections, this expectation is unreasonable. Instead, primary voters generally choose the candidate they, as individuals, would most like to see elected. Thus, even if Democratic primary voters were typical of Democrats (and likewise for the Republicans), the result ought to be two candidates, neither of whom would be the choice of the whole electorate given an unrestricted field. While this problem is mitigated to some extent by the overlap of the electorates of the two parties, it worsens through the tendency of their primary electorates to be more extreme than their average general election voters.

Obviously, no democrat can completely distrust the judgment of the voters. In the view of more elitist democrats, however, voters really can be trusted only to choose among candidates whose moderation or competence has already been certified. From the Schumpeterian perspective in particular, this is an important function of party leaders. The primary short-circuits this control. The more general fear is that modern campaign techniques and the private nature of voting excessively weigh superficial personal appeal over practical competence and that use of the primary to make nominations removes an important check on this tendency.

Implicit in many of the criticisms of the use of primaries is the view that party professionals would do better. The basic claim is that party leaders are interested in winning elections, and so will nominate candidates with broad popular appeal, while party voters are interested only in expressing their private opinions.

At the very top, this claim may be true. Prime ministerial candidates generally have long experience in the parliament and have moved progressively through the ranks of lesser to more important cabinet office. This may, however, be more a function of parliamentary versus presidential government, rather than selection of nominees by party processes versus public election. Nomination of individual parliamentary candidates, however, generally is controlled at the local level,[1] and these choices appear to have most of the same problems as those made by primary. As the experience of the British Labour Party during the 1970s attests, Ranney's conclusion that local selectorates are looking for loyal supporters of the national leadership is not an invariable rule. Indeed, during this period of left-wing activism, several Labour candidates were deselected for being too loyal to national policies and leaders. In other cases, the problem has not been the "loony left" (or equally loony right), but that local choices are "mostly based on purely internal criteria worthy of a social club rather than political criteria that may interest the voters."[2] It is far from clear that returning choice of American candidates to party organizations would improve the quality, or even the general popularity, of nominees.

Campaign Subsidy

As the number of British candidates who can only be assumed to know that they will lose their £500 deposits forcefully suggests, hope of being elected is not the only reason why a candidate might contest an election. Some may only be exhibitionists, but others may have substantial reasons for candidacy. A candidate may hope that by making a credible showing in a hopeless contest, his or her chance of nomination in a winnable district or for some other office will be improved. Repeated contests may chip away at an incumbent's support, so that the hopeless becomes winnable. Even when there is no hope of election, yeoman service for the party may put a candidate in line for appointive office. Some candidates and minor parties may use elections to proselytize for their ideological or policy preferences in the hope that they will gain support, or just for the satisfaction of campaigning. And for some candidates, self-advertisement itself may be a rational objective. Although political analysts generally think of name recognition in terms of the advantage it offers a candidate, candidacy can also be a way for individuals to gain name recognition for their private businesses.

Ballot access requirements limit the possibility (or raise the cost) of using public elections for private ends, and indeed in some cases limit the use of the electoral forum for the public ends of small groups. The underlying conflict between freedom and fairness in election contests on one side and manageable and meaningful elections on the other becomes all the more acute, however, when the state not only provides the forum but also pays some or all of the bills.

Public subsidies of election campaigns are of three basic kinds. The simplest is direct cash payment. The second is the direct provision of services (postal delivery of campaign propaganda, broadcasting time, meeting halls) either free or at reduced rate. Finally, there is indirect subsidy, for example through tax deductions for political contributions or regulations compelling commercial broadcasters to make time available to candidates at below-commercial rates. In this section, the primary focus will be on the first two forms of public subvention, although the last may be significant in some cases.

The immediate impetus for subsidies has been the high cost of modern campaign tools (surveys, computers, media consultants). Although levels of use vary, the result virtually everywhere has been an explosion of campaign-related spending. As in the use of modern campaign techniques, the United States has led the way in exploding political expenditures. Candidates for the House and Senate reported spending $459 million in the 1987–1988 election cycle, more than double the corresponding total of 10 years before.[3] To this must be added the $250 million spent by presidential primary candidates and the more than $90 million spent by the two major presidential candidates in the general election. Although the American figures are an order of magnitude bigger than those elsewhere, the trends are the same. Expenditures by the three major British parties in 1987 totaled over £22.4 million, up from £13.2 million in 1983.[4] Estimated spending in Ireland rose from IR£1.3 million in February 1982 to at least IR£2.5 million in 1989 and in Sweden it rose from SEK 37.23 million in 1982 to SEK 70.44 million in 1988.[5]

Using public funds to help defray these costs may be justified in a variety of ways. Since the decision to subsidize is made by elected governments, however, it is perhaps useful to consider justifications in order of their increasing self-serving nature, bearing in mind that even if the ostensible justification is altruistic, those who are deciding to provide subsidies will also be among their primary recipients.

Most altruistic is the argument that democracy requires the widespread dissemination of information and ideas and the vigorous debate of opposing viewpoints. This argument has been used to justify state subvention of newspapers, research and educational initiatives of parties and their "front" organizations, and even the day-to-day administrative expenses of party organizations. In the particular context of election campaigns, it calls for assuring candidates adequate resources to make their views generally known. This justification focuses on the general public benefit presumed to follow from the campaign, so the seriousness of the arguments raised, rather than the popularity of the viewpoint or the candidate espousing it, ought to be the criterion for allocation of resources.

Only slightly less altruistic is the argument that freedom to contest an election is only meaningful if a candidate or party has adequate resources to communicate with the electorate effectively, and analogously, the electorate is only free if the voters have been informed adequately of the options available to them. Although quite similar to the first justification, the implications of the two differ in important respects. Where the previous argument is rooted in participationist and developmental communitarian democracy, and so stresses the impact of the campaign on the citizens, this argument stresses the impact of the campaign on the outcome of the election. On one hand, the potential popularity of a party or candidate is a relevant criterion for allocating resources, suggesting that those with no real chance of winning may be denied subsidy. On the other hand, where personal development requires only adequate resources for each viewpoint, the emphasis on fairness of this outcome-oriented argument suggests that substantially equal resources be made available to all seriously viable candidates or parties. (One should remember here, especially in the institutional context of PR or the theoretical context of legislative popular sovereignty or liberal democracy, that viability may require only a real chance to win a single seat.)

A third justification for public support is that the expense of modern campaigning makes politicians excessively dependent on major contributors. The claim that the United States has *The Best Congress Money Can Buy* merely expresses this concern as an epigram.[6] The emphasis shifts from the present campaign to the influence of future campaign needs on the behavior of those in office. Discounting the commitments made by challengers in attempting to raise support for their initial campaigns as unenforceable, this concern could be satisfied by subsidy of incumbents, or more broadly the parties already represented in office. Of course, this would violate fundamental norms of fairness intolerably, but in more palatable form this argument is compatible with subsidies limited to, or concentrated on, the most major contenders.

Finally, an idea rarely expressed by politicians but sometimes imputed (not necessarily disapprovingly) to them by political commentators is that public subsidy is desirable because it frees politicians from dependence on the members of their own parties. Here one returns to the same arguments raised about the direct primary. If leaders are more interested in winning and more concerned with the public interest in governing, while likely contributors are more extremist and more interested in ideological purity, perhaps it is better for parties to depend only on the support of the electorate at the polls.

Turned around, of course, many of these become the principal arguments against government subsidy. Ruud Koole summarizes three reasons for official opposition to public funding in the Netherlands:

> First, public subsidies are thought to reinforce the status quo of the party system. Secondly, the danger of manipulation and control by the state would be enhanced. Thirdly, the distance between elite and grassroots would increase because the parties would no longer have to rely financially on their members.[7]

At a practical level, two basic rules govern the allocation of resources. First, every party or candidate can be given equal support, which has the obvious appearance of fairness and reflects that the costs of many forms of campaigning are independent of the size of the intended audience. It avoids the problems of prejudging the viability of candidates. But it also has two problems of its own. It encourages candidacies motivated by the availability of resources. Is it fair for the party of 40% of the people to be given only as much support as the party of 4%? Or does not fairness dictate that the first be given 10 times the support of the second? Should the standard be an equal share per candidate, or an equal share per voter? Hence the other basic rule for allocation, that parties and candidates should be supported in proportion to their popular support. To these rules may be added a compromise position: equal shares, but only for those candidates or parties reaching a threshold of support.

If subsidy is allocated on the basis of public support, the further questions of how and when that support is to be demonstrated arise. Three major ways of assessing support are in common use. First, support is most directly indicated by votes received; second, by seats won; third, by ability to raise contributions. Beyond the obvious likelihood that each of these three standards will result in a different distribution of subsidies, they also differ in their interactions with questions of timing.

The two important questions about timing are when the amount to be given is determined and when the subsidy is received. Early payment is especially useful for new contenders, because they need to use the subsidy to generate the public support that will in turn justify their subsidy. Even for major parties, however, cash in advance is far more useful than a promise of reimbursement at a later date.

In general it is to the advantage of strong and established parties to base the allocation of resources on prior election results, because that denies resources to newcomers. New parties, on the other hand, need to capitalize on and compound their immediate support, ideally receiving subsidy before the election either on the basis of a match of current contributions or in anticipation of the present electoral result.

With cash subventions, excess payments can be refunded, so there is no reason why the subsidy cannot be paid wholly or partially in advance of the election, even if the final entitlement is not determined until later. To this extent, the two questions of timing are independent. Some forms of subsidy, however, can be given only in advance of an election; broadcasting time, for example, is of little use after the fact. Resources that must be distributed before the election and cannot be repaid by a candidate whose "advance" proves to have been too large require that the allocation be determined before the election as well. If allocation is to be based on vote or seat share, however, it must rely on the results of the previous election, so that the system of public subsidy necessarily reinforces the position of strong parties.

Table 14.4 summarizes the systems of national government support—both direct financial aid and the provision of free broadcasting time—for the electoral activities of political parties in a sample of countries.[8] The table suggests a number of generalizations as well as a number of differences between the provision of direct monetary support and provision of television access. In most systems, most of the questions raised above have been answered to the advantage of large and previously established parties. Direct financial aid generally is given only as reimbursement after the fact, and the principal exceptions (Germany, Israel, the United States) are only for parties that can demonstrate entitlement on the basis of previous elections. Most systems of financial aid are based on party strength, giving the already strong parties additional resources with which to remain so. Broadcasting time, on the other hand, is more likely to be allocated on the basis of equal shares, and when it is allocated on the basis of strength in parliament, small but established parties generally do better proportionately than the largest parties. Minimal time at the least desirable hours may be given to unrepresented parties putting up a large enough number of candidates.

Spending and Other Limitations

Long before the question of subsidizing candidates or parties was raised, most countries attempted to promote fairness by prohibiting or requiring various practices. As with any legal provision, the first two descriptive questions are (1) who is required or prohibited to do what? and (2) what are the mechanisms and sanctions used to ensure compliance?

Nonfinancial Requirements and Prohibitions

Most significant campaign regulations can be grouped into a small number of general categories. The first, and least problematic, include those concerning complicity in overt fraud. Much of the apparently cumbersome machinery surrounding elections is designed to make such frauds difficult to perpetrate, although no system is likely to fully suppress frauds. The main requirements are independent investigative and judicial agencies and penalties that guarantee that the game is not worth the candle.

A second group is designed to protect voters from undue pressure. Generally prohibited are the making of threats and the payment of direct bribes. The secret ballot goes a long way toward eliminating such practices, but some problems remain. First, even if the ballot is secret, many other forms of electoral activity (display of posters, wearing of buttons, attendance at meetings) are not. Second, especially with regard to these activities, it is difficult to frame an enforceable law that distinguishes corrupt practices from informal social pressures.[9] Third, if aggregate election returns are reported at a sufficiently local level (e.g., polling place or ballot box), it may be possible to make a shrewd guess about individual voters or to apply pressure to a small community as a whole. Avoidance of this is one of the reasons the electoral laws of some countries (e.g., Ireland and the UK) require that all the ballots from an entire constituency be mixed before they are counted.

A third set of regulations aims to protect the openness and fairness of elections. An example here would be the quite common requirement (e.g., in 42 American states) that any campaign literature include the name of the printer, publisher, or some other responsible party. More controversial, and less common, are regulations to limit libelous, false, or otherwise misleading advertising. With regard to personal attacks, British law comes close to one extreme whereas American law approaches the other. In Britain, it is an illegal campaign practice for a person to publish "any false statement of fact in relation to the candidate's personal character or conduct . . . , unless he can show that he had reasonable grounds for believing, and did believe, the statement to be true." This law allows both for injunctive relief and, if the offender is a candidate or his agent, the possibility of disqualification, in addition to the possibility of a libel action at common law.[10] In the United States, only the common law remedy is available. Moreover, under the standard of "actual malice" applied to public figures, this relief is largely illusory.[11] Even in the British case, however, the law applies only

TABLE 14.4 State support to candidates and parties.

Country	Broadcasting	Financial support	Timing of financial support
Australia	Free television time given to major parties in rough proportion to vote in previous election.	Based on 1984 prices, indexed for inflation, A$ 0.60 per House first preference vote and A$ 0.30 per Senate first preference vote (A$ 0.45 for half-Senate elections separate from House elections). Funds are provided only to reimburse receipted expenses incurred during the formal campaign. To be eligible, parties and candidates must achieve a 4% vote threshold	After the election
Austria	Shares given in proportion to party strength in the Nationalrat	ÖS 85 million (1991) divided among parties in Nationalrat in proportion to vote at last election.	Annually
Belgium	French media: 8-minute programs awarded on basis of seats in the Conseil Culturel. 1 program for groups with 2% of seats; 2 for groups with 5% of the seats; 4 for groups with 10% of the seats; 6 for groups with 15% of the seats; 8 for groups with 20% of the seats; 10 for groups with 30% of the seats; 12 for group with more than 40% of the seats Flemish media: Every group represented by 10 members in the Nederlandse Cultuurraad can create an organization with the right to make programs. Political groups with 2 members in the Cultuurraad can also be recognized. Time allocated 50% equally, and 50% in proportion to strength in the Cultuurraad	None	
Brazil	2 hours per day in the two months before the election, allocated in proportion to representation in the Federal Chamber		
Canada	Free television time given to parties based on seats held and vote in previous election and number of seats contested in current election	Candidates receiving at least 15% of the vote receive the lesser of (a) actual expenses or (b) cost of first-class postage for a one-ounce item sent to each elector in	After the election

(continued)

TABLE 14.4 (continued)

Country	Broadcasting	Financial support	Timing of financial support
		constituency plus C$0.08 (1974 prices, adjusted for inflation) for each of the first 25,000 electors in the constituency plus C$0.06 for each additional elector. In addition, candidates receive C$250 to cover auditor's fee	
Denmark	Recognized parties receive equal amounts of free radio and television time	No direct monetary campaign support	
Finland	Equal shares to all parties	Party support based on number of MPs	Annual
France	Presidential candidates are given 2 hours of free time on both radio and television in each round of voting	Presidential candidates with at least 5% of the vote receive FF100,000 and costs of printing and sending platform to each voter as well as printing campaign posters. Parliamentary candidates with at least 5% of the vote reimbursed for costs of printing ballots and posters for polling places	Monetary subsidy is paid after the election
Germany		DM 5.00 per vote received, not to exceed the party's other income in the second calendar year following the election, or any of the three preceding years. Paid to parties receiving at least 0.5% of the vote in a given Land, or 10% of the vote in a single-member district if no Land list is presented	After the election except that parties qualifying in the previous election may receive advances totaling no more than 60% of the reimbursable amount
Ireland	Party political broadcasting time allocated on the basis of party strength in the outgoing Dáil and to groups fielding at least 7 candidates	No direct monetary campaign support	
Israel	Each list is given 10 minutes of television time plus 6 minutes per Knesset member	Financial support based on equal shares per seat in the incoming Knesset	Parties in the outgoing Knesset: 60% of the per member allocation times the number of members in the outgoing Knesset on presenting candidate lists; up to a total of 85% of allocation based on incoming seats on

Country			
Italy		Lit. 15 billion divided among all parties (a) with lists in at least 2/3 of the constituencies; (b) which elect at least one member and have at least 300,000 votes or 2% of the votes cast. 15% is divided equally, the remainder in proportion to votes obtained	publication of election results; balance following positive report of controller Parties not in outgoing Knesset: 85% of allocation on publication of election results; balance following positive report of controller
Japan	One 2½ minute television broadcast is given to each candidate	Candidates polling over a minimum vote are reimbursed a fixed percentage of promotional costs	Reimbursement after election
Netherlands	Equal broadcasting time and production subsidies for all parties presenting lists of candidates in all 19 electoral districts		In advance
New Zealand	Free television time is given to parties based on relative strengths, but with equality between two major parties and more than proportional time given to smaller established parties	No direct monetary support	
Norway	Equal shares for parties participating in elections in all electoral subdivisions. Between elections, equal shares for all parties represented in the Storting	Nkr 22.10 (1991) per vote received. 2.5% of vote required to qualify	Annual
Sweden	Time allocated to all parties represented in at least one of the last two parliaments; nominating candidates in a majority of constituencies and having a national organization	Skr 274,850 (1989) per seat in Riksdag.	Annual

(continued)

TABLE 14.4 (continued)

Country	Broadcasting	Financial support	Timing of financial support
United Kingdom	Broadcasting time is allocated according to party strength as perceived by broadcasting authorities. One 5-minute broadcast is guaranteed to any party fielding at least 50 candidates (e.g., in 1987, Alliance, Labour, and Conservative parties were each given 5 10-minute broadcasts)	No direct monetary campaign support	Before the election
United States	Equal access at controlled rates to all legally qualified candidates for federal office	Presidential candidates only Primary election: Matching of private contributions of $250 or less for candidates who (a) agree to limit total spending to $10 million (1974) plus COLA; (b) have received at least $5,000 in contributions in each of at least 20 states; (c) has not polled under 10% of the vote in two successive primaries unless has certified not to have been actively campaigning in those states General election: Candidate of a party polling at least 25% of vote in preceding election and who agrees to raise or spend no additional funds receives $20 million (1974) plus COLA; candidate of a party polling between 5% and 25% of vote in the preceding election receives a share of funds given to major party candidates proportional to party's previous vote and may raise additional contributions up to the limit for major party candidates; candidate of a new party receives a share of funds given to major party candidates proportional to vote in the current election provided it is at least 5% of total	As certification of qualifying contributions is processed In advance for major and minor party candidates; after the election for new party candidates

to "statements in relation to the candidate's personal character or conduct" and does not include statements about an incumbent's official conduct or a candidate's qualification for office.[12]

A fourth set of requirements might be described as "nuisance laws," although their existence and the potential for enforcement may significantly raise the level of technical expertise required to mount a legal campaign. Regulations concerning the placement of campaign posters would be only one example of this residual category.

Campaign Spending

The fifth, and generally most numerous and complex, class of regulations concerns campaign finance. This category in turn can be divided between regulations concerned with expenditure and those concerned with contributions and other forms of income. At the risk of only slight oversimplification, the former are intended to prevent candidates from buying elections, while the latter are intended to prevent other individuals or groups from buying candidates.

A number of questions must be addressed in formulating rules limiting expenditure. First, to whom does the limitation apply? In general, list-oriented systems limit spending by parties, under which not only local organizations but also candidates as individuals are subsumed. Candidate-oriented systems, on the other hand, in part because their laws often do not take cognizance of parties, may limit only the spending of candidates and their direct agents, although the fiction that elections are not really contests among parties gradually is being abandoned. Difficult as the problem of party spending may be, however, the more intractable problem is spending on behalf of a candidate or party by supporters who are not formally connected to either. Again, the exercise is seriously undermined if candidates or parties can multiply their spending, or evade control altogether, by creating many nominally independent organizations to campaign on their behalf. One possibility, used in Britain and New Zealand with regard to campaigning in favor of (or in opposition to) specific candidates, is to prohibit all spending unless authorized by the candidate/party (or his or her or its agent) and counted against the allowable total. In India, on the other hand, spending by parties, associations or groups, or individuals other than the candidate or his or her agent are (since 1974) specifically *excluded* from the controls imposed on candidates, rendering those limits practically irrelevant. In the United States, spending by candidates is unregulated, except for presidential candidates who elect to accept federal funding.[13] Spending by parties on behalf of their candidates is limited, however.[14] State parties are allowed an equal amount and may designate the national party as their agent, effectively doubling its limit. "Independent expenditures," those made without consultation with the candidate's organization, are excluded from the spending limits that apply to direct expenditures.

Second, what is included as an expenditure subject to limitation? Many countries exclude fees for attorneys and accountants required to comply with campaign regulations. The rental of campaign premises generally is subject to expenditure limitation, but how does one apportion the expense of a regular party headquarters that also provides space to a candidate or handle the candidate who uses his or her private home or business for this purpose? This points to the more general problem of noncash or below–market value transactions. These usually are regulated as contributions. Indeed, in Canada if a self-employed individual volunteers services for which he or she would normally charge, the value of those services must be included in the candidate's reported election expenses.[15]

One of the most difficult problems is whether expenses that are not overtly directed at garnering votes, but that nonetheless have that effect, should be included as campaign expenses. Although commercial advertising may make no mention of politics or issues, it can increase name recognition and turn a would-be candidate from a "nobody" into a local "personality." It is not clear, however, how undeclared potential candidates who can afford a campaign of self-promotion under the guise of regular business activity could be barred from doing so. Even more a problem is the "nonpolitical" activity of incumbent officeholders. Members of Congress, for example, have an impressive array of facilities—free postage, district offices, television and radio studios, staff assistance—to help them communicate with and serve their constituents. Although the opportunities to do favors for constituents and to wear the mantle of office give incumbents an advantage in any system, this problem is particularly acute in the United States because of the scale of facilities members of Congress (and many state legislators) have voted themselves.

In part, whether use of these sorts of goods and services should be regulated as campaigning depends on the type of activity, but in part it depends on timing. This point leads to the third question, when do the limitations (and any related reporting requirements) begin? Not only are congressional mass mailings limited to two per year, in the interest of economy as well as fairness, they also are prohibited within 60 days of any election in which the member is a candidate. In more general terms, spending limits usually are triggered in one of two ways. They may begin on a fixed date, either specified in the law or relative to the announcement or holding of the election. Alternatively, they may be triggered by some action of the candidate or party involved. For example, the primary spending limits imposed on American presidential candidates who accept federal matching funds are triggered by the filing of a statement of organization with the Federal Election Commission (FEC).

Whether triggered by the candidate or the calendar, however, these limits often are legal fictions. Major parties begin the real jockeying for position, building of organization, and cultivation of public opinion for the next election within a few days of the conclusion of the last one. Pierre Avril, for example, attributes the main deficiencies of pre-1988 French regulation of campaign expenses to the fact that they applied only during the official campaign period of three weeks preceding the election.[16] For individuals, a campaign for high office may span several election cycles. One might reasonably date the beginning of Ronald Reagan's 1980 presidential campaign to 1974, or even 1968,[17] for example, although the first statements of organization by any of the candidates were not filed until fall 1978. Nonetheless, the regulated period in the United States is sufficiently long to give some substance to the spending limits imposed. Shorter limits, on the other hand, may be evaded by prepaying, as has been the experience in New Zealand in which a stringent limitation of NZ$5,000 applies only to the three months before the election.[18] Where premature elections are possible, the real limitation may derive from ignorance about when the election will be held, rather than from legislation, with spending limited by a candidate's inability to plan a campaign, stimulate interest, raise funds, or maintain an organization for an election that may be next year or next month.

Political Contributions

Turning from expenditures to income, most regulations fall into three major categories: those limiting the acceptable source of a contribution, those limiting the maximum size of an acceptable contribution, and those requiring disclosure of the sources of contributions.

The earliest limits on campaign income generally were introduced by coalitions of agrarian interests that were deeply suspicious of the power of business and other moneyed groups. In the United States, the Tilman Act (1907) for example, prohibited monetary contributions to any political campaign from federally chartered banks and corporations and to federal campaigns from any corporation. A similar ban was introduced in Canada in 1908, although it proved totally ineffective because it barred only contributions to candidates, not to parties. This Canadian ban was extended in 1920 to all companies and associations, thus including trade unions. Unions in the United States were prohibited from making any contribution in connection with a federal general election in the War Labor Disputes Act of 1943, a ban made permanent for both unions and corporations and extended to include "expenditures" as well as "contributions" by the Taft-Hartley Act of 1947.[19] These bans were weakened, in substance if not in form, by the 1971 FECA (Federal Election Campaign Act), which allowed unions and corporations to establish political action committees, so long as the funds collected are kept segregated and contributions were voluntary.[20]

In some cases a ban on contributions may protect the contributor from undue pressure, as with civil servants who might fear for their jobs, or government contractors whose "concern was not to obtain favors but to avoid possible government discrimination against them if they did not contribute."[21] A related argument, applied particularly to associations like trade unions, is that a majority should not be able to use funds collected from all to support causes or candidates that the minority oppose.

Short of an outright ban, an attempt may be made to limit the concentration of influence in a few hands by limiting the amount that may be contributed by or accepted from a single individual. The first federal regulation of this type in the United States was included in the Hatch Act of 1940, which imposed a limit of $5,000 per year on individual contributions to a candidate or political committee and $3 million per year in total for any political committee. Since a single person could make $5,000 contributions to each of several committees all supporting the same candidate, however, massive contributions remained legal. These limits remained in effect until 1972, when they were replaced by comprehensive reporting requirements and limits on the amount of personal money spent by candidates and their immediate families.[22] In 1974, general contribution limits were reintroduced, with individuals limited to $1,000 for each primary, run-off, or general election, up to a total of $25,000 for all federal candidates, while organizations, political committees, and parties (with state and federal parties counted separately) were limited to $5,000 per candidate per election with no aggregate limit. The provisions were supplemented in 1976, with the result shown in table 14.5. Just as the Watergate scandal stimulated regulation of contributions in the United States, so the Lockheed scandal led to regulation in Japan. In both cases, the effectiveness of the limits on giving to a single candidate is reduced by the possibility of giving to many separate committees, all of which support the same individual. Under the simpler circumstances of a party-oriented electoral system, Spain in 1985 limited individual contributions to a party to 1 million pesetas. With a candidate-oriented system, French law limits contributions from individuals to FF30,000 in a single election, and for corporate bodies (including parties) to 10% of the legal spending limit for the office.[23] Donations to parties by individuals and corporate bodies are limited to FF50,000 and FF500,000 per year, respectively.

The third aspect of regulations about contributions is the requirement that candidates disclose the sources of their support. Such requirements may dissuade candidates from accepting questionable contributions, while also allowing voters to know which candidates are beholden to which interests. The first such requirements in the United States were included in the Publicity Act of 1910 and Publicity Act Amendments of 1911. Although these requirements were overturned for primary elections,[24] they were continued for general elections in the Federal Cor-

TABLE 14.5 Contribution limits, United States.

Limited entity	To candidate per election[a]	To state and local party committee per year	To national party committee per year	To any other committee per year	Other limits
Individual	$1,000	$5,000	$20,000	$5,000	$25,000 per year in total
Political committee[b]	$1,000	$5,000	$20,000	$5,000	
Multicandidate committee[c]	$5,000	$5,000	$15,000	$5,000	
State and local party committee	$5,000	No limit	No limit	$5,000	
National party committee	$5,000	No limit	No limit	$5,000	$17,500 to Senate candidates[d]

[a]The same amount of money may be donated in the primary and general election. This effectively doubles the amount of money one may contribute to each candidate.
[b]Refers mostly to individual candidates' political committees, or reelection committees.
[c]Refers mostly to PACs and political parties.
[d]Shared by the national committee and the Senate campaign committee.

rupt Practices Act of 1925. Between loopholes and nonenforcement, they had little apparent impact.[25] They were superseded by the FECA of 1971, which, as amended in 1979, requires candidates and political committees to report the name, address, and other particulars of any donor contributing $200 or more in a single year. Moreover, the new legislation required that these reports be filed quarterly (plus two pre-election reports) rather than only after the election.

Requirements that significant contributions be disclosed can supplement restrictions on contributing, but more generally they substitute for them. Thus, when the Canada Elections Act of 1974 introduced the requirement that all contributions over $100 (Canadian) be reported, it repealed the earlier bans on corporate and union contributions. While several countries have reporting requirements, there are significant differences regarding the maximum size of a contribution that can be accepted without individual disclosure. In Canada or Spain, even modest contributions must be reported, while in other cases only quite sizeable donations must be itemized (e.g., DM 10,000 in West Germany or ÖS 100,000 in Austria).

Reporting

The most common mechanism for implementing financial limits is a requirement that detailed accounts be filed or published. One compilation found some requirement of this sort in 14 of 20 democratic countries surveyed.[26] Instituted in many cases in conjunction with public subsidy of campaigns or party organizations, requirements vary tremendously in breadth and effectiveness. In general, fully effective disclosure would require that all the following conditions be satisfied:

- that the reports be public and timely;
- that the reports be detailed;
- that the disclosure be comprehensive, rather than applying only to some parts of the party/campaign apparatus or only to some activities;
- that the reports be subject to effective audit.

If one objective of disclosure is to allow candidates to bring the behavior of their opponents to the public's attention as a campaign issue, only reports made available before the election will do. Even if this is impossible, as where the regulated period is extremely short, or when the reports concern expenditures concentrated in the few days before an election, reports filed well after public interest in an election has waned are likely to have very limited deterrent effect. Moreover, reports will have very little effect unless their contents are available to opponents, the press, and the public. In part, disclosure is a question of ease of retrieval—one of the ways the National Republican Congressional Committee, with the complicity of the FEC, tried to limit the impact of disclosure laws in the United States, was to try to block electronic publication of donor reports[27]—but in other countries even the principle is in doubt. For example, in 1989 the extent to which the public would be allowed access to party reports required by the Spanish electoral law of 1985 still was not clear.[28]

To be effective, reports must also be sufficiently detailed to convey meaningful information. Reports of the kind required of Italian parties, for example, which only list private donations as an aggregated total, are less significant than reports that detail every donation over a relatively small threshold.

Unless all relevant levels of political organization and the full range of political activities are brought within the scope of disclosure laws, parties and politicians can conceal many contributions or expenditures that otherwise would be illegal, or at least highly questionable, by transferring them to an uncontrolled budget. While Britain requires timely and detailed reports from candidates, the exclusion of spending by the parties means that, at best, the system can control petty corruption while ignoring even the possibility of national-level influence peddling or unfairness. Conversely, Austrian, Italian, and Swedish parties issue reports that include only the finances of the central party; local parties, ancillary enterprises, and independent factions are all excluded.

The final requirement of effective reporting is that the reports filed be subject to audit. The FEC provides an outstanding negative example. Although presidential campaign reports are audited, reports from other campaigns are audited only if the commission receives a notarized complaint *and* at least four commissioners vote to pursue the investigation. Since the commission consists of three Democrats and three Republicans, the chance that four votes will be mustered to investigate any but the most flagrant violations by major party candidates is slim indeed. In Canada, on the other hand, all reports must be audited before filing.

Enforcement and Sanctions

As with all regulations, there may be a great gulf between the articulation of a norm and regular compliance, raising questions both of enforcement mechanisms and sanctions.

One important question is whether enforcement proceedings are instituted by the government or triggered only by a complaint. The FEC cannot audit candidates except for cause; thus, except for reports inaccurate or incomplete on their face, audit requires an outside complaint. The FEC does, however, enforce requirements concerning the form and timing of reports, with the effect that much of its time is spent investigating petty infractions by insignificant candidates.

A second question concerns the availability and powers of staff to investigate alleged violations. As Brooks Jackson reports, one major problem with FEC enforcement is that "[t]he FEC lacks the most basic tool for conducting investigations—investigators."[29] Although it once had them, they were eliminated, in part because of pressure from Congress.

The principal British mechanism for enforcement is the election petition filed with an Election Court by an unsuccessful candidate, a voter, or "a person claiming to have had a right to be elected or returned at the election."[30] The director of public prosecutions may take action after a corrupt practice is found to have occurred, but is not involved in bringing petitions in the first place. These are extremely rare, in part as the result of a tacit conspiracy between the parties. As one senior official put it:

If we lost a seat by one vote and I could clearly prove illegal practices by the other side I wouldn't try. It would cost perhaps £5,000 and they might be able to show that our man had slipped up in some way. But worse than that, it might start tit-for-tat petitions and no party could afford a lot of them. On the whole, we're both law-abiding and it's as well to leave each other alone.[31]

Once an offense is detected, the question of sanctions arises. In general, these are of four types. The first two are available in the United States, as well as abroad. Most severe would be jail. Although virtually always an option, it is virtually never imposed. A second type is a fine, far more common, but often so small as to have more nuisance than deterrent value. The two other sanctions are employed in other countries. One is to reduce the subsidy payable to the offending party—just another name for a fine. The final, and perhaps most effective, sanction is that available in Britain—the Election Court (in reality the House of Commons acting on its recommendation) can declare the election void and the offender disqualified from election for five years. The penalty of being declared ineligible is also available in France, where the Constitutional Court in 1992 declared ineligible two candidates who had failed to submit their campaign accounts within the required period.[32] Disqualification may appear rather draconian, and it has the potential to subvert the public will. However, it is not clear that lesser penalties will deter violations, especially since, as the Watergate example illustrates, serious campaign violations may be perpetrated by a candidate who was virtually certain to win anyway.

The structuring of the FEC so that either major party can block action and pressures from Congress to leave incumbents alone, as well as the virtual desuetude of British election petitions to enforce spending regulations, illustrate the limitations of the liberal belief that separation of powers and electoral competition can keep public officials in check. As in many other fields, major parties and many elected officials appear to be guided more by the interest they share with their electoral opponents in avoiding vigorous enforcement than by the spirit of competition. Thus one recent book on electioneering divided (with only two exceptions) expenditure limits in 16 countries into two categories: "no" and "ignored." And the two exceptions, spending limits on French and British candidates, lose much of their force when one remembers that they are coupled with unlimited spending by parties.[33]

Elections and Democracy

In a seminal work on the relationship between political institutions and models of democracy, Arend Lijphart proposes a bipolar categorization of democratic governments. Lijphart initially suggests that the two poles, the "Westminster" or majoritarian model of democracy and the consensus model, can be distinguished on the basis of nine characteristics. In the course of analyzing the patterns of characteristics found in 21 democracies, Lijphart ultimately develops a two-dimensional scheme and four classes of democratic regimes. The four classes (whose labels implicitly name the dimensions defining them) are, together with the most extreme example in each, majoritarian (New Zealand), majoritarian-federal (United States), consensual-unitary (Israel), consensual (Switzerland). The first and last categories correspond to Lijphart's two original polar types; the second and third, however, combine features of each.[1]

Lijphart associates plurality election with the majoritarian model of democracy and PR with the consensual; in the final quantitative analysis, the operational measure is disproportionality. Other characteristics and their corresponding operational measures are influenced by the electoral system as well. In each case, the more majoritarian value of the indicator would be associated with plurality election, while the more consensual value would be associated with PR. Thus, although among the indicators that define the majoritarian/consensual factor, disproportionality itself is the one that loads most weakly (.42), a simple dichotomy of PR versus not PR (modified to score the Japanese SNTV system at the midpoint) has a correlation of .52 with this factor.

While this dimension may help sort democratic systems into empirically defined categories sharing certain structural or behavioral characteristics (which is all Lijphart claims for it), the attempt to relate electoral system characteristics to democratic values in the preceding chapters strongly suggests that a discussion of the relationship between plurality and PR electoral systems, on the one hand, and models of democracy, on the other, needs to be more nuanced. In particular, Lijphart essentially posits only two "pure" models, with everything else somehow an intermediate case or compromise—and indeed this is how he describes the majoritarian-federal and consensual-unitary categories. In fact, as was shown in the first part of this book, even if one ignores the more metaphysical values of personal development and community, there are two *classes* of democratic theories, one emphasizing liberalism and the other popular sovereignty, each encompassing a number of alternative models of democracy, in turn depending on alternative assumptions about the character of elites and social structure. In general terms, Lijphart's two polar cases correspond to the distinction between popular sovereignty and liberalism, but in particular they relate only to *some* popular sovereignty theories (especially the binary, Downsian, Tory, and socialist models) and to *some* liberal theories (especially the concurrent majorities or consociational models).

Lijphart's analysis also implicitly ignores the consequences of societal differences, in effect assuming that the same institutions will engender the same kind of democracy regardless of the society in which they are found—an assumption whose truth is limited. The institutions most likely to support liberty in a society with high levels of social homogeneity and mobility and in which citizens feel sympathy for and empathy with their fellows (i.e., one that meets the assumptions of Benthamite liberal democracy) are virtually assured of destroying liberty in a society characterized by fixed and rigid segmentation and mutual hostility and suspicion (i.e., one that meets the assumptions of consociational democracy). Similarly, the institutions that should produce reasonably stable majorities in a bipolar society or one with a single overriding issue dimension are likely to produce incoherence, instability, and majorities that on many issues appear arbitrary and out of touch with popular concerns where the issue space is multidimensional.

In this concluding chapter, I return to the original question—which electoral system is best, or most democratic—but now informed both by the discussions of democratic values in the first part and the analysis of the operation and consequences of electoral institutions in the second part. By now it should be clear that this question has no single answer. Rather, as just suggested, the answer depends on two sets of considerations, those concerning the values to be encouraged and those concerning the political and social environment in which one is working. Moreover, these considerations are not independent. The nature of the political and social environment is likely to bear heavily on the relative weight given to different values. Not only are the institutions best suited for the protection of minorities in a segmented society different from those most appropriate in a society characterized by crosscutting and fluid cleavages, the importance of providing such protection is likely greater in the first case as well.

The discussion of the relationships between institutions and democratic values in the preceding chapters was framed in terms of polychotomous choice; one was assumed to be trying to maximize popular sovereignty *or* liberalism *or* personal development *or* community. In real political situations, however, the choice is not to maximize one value and ignore the others, but rather to strike a balance among them. Although one may be prepared to accept a diminution in one value as the price for an increase in another, no democratic system can survive without adequate achievement of all four of the values that have been the focus of this book. But how much achievement is "adequate achievement"? Undoubtedly there are minima below which democracy would cease to exist. Beyond that, however, adequate achievement of the various democratic values appears to be part of the essential contestation of the definition of democracy itself; in practical terms it is a matter of taste. Nonetheless, history suggests that the value likely most emphasized is the one perceived to be the most threatened or, if there is no perception of immediate threat, the one least emphasized in the recent past.

The demands for increased participation and community made by the contemporary theorists cited in chapters 5 and 6, as well as those in the programs of the "new politics" or "left-libertarian"[2] parties are predicated on the lack of substantial threats to the values of popular sovereignty or liberalism. On the other hand, where the value of popular sovereignty cannot be taken for granted, for example in South Africa, or indeed even in the UK after four general elections that allowed a party that never won more than 44% of the vote to impose radical changes on the fabric of British society and economy, those interested in institutional reform are far more likely to stress that value.[3] Similarly, where majority tyranny appears a real threat, for example in Northern Ireland, institutions promoting liberal values of compromise and restraint of the majority are likely to be favored.

In this chapter, I have two goals. The first is to draw together the theoretical and empirical discussions by asking how each of the major democratic theories might be institutionalized in the electoral sphere. While this will repeat some of the discussions in the conclusions of the other chapters, here I can pay more attention to interactions among various aspects of an electoral system, to the possibility that the same result (e.g., a weakly disciplined party) might be encouraged in more than one way, and to the need in designing institutions to attend to many values simultaneously.

The second objective is to illustrate the way in which the mutual incompatibility of the core values leads to an inherent unsettledness of democratic institutions by focusing on three case studies: the collapse of consociationalism in Belgium, the reform of the Italian electoral system in the early 1990s, and the reform of the electoral system of New Zealand at the same time. In the last case I also want to compare the utility for understanding electoral reform of the more elaborate classification of democratic theories advanced in this book with that of the simple majoritarian/consensual or populist/liberal dichotomies that have dominated the literature in the past.[4]

Institutionalizing Democracies

Binary Democracy

Binary democracy assumes a bipolar or bimodal society with regard to the political questions of the day. Its conception of popular rule—the choice of the majority—requires two policy-oriented and nationally cohesive parties competing for a majority of popular votes to be translated into a majority/monopoly of political power (i.e., a majority of the parliamentary seats). Governments should be stable between elections, because direct electoral choice of one party and its program is the only legitimizer of authority.

While this might appear to be the quintessential case for single-member plurality, which is most likely to be associated with a two-party system and with stable, and electorally determined, governments, single-member plurality entails a substantial danger, illustrated in recent years by the British case, that the "wrong party" (most mildly, a party without a majority of the votes; worse, a party that would be beaten by another if only third parties had not intruded; worst of all, a party with fewer votes than another in the actual election) will win. In this light, binary democracy might better be institutionalized through PR, perhaps with a provision like that introduced in Malta in the 1980s to give the party with an absolute majority of the popular votes enough bonus seats to give it a bare majority in the parliament if it does not already have one. The association of PR with multiparty politics might then be countered with a high electoral threshold, ultimately arriving at a system akin to Greek reinforced PR. While this runs counter to the general perception of PR as a system that allows the representation of many distinct points of view, the fundamental sociopolitical premise of this model of democracy is that there are only two significant points of view. Where this assumption is violated, but approximated sufficiently to maintain the myth of bimodality, a high threshold coupled with a device pooling votes of supporters of smaller parties with those for one of the large parties (i.e., some form of apparentement) at least would encourage a two-block, if not a two-party, system, and in any case would treat supporters of ultimately excluded parties no worse than single-member plurality.

Whether elections are held under single-member plurality, PR, or some other formula, binary democracy also implies that two-partyism should be encouraged through institutions that favor large or established parties (high thresholds, or biased distributional formulas—for state subventions, media access, ballot access). If there are multiple offices, elections should be timed and the ballot should be structured to encourage party line voting.

Beyond the possibility of a minority winner, a further danger with single-member plurality (and potentially a problem with PR as well) is that the parties will not be cohesive, so that a majority for a party will not be equivalent to a majority for a particular program. To minimize this problem, each party's central leaders should have strong control over recruitment and reselection of their parliamentary colleagues. Institutionally, this means opposition to direct primaries or intraparty preference voting. The emphasis on popular choice between parties, and on party autonomy in the selection of candidates, suggests that there should be few, if any, formal restrictions (age, wealth, residence) on eligibility to become a candidate.

The obvious problem is enshrinement of two oligarchies. If entry by third parties is difficult, it is also difficult for a new organization to replace one of the two established parties. But centralization of nomination may make the leadership cadres of each of the existing parties into self-perpetuating and irresponsible cliques. If the liberals are correct about the inherent self-regard of political elites, one might even predict a conspiracy among the leaders of both parties to put their private interests ahead of implementation of the will of the people. This danger might be contained by enforcing internal democracy as a precondition for enjoying the benefits of established-party status.[5] If done at the central level, this solution need not undermine party coherence.

Since its notion of democratic legitimacy is based heavily on the majority principle, it is important to the institutionalization of binary democracy that the one-(wo)man-one-vote-one-value principle be maintained. Obviously, this principle militates against suffrage requirements, including burdensome registration regulations or linguistic obstacles, that tend to limit or discourage participation, although it does not require an affirmative effort to encourage voting. More important, it requires that district lines be drawn to equalize political influence. But since equality is inherently impossible with single-member districts, binary democracy is better implemented with high-threshold PR.

If there are some questions whose impact is restricted geographically, or for which different policies are possible in different areas, "the people" whose will is to be implemented might be similarly restricted or divided. In these cases, local autonomy would be consistent with binary democracy. On other issues, however, local autonomy is more likely to be an impediment to the implementation of the popular will, with local majorities of one persuasion obstructing the national majority of the other. Similarly, at each level of government there ought not to be rival centers of power (e.g., both a parliament and a directly elected president). For this reason, binary democracy is most consistent with a strongly centralized political structure, and so might call for restricting the number and range of elected officials, and in any case for tying their election to a single national choice. At the same time, local autonomy has an important advantage in that it provides some experienced leadership and other resources to help the minority party mount an effective challenge at the next national election. The need for an effective challenge also means that state subventions and other resources ought to be given equally to the major parties (or that, as in Britain, the *opposition* might even be given disproportionate resources[6]), notwithstanding that this equality among the two major parties might be coupled with strong discrimination against third parties.

Although these prescriptions are appropriate to binary democracy understood on its own terms as a system for the implementation of the popular will, they present a number of problems with regard to the other democratic values. The first and perhaps fatal problem is the possibility that one political pole will remain more popular than the other, with a result indistinguishable from the fear of all but the majoritarian liberals—a permanent oppressive majority and a permanent oppressed minority. Even without overt oppression, a permanent minority is likely to feel excluded from full membership in the political community. Echoes of this concern are heard even from the essentially liberal American system in suggestions that simply guaranteeing representation to minorities will be ineffective if those representatives are nonetheless permanently excluded from influence,[7] but it is far more significant when coupled with the unrelievedly majoritarian focus of binary democracy. Moreover, this problem is likely to be exacerbated by the polarization inherent in this system; in dividing citizens politically into one camp or the other, community is undermined, and the likelihood that those in the majority will trample on the interests of the minority increases. If the social and political conditions assumed by binary democracy obtain, majority tyranny likely can be avoided only if the majority exercises self-restraint, either voluntarily or because the minority commands nonelectoral resources (e.g., control over the economy, moral suasion, or a credible threat to create chaos) adequate to compel compromise. Voluntary restraint implies the infusion of a large element of communitarianism, while restraint imposed by prudence tends to convert binary democracy into a variety of Benthamite or Madisonian liberalism.

A second problem is that the emphasis on government by, and centralization of power in, cohesive parties may reduce the ordinary citizen to an extremely passive role, making the benefits valued by participationist democrats quite problematic. Basically, all the citizen can do is to make periodic choices between parties. This passivity can be countered to a limited extent by internal party democracy, but a more likely outcome is popular dissatisfaction and the channeling of participation into nonparty groups. There is, however, no real place in the scheme of binary democracy for such groups, which are more appropriate to liberal theories, especially polyarchy.

Downsian Democracy

Downsian democracy is similar to binary democracy in its initial call for two cohesive parties competing on the basis of policy and forming governments that endure from one election to the next. It differs, however, in assuming that opinions are distributed more or less continuously along a dimension, so that the political center, which for binary democracy is assumed to be virtually empty, may be the most densely populated part of the political space. This crucial difference translates into different institutional prescriptions.

Although Downsian democracy shares the concern that (mal)apportionment or the appearance of third parties will mean that the "wrong party" wins an election, the solution of adopting PR instead of single-member plurality will not work for two related reasons. First, because more of the political spectrum is assumed to be occupied, the danger that PR will result in a multiparty system increases. The solution proposed for binary democracy, a high threshold, is unavailable because there is no reason to suppose that the largest parties in a free competition will be those closest to the center of the political space, yet those are the two that, according to this model, "ought" to survive. Second, a multiparty system is likely to result in coalition government, thus reducing the incentive for individual parties to converge on the median position, while the policy adopted by a coalition is more likely to reflect the median position of its members than the median position of the electorate as a whole. On the other hand, since the object is to elect a party whose policy proposals closely approximate the Condorcet choice, if the proposals of the parties do converge on that position, then the consequences of electing the wrong party are relatively minor.

High barriers to entry will not satisfactorily allow Downsian democracy to be institutionalized with PR for another reason. Although in most cases, the Downsian argument about blackmail parties is internally inconsistent, in two respects they play a vital role. First, if both parties are on the same side of the median (whether as a result of miscalculation or a shift in the distribution of opinion), then the entry of a blackmail party to pull them back to the center is vital. Second, the assumption that politicians are motivated by self-interest makes the problem of an interparty cartel particularly serious. Extending the economic analogy that underlies Downs' analysis, just as economists expect duopolistic firms to exact rents, so one should expect two parties that have a lock on the political market to exact benefits for themselves at the expense of the public.[8] While this danger can be reduced through the threatened entry of additional competitors, the same barriers that would prevent the entry of permanent third parties would also prevent the entry of temporary blackmail, or replacement major, parties. At the same time, however, incentives to two-partyism that simply disadvantage third parties, such as single-member plurality's tendency to leave them underrepresented, are perfectly acceptable, since the key to the blackmail party is not that it wins, but that it credibly threatens one of the major parties with loss to the other. Third, the possibility of blackmail parties is also important because internal party democracy or intraparty choice of candidates cannot be used to prevent an irresponsible oligarchy from taking control of one (or both) of the major parties, because they force politicians to move their policy proposals toward the median position of those supporters, and hence away from the median position in the electorate as a whole. The same can be said as well for dependence on campaign contributors, so that public finance of politics would also be necessary if complete convergence were desired.

One may, however, question the degree to which full convergence ought to be desired, notwithstanding its necessity if the popular will is to be implemented. First, Downsian democracy is even more antiparticipationist than binary democracy, a problem exacerbated since even if there is partisan alternation in office, full convergence would mean that the policies implemented would never change, giving the whole exercise the appearance of futility. Second, the problem of permanent losers would arise in substance (policy) even if not in form (which party is in office). Although the aggregate will of the people would be implemented, all those whose opinions were not roughly in the middle of the social distribution of opinion would find themselves cast in the position of permanently excluded losers. Failure of complete convergence, on the other hand, would mean that even if those near the extremes of the policy space never get their most preferred outcome, there would be a noticeable difference between winning and losing.

Ostrogorskian Democracy

In many respects, Ostrogorskian democracy is simply binary (or possibly Downsian) democracy in the short run, so many of the comments and prescriptions offered above apply here as well. There is, however, one significant difference: where binary and Downsian democracy assume a stable two-party system, Ostrogorskian democracy assumes a succession of transitory two-party systems. As a result, the danger of an entrenched two-party oligarchy becomes a central, rather than a marginal, concern, and those institutional devices favored in the first two cases because they would protect against third-party challenges need to be modified to facilitate the regular replacement of major parties. This difference, in turn, has implications for a number of other aspects of the electoral process, suggesting still further variations in institutional prescription.

Ostrogorskian democracy appears to call for single-member plurality for the same reasons as Downsian democracy. The danger of the wrong party winning is mitigated first by the assumption of frequent party realignment, so that this will be a transitory problem, and second by a tendency to see politics in technocratic terms so that the consequences of allowing the wrong party to win are likely to be less severe. Moreover, since the vestiges of old lines of political division and the germs of new ones are likely to coexist with the division underlying the current party system, the danger that PR will result in a multiparty system, and precisely the lack of clarity of result about which Ostrogorski complained, is enhanced.

In contrast to the previous two systems, established parties ought not be given privileged access to the ballot or to other resources based on outdated enrollment figures or votes received in previous elections. More acceptable barriers to extraneous candidacies would be requirements of nominating petitions or recently renewed enrollments amounting to a significant percentage of the electorate.

The danger of party leadership cadres becoming self-perpetuating is mitigated by the assumption that the parties themselves will not last long. Further, because the Ostrogorskian conception of a party is very much akin to what are now called citizens' movements, internal democracy is clearly appropriate. This, however, has its own danger. Even when a party avoids the "Iron Law of Oligarchy," decisions may be made not by the most numerous but by the most stubborn members, or simply by those whose lack of other responsibilities in life allows them the indulgence of greater staying power at meetings. Additionally, since lack of structure may mean no decisive locus of decision, internal democracy, rather than empowering the party's members to make decisions, may simply mean that there are no decisions.

If, as students of voting behavior repeatedly say, durable parties are important to simplify the information-gathering and decision processes of voters,[9] then one must conclude that Ostrogorskian democracy requires a special kind of citizen. Only those highest in cognitive mobilization are likely to be able to participate effectively, even at the relatively low intensity of voting.[10] In this light, strong tests of competence for the suffrage may be only necessary evils. Additionally/ alternatively, barriers of inconvenience, such as periodic registration, might be used to filter out the uninterested. All these possibilities present obvious problems from the point of view of participationist democrats.

The fluidity of the politics of Ostrogorskian democracy also suggests that more attention be paid to qualifications for office than was necessary with either binary or Downsian democracy. The idea, explicit in Schumpeterian liberalism, and implicit in the first two forms of individualist popular sovereignty, that established party leaders will screen their successors, cannot apply when there are no durable party organizations. Most especially, this model of democracy would justify term limitations to prevent the establishment of a permanent class or cadre of professional politicians. The problem then is that the possibility of reelection is removed as an incentive to responsible behavior in office.

Legislative Democracy

In contrast to the other popular sovereignty theories, under which a particular government is legitimated by having itself won an electoral majority, under legislative democracy a government is legitimated by the endorsement of individual parties that collectively represent an electoral majority, even if the particular government (coalition) itself was never an option presented to the people for ratification or choice. Thus there is no virtue inhering in governments formed in the immediate aftermath of an election, and correspondingly no prejudice against changes in government between elections.

Legislative democracy requires a multiparty system and can be implemented only through PR or STV. The only question is the appropriate number of parties, the trade-off being between fidelity of representation, on one hand, and the clarity and tractability of the negotiating process in the legislature, on the other. Concerns here are district magnitude and devices that encourage party coalescence (electoral thresholds, barriers to the entry of new parties, distribution of resources in a way that privileges large parties) or proliferation (apparentement, distribution of resources according to an equal shares scheme).

The same trade-off returns in another guise with the question of intraparty choice. On one hand, intraparty choice might increase the correspondence between the distribution of views in the party's electorate and its legislative delegation. On the other hand, allowing an intraparty choice may undermine party cohesion. Moreover, if the party elite uses a criterion of balance rather than one of majority or plurality control, an elite-dominated selection of candidates may result in "better" representation than would choice by the party's supporters.

With this exception, internal party democracy is not a major concern for legislative democracy as a model of popular sovereignty theory, since a party's supporters have plenty of alternatives and can "vote with their feet," if policies drift away from those they support. On the other hand, concern with popular sovereignty also implies no reason to oppose internal democracy, which might be supported as a means to increase participation.

Because many alternative coalitions are possible, coalitions likely will form in some localities incompatible with the one formed at the national level. The possibility of local obstruction of national policies emerges and suggests that the autonomy of local governments ought to be restricted. At the same time, in addition to the possibility that local and regional councils will prove useful training and screening devices for future national leaders, some local autonomy can provide valuable opportunities for popular participation.

That the legislature accurately reflect the distribution of popular opinion implies strict attention to the principle of one-(wo)man-one-vote-one value. This principle is relatively easily implemented with a PR electoral formula, but it also means no high barriers of inconvenience to voting. Since the actual negotiating of compromises is delegated to party elites, all that is required of a voter is that he or she be able to identify a party whose platform reasonably approximates his or her own views. Hence, there are no grounds for severe voter qualifications based on competence. Analogously, since party elites are assumed to be pursuing their own most preferred policies, there is no reason for restricting candidacy. Maintaining a policy of equality in the allocation of resources is impossible, both because of the danger of financially motivated proliferation and because of the danger that serious contenders will be lost in a sea of insignificant parties. Thus, allocation according to strength, or on the basis of equality over some reasonably high threshold, although tending artificially to preserve the current balance of power, becomes the best available alternative.

Socialist Democracy

Socialist democracy assumes two cohesive parties that reflect the fundamental conflict between two strong social segments or classes. Governments must command parliamentary majorities and should be stable between elections since only electoral victory authorizes the formation of a government. So far, this is binary democracy revisited, except for the explicitly sociological basis assumed for the two parties. There is, however, an additional difference that stems from the communitarian orientation of socialist democracy and makes this model accept single-member plurality as an electoral formula. Whereas majority support is the fundamental legitimizer of a party's program under binary democracy, the program of the socialist party under socialist democracy has already been legitimized; the role of the electoral system is to assure the peaceful acceptance of its result. Thus conformity to social norms is more important than conformity to abstract principles of majority rule, and the key reason why single-member plurality might be replaced by PR in binary democracy is undercut. Moreover, the underlying communitarianism of socialist democracy is compatible with the idea that a single deputy should represent an entire constituency in a way that individualism is not.

Socialist democracy makes the strongest demands of any of the theories considered regarding internal party democracy, and in particular about the primacy of the party congress over both the leadership and the party's electorate. As a consequence, socialist democracy is fundamentally incompatible with such devices as direct primaries. At the same time, the party authorities must be responsible to the membership through the party congress.

Socialist democracy is associated with a particular class and a particular political orientation. Since they were excluded in the past by suffrage restrictions, it is understandable that this theory calls for a broad franchise. Similarly, there need be few if any legal qualifications for candidacy, since the party itself is the primary filtering device to eliminate unworthy candidates. Public subsidy of campaigns is desirable, and private contributions to political parties ought to be restricted to ensure that number of supporters rather than their "quality" is the basis for party strength. On the other hand, strong barriers to the entry of new parties are appropriate, especially to prevent splits in the working class. The ballot should be structured and subnational elections should be timed to encourage party line voting and national political supremacy.

Tory Democracy

Like socialist democracy, Tory democracy requires two disciplined national parties, thus guaranteeing stable majority governments. Even more important than in the socialist model are legitimation according to tradition rather than raw numbers; the representation of organic communities, with the representative as interlocutor for all constituents; and the (ordinarily) unchallenged supremacy of a single head of government. Hence this model of democracy most obviously calls for single-member plurality elections, as well as other institutional devices that will encourage or enforce a two-party system.

Given the centrality of party discipline and leadership, it is clear that nominations ought at least to be subject to central approval; any form of intraparty electoral choice would be inappropriate. Indeed, the degree to which this prescription fits both Tory and socialist democracy may help explain why the "conventional wisdom" of British politics has tended to exaggerate the degree to which the national parties control local nominations. In contrast to socialist democracy, however, Tory democracy is hostile to internal party democracy. Party members are assumed normally to be supporters rather than choosers or directors of the party's leader, at least until they are prepared to depose him or her; like the Czarist regime in Russia, the proper constitution of a political party in the Tory view might be described as "absolutism moderated by assassination."[11]

Since the nation is assumed to be a single community with a single will, devolution is appropriate only as an administrative convenience. Local elections ought to be about competence rather than policy, so a candidate-oriented electoral system is more appropriate than list PR. National dominance of politics is essential and may be furthered by appropriate ballot format and coincident timing of elections. Local units important enough to rival or challenge the national government either in power or in public perception ought to be avoided.

Tory democracy requires an electorate that represents the nature of the community, but since a community is not simply the aggregation of a large number of unconnected individuals, this does not require slavish adherence to a one-(wo)man-one-vote principle. Restrictions on suffrage that are sanctioned by tradition might be acceptable, particularly as they relate to membership in the community, although their acceptability would evaporate if the social consensus as to their reasonableness were challenged. Tory democracy does not accept the participationist view that everyone ought to take an active part in political life, and citizens ought not to be overencouraged or required to vote; if they prefer to defer to the judgment of other citizens, they should be allowed to do so. Yet no significant group that is a part of the community should be systematically excluded either by explicit bars to voting or by inconvenience.

Modern norms clearly make stringent de jure personal qualifications for candidacy impossible, but at the same time Tory democracy, with its emphasis on a natural ruling class, ought to continue to favor the de facto imposition of such qualifications, perhaps by structuring politics to make candidacy impractical for those who are to be discouraged from pursuing a political career, or to make it less likely that they will be elected. For example, a significant class bias might be introduced to the recruitment process by not paying members of the legislature. Similarly, an electoral system like single-member plurality and campaign practices that emphasize the verbal skills and personability of candidates should aid particular kinds of individuals to "float to the top."

Tory democracy also is inherently ambivalent about political campaigns. On one hand, election campaigns should not be necessary since even ordinary citizens should already know who the leaders of their community are. On the other hand, campaigns are important for mobilizing citizens to express their support and as occasions in which the ties of leadership and deference that bind the political community together are renewed. Restrictions against the buying of votes clearly are needed, but traditional forms of patronage and loyalty are appropriate. Although Tory democracy looks favorably on the monied class, the primary resources ought to be status and respect. Restrictions on political uses of money, especially during a narrowly defined campaign period, are appropriate as a defense against plutocracy.

Benthamite Democracy

Benthamite democracy requires that majorities be formed both in the legislature and in the individual constituencies, because it is by the votes of the majority that one tests proposals against the criterion of "the greatest good for the greatest number." Whether this system requires a two-party system depends on other institutional arrangements. Bentham himself proposed that the prime minister (one would now be more likely to call this official a president) be elected by the parliament for a fixed term. In this case, ad hoc majority formation would be adequate to check executive excesses, and strong party organization would be unnecessary. In a strictly parliamentary system, more partisan structure would be required for government stability, but one may for this reason question the degree to which Benthamite democracy is compatible with a parliamentary system.

If the legitimacy of election depends heavily on the votes of a majority, but strict adherence to a two-party format is not required, then the logical electoral system would be single-member majority or alternative vote. These would also reflect the idea that electoral choices ought to be personal rather than ideological or partisan. Moreover, each allows the functional equivalent of an intraparty choice, thus institutionalizing the idea that MPs should be individually responsible to their constituents. Were single-member plurality to be implemented, it ought to be coupled with a direct primary. In contrast to popular sovereignty theories, ballots ought to be constructed and elections timed to emphasize the individual rather than the party.

The importance of personal ties between representatives and constituents suggests that constituencies ought not to be changed frequently and that they should correspond to natural communities. At the same time, reasonable population equality is required if the idea of majority rule is to be maintained. Bentham himself appears to have resolved this potential conflict largely in favor of stable constituencies and community representation, in that he specified a maximum allowable range of constituency populations of 4:1.

Given the relatively heavy demands it makes of voters, Benthamite democracy calls for suffrage requirements based on competence. Suffrage requirements based on community membership are also appropriate. Similarly, the mature judgment of representatives is important, but Bentham himself feared that once formal requirements for candidacy were substituted for reliance on the judgment of the people, those requirements might become the basis for tyrannical exclusion of some individuals. As a result, he proposed only that candidates be supported by the oaths of their nominators attesting to their belief that the candidate "is at least as qualified in probity, intellect, and active talent as anyone else who might be elected." [12]

Since the point of election is not the direction of policy but its restraint, the danger of local majorities obstructing the national authorities becomes a virtue. Hence, Benthamite democracy is compatible with strong and autonomous local governments. Likewise, rather than seeing frequent elections as an impediment to representatives' implementation of policy, Benthamite democracy suggests that short terms allow representatives who attempt to trespass on the people's rights to be removed before they can do much damage.

The logic of Benthamite democracy suggests that campaign expenditures must be restricted; if all people are motivated by self-interest, one can only assume that candidates who have spent heavily to secure election will expect a return on their investments, which could come only at the expense of the public interest. One reasonable response would be public finance of campaigning. Although there is some risk of candidates coming forward to advertise themselves at the public expense rather than to seek office, the size of the public payment need not be large and could be predicated on the payment of a substantial deposit returnable only to candidates polling a respectable percentage of the vote.

Finally, returning to the problem of parliamentary government, liberal theories are concerned primarily with what the government ought not do. This concern makes sense if government already exists and needs only to be restrained. If there is no prior source of direction, or if the people are to provide direction, then the problem is that the same institution cannot be expected both to provide impetus and to restrain itself. The parliament, as the bastion of liberalism, is ill-suited to formulate policy and needs instead something to which it may react. Thus, with the possible exception of consociational democracy (see below), liberal democracy appears to require a presidential system.

Schumpeterian Democracy

The Schumpeterian model of liberal democracy differs in several ways from its Benthamite sibling in addition to the basic distinction of putting greater faith in the self-restraint of the elite. Schumpeterian democracy also assumes a more active government, and therefore one whose stability and capacity to govern is more important. Its conception of the electorate is more national, giving correspondingly less weight to community representation. The net result implies competition between two national teams of leaders.

Where the key element of Benthamite democracy is the threat that individual MPs will be turned out of office, for Schumpeterian democracy the corresponding threat is that the party in power collectively will be turned out of government, if not necessarily altogether from the parliament. To increase the threat of turnover at the top, electoral institutions that magnify the swing of seats relative to the swing of popular votes are desirable. Thus single-member plurality, along with the usual panoply of institutions that tend to maintain a two-party system, is appropriate. Even more, a presidential system should both encourage a two-party system and magnify the consequences of small swings in the vote.

Although marginal responsiveness is more important than proportionality to the basic logic of Schumpeterian democracy, the appearance of fairness is also significant. Slavish adherence to equality of district populations is unnecessary, and indeed because the perceived fairness of the district drawing process is important, respect for local subdivision boundaries would be desirable precisely because they are not subject to obvious partisan manipulation.

Governance in this view is primarily an elite function. Intraparty democracy is undesirable because it implies constraints on elites. Intraparty choice of candidates is also undesirable because it limits the capacity and responsibility of elites to vet their colleagues and successors. Terms should be long enough to establish the clear responsibility of the incumbent government before voters decide whether to retain or replace it.

The emphasis on self-vetting by the elite implies that formal qualifications for holding office are superfluous. While widespread opportunities for popular participation are important, the uninterested need not be encouraged to participate.

Madisonian Democracy

Only Madisonian liberal democracy has actually been implemented by its original proponents, so the institutions of the original United States government may be taken as a reasonable approximation of those required. At the same time, however, those institutions represent the result of political compromise and were framed for a social system and set of assumptions about the conduct of politics that are no longer valid. As a result, some departure from the early American model may be appropriate.

The key element of the Madisonian model is division and separation of powers, which in the electoral context means multiple sites and times for elections, and where that is not done, a ballot structure that separates one office from another as much as possible. A basic hostility to parties, especially at the national level, requires a candidate-oriented electoral system, although modern realities, as well as the need for some structure within and coordination between the various branches and levels of government, suggest that parties are necessary and therefore that a nonpartisan ballot is not desirable.

The original Madisonian system involved a variety of candidate-oriented electoral systems, including single-member plurality, single-member majority, and some multimember districts. In general, however, all of these reflected the idea that communities with a basic harmony of interest were the correct objects of representation. In modern times, the assumption of a harmony of community interest has often been proven false, suggesting that single-member plurality might be abandoned in favor of STV or one of the semiproportional schemes like limited vote or cumulative voting, which would allow representation of sizeable minorities while still maintaining a candidate-oriented approach. These could also provide an intraparty choice (minimizing party discipline, encouraging personal and local ties). If single-member plurality were preserved, primary elections clearly would further the aims of Madisonian liberalism. As in Benthamite democracy, a separately elected executive would bring some coherence to an otherwise fissiparous system.

Originally, the Madisonian model was seen as compatible with restrictive qualifications for voting for some branches of government, so long as there was a broad franchise for at least one body. In the twentieth century, diversifying the electoral base of the various organs of government through restrictive suffrage requirements is no longer acceptable, but the goal of representing different definitions of the political community in the various branches of government remains. One implication is that the principle of one-(wo)man-one-vote-one value ought not to be applied to all branches of government.

Polyarchal Democracy

Polyarchy, as the late twentieth-century version of Madisonian democracy, needs little additional discussion. One major difference between the updated version of the Madisonian model just sketched and polyarchal democracy is the latter's greater stress on nonelectoral avenues of influence—interest groups, media access, threats of civil (or not-so-civil) disobedience, and so forth. Because it tries to secure diversity of access to power by seeing elections as just one point of access among many, rather than trying to secure institutionalized diversity within the electoral process, polyarchal democracy can support greater adherence to a universal principle of equality in elections. Thus equalization of member-to-voter ratios in all elections, even at the expense of adherence to established community boundaries, is more acceptable. Polyarchal democracy is also, as the emphasis on interest groups implies, more inclined to recognize overtly the existence of "constituencies" that require representation without being geographically defined. Coupled with the fluidity of district boundaries required by equality (at least if single-member districts are used), this model suggests the possible necessity of affirmative gerrymandering.

A second difference is that the polyarchal model is more favorably disposed toward elites and parties. Although parties ought to be loosely organized, diverse, and broadly representative of local and other differences in the population, party line ballots and some space for party organizational elites to screen potential entrants into the political elite are appropriate.

Concurrent Majorities

Although the theory of concurrent majorities effectively was killed in the United States by the Civil War, a modern version has returned in recent years in some proposals for the multiethnic states of central and eastern Europe as well as for the European Union. In simple terms, the theory of concurrent majorities can be decomposed into two parts: some system of popular sovereignty democracy *within* each of the major groups that make up society, and the right of each of those groups to veto, or at least to opt out of, any decision it believes threatens its vital interests.

Although concurrent majorities is a theory of liberal democracy when viewed from the perspective of the society as a whole, within each of the groups presumed to make up that society it calls for some variety of popular sovereignty. This inconsistency is only apparent, however. The theory presumes a fundamental harmony of interest within groups, so that the kinds of threats against which liberals feel defense is necessary can only be external. Although the close identification of elites with their own groups means that elite self-restraint at the level of the whole system cannot be relied upon to prevent tyranny, there is a presumption that elites will be responsible within each group. Indeed, if a particular theory of popular sovereignty were to be attributed to Calhoun himself, it would almost certainly be Tory democracy, the most overtly elitist of those theories. Depending on the characteristics of the groups, however, any popular sovereignty model might be appropriate, and indeed, the same model need not be applied within each group, and elections within the groups need not be simultaneous.

Institutionalization of the group veto is relatively simple. Presumably, subnational governments will correspond to the societal groups, and the group veto could be exercised by those governments. Alternatively, various group delegations in the national legislature might exercise the veto power, again on the presumption that the constituencies for the national legislature will be homogeneous with respect to group. Indeed, this possibility allows some departure from the assumption of geographic segregation, given that it is possible to define constituencies in ethnic terms as well as geographically. Finally, since each group has an independent and absolute veto, apportionment of representation among groups is not especially important.

Consociational Democracy

In the consociational democracy model, the group veto power is conventional rather than constitutional, and so contingent on the acceptance of the majority rather than absolute. The primary defense against both tyranny and system collapse is the self-restraint of the group leaders, on one side the willingness of the leaders of majority groups to defer to minorities, and on the other side the willingness of the leaders of minorities not to abuse this generosity. Concomitantly, consociational democracy does not assume intragroup popular sovereignty, and indeed its emphasis on the deference of followers to leaders and the autonomy of the latter make it doubtful that effective intragroup choice or internal party democracy would be compatible with this theory. Whereas concurrent majorities calls for significantly mass-responsive representation, consociational democracy requires mass-directing representation.

Once proportional sharing replaces absolute veto as the core principle, and once the assumption that the societal groups are divided into local communities that can serve as legislative constituencies is relaxed, the only acceptable electoral system is some form of list PR. Moreover, that legislative representation be proportional to group strength is so important that compulsory voting to assure the proportionate representation of groups whose members are less likely to vote makes sense. PR also has the advantage of favoring minority or oversized majority governments, either of which consociationalists would regard as superior to a self-confidently legitimate minimum winning coalition.

Because consociational democracy envisions a relatively active government, and because executive office is itself one of the values that must be distributed among the social groups, a single directly elected head of government clearly is unacceptable, even if the parliament remains able to restrain the president in ways that avoid overt tyranny. Probably the best solution is a proportionately divided collective presidency, like the Swiss Federal Council, but failing that, government by grand, or at least oversized, coalition. In this respect the high demands made on, and altruistic assumptions made about, elites become most apparent. Unlike the other elite-centered liberal theories, consociational democracy relies on elites to restrain themselves without the external incentive of possible electoral defeat. Because this restraint is assumed to come from the character of the person, rather than from the logic of institutional placement, the cartel of group leaders can be assumed to provide both direction to society as a whole and protection to individual groups at the same time.

Although proportionality is important, suggesting, for example, large districts, it is also important to avoid the splintering of group representation. Competition among parties claiming to represent the same group would have the same deleterious effect on the possibility of elite accommodation as intraparty competition. Thus high barriers to ballot access for new parties, an electoral threshold, and a system of campaign subsidy proportional to previous electoral success would be consistent with the consociational model.

Finally, one cannot rule out the likelihood that one group or another will achieve a (semi)permanent majority in some areas. Such a majority has no need to compromise and little incentive to self-restraint. In addition, it is not clear that the factors that might incline national elites to self-restraint (e.g., fear of system collapse or foreign intervention) would apply in local arenas whose existence is guaranteed by the national government. Thus local autonomy must be suspect in the consociational model. Where it is possible to grant the actual groups, rather than geographic units that only approximately correspond to those groups, autonomy, however, that may be done.

Participationist Democracy

The most important condition regarding elections imposed by concern for participationist democracy is that individual citizens perceive voting to make a difference, or alternatively that the number of wasted votes be minimized. Single-member districts must be avoided. Among multimember systems, those that allow an effective intraparty choice should be preferred, since the psychological effect of having a large proportion of the legislature effectively guaranteed (re)election by virtue of their places on party lists should be nearly as deleterious as having to vote in a safe single-member district. In this sense, STV is probably the best electoral system for participationist democracy, because under this system the maximum possible number of votes demonstrably contributes to the electoral quota of some particular candidate who was preferred by the voters who cast them to some other candidate who was defeated. STV has the additional advantage of furthering the personal involvement of representatives and represented, since, although party may play a significant role in electoral choice, the actual coalition that elects a representative is personal rather than partisan.

Partisan organization of government increases participation and thus should be encouraged. Since this stems from the parties' incentive to fill positions both as candidates and in offices, the number of such positions should be multiplied, especially at the local level. And since participation that involves the making of meaningful decisions is crucial, these local governments must have substantial autonomy within their fields of competence. Along with autonomy of local governments once they are chosen, the election of local government officials should be separated from national elections so that candidates do not feel themselves to be merely place-holders.

Restrictions on candidacy ought to be minimized, although at the same time the choice offered to those who are simply voting must be clear enough for their participation to be meaningful. Even if restrictions on the entry of candidates into the electoral contest should be minimized, their activities once in the contest may be more substantially limited. In particular, regulations that force candidates to adopt labor-intensive rather than capital-intensive strategies should be favored. For example, one might argue that broadcasting should be highly restricted since broadcast campaigns tend to convert the electorate from participants into an audience.

Finally, voting may legitimately be made compulsory, both because citizens may not be able to anticipate the benefits of participation, and because some of those benefits accrue to the public at large, making active engagement in public life a duty, not merely an opportunity. While attention to individual liberty imposes obvious limits on the power of the state to enforce such engagement, compulsory attendance at the polls infringes on individual rights no more than compulsory payment of taxes or compulsory elementary education.

Communitarian Democracy

The difficulties in institutionalizing communitarian democracy were discussed at length in chapter 6, and need not be rehearsed here. Moreover, even more than participationist democracy, in the world of practical politics communitarian values must be seen as correctives to the possible consequences of excessive attention to the values of popular sovereignty or liberalism, rather than as the primary criteria for the construction and evaluation of institutions. Hence, only a few supplementary comments are necessary.

First, an electoral system should encourage political talk that aims toward the building of consensus. PR, which encourages politicians to appeal to that which divides citizens and ultimately may lead to the encapsulating strategies associated with the mass party of integration, is less attractive than single-member plurality or single-member majority. Constituencies should be drawn to encompass true communities, presumably respecting local subdivision boundaries (which themselves should reflect communities), with the natural implication that equality of population must have a relatively low priority. Strong parties should be discouraged, as partial associations that undermine community, as oligarchies that vertically divide the community, and as organizations that foreclose discussion by taking fixed positions and requiring citizens simply to choose between them. Thus the institutions that might further strong party organizations should be avoided.

Second, from the communitarian perspective democracy is the self-government of a community, not just of a group of individuals who happen to reside in geographic proximity. Hence, suffrage requirements (and other standards defining full citizenship) that demand commitment to the community may legitimately be imposed. Although clearly obnoxious on other grounds, under some circumstances racial or religious tests may be necessary for the implementation of communitarian democracy, and indeed that fact underscores one of the dangers of the communitarian argument. More moderately, however, restricting the vote to those willing to endure some inconvenience or insistence that all electoral activity take place in the national language could be defended as reasonable tests of membership in and commitment to the political community.

Incompatibility of Values

Any institutional embodiment of democracy necessarily involves a trade-off among the various democratic values. Especially as the internal or external circumstances that led to a particular choice change, so too may the attractiveness of the institutions chosen. In this concluding section, the cases of Belgium, Italy, and New Zealand illustrate this point; in 1993, Belgium and Italy both had substantially reformed their political institutions and New Zealand appeared committed to do so, all in response to dissatisfaction with the "undemocratic" way in which democratic institutions were working. More generally, these cases illustrate the utility of the approach to the analysis of institutions taken in this book, showing that the problems and debates can be understood in terms of the alternative models of democracy discussed.

Consociationalism in Belgium

At least until the early 1960s, Belgium was one of the leading examples of a successful consociational democracy.[13] Unlike the prototypical Dutch case, however, the major societal cleavage, that between Francophone Wallonia and Flemish-speaking Flanders, was subsumed within the party system rather than forming its basis. The actual party system was based on a division among socialist, liberal, and Catholic camps, but within each camp rules and practices explicitly recognized the language divide. The electoral system was, as appropriate for a consociational democracy, list proportional representation with an individual preference vote allowed, but structured so as virtually never to alter the order of the party lists; the provinces, which were basically homogeneous with respect to language (with the exception of Brussels), formed the constituencies. The established parties enjoyed some minor privileges with regard to ballot access, but the real bar to new parties was the loyalty of the overwhelming number of voters to the big three, which among them won over 90% of the vote and nearly 95% of the lower house seats in 1961, both of which were *declines* from previous elections.

Party leaders played a key role in governing while containing conflict, which required them to make substantial compromises across subcultural boundaries and, in turn, required that each of the leaders maintain firm control over his or her own subculture, so that compromises would be accepted and implemented. On one hand, leaders had to represent their subcultures, and on the other hand they had to compromise their interests.

Maintenance of this system required that the public be satisfied with its almost unrelievedly liberal and elitist emphasis, and that parties be held together by feelings of group solidarity and the delivery of material advantages rather than through ideology. Elections, thus, were about identity rather than policy, and their outcome was reasonably stable because each party merely tried to mobilize its own natural supporters. Within parties, policy was the preserve of the leadership. The language/regional problem was defused by what might be described as an elite conspiracy to keep the lack of a national political community off the political agenda. So long as the overwhelming majority of citizens were prepared to accept a marginal position in politics as well as the elite's decision to subsume the language divide within each of the big parties, and so long as each party concentrated on mobilizing its own subculture and ignored the clienteles of the other parties, consociationalism provided a stable system of power sharing.

In the mid-1960s, all of these conditions unraveled. The Liberal Party changed its name and attempted to shed its anticlerical image (the essence of its cultural identity) and compete on policy grounds for the economically conservative element of the Christian Democratic subculture; in 1965 the new Party of Liberty and Progress nearly doubled the liberal vote and more than doubled their parliamentary representation, roughly equally at the expense of Christians and of socialists. At the same time, (sub)nationalist parties (which had always been there, but with little electoral significance) more than doubled their vote, to 8.8%; in 1968, they had 15.7%, and in 1971 over 22%. These parties raised the immediacy of the language issue and ultimately made accommodation of two language wings within each of the major parties impossible. However, they also attacked the "poor quality" of Belgian democracy, with its domination by a secretive and unresponsive cartel of party elites. This point was echoed in the 1980s by new left libertarian parties, while a succession of right-wing nationalist parties arose, each making its predecessors seem tame in comparison. The results—that each of the major parties split into two independent parties, one Flemish and the other Walloon; that the "responsible" parties shared a smaller fraction of the seats; that the electorates of the responsible parties came under attack from nationalists, left libertarians, and indeed from the other responsible parties—have meant that the compromises required by consociationalism have been more difficult to achieve, both because they require the agreement of more parties, and because the leaders of those parties have less freedom to be responsible. One consequence has been a series of institutional reforms to increase the autonomy, and purity, of the linguistic regions nearly to the point of dismantling the Belgian state.

This brief narrative can be restated in terms of the four underlying democratic values. Consociationalism guaranteed the interests and internal autonomy of each of the major segments of Belgian society; that is, it achieved the goal of political liberalism, but only at the expense of popular sovereignty (elections did not decide government policy), participation in governing, and community (rather than attempting to build a political community, consociationalism implies that existing cleavages will be maintained). Moreover, the unreasonable encroachments against which the subcultures were protected could be defined only relative to the status quo. Thus even the value of liberalism was achieved only to the extent that Belgians were prepared to accept the fairness of the initial position. But, since that included a large residue of the prior system of overt Francophone domination of Flanders, not everyone was prepared to accept its fairness. Further, as the balance of economic power shifted from the old industries of Wallonia to the new high-tech industries that grew in Flanders, and as the threat of domination/invasion from Spain (eighteenth century), France or the Netherlands (nineteenth century), or Germany (twentieth century) faded, they had less reason to submit to a status quo they believed unfair.

The ignoring of popular sovereignty, communitarian, and participationist values was not coincidental, but rather a necessary condition for consociational liberalism to survive. But at the same time, in using solidary incentives to maintain the subculturally-based parties, leaders increased the salience of the lack of community; those relatively worse off subcultures (in this case, the Flemish) were encouraged to call for separation as a way to end their "subjugation." For other citizens, the success of the consociational system in mitigating intercultural conflict and providing security and prosperity allowed values like participation and popular sovereignty to become more important; people became less willing to be excluded from meaningful participation and more insistent on a direct linkage between popular choice and government formation and policy. But these demands cannot be met within the consociational framework.

Electoral Reform in Italy: 1993

Given that more models of democracy have been proposed than, at least in gross terms, electoral formulas, it is natural that the same formula appears appropriate for more than one democracy; in particular, PR has been the electoral formula of choice for both consociational democracy and legislative democracy. Which version of democracy is furthered by use of PR depends on the details of the electoral system, the social and political environment, and the will of politicians.

The Italian Republic could have evolved into a consociational system, and indeed the existence of three clear subcultures (Catholic, socialist/communist, and liberal), postwar government by grand coalition, and a proportional electoral system all pointed in this direction. Movement toward consociationalism was halted, however, by three countervailing facts, which help distinguish the Italian case from that of the classic consociational states: (1) the unwillingness of the Catholic church to countenance cooperation with atheistic communism; (2) the Christian Democrats (DC), rather than facing a situation of "hang together or the system will collapse or be taken over by outsiders," saw the communists as the agents of Soviet domination while the American government both pressed strongly for communist exclusion from government and stood as guarantor against outside (other than American) domination; and (3) perhaps most importantly, in 1948 the DC won an absolute majority in the Chamber of Deputies and did not need to compromise with their major opponent. A second overture to consociationalism came in the period of "national solidarity" in the 1970s. This time movement was halted by the communists, who found that the compromises required to be responsible carried too high a price within their own subculture.[14] (An alternative interpretation is that the DC intentionally kept increasing the price demanded of the communists until they were no longer willing or able to pay it.) Instead, the Italian Republic more nearly approximated a legislative democracy.

Pre-1994 Italian electoral institutions were more appropriate for legislative than consociational democracy. First, the system was hyperproportional, with extremely low barriers both for entry onto the ballot and for election of deputies. One result was at least nine parties represented in the Chamber of Deputies. Second, list PR was coupled with a system of effective intraparty preference voting,[15] which contributed to the early and thorough factionalization of all of the major parties. Thus both the manageability of coalition negotiations and the autonomy of party leadership required by consociationalism were undermined from the beginning. Neither condition, however, is as important for legislative democracy.

Although there were occasional voices to the contrary,[16] the general opinion both in Italy and abroad was that the Italian system worked poorly. The fragmentation of the party system increased, and cabinets were short-lived; in mid-1993 there were 16 parties in the Chamber of Deputies, and Italy had its fifty-second government since 1945. At the same time, however, there was very little actual turnover in government with both the same parties (particularly the DC), and indeed the same individuals, permanently in office.

Beginning in the late 1980s, three events happened to undermine this system. A number of "antiparty parties" (Radicals, Greens, and especially the Northern Leagues and the Sicilian Network) developed, both expressing public discontent with the status quo and further cutting the share of the parliamentary seats from which the governing parties had to form a majority. In the midst of this process, the Communist Party (PCI) dissolved itself and was transformed (minus a rump calling itself the Communist Refoundation) into the explicitly noncommunist

Democratic Party of the Left (PDS). Coupled with the collapse of communism in eastern Europe, this reopened the question of the necessity and inevitability of DC-dominated governments. Then, beginning in 1992, a growing scandal revealed corruption in all the parties, including the former communists, on a staggering scale. One result was the approval in April 1993 of a referendum that in essence called for the replacement of the PR electoral system with an alternative heavily weighted in favor of single-member districts.

Even three years after enactment of a new electoral system in August 1993, it is impossible to predict the ultimate result. It is possible, however, to relate events and arguments during the reform process to the different models of democracy and to the tensions among the democratic values that underlie them, as well as to the importance of the social and political environment in which institutions operate.

The first point to make is that the system of legislative democracy worked more or less as one might have anticipated. The decisions to emphasize representation rather than clear choice of government (implicit in the choice of a highly proportional electoral system) and responsibility of members of parliament to individual electorates rather than to their party leaders (implicit in a strong intraparty preference vote) meant that short-lived coalitions would be formed after elections rather than before. This result is precisely what the model of legislative democracy prescribes, and although here described pejoratively, what the framers of the Italian constitution, who feared that the communists would prove the largest party, wanted. Once that fear was proven groundless, however, the costs of these arrangements loomed larger in the minds of observers. While the tangentopoli scandal may have been the catalyst making reform irresistible even for those who owed their positions to the old system, there had been calls for reform for at least 20 years before 1993.[17]

The basic problem was that the DC was not strong enough to govern effectively but was too strong to be turned out of office. Even the feared sorpasso (the PCI overtaking the DC as the plurality party) would have left the DC securely in office. If all parties were considered potential coalition partners, and if the political center were unoccupied, or even occupied by a small party whose influence in any coalition would be marginal, legislative democracy might produce effective turnover in government, but in the Italian circumstance permanent centrism was the only possibility.[18]

The Italian experience also illustrates the danger that the vote trading that characterizes legislative democracy will decrease rather than increase aggregate welfare.[19] The legislative output of the Italian parliament was typified by hundreds of leggine (little laws), often conferring special privilege or exemption on a small group in exchange for the support of "its" representatives on other issues. The result was widespread waste and inefficiency and an inability to make short-term particular sacrifice, no matter how small, for long-term general benefits, no matter how great. Because shifting coalitions make policies, legislative democracy means that no single and identifiable group is responsible for policy overall, and therefore no group has an incentive to take care of "the big picture."

These problems are the price one pays for the benefits of legislative democracy, and this may indeed have been a wise choice in the early days of the Italian

Republic, when the experience of eastern Europe made the possibility of communist takeover appear quite real. As the perceived benefits shrank, so did willingness to pay the costs.

The key desire expressed by Italian reformers was for alternation in government for several specific reasons. One was to give the voters an effective choice of governments; under the old system, the same government would form in any event, no matter how they voted. A second was the belief that alternation in office at elections would be accompanied by government stability between elections. Third, it was argued that alternation would give politicians in the center an incentive (the threat of defeat) to be responsive, and politicians on the extremes an incentive (the possibility of office) to be responsible.

Although these demands were not often distinguished in the debate over reform, they followed from two rather different conceptions of the ultimate aim. One may be characterized as calling for the system of legislative democracy to be replaced by one of binary democracy, emptying the political center so that instead of a politics of center versus extremes, one would have a politics of moderate left versus moderate right. Alternatively, one could call for the replacement of legislative democracy by Schumpeterian or polyarchal liberalism. To do this fully would presumably require a presidential system, but reforms to strengthen the independent standing of the government in relation to the parliament would represent movement in this direction, and there were indeed such proposals. In particular, some have called for the direct election of the government or prime minister who then would not require an affirmative vote in parliament to assume office.

The Italian case illustrates some of the difficulties of framing an electoral system. The first is that an attempt to implement a system of democracy with unmet social and political preconditions will likely have results quite different from those desired. For example, the first postreform election (1994) saw the number of parties represented in parliament increase. With the inclusion of the Alleanza Nazionale (the reformed neofascists) in one of the major electoral alliances and then in the government, one could at least ask whether there had been any moderation. Although a government formed that apparently had majority electoral and parliamentary support, within nine months it had been brought down by the defection of one of its component parties. Rather than increasing legitimacy, the reform opened a debate over whether majority support in parliament or leadership of a coalition that won a general election (even if the coalition then dissolved) gave the right to form a government.

A second point is that although reformers often look to foreign examples, they often engage in a good deal of wishful thinking. Even within the context of the single-member plurality formula, Italians showed a desire to "have it both ways." Pointing to the UK, the reformers claimed that single-member plurality would produce stable and effective governments. But pointing to the United States, they also claimed that single-member plurality would break the hold of the "party barons," and make individual deputies more responsive to their individual constituencies. They ignored the basic incompatibility of these two models. Illustrating the principle that people tend to rate most highly those values in the shortest supply, features of electoral politics generally regarded as the vices of single-member district systems became virtues in Italy. For example, arguments were advanced claiming that choice based on the personal character and behavior of candidates, and indeed of their spouses and children, would be superior to choice based on party, ideology, or policy.

Finally, the reform process demonstrates that, notwithstanding the references to principle that abound in debates about institutional reform, politicians also are likely to look to their own interests. In the days before the April referendum, the leader of La Rete (the Network), who had been actively supporting electoral reform, switched sides, apparently suddenly realizing that a majoritarian electoral system could have devastating consequences for his movement.[20] Self-interest also explains the early support of the smaller parties for a two-round system rather than single-member plurality and their insistence that a significant number of PR seats be retained. Most significantly, fear that the second round of a two-round system would become "everyone against the DC" was one strong reason for the DC to insist on single-member plurality rather than single-member majority. In the end, however, a majority clearly concluded that the costs of failing to follow through after the overwhelming approval of the April referendum would have exceeded those implicit in the reforms adopted.

Electoral Reform in New Zealand: 1985–1993

As Italians were abandoning PR in favor of a system in which the predominant electoral formula would be single-member plurality, New Zealand was abandoning single-member plurality in favor of a system in which 60 of the members of a newly expanded House of Representatives would be chosen using single-member plurality while another 60 would be chosen from party lists to make the overall result proportional to the party list votes cast. Unfortunately, at least for the purposes of this book, this system entered the New Zealand electoral lexicon as mixed-member proportional (not to be confused with multimember plurality election).

The pre-reform New Zealand political system was widely regarded as the best contemporary example of Lijphart's Westminster model of democracy. Although the Social Credit Party won at least 6.2% of the popular vote at every general election from 1954, the use of single-member plurality assured that the two major parties, Labour and National, monopolized political office, alternately (with a strong bias in favor of National) forming strong majority governments. Since 1950, New Zealand has had a unicameral parliament, which—combined with strong party discipline, a weak judiciary and the absence of any constitutionally enshrined bill of rights, and unquestioned authority of the center to alter the powers of local bodies—has meant that the government's power has been restrained only by its own sense of what is legitimate and by the requirement that it face the electorate at least every three years. Notwithstanding the Labour Party's name, neither of the major parties is class-based. Although Castles and Mair remark on the "sheer narrowness" of the political spectrum identified by their expert judges,[21] the parties nonetheless had quite distinct programmatic identities, and indeed one of the complaints raised against the single-member plurality system was that it encouraged adversarial rather than consensual politics. Thus, in the terms of this book, New Zealand closely approximated binary democracy.

The immediate source of the proposal for mixed-member proportional was the report of the five-member Royal Commission on the Electoral System.[22] The question of electoral reform had been given increased salience by the general elections of 1978 and 1981. On one hand, both of these elections resulted in parliamentary majorities for the National Party, notwithstanding that it had fewer popular votes than Labour. On the other hand, popular discontent was furthered by the discrepancy between the large and growing share of the popular vote received by third parties (particularly Social Credit) and their continued derisory (or nonexistent) representation in Parliament.[23] One consequence was that the Labour Party's manifestos in both 1981 and 1984 called for the creation of a Royal Commission to review the electoral system. Seven months after Labour was returned to power in July 1984 (with a solid parliamentary majority based on only 43% of the valid poll—as opposed to 35.9% for National), the commission was appointed.

In evaluating proposals, the commission referred frequently and explicitly to a set of 10 criteria. The commission recognized at the outset that, as I have argued about the four values around which the analyses in this book have been structured, some of these criteria, "if carried to their full extent, are mutually incompatible. . . . If a system is designed to achieve one particular objective, the likelihood of meeting other objectives may thereby be lessened."[24] Not surprisingly, the commission's recommendations and arguments do not always appear mutually consistent. Clearly, however, both the recommendations of the Royal Commission and the circumstances that led to its creation reflect dissatisfaction with the system of binary democracy then in place.

Although the commission's criticisms of the existing system were not limited to the direct effects of single-member plurality, these were its primary concern. Perhaps the most pressing complaint was the possibility that the "wrong" party might win, as had happened in 1978 and 1981. The commission also found the underrepresentation of small parties, and indeed the tendency to overrepresent the largest party, to be defects of single-member plurality.

A second complaint was the potential for the abuse of executive power that accompanies single-party government. This issue arose prominently in the ensuing debate, in which the most notorious case was the passage of legislation to privatize New Zealand Telcom "late at night and close to the end of the parliamentary session, with less than 13 hours of debate in Parliament,"[25] but in early 1990 there was widespread "dissatisfaction with the way the Government has departed from its manifesto and rushed through dozens of pieces of legislation."[26]

Binary democracy assumes a society divided into two homogeneous sociopolitical groupings. The commission noted that New Zealand fails to meet this condition. Indeed, provision of effective representation for the Maori people was one of the commission's 10 evaluative criteria. In critiquing the provision of four reserved Maori seats, it made many of the arguments raised in the United States about "affirmative action" gerrymanders.

The same problem was considered with somewhat less urgency, but with the same conclusion, for other minority interests and viewpoints under the heading of "political integration."[27]

Other criticisms noted (but not endorsed) were that politics was excessively adversarial and that changes in government entailed the "complete removal from power of all members of the defeated government" with the potential for a complete turn-around in policy.[28] Ironically, it was in part to get "the complete removal from power of all members of the defeated government" that many Italians wanted to adopt a more binary system, and one of the Italian complaints against PR—that it encourages ideological polarization—was raised in New Zealand, under the guise of encouraging adversarial rather than consensual politics, but this time as a defect of single-member plurality.

In Lijphart's view, the commission's report "appears to be based on a general philosophical dislike of the underlying Westminster principle of concentrating power in the hands of the majority and great sympathy for the contrasting consensus principle of sharing, dispersing, and limiting power."[29] However, this interpretation of the report is strongly conditioned by the original framing of a dichotomous choice. A closer reading, coupled with a wider set of alternatives, suggests that the commission instead was proposing an alternative institutionalization of popular sovereignty, which is to say majoritarianism. While there is some evidence of concern for the liberal values at the core of the consensual model, they are to be advanced primarily as a result of a furthering of community.

The choice between these two interpretations hinges on several specific points. The first is the commission's attitude toward majority rule. If the commission indeed favored the consensual model of democracy, it ought to be reflected in a preference for grand coalitions, or at least super-majorities; if it favored a version of popular sovereignty, this should be reflected in a preference for minimum winning coalitions. Second, when the commission expresses concern about possible abuses by single-party governments, is it primarily concerned that the majority will run rough-shod over the minority (consensual), or that the government will be able to ignore the will of the majority by ignoring its own caucus in Parliament or its electoral manifesto (majoritarian or popular sovereignty)? Does the commission see elections primarily as a mechanism by means of which majorities and governments are restrained (consensual) or primarily as a mechanism by which government is directed (popular sovereignty)? Third, what is the commission's attitude about adversarial politics? Finally, does the commission welcome the introduction of ethnicity and other dimensions of conflict into the legislature (consensual, but equally appropriate to the legislative democracy variant of popular sovereignty), or are its proposals rather aimed at the communitarian objective of defusing such questions and preventing them from becoming objects of partisan conflict?

Although the commission suggests from the outset that there ought to be "important limits on any unqualified version of majority rule," the limits to which it refers are "understandings of what is basic in our society," rather than institutional limits. In contrast to the liberal idea that external restraints are necessary, these are not limits to what the majority can do, but limits on what the majority will choose to do. The commission mentions entrenched features of the constitution, but precisely these clauses protect the majority principle itself.[30]

With regard to the normal operation of elections and government, the commission remains clearly majoritarian in outlook. It observes, for example, that "democratic Governments need majority support in the legislature before they can implement their policies";[31] when it writes about the desirability of compromise, it is looking for "a compromise solution acceptable to a majority of the population";[32] most of the problems of Westminster democracy are attributed to governments that have less than majority support, not to those with bare majorities.[33] The commission suggested that elections under mixed-member proportional would still be choices between alternative governments, and thus in essence majoritarian, with potential coalitions announced in advance.[34] The commission, in fact, suggested a clear preference for single-party majority governments, followed by majority coalitions; while it recognized that mixed-member proportional might lead to a situation in which minority governments would form, it argued that this was not necessarily terrible rather than ever suggesting that minority governments might be positively good.[35] The virtue of mixed-member proportional from this perspective is not that it makes coalitions more likely, but that it makes more likely that whatever government forms, whether single-party or coalition, will have received the votes of a majority of the electorate. Indeed, in this respect the commission appears to have reached the conclusion suggested earlier in this chapter—that so long as barriers are erected against excessive proliferation of parties (the commission proposed a 4% threshold), binary democracy may be best implemented through PR.

In evaluating the prospects of government formation under mixed-member proportional, the commission addressed the possibility of "a minor party . . . exacting excessive concessions from a coalition partner or a minority government."[36] This concern is particularly illuminating because concern with the proportionality of power to votes makes sense only within the context of a majoritarian orientation. From the consensual or liberal perspective, influence need not be proportional to voting strength; rather, the concern should be that every significant group have adequate power to protect its interests.

While the commission did express concern about potential abuse of executive power under single-party governments, its primary concern was that, given party discipline, the government caucus might prove unable to restrain the government it supports.[37] In this respect, the problem is not so much protection of minorities (the concern of consensual or liberal democracy) as it is keeping the government in touch with the majority that elected it (the concern of popular sovereignty democracy). This conclusion is reinforced when one looks beyond the electoral formula. In the consensual model, government is restrained by separation of powers. The commission, however, specifically declined to recommend such a separation for New Zealand. In declining to recommend that New Zealand return to bicameralism, the commission again displays a fundamentally majoritarian approach, observing that if a second chamber were under the control of the opposition, "its use of the power to block would be seen as democratically illegitimate, an attempt of the minority to overrule the majority."[38] The commission clearly did not regard elections as the minority's primary protection, observing that, "[i]f a minority group needs or is entitled to other protections [beyond effective representation] for its rights, these must largely be found outside an electoral system based on equality of the vote."[39] The commission was even more explicit about the Maori, concluding "that the burden of responsibility for the protection of these rights is more appropriately borne by arrangements outside the electoral system. . . ."[40]

Single-member plurality generally is associated with an "adversarial" style of politics.[41] If "consensual" politics is the opposite of "adversarial politics," then it is natural to infer that the proposed shift from single-member plurality to mixed-member proportional reflects an antipathy toward adversarial politics. The commission clearly wanted to encourage more compromise in the formulation of policy and to limit the swings in policy attendant on a change of government, but this interpretation should not be accepted uncritically as evidence of a desire to eliminate adversarial politics. In the first place, the commission attributes the swings in policy to governments that have less than majority electoral support. Second, while a "compromise solution acceptable to a majority" may be more moderate than other solutions, it need not be. Moreover, more moderate policies are not necessarily more inclusive; they may simply be unacceptable to citizens on both extremes.

More important, at other points in its report the commission appears positively to value an adversarial approach to politics, regretting only that MPs often are ill-informed and unprepared, and that the "traditions of the House encourage MPs to adopt a style of debate which concentrates on partisan attack and that often appears to the public as little more than petty point-scoring."[42] The commission attributed this perception, however, to "a misunderstanding of the valuable role performed by the Opposition." Moreover, this valuable role is specifically identified as adversarial, and the "value of both Parliament and elections as arenas where competing ideas and policies can and should clash" is emphasized. While the commission records "that a constant theme in the submissions made to us was the strong desire for a process which is less adversarial and more consultative," the commission itself did not endorse this view.[43] The frequent references to elections as choices between alternative governments, rather than merely as selections of representatives, underlines this fundamentally adversarial orientation.[44] The commission rejected the idea of staggered terms because "the electorate would never have a single and decisive opportunity to select or reject a Government."[45]

The commission, extremely concerned with securing effective representation for Maori interests, made two specific recommendations in the context of its advocacy of mixed-member proportional that have a bearing on this problem. The first proposes a waiver in the proposed threshold of 4% of the popular vote or victory in one of the single-member districts for parties representing the interests of Maori or other ethnic groups. The second proposes to abolish the separate Maori electoral roll and constituencies. While the commission clearly expected these proposals to increase Maori representation, this recommendation does not mean, as Lijphart suggested, that it would welcome ethnicity as a point of partisan conflict. In fact, the commission apparently wanted to secure effective representation for Maori interests while *discouraging* the introduction of ethnicity as a point of partisan conflict.

Even though the commission proposed that the 4% threshold be waived for a Maori political party, it did not favor the establishment of such a party. Rather, it saw the possibility of a Maori party—"in the event that Maori were to become dissatisfied with the performance of the existing parties"[46]—as an additional incentive for the major parties to take Maori interests into account. Indeed, if a specifically Maori party may be taken as the PR equivalent of reserved constituencies under single-member plurality, the commission's observation that "[s]eparate representation gives the majority culture a license to ignore the political interests of the Maori people" and "works against the development of mutual understanding between the races"[47] suggests their opposition to such an outcome. Moreover, one may infer from the location of related discussions in the sections on "political integration"[48] that the commission was relying on the defusing, rather than the party politicization, of Maori separateness to assure that the major parties take Maori interests into account. That is, the solution is essentially communitarian rather than liberal.

Once one recognizes more than one conception of popular sovereignty democracy and more than one set of institutions that may be used to implement these conceptions, one perceives that the commission's proposals were aimed at improving rather than replacing majoritarianism and indeed represent a challenge only to the institutions of Westminster democracy, not to its fundamental ethos. An additional advantage of the richer set of democratic theories is that it provides a framework to which many of the commission's other concerns can be related. Three such concerns illustrate this point.

The first is the question of internal party democracy. The problem that the leaders of the two parties associated with binary democracy will become unresponsive to their followers has no real place in the bipolar classifications of democracies, but the commission was quite sensitive to it. Thus they believed a closed-list system necessary to ensure that "democratic procedures for selection of candidates are safeguarded. . . . The law should specifically require that anyone who stands as a candidate for a particular political party should be selected according to procedures which allow any member of the party . . . to participate."[49]

A second concern was the question of suffrage. Again, this question is not raised by the bipolar classifications, but it is central to communitarian values, and the commission considered suffrage in precisely those terms, pronouncing itself "disinclined to suggest the removal of rights . . . which may help integrate new members into our community."[50]

Third, the commission gave explicit attention to participationist values stressing the importance of electoral participation for civic education and personal development. For example, the educational function of electoral campaigns was one of the reasons why the commission rejected the idea of making early voting more generally available.[51] Similarly, the commission appears to have given as much weight to encouraging public understanding as to measuring public approval in its recommendation that the electoral formula be changed only after a referendum and a "period of public consideration . . . during which the advantages and disadvantages of change may be discussed and debated."[52]

Experience and Reform

The end of the 1980s and the first years of the 1990s have seen widespread electoral reform. Aside from the reforms in Italy and New Zealand just discussed, significant reforms have been adopted in Austria, Finland, Israel, Japan, Portugal, and Switzerland among the established democracies, with serious proposals for reform on the table in France and the UK. Attempts to forge a common electoral system for the European Parliament that began in the 1970s have continued. Even more, the period saw the collapse of communism in Europe, with the attendant need for all of the states of eastern Europe and the former Soviet Union to reform their electoral systems. Regimes aspiring to be democratic in the western sense have burgeoned in Africa and Latin America as well, again with widespread writing or rewriting of electoral laws. The problem of how the quality and survivability of democracy may be enhanced through the judicious design of electoral institutions has taken on a practical urgency. In each of these cases claims that particular sets of institutions would further the achievement of democracy figure prominently in the process of reform.

Some of these claims were better described as rationalizations than as arguments about the achievement of democracy. Many electoral institutions have reasonably predictable consequences. Replace PR with single-member plurality and small parties will be disadvantaged, if not wiped out altogether. Eliminate intra-party preference voting and the independence of legislators vis-à-vis the leaders of their parties will diminish. Make registration and voting more convenient or compulsory and the relative weight of the working class in the electorate will increase. One can make plausible arguments that each of these reforms would advance the cause of democracy, but they also have predictable consequences for the self-interest of some parties and individuals. Politicians rarely say, "I favor this reform because it is good for me." Instead they say, "I favor this reform because it will serve the national interest and advance democracy. That it happens to be in my interest as well merely shows what a good democrat I am."

Some disingenuous arguments about institutions and democracy do not alter the fact that institutions do make a difference. The difficulty is that there is no universally correct, most democratic electoral system, notwithstanding a variety of "one size fits all" prescriptions offered by committed advocates of particular systems. Rather, the appropriateness of electoral institutions depends on three mutually contingent considerations that may be summarized as who you are, where you are, and where you want to go.

Democracy has many meanings not just because it is a complicated concept, but because it is constituted of many ill-fitting parts. Trying to define democracy is rather like trying to assemble a jigsaw puzzle that has several extra pieces and too much play in the joints; the pieces may be put together in many ways, yet none of them will ever appear quite right. The first part of this book set out the pieces of the democratic puzzle. In it, I suggested that democracy is valued because it is expected to produce some mix of four valued ends: governmental or other collective decisions that embody the "will of the people," protection of individuals and groups from tyrannical exploitation by government, the development the human potential and personal powers of the citizens, and the encouragement and preservation of community among citizens. Each is valued to some extent by all democrats, if only because some minimal level of each is necessary for the maintenance of the others. But at another level, each is also incompatible with the others, and thus one is compelled to make trade-offs and choices. The institutions one can reasonably expect to increase the level of democracy in a political system depend on the kind of democracy one wishes to achieve.

Changing metaphors, once one knows the kind of democracy to be achieved (where you want to go), the question becomes how to get there. In the second part, I provided a kind of road map, inquiring into the consequences of taking one institutional path rather than another. The first and central concern was the classic question of electoral formula. How do choices among candidate-oriented versus party-oriented systems, or among single-member versus multimember systems, affect the accuracy of the representation of groups and interests, the party system, the stability, and majority status of governments? Other questions concerned the range of offices to which the electoral principle is to be applied and the degree to which elections for various offices are connected to one another; the qualification, selection, and regulation of candidates and parties; and the nature of the electorate and methods by which the voters may express their preferences. Although it was sometimes possible to say unequivocally what the consequences of an institutional choice might be in a narrowly empirical sense, in many cases consequences were contingent on other factors. As with bridges, the carrying capacity of many political institutions is limited; depending on the kind of vehicle they are driving and the baggage it is carrying, a secure shortcut for one set of travelers may be hazardous for some and lead to disaster for others. Who you are contributes to determining the efficacy of institutional choices.

The impact of an institutional change also depends on the prior situation. How to get there depends not only on where "there" is, but also on where one starts. For example, whether reforms that will increase the protection of minority rights are appropriate depends not only on the degree to which those rights might be infringed upon in the absence of institutional protection (who you are), but also on the degree to which institutional protections already are in place (where you are). The meaning of a reform depends not just on what is adopted but also on what is abandoned and on the circumstances under which the change is made. Already it appears that the effect of the reforms introduced in Italy will extend beyond those normally associated with a reduction in proportionality to reflect the fact that the reforms represent an explicit repudiation of the previous political style.

The lesson is that while analysis of the experiences of other countries and other times may make a valuable contribution to consideration of reforms, to prescribe the whole-cloth translation of institutions from one setting to another is wrong. It is wrong because different societies have different needs and desires concerning to the core values of democracy. And it is wrong because the effects of institutions are contingent upon the contexts in which they are set. To conclude a book of this length with the observation that the answer to its central question is, "It all depends," might be disappointing, but that is often the way of political life. To accept the complexity and contingency of political life is better than to emulate the free marketeers who have charged in to impose their view of the only correct economic institutions on societies where they are doomed to fail.

Notes

Chapter 1. Values and Institutions

1. Graham Gudgin and Peter J. Taylor, *Seats, Votes, and the Spatial Organisation of Elections* (London: Pion, 1979), p. 1.

2. Joseph Schumpeter, *Capitalism, Socialism and Democracy* (New York: Harper and Row, 1962), pp. 240–42.

3. For a discussion of the technical meaning of these terms, see, for example, John T. Holt and John M. Richardson, Jr., "Competing Paradigms in Comparative Politics," in John T. Holt and John E. Turner (eds.), *The Methodology of Comparative Research* (New York: Free Press, 1970), pp. 21–72.

4. Douglas W. Rae, *The Political Consequences of Electoral Laws* (New Haven: Yale Univ. Press, 1971); Richard S. Katz, *A Theory of Parties and Electoral Systems* (Baltimore: Johns Hopkins Univ. Press, 1980).

Chapter 2. Early Voting and Elections

1. Aristotle, *The Politics of Aristotle* (New York: Random House, 1943), 1300b, p. 206.

2. J. A. O. Larsen, "The Judgment of Antiquity on Democracy," *Classical Philology* 49 (January 1954), 1–14.

3. Aristotle, *Constitution of Athens* in *Aristotle's Constitution of Athens and Related Texts* (New York: Hafner, 1950), 7:4. Staveley, however, doubts whether so radical a reform as the admission of the landless Thetes to participation even in the Assembly was consistent with the underdeveloped notion of citizenship at that time. E. S. Staveley, *Greek and Roman Voting and Elections* (Ithaca, NY: Cornell Univ. Press, 1972), p. 26.

4. Aristotle, *Politics*, 1281b, p. 147, 1274a, p. 121.

5. Aristotle, *Constitution of Athens*, 8:1.

6. Aristotle, *Constitution of Athens* 16:2.

7. Thucydides, *The Peloponnesian War* (Baltimore: Penguin Books, 1954); J. Cadoux, "The Athenian Archons from Kreon to Hypsichides," *Journal of Hellenic Studies* 68 (1948), 109ff.

8. Staveley, pp. 59–60.

9. The lot also had some religious significance in that it left the final choice to the

gods. For this reason, it was always used to select officials whose functions dealt especially closely with the gods, for example the Treasurer of Athena. The extension of the lot to purely political offices, however, appears to have been more practically motivated, or at least was so explained by later commentators.

10. Moses I. Finley, *Democracy Ancient and Modern* (New Brunswick, NJ: Rutgers Univ. Press, 1973), p. 26.

11. Thucydides, pp. 118–19.

12. Aristotle, *Constitution of Athens*, 8:5.

13. Aristotle, *Constitution of Athens*, 41:3.

14. Frank E. Adcock, *Roman Political Ideas and Practice* (Ann Arbor: Univ. of Michigan Press, 1964), p. 29.

15. Marcus Tullius Cicero, *De Republica*, 2, 39–40, cited in Staveley, p. 128.

16. This right was also available to the magistrate's opponents, who could take advantage of the fact that there were only 195 days during the year on which voting assemblies could meet to prevent a magistrate from being able to call a vote before his term expired.

17. Q. Cicero, *Commentariolum Petitionis*, 53.

18. M. Dessau, *Inscriptiones Latinae Selectae* (Berlin, 1892–1916), 6398ff.

19. Leo Moulin, "Les origines religieuses des techniques electorales et deliberatives modernes," *Revue Internationale d'Histoire Politique et Constitutionnel* (April–June 1953), 106–48.

20. David Knowles, *The Monastic Order in England* (Cambridge: Cambridge Univ. Press, 1941), pp. 396–97.

21. Robert L. Benson, *The Bishop Elect* (Princeton: Princeton Univ. Press, 1968).

22. St. Cyprian of Carthage, Ep. 48,4, Ep. 55,8, Ep. 59,5, Ep. 66,1, Ep. 66,4, Ep. 66,9.

23. F. Homes Dudden, *Life and Times of St. Ambrose* (Oxford: Clarendon Press, 1935), v. I, p. 66.

24. *History of the Franks*, trans. O. M. Dalton (Oxford: Clarendon Press, 1927), v. II, p. 57.

25. Thomas F. O'Meara, "Emergence and Decline of Popular Voice in the Selection of Bishops," in William W. Bassett (ed.), *The Choosing of Bishops* (Hartford: Canon Law Society of America, 1971), p. 28.

26. "Qui praefuturus est omnibus, ab omnibus eligatur." (J.-P. la Migne, *Patrologie latine* [Paris: Garnier Frates, 1881], vol. 54, col. 634, Ep. 10).

27. Luigi Einaudi, "Major et sanior pars," in *Il Buongoverno* (Bari: Editori Laterza, 1954), pp. 92–112.

28. Benedict's fear that an unworthy monk would be chosen abbot was so strong that even in the case of a unanimous decision, the bishop, neighboring abbots, or even laymen were to intervene to prevent scandal (*Sancti Benedicti Regula Monasteriorum* [Freiburg: Herder, 1927] ch. 64).

29. One early reference is Lanfranc. As late as the fifteenth century, Panormitanus wrote "Non sufficit maioritas numeri sine sanioritate" and "Non ergo sufficit sanioritas nisi etiam concurrat maioritas." Niccolo de' Tudeschi, *Abbatis Panormitani in qvinqve Decretalivm epistolarvm libros, commentaria, sev lectvrae* (Lyons: Philippi Tinghi, 1578), Tit vj "De Electione," cap. 57, 7 and cap. 42, 7.

30. Leo Moulin, "Les origines," p. 127.

31. The problem of election did arise for the House of Lords after the Act of Union with Scotland in 1707, which added 16 representatives of the Scottish peerage to be elected at the beginning of each parliament.

32. In 1212, John summoned representatives from each county to meet with him as soon as possible, i.e., not necessarily all together. Earlier in 1213, he summoned the reeve

and four men from each township to meet in St. Albans, but this was limited to the royal demesne. See J. C. Holt, "The Prehistory of Parliament," in R.G. Davies and J. H. Denton (eds.), *The English Parliament in the Middle Ages* (Philadelphia: Univ. of Pennsylvania Press, 1981), pp. 5–8.

33. Edward Miller, "Introduction," in E. B. Fryde and Edward Miller (eds.), *Historical Studies of the English Parliament* (Cambridge: Cambridge University Press, 1970), vol. 1, pp. 7–8.

34. J. G. Edwards, "The *Plena Potestas* of English Parliamentary Representatives," in Fryde and Miller, p. 148. The term "attorney" actually was used in several returns in the 1330s.

35. *Statutes of the Realm*, 7 Hen IV c 15.

36. *Statutes of the Realm*, 8 Hen VI c 7.

37. Goronwy Edwards, "The Emergence of Majority Rule in English Parliamentary Elections," *Transactions of the Royal Historical Society*, 5th series, v. 14 (1964), 189.

38. Derek Hirst, *The Representative of the People* (Cambridge: Cambridge Univ. Press, 1975), p. 14. By the end of the sixteenth century, plurality was also established for election to the French Estates General. See J. Russell Major, "The Electoral Procedure for the Estates General of France and Its Social Implications, 1483–1651," *Medievalia et Humanistica* 10 (1956), 133.

39. John Ernest Neale, *Elizabethan House of Commons* (London: Jonathan Cape, 1949), p. 70.

40. Theodore F. T. Plucknett, *Taswell-Langmead's English Constitutional History* (Boston: Houghton Mifflin, 1960), p. 564.

41. Even William Pitt the younger sat for a pocket borough. After being returned in 1780, he wrote of his patron that "no kind of condition was mentioned but that if ever our lines of conduct should be opposite, I should give him the opportunity of choosing another member." Quoted in Samuel H. Beer, *British Politics in the Collectivist Age* (New York: Random House, 1969), p. 23.

42. *The Weekly Register or Universal Journal*, London, March 31, 1733. The letter, with a slightly different text, is quoted by Romney Sedgwick in *The House of Commons 1715–1754* (History of Parliament Trust, 1970) vol. 2, p. 126. According to Sedgwick, the letter was a joke, with a "short and extremely proper" letter actually dispatched to the corporation.

Chapter 3. Popular Sovereignty

1. Mancur Olson, *The Logic of Collective Action* (New York: Schocken, 1970).

2. Some communications theorists would dispute the acceptability of this substitute. It is not at all clear that one can "reach out and touch someone" electronically in the same way that is possible in person. See, for example, Marshall McLuhan, *Understanding Media* (New York: McGraw Hill, 1964).

3. John Stuart Mill, *Considerations on Representative Government* (Chicago: Henry Regnery, 1962), p. 74.

4. L. S. Amery, *Thoughts on the Constitution* (London: Oxford University Press, 1947), p. 19. Samuel Beer in *British Politics in the Collectivist Age* (New York: Random House, 1969) refers to the Conservative Party's model of democracy as "Tory Democracy." In many places, this discussion follows his quite closely. Use of his term has been avoided here, however, first because aspects of the theory that more properly relate to other democratic values are ignored and second because added explanations and elaborations do not necessarily reflect the Conservative Party's philosophy. My concern is more to present a consistent theory and its implications than to reflect and criticize an existing body of thought.

5. Amery, p. 31.

6. Except as a matter of English history, this argument need not be made in monarchist terms.

7. Beer, p. 93.

8. A. K. White, *The Character of British Democracy* (Glasgow: Craig and Wilson, 1945), p. 20.

9. The change to election of the Conservative leader is actually a retreat from "real" Toryism, which always would prefer decision by consensus to a vote.

10. F. J. C. Hearnshaw, *Conservatism in England* (London: Macmillan, 1933), pp. 293–94.

11. Herbert Morrison, at the 1947 Labour Party Conference.

12. Clement Attlee, *The Labour Party in Perspective* (London: Gollancz, 1949), p. 91.

13. "Simple majority rule" is that system of choice between two alternatives in which the one chosen by more than half of those voting is adopted. The system in which the alternative, potentially of several, that has the most votes regardless of whether or not they constitute an absolute majority will be called "simple plurality rule."

14. Douglas W. Rae, "Decision Rules and Individual Values in Constitutional Choice," *American Political Science Review* 63 (March 1969), 40–56.

15. I refer here only to technical problems with majority rule as a social decision rule. Such problems as the possibility that the majority may be nasty are definable only in terms other than those of popular sovereignty and so are beyond the scope of this chapter. On the other hand, some minor technical problems, for example the possibility that some citizens have no preferences, are also ignored. Some of these are discussed in Robert A. Dahl, *A Preface to Democratic Theory* (Chicago: Univ. of Chicago Press, 1956), pp. 38–44.

16. Kenneth J. Arrow, *Social Choice and Individual Values* (New York: John Wiley, 1963). The conditions are unrestricted domain, positive association of social and individual values, citizen sovereignty, and independence of irrelevant alternatives.

17. Gerald H. Kramer, "On a Class of Equilibrium Conditions for Majority Rule," *Econometrica* 41 (1974), 285–97; Charles A. Plott, "A Notion of Equilibrium and Its Possibility under Majority Rule," *American Economic Review* 57 (1967), 787–806; Richard G. Niemi and Herbert F. Weisberg, "A Mathematical Solution for the Probability of the Paradox of Voting," *Behavioral Science* 13 (1968), 317–23.

18. Robin Farquharson, *Theory of Voting* (New Haven: Yale University Press, 1969). A practical example comes from the debate over direct election of U.S. senators. By introducing an amendment to the proposal that would have called for federal supervision of elections so as to prevent racial discrimination, Republican opponents of direct election were able to delay its adoption by 10 years.

19. Maurice Duverger, *Political Parties* (New York: John Wiley, 1959), p. 215.

20. E. E. Schattschneider, *Party Government* (New York: Holt, Rinehart, and Winston, 1942), p. 52.

21. Woodrow Wilson, *Congressional Government*, (Boston: Houghton Mifflin, 1885), p. 332.

22. Austin Ranney, *The Doctrine of Responsible Party Government* (Urbana: Univ. of Illinois Press, 1962), p. 156.

23. For the most part, the distinction between members and supporters reflects the difference between European and American conceptions of party.

24. Duverger, pp. 372–92.

25. "We will refer to a curve which is either always upward-sloping, or always downward-sloping, or always horizontal, or which is upward-sloping to a particular point and downward-sloping beyond that point . . . , as being a single-peaked curve. On this

definition *a single-peaked curve is one which changes its direction at most once, from up to down.*" Duncan Black, *The Theory of Committees and Elections* (Cambridge: Cambridge Univ. Press, 1958), p. 7 (emphasis in original).

26. Anthony Downs, *An Economic Theory of Democracy* (New York: Harper and Row, 1957), p. 25.

27. Moisei Ostrogorski, *Democracy and the Organization of Political Parties* (New York: Macmillan, 1902), vol. II, p. 658.

28. Ostrogorski claims that the apparent incompetence of voters is actually the fault of the system: ". . . confronted with a single well-defined question, the elector will be able to understand what is said to him, whereas now he is not. Those who have conducted elections campaigns . . . all agree that it is impossible to make the electors understand more than one question at a time, but that, on the other hand, if one deals with a single problem and takes the trouble—one must take a great deal—to explain it well, one can drive it into the popular mind," vol. II, p. 660.

29. Ranney, p. 129.

30. Dahl, p. 132; Douglas W. Rae and Hans Daudt, "The Ostrogorski Paradox: A Peculiarity of Compound Majority Decision," *European Journal of Political Research* 4 (1976), 391–98.

31. James M. Buchanan and Gordon Tullock, *The Calculus of Consent* (Ann Arbor: Univ. of Michigan Press, 1962), chap. 7–12; Gordon Tullock, "A Simple Algebraic Logrolling Model," *American Economic Review* 60 (June 1970), 419–26; James S. Coleman, "The Possibility of a Social Welfare Function," *American Economic Review* 56 (December 1966), 1105–22; Edwin T. Haefele, "Coalitions, Minority Representation, and Vote-Trading Probabilities," *Public Choice* 8 (Spring 1970), 75–90; Dennis C. Mueller, Geoffrey C. Philpotts, and Jaroslav Vanek, "The Social Gains from Exchanging Votes: A Simulation Approach," *Public Choice* 13 (Fall 1972), 55–80.

32. The falsity of this assumption is one reason for government intervention in the so-called free market.

33. William Riker and Steven J. Brams, "The Paradox of Vote Trading," *American Political Science Review* 67 (December 1973), 1235–47.

34. There are reasons for wanting to ensure minority representation, but they are not directly related to popular sovereignty. Examples include desire for a legitimate arena for dissent to be voiced, a training and recruitment ground for alternative government, a forum to keep the public informed so it can make intelligent decisions in future elections.

35. David H. Koehler, "Vote Trading and the Voting Paradox: A Proof of Logical Equivalence," *American Political Science Review* 69 (September 1975), 954–60. See also Peter Bernholz, "Logrolling, Arrow-Paradox and Decision Rules—A Generalization," *Kyklos* 27 (1974), 49–62.

36. For arguments against the likelihood of this occurring, see Richard S. Katz, "Party Government: A Rationalistic Conception," in Francis Castles and Rudolf Wildenmann (eds.), *Visions and Realities of Party Government* (Berlin: de Gruyter, 1986), pp. 31–71.

37. Steven J. Brams and Peter C. Fishburn, *Approval Voting* (Cambridge: Birkhauser Boston, 1983).

Chapter 4. Liberal Democracy

1. Joseph A. Schumpeter, *Capitalism, Socialism and Democracy* (New York: Harper and Row, 1962), p. 242, emphasis in original.

2. C. B. Macpherson, *The Real World of Democracy* (Oxford: Oxford Univ. Press, 1966), p. 6.

3. *The Federalist* (New York: Random House, n.d.), number 51, p. 337.

4. John C. Calhoun, *Disquisition on Government* (New York: Peter Smith, 1943), p. 4.

5. C. B. Macpherson, *The Life and Times of Liberal Democracy* (Oxford: Oxford Univ. Press, 1977), p. 34.

6. Women's suffrage has been a special case in the liberal definition of democracy. Because the liberal justification of the right to vote is to allow those whose interests were threatened by the government to defend themselves, and because women were not perceived as having any interests distinct from those of their male relatives, liberals could argue that universal *manhood* suffrage was sufficient for full democracy.

7. Jeremy Bentham, *Principles of the Civil Code*, in *The Works of Jeremy Bentham* (New York: Russell and Russell, 1962), vol. l, p. 305.

8. Jeremey Bentham, *Constitutional Code*, in *The Works of Jeremy Bentham* (New York: Russell and Russell, 1962), vol. 9, p. 47.

9. Bentham, *Constitutional Code*, pp. 48–49.

10. Bentham, *Constitutional Code*, p. 95.

11. Bentham, *Constitutional Code*, p. 51.

12. Bentham, *Constitutional Code*, p. 96.

13. It is important to distinguish between the reforms that Bentham the theorist advocated as desirable and those that Bentham the political reformer was prepared to accept. In contrast to the variety of exceptions to universality that Bentham and James Mill at one time or another appeared willing to accept, the argument I consider here permitted disenfranchisement only of children, the insane, and criminals actually incarcerated. Literacy was to be allowed as a qualification for voting, but only on the presumption that "two to three months social pastime, at the hours of repose from work, would give it to all adults in whose eyes the privilege were worth that price." ["Radical Reform Bill with Extracts from the Reasons," in *The Works of Jeremy Bentham* (New York: Russell and Russell, 1962), vol. 3, p. 560; see also, Bentham, *Constitutional Code*, p. 99.]

14. Bentham, *Constitutional Code*, p. 100.

15. Bentham, "Radical Reform Bill," p. 561.

16. Bentham, "Radical Reform Bill," p. 559, emphasis in original.

17. Schumpeter, p. 256, emphasis in original.

18. Schumpeter, p. 262.

19. Schumpeter, pp. 262–63.

20. See Bernard Berelson, Paul Lazarsfeld, and William McPhee, *Voting* (Chicago: Univ. of Chicago Press, 1954), chap. 14, for the classic statement of this position.

21. Giovanni Sartori, *Democratic Theory* (New York: Praeger, 1965), p. 91.

22. Sartori, p. 124.

23. Schumpeter, p. 278.

24. Samuel Beer, *British Politics in the Collectivist Age* (New York: Random House, 1969), chap. 2.

25. Schumpeter, p. 283.

26. As Dahl points out for Madison, and as is true of other liberals as well, although tyranny is the central concern, and although the term is used frequently, it is never clearly defined. Robert A. Dahl, *A Preface to Democratic Theory* (Chicago: Univ. of Chicago Press, 1956), pp. 6–7.

27. *Federalist*, number 10, p. 59.

28. *Federalist*, number 10, p. 60.

29. *Federalist*, number 10, p. 61.

30. *Federalist*, number 39, pp. 243–44.

31. *Federalist*, number 51, p. 339.

32. Compare *The Federalist*, number 49, with Bentham's "Radical Reform Bill," p. 561.

33. *Federalist*, number 51, p. 337.

34. Dahl, *Preface*, p. 20.

35. Dahl, *Preface*, p. 21.

36. David Mayhew, *Congress: The Electoral Connection* (New Haven: Yale Univ. Press, 1974), esp. pp. 84–85.

37. Richard Hofstadter, *The Idea of a Party System* (Berkeley: Univ. of California Press, 1970).

38. Robert A. Dahl, *Polyarchy* (New Haven: Yale Univ. Press, 1971).

39. Dahl, *Polyarchy*, pp. 1–2.

40. Dahl, *Polyarchy*, p. 1.

41. Michael Parenti, *Democracy for the Few* (New York: St. Martin's Press, 1977), pp. 1–2. One should note that although Parenti disputes this rosy picture of the United States, his disagreement is largely factual. He does not dispute the fundamental liberal argument, merely the assumptions of some (most?) American liberals about "how the resources of power are distributed within the entire politico-economic system."

42. Dahl, *Polyarchy*, p. 15.

43. In principle, polyarchy might instead be maintained by diffusion of politicized military power, but as the example of Lebanon demonstrates, this solution is unlikely to be stable since the competition engendered quickly becomes military rather than electoral.

44. Seymour Martin Lipset, *Political Man* (Garden City, NY: Doubleday, 1960), pp. 77–78.

45. Dahl, *Preface*, p. 132.

46. Mancur Olson, *The Logic of Collective Action* (New York: Schocken Books, 1968).

47. Calhoun, p. 7.

48. Calhoun, pp. 13–14.

49. Calhoun, pp. 15–16.

50. Calhoun, p. 34.

51. Calhoun, p. 24.

52. Calhoun, pp. 37, 47, 40–41.

53. Calhoun, p. 25.

54. Calhoun, p. 46.

55. Calhoun, p. 45.

56. Arend Lijphart, *The Politics of Accommodation* (Berkeley: Univ. of California Press, 1968), p. 200.

57. Arend Lijphart, *Democracy in Plural Societies* (New Haven: Yale Univ. Press, 1977), p. 25.

58. Lijphart, *Politics of Accommodation*, p. 206.

59. For example, time on the Dutch state broadcasting networks is allocated in proportion to membership in listener/viewer associations.

Chapter 5. Participationist Democracy

1. John Stuart Mill, *Considerations on Representative Government* (Chicago: Henry Regnery, 1962), p. 58.

2. Peter Bachrach, *The Theory of Democratic Elitism* (Boston: Little, Brown, 1967), p. 4.

3. Mill, pp. 49–52.

4. Mill, pp. 71–73.

5. For example, see Bachrach.

6. Margaret Mead, quoted by Robert Lane, *Political Ideology* (Glencoe: Free Press, 1962), p. 161.

7. Carole Pateman, *Participation and Democratic Theory* (Cambridge: Cambridge Univ. Press, 1970), chap. 3.

8. John Stuart Mill, in G. Himmelfarb (ed.), *Essays on Politics and Culture* (Garden City, NY: Doubleday, 1963), p. 229.

9. Pateman, chap. 4.

10. Sidney Verba, *Small Groups and Political Behavior* (Princeton: Princeton Univ. Press, 1961), pp. 220–21.

11. Giovanni Sartori, *Democratic Theory* (New York: Praeger, 1965), p. 89.

12. Alexis de Tocqueville, *Democracy in America* (New York: Oxford Univ. Press, 1947), p. 53.

13. Gabriel Almond and Sidney Verba, *The Civic Culture* (Boston: Little, Brown, 1965), p. 145.

14. Sartori, p. 124.

15. John Stuart Mill, *Principles of Political Economy* (New York: D. Appleton, 1876), vol. 2, p. 569.

16. Bachrach, p. 96.

17. Joseph Schumpeter, *Capitalism, Socialism and Democracy* (New York: Harper and Row, 1962), p. 283.

18. Pateman, p. 25.

19. Robert Michels, *Political Parties: A Sociological Study of the Oligarchical Tendencies of Modern Democracy* (New York: Free Press, 1962), p. 365.

20. Michels, p. 366.

21. Michels, p. 369.

22. F. H. Blum, *Work and Community* (London: Routledge and Kegan Paul, 1968), pp. 374–75.

23. Pateman, pp. 82–83.

24. Robert Pranger, *The Eclipse of Citizenship* (New York: Holt, Rinehart, and Winston, 1968), p. 52.

25. See Alan Wertheimer, "In Defense of Compulsory Voting," in J. Roland Pennock and J. W. Chapman (eds.), *Participation in Politics*, pp. 276–96.

26. David E. RePass, "Issue Salience and Party Choice," *American Political Science Review* 65 (June 1971), 389–400.

27. Sidney Verba and Norman Nie, *Participation in America* (New York: Harper and Row, 1972), pp. 32–40.

28. Mill, *Considerations*, p. 134.

29. Mill, *Considerations*, pp. 194–95.

30. Mill, *Considerations*, p. 235.

31. Mill, *Considerations*, pp. 95–101.

32. C. B. Macpherson, *The Life and Times of Liberal Democracy* (Oxford: Oxford Univ. Press, 1977), p. 60.

33. For example, see Peter Bachrach and Morton Baratz, *Power and Poverty* (New York: Oxford Univ. Press, 1970).

34. Macpherson, p. 99.

35. Macpherson, pp. 65–66.

36. G. D. H. Cole, *Social Theory* (London: Methuen, 1920), p. 208.

37. See Pateman, p. 77.

38. Benjamin Ginsberg, *The Consequences of Consent: Elections, Citizen Control and Popular Acquiescence* (Reading, MA: Addison Wesley, 1982), ch. 1, 5.

Chapter 6. Communitarian Democracy

1. Benjamin R. Barber, *Strong Democracy: Participatory Politics for a New Age* (Berkeley: Univ. of California Press, 1984), p. 221.

2. Barber, p. 219.

3. Barber, p. 226, emphasis in original.

4. Joseph Stalin, *The Foundations of Leninism* (New York: International Publishers, 1932), p. 50.

5. V. I. Lenin, *State and Revolution* (New York: International Publishers, 1932), p. 74; see also, Mao Tse-Tung, "On People's Democratic Dictatorship," excerpted in Carl Cohen (ed.), *Communism, Fascism, and Democracy* (New York: Random House, 1962), p. 206.

6. Karl Marx, *Critique of Political Economy*, in Max Eastman (ed.), *Capital and Other Writings* by Karl Marx (New York: Modern Library, 1932), p. 343.

7. Marx and Engels, in Eastman (ed.), p. 321.

8. Eduard Heimann, "Marxism and Underdeveloped Countries," *Social Research* 19 (September 1952), 326–27.

9. Marx and Engels, pp. 342–43.

10. The word "apparent" is used to describe both the political power and the political rights of the working class because one could argue that the working class has only gained the power to choose their oppressors and that their political rights are limited to the right to support the existing capitalist hegemony. Additionally, and of great significance for the theory of guided democracy, there is the Leninist argument that the improved living conditions of the working class in western countries is supported only by the exploitation of the Third World.

11. Heimann, p. 327.

12. V. Chkhikvadze, *The State, Democracy and Legality in the USSR: Lenin's Ideas Today* (Moscow: Progress Publishers, 1972), pp. 220–21.

13. Chkhikvadze, p. 219.

14. Heimann, p. 331.

15. A. Denisov and M. Kirichenko, *Soviet State Law* (Moscow: Foreign Languages Publishers, 1960), p. 336.

16. Etienne Balibar, *On the Dictatorship of the Proletariat* (London: NLB, 1977), p. 70.

17. Denisov and Kereshenko, p. 336.

18. Stalin, p. 115.

19. V. I. Lenin, *What Is To Be Done?*, in *Collected Works* (London: Lawrence and Wishart, 1960), vol. 5, p. 384, emphasis in original.

20. Stalin, p. 50, quoting Lenin, *State and Revolution*. See also, Chkhikvadze. pp. 202, 211.

21. Mao, p. 207.

22. *Pravda* (Bratislava), 4 Dec. 1971, quoted in Frank Dinka and Max J. Skidmore, "The Functions of Communist One-Party Elections: The Case of Czechoslovakia, 1971," *Political Science Quarterly* 88 (September 1973), 415.

23. Everett M. Jacobs, "Soviet Local Elections: What They Are and What They Are Not," *Soviet Studies* 22 (July 1970), 70.

24. Dinka and Skidmore, 419.

25. Chkhikvadze, pp. 207, 211–12.

26. For example, Daniel S. Lev concludes that while Sukarno "speaks the language of the early Marxists and insists that Marxism is a basic element in his thinking . . . a careful reading of his many speeches brings to light little evidence to show that he was in fact deeply affected by Marxist analysis, even though he may rely on its terminology." *The Transition to Guided Democracy: Indonesian Politics, 1957–1959* (Ithaca: Cornell Univ. Department of Asian Studies, 1966), pp. 46–47.

27. Ruth T. McVey, introduction to *Nationalism, Islam and Marxism* (Ithaca: Cornell Univ. Department of Asian Studies, 1970), p. 3.

28. Madeira Keita, "The Single Party in Africa," in Paul Sigmund (ed.), *The Ideologies of the Developing Nations* (New York: Praeger, 1967), pp. 229–30.

29. McVey, p. 23; Sékou Touré, *La Lutte du Parti Démocratique de Guinée pour Emancipation Africaine* (Conakry: Imprimerie Nationale, 1959), translated and excerpted in Paul Sigmund (ed.), *The Ideologies of the Developing Nations* (New York: Praeger, 1967), p. 220; Sékou Touré, *The Doctrine and Methods of the Democratic Party of Guinea,* (Conakry: 1963), vol. 1, p. 30.

30. Sékou Touré, *Doctrine and Methods,* vol. 1, p. 21, emphasis in original.

31. As Sigmund remarks in observing that legitimacy may derive as much from what the people should desire as it does from what they do desire, "That there should be some confusion on this point is not surprising since democratic theory has always been ambiguous in this respect." Sigmund, p. 24.

32. Sukarno, quoted in Bernhard Dahm, *Sukarno and the Struggle for Indonesian Independence,* Mary F. Somers Heidhues (trans.), (Ithaca: Cornell Univ. Press, 1969), p. 203; see also the statement of the Cabinet of Kenya, "African Socialism and Its Application to Planning in Kenya," in Sigmund, p. 271.

33. Sékou Touré, *Doctrine and Methods,* vol. 1, p. 27.

34. McVey, p. 8.

35. Julius Nyerere, "Democracy and the Party System," in Sigmund, p. 300. Nyerere continues, "There can, therefore, be only one reason for the formation of such parties in a country like ours—the desire to imitate the political structure of a totally dissimilar society." See also Madeira Keita, p. 230.

36. Sékou Touré, *Doctrine and Methods,* vol. 1, pp. 27–28.

37. Kwame Nkrumah, "Consciencism," in Sigmund, p. 260.

38. Madeira Keita, p. 233.

39. Sigmund, p. 26; McVey, p. 5; Dahm, p. 156; Sékou Touré, *Doctrine and Methods,* vol. 1, p. 161.

40. Nyerere, p. 301.

41. That is, although a large proportion of incumbent candidates, even at the ministerial level, may be denied reelection, the social stratum from which successful candidates are drawn is not changed. Goran Hyden and Colin Leys, "Elections and Politics in Single-Party Systems: the Case of Kenya and Tanzania," *British Journal of Political Science* 2 (October 1972), 389–420; Guy Hermet, Richard Rose, and Alain Rouquié (eds.), *Elections without Choice* (New York: John Wiley, 1978).

42. This is a distinction that C. B. Macpherson overlooks in his assessment of the claims of Third World, nonliberal democracy to be called "democracy." *The Real World of Democracy* (Oxford: Oxford Univ. Press, 1966), pp. 23–34.

43. In this respect, elections in guided democracies can be likened to early ecclesiastical elections, in which an informal discussion would result in a choice later confirmed by formal unanimity. In these terms, elections in people's democracies might then be compared to church elections ratifying the nominee of a prince or bishop.

44. Sékou Touré, *Doctrine and Methods,* vol. 1, p. 52, emphasis in original.

45. Sékou Touré, vol. 1, p. 159.

46. Bechir Ben Yahmed, "For or Against the Single Party?" in Sigmund, pp. 184–85.

47. Barber, part 1.

48. Robert Paul Wolff, *The Poverty of Liberalism* (Boston: Beacon Press, 1968).

49. Barber, pp. 35, 171.

50. John Rawls, *A Theory of Justice* (Cambridge: Harvard Univ. Press, 1971), p. 12.

51. Michael J. Sandel, *Liberalism and the Limits of Justice* (Cambridge: Cambridge Univ. Press, 1982), p. 149.

52. Sandel, p. 173.

53. Sandel, pp. 179, 65, 179.

54. Rawls, p. 3.

55. Barber, pp. 32–35.

56. Barber, p. 64.

57. Barber, p. 136.

58. John Dewey, *The Public and Its Problems* (New York: Henry Holt, 1927), p. 150.

59. Barber, p. 158. In these terms, it is obvious that there can be no citizens unless they have a (not necessarily all the same) prior conception of the public good.

60. Carole Pateman, *The Problem of Political Obligation: A Critical Analysis of Liberal Theory* (Chichester: John Wiley and Sons, 1979).

61. Pateman, esp. pp. 80–88.

62. Pateman, p. 174.

63. Barber, p. 145; see also Pateman, p. 161.

64. Peter Bachrach, *The Theory of Democratic Elitism: A Critique* (Boston: Little, Brown, 1967).

65. Dewey, p. 143.

66. Dewey, p. 188.

67. Elaine Spitz, *Majority Rule* (Chatham, NJ: Chatham House, 1984), p. xii, emphasis in original.

68. Barber, p. 132. See also, p. 151.

69. Barber, p. 118, emphasis added.

70. Barber, pp. 120–21.

71. Barber, p. 158.

72. Barber, p. 126, emphasis in original.

73. Barber, pp. 175, 136.

74. Barber, chap. 10.

75. Barber, pp. 269–81.

76. See especially Barber, pp. 186–87, for criticism of the secret ballot.

77. The reservations Barber expresses are of such force and of such a character as to make one wonder why he lists this proposal at all. As he himself observes, "the libertarian spirit of the voucher scheme . . . is inimical to the very idea of a public good and of public judgments politically generated" (p. 296).

78. For example, Robert Dahl seems to favor a more thorough program of workplace democracy than Barber himself. *Dilemmas of Pluralist Democracy: Autonomy vs. Control* (New Haven: Yale Univ. Press, 1982), pp. 199–201.

79. Douglas Yates, *Neighborhood Democracy* (Lexington: D.C. Heath, 1973), p. 160.

80. For example, see James A. Morone and T. R. Marmor, "Representing Consumer Interests: The Case of American Health Planning," *Ethics* 91 (April 1981), 431–50.

81. Spitz, p. 184.

82. Barber, p. 192.

83. Barber, p. 198.

84. George Kateb, "The Moral Distinctiveness of Representative Democracy," *Ethics* 91 (April 1981), 371.

85. Kateb, 363.

86. Kateb, 373.

87. Amy Gutmann, "Communitarian Critics of Liberalism," *Philosophy of Public Affairs* 14 (Summer 1985), 319. Barber admits that "a healthy democratic community [should] leave room for the expression of distrust, dissent, or just plain opposition, even in lost causes where dissenters are obviously very much in the minority" (Barber, p. 192). He does not offer any convincing argument that it *will.*

88. For a fuller discussion of these issues, see my review of Elaine Spitz's *Majority Rule* in *Political Theory* 13 (November 1985), 634–38.

Chapter 7. The Roles of Elections

1. Although it is fundamentally different in approach, this chapter draws heavily on Richard Rose and Harve Mossawir, "Voting and Elections: A Functional Analysis," *Political Studies* 15 (June 1967), 173–201.

2. For example, see Ronald M. Glassman, *Democracy and Equality* (New York: Praeger, 1989); Sanford Lakoff, *Equality in Political Philosophy* (Cambridge: Harvard Univ. Press, 1964); George L. Abernethy (ed.), *The Idea of Equality* (Richmond: John Knox Press, 1959).

3. Anonymity means that the collective decision is determined only by the aggregate distribution of preferences, not by which preferences are held by which particular individuals. See Dennis C. Mueller, *Public Choice* (Cambridge: Cambridge Univ. Press, 1979), pp. 208–10.

4. Giovanni Sartori, *Democratic Theory* (New York: Praeger, 1965), p. 346.

5. As an historical matter, this statement needs important qualification. Many writers from the eighteenth and nineteenth centuries cited as advocates of one or another of the theories discussed were apparently content with systems that denied the vote to women, the poor, and in the American case to nonwhites as well. Presumably contemporary advocates of these theories would demand universal adult suffrage.

6. Bernard Berelson, Paul Felix Lazarsfeld, and William N. McPhee, *Voting* (Chicago: Univ. of Chicago Press, 1955).

7. Jean Jacques Rousseau, *The Social Contract* (New York: Hafner, 1947), p. 91.

8. J. Roland Pennock and J. W. Chapman (eds.), *Representation* (New York: Atherton Press, 1968); Hanna Pitkin, *The Concept of Representation* (Berkeley: Univ. of California Press, 1967).

9. Samuel Finer, cited in Herbert Döring, "Party Government in Britain—Recent Conspicuous Constraints," in Richard S. Katz (ed.), *Party Governments: European and American Experiences* (Berlin: de Gruyter, 1987), p. 146.

Chapter 8. The Description of the Electoral System

1. Douglas W. Rae, *The Political Consequences of Electoral Laws* (New Haven: Yale Univ. Press, 1971), p. 14.

2. For example, accurately reflecting its contents, Rein Taagepera and Matthew Soberg Shugart title their book, whose subtitle is "The Effects and Determinants of Electoral Systems," simply *Seats and Votes* (New Haven: Yale Univ. Press, 1989). Similarly, the summary descriptions of electoral systems in Stein Rokkan and Jean Meyriat (eds.), *International Guide to Electoral Statistics* (The Hague: Mouton, 1969) and in Thomas T. Mackie

and Richard Rose, *International Almanac of Electoral History* (New York: Facts on File, 1982) focus only on electoral formula and suffrage, as do the longer descriptions in Andrew McLaren Carstairs, *A Short History of Electoral Systems in Western Europe* (London: Allen and Unwin, 1980).

3. Enid Lakeman, *Voting in Democracies* (London: Faber and Faber, 1955); *Power to Elect* (London: Heinemann, 1982).

4. Ferdinand A. Hermens, *Democracy and Proportional Representation* (Chicago: Univ. of Chicago Press, 1940).

5. From 1971 to 1974, the spending for advertising time in communications media of American candidates for federal office was limited to $50,000 or 10 cents per voter, whichever was greater. Of this, no more than 60% could be spent on broadcasting. Federal Election Campaign Act of 1971, PL92-225.

6. The clearest exception is Israel. The Netherlands has electoral subdistricts, but the initial allocation of seats among parties is made at the national level, with the subdistricts relevant only to the allocation of seats within a party.

7. This formulation ignores the possibility, used in the nomination of American presidential candidates, of a primary election to choose delegates to a nominating convention. Although the ultimate objective of the exercise is the nomination of candidates, these "primaries" are perhaps better seen as final elections, albeit with restricted electorates, to the office of delegate.

8. As with many simple dichotomies, this oversimplifies a complicated reality. Among "parliamentary" systems, one can distinguish bipolar systems, in which parliamentary election victory for one party/coalition more or less mechanically translates into the choice of its previously announced candidate as chief executive, from coalitional or dominant party systems, in which the choice of chief executive is the result of postelection negotiations between and within parties. See Richard S. Katz, "Party Government and Its Alternatives," in Richard S. Katz (ed.), *Party Governments: European and American Experiences* (Berlin: de Gruyter, 1987), pp. 12–14, and chapter 12, below. The American president is only directly elected so long as one candidate receives a majority of the electoral votes; in the absence of electoral college majorities (due at least in part to the use of proportional representation to elect the electors), the Finnish president was indirectly elected until 1987. Several countries (e.g., Ireland and Austria) have directly elected presidents who are nonetheless *not* the chief executives, while in the case of 1958 France, the indirectly elected president (Charles de Gaulle) was the chief executive.

9. The best example here is Switzerland's refusal to allow women to vote until 1970.

10. See V. O. Key, Jr., *Politics, Parties and Pressure Groups* (New York: Thomas Y. Crowell, 1964), p. 613.

11. William Blackstone, *Commentaries on the Laws of England*, Book I, chap. 2, p. 171.

12. See Michael Gallagher and Michael Marsh (eds.), *Candidate Selection in Comparative Perspective: The Secret Garden of Politics* (London: Sage, 1988).

Chapter 9. Representation: The Relationship between Seats and Votes

1. Douglas W. Rae, *The Political Consequences of Electoral Laws* (New Haven: Yale Univ. Press, 1971).

2. Arend Lijphart, "The Political Consequences of Electoral Laws, 1945–85: A Critique, Re-Analysis, and Update of Rae's Classic Study," presented at the XIVth World Congress of the International Political Science Association, Washington, DC, 1988. Also see his *Electoral Systems and Party Systems* (New York: Oxford Univ. Press, 1994).

3. Note that by this rule the one postwar election in Antigua for which data were collected contributes the same weight to the analysis as the 13 postwar elections in Iceland.

4. Stein Rokkan is one of the pioneer investigators of threshold of representation. "Elections: Electoral Systems," in D. L. Sills (ed.), *International Encyclopedia of the Social Sciences* (New York: Macmillan, 1968), vol. 5, pp. 6–21. Douglas Rae et al. extend the analysis to include thresholds of exclusion. "Thresholds of Representation and Thresholds of Exclusion: An Analytic Note on Electoral Systems," *Comparative Political Studies* 3 (January 1971), 479–88. See also John Loosemore and Victor J. Hanby, "The Theoretical Limits of Maximum Distortion: Some Analytic Expressions for Electoral Systems," *British Journal of Political Science* 1 (October 1971), 467–77.

5. Arend Lijphart and Robert W. Gibberd, "Thresholds and Payoffs in List Systems of Proportional Representation," *European Journal of Political Research* 5 (September 1977), 219–44. See also Michael Gallagher, "Comparing Proportional Representation Electoral Systems: Quotas, Thresholds, Paradoxes and Majorities," *British Journal of Political Science* 22 (October 1992), 469–96.

6. The last conclusion merely repeats the observation of chapter 8 that what is important for small parties is not that the quota be small, but that as large a proportion as possible of the votes of the larger parties be consumed in fulfilling the quota.

7. Enid Lakeman, *Power to Elect: The Case for Proportional Representation* (London: Heinemann, 1982).

8. For a discussion of alternative measures of proportionality, see Gallagher.

9. Lijphart, "The Political Consequences of Electoral Laws, 1945–85," 13.

10. Single-member plurality is retained as a separate category because the parameters estimated for it are significantly different from those for multimember plurality and block vote.

11. The first step was to estimate the effect of second-stage distributions based on national vote totals. Logically, the disproportionality of systems with these procedures should be a weighted average of the expected result of the two stages, each taken as if it were the only stage. For the first stage, this would mean ignoring any supplementary seats, while for the second stage it would mean computing the number of districts and district magnitude as if all members were elected directly in the highest stage districts. The weight, then, should be a function of the relative numbers of seats actually filled at each level. As already observed, when more than 20% of the seats are filled at the higher level, the electoral system behaves as if that were in fact the only level. Although ideally the weighting function for cases between 0% and 20% would be an S-shaped curve, there is insufficient variance in the data for such a curve to be estimated, and so a straight-line approximation was used. The second step was to estimate the effect of thresholds on both simple systems and on those using national distributions of remainders. Here a distinction was made between thresholds applied at the district level, the only kind in fact found coupled with single-stage systems, and those applied at the national level, associated with second-stage supplementary seats. In each case, it seemed wise to allow for a curvilinear relationship in which after a certain point a threshold would increase proportionality by discouraging minor parties from competing in the first place. This was approximated by a quadratic function forced to go through the origin (representing the principle that a threshold of 0% must be equivalent to having no threshold). For the single-stage systems, the no-threshold expectation was based on the functions in Table 9.6, while for the two-stage national total systems it was based on the results of step 1. The final stage was to estimate the impact of distributions of remainders, now using the estimates of threshold effects computed in stage 2. In this case, simple averaging of first- and second-stage results is inadequate, because the result of the first stage will be less proportional than it would have

been had it been the only stage, since the seats not won with full quotas are carried forward rather than being distributed. The number of seats carried forward, and hence the weight given to the second-stage formula, should be a function of district magnitude. Subtracting the threshold effects from those systems that employ thresholds allows the full set of systems with distributions of remainders to be used to estimate parameters of the function $D = s (st_2) + (1-s)(st_1)(a + b\ m_1)$, where s is the share of seats awarded in the second stage, st_1 and st_2 are the predicted proportionalities for first- and second-stage (this time based on the numbers of seats actually awarded at each level), and $(a + b\ m_1)$ is the "discount factor" for first-stage proportionality.

12. The numbers in this table are, in effect, squared part correlations, and the difference between the figure cited for the model with one set of parameters constrained and the full model indicates the *loss* in explanatory power resulting from the elimination of a particular class of variables. It should be noted that this procedure implicitly gives "credit" for any shared (covariant) explanatory power to the classes of variables that remain in the restricted model.

13. M. G. Kendall and A. Stuart, "The Law of the Cubic Proportion in Election Results," *British Journal of Sociology* 1 (September 1950), 183–96.

14. Edward R. Tufte, "The Relationship between Seats and Votes in Two-Party Systems," *American Political Science Review* 67 (June 1973), 540–54.

15. Henri Theil, "The Desired Political Entropy," *American Political Science Review* 63 (1969), 521–25. See also Terence H. Qualter, "Seats and Votes: An Application of the Cube Law to the Canadian Electoral System," *Canadian Journal of Political Science* 1 (1968), 336–44.

16. Gary King, "Electoral Responsiveness and Partisan Bias in Multiparty Democracies," unpublished manuscript, August 1988.

Chapter 10. Parties and Governments

1. Maurice Duverger, "Duverger's Law: Forty Years Later," in Bernard Grofman and Arend Lijphart (eds.), *Electoral Laws and Their Political Consequences* (New York: Agathon Press, 1986), p. 70, citing his own *Droit Constitutionnel et Institutions Politiques* (Paris: Presses Universitaires de France, 1955).

2. Whether this should be taken as a clarification or a retraction depends in part on how one takes Duverger's other statements of the law in the 1950s. E.g., "*[T]he simple-majority single-ballot system favours the two-party system. . . .* An almost complete correlation is observable between the simple-majority single-ballot system and the two-party system. . . . The exceptions are very rare and can generally be explained as a result of special conditions." Maurice Duverger, *Political Parties* (New York: John Wiley, 1954), p. 217. Emphasis in original.

3. "Duverger's Law," p. 71, citing *Political Parties*, p. 252.

4. John Grumm, "Theories of Electoral Systems," *Midwest Journal of Political Science* 2 (November 1958), 357–76; William Riker, "Duverger's Law Revisited," in Grofman and Lijphart (eds.), pp. 19–42; Giovanni Sartori, "The Influence of Electoral Systems: Faulty Laws or Faulty Method?" in Grofman and Lijphart (eds.), pp. 43–68.

5. Rein Taagepera and Matthew Soberg Shugart, *Seats and Votes: The Effects and Determinants of Electoral Systems* (New Haven: Yale Univ. Press, 1989), pp. 78–80.

6. Suggested by Riker as a reason why early Danish elections may be discounted.

7. Imperiali is combined with d'Hondt rather than Modified Ste.-Laguë (as by Lijphart) for two reasons. First, since the Imperiali quota denominator is one more than the Droop quota denominator, just as the Droop denominator is one more than Hare, consis-

tency suggests that it should be in the "next category over." Second, the data show the mean EFF.V for Imperiali to be closer to that observed for d'Hondt than for Modified Ste. -Laguë in the same range of magnitude.

8. For example, the Bader-Ofer law in Israel in 1969, which restored the d'Hondt highest average electoral formula. See Avraham Brichta, "1977 Elections and the Future of Electoral Reform in Israel," in Howard Penniman (ed.), *Israel at the Polls* (Washington, DC: American Enterprise Institute, 1979), pp. 41, 50–52.

9. The legal possibility of apparentement was not eliminated until 1964, when para. 56, section 3 of the *Vallagen*, which had regulated the existence of allied lists, was dropped, and para. 79, which regulated the format of ballots, was changed to allow only one designation above candidate names. The change in formula in 1952 was motivated by a desire to guarantee the Agrarian Party a proportionate share of the seats without obliging it to enter into a formal alliance, either with the socialists (with whom they were in government, but for whom it would be hard to get the Agrarian Party's supporters to vote) or the bourgeois parties (which were in opposition). Its effect was to make alliances among the bourgeois parties unnecessary. Bo Särlvik, "Scandinavia," ch. 7 in Vernon Bogdanor and David Butler (eds.), *Democracy and Elections* (Cambridge: Cambridge Univ. Press, 1983).

10. Ferdinand Hermens, *Democracy or Anarchy* (Notre Dame: Notre Dame Univ. Press, 1941).

11. See C. Waxman (ed.), *The End of Ideology Debate* (New York: Funk and Wagnalls, 1968); John Clayton Thomas, "The Decline of Ideology in Western Political Parties," *Sage Professional Papers in Contemporary Political Sociology*, ser. 06–012 (1975). Note that this literature accepted Marxism as virtually synonymous with ideology to the extent that the decline of social (especially working) class solidarity was taken to be a prime indicator of the end of ideology.

12. Philip E. Converse, "The Nature of Belief Systems in Mass Publics," in David E. Apter (ed.), *Ideology and Discontent* (New York: Free Press, 1964), pp. 206–61.

13. Otto Kirchheimer, "The Transformation of the Western European Party Systems," in Joseph LaPalombara and Myron Weiner (eds.), *Political Parties and Political Development* (Princeton: Princeton Univ. Press, 1966), pp. 177–200.

14. Francis Castles and Peter Mair, "Left-Right Scales: Some 'Expert' Judgments," *European Journal of Political Research* 12 (March 1984), 73–88.

15. Michael Laver and W. Ben Hunt, *Policy and Party Competition* (New York: Routledge, 1992).

16. Kenneth Janda, *Political Parties: A Cross-National Survey* (New York: Free Press, 1979). These data were provided by the Inter-University Consortium for Political and Social Research. Neither the Consortium, nor the original investigator, bear any responsibility for the analyses and interpretations presented here.

17. Although not all parties are included in the data sets, they do include all those parties that won significant proportions of the vote. Hence the bias introduced by the exclusion of minor parties should itself be minor.

18. See Karlheinz Reif, "Party Government in the Fifth French Republic," in Richard S. Katz (ed.), *Party Governments: European and American Experiences* (Berlin: de Gruyter, 1987), pp. 27–77.

19. Philip Converse, "The Nature of Belief Systems in Mass Publics," in David E. Apter (ed.), *Ideology and Discontent* (New York: Free Press, 1964), pp. 206–61.

20. All of the survey data were provided by the Inter-University Consortium for Political and Social Research. Neither the Consortium, nor the original investigators, are responsible for the analyses or interpretations presented here.

21. The issues addressed in the Eurobarometer were efforts to reduce inequality of

income, development of nuclear energy, reduction in the number of laws and stricter enforcement of those remaining, reducing hours of those working to provide jobs for the unemployed, penalties for terrorism, public ownership of industry, military defense, government control of the economy, aid to Third World countries, protection of the environment, regional autonomy. In the Political Action Study, respondents were asked to rate the importance and level of government responsibility for a series of problems: looking after old people, guaranteeing equal rights for men and women, seeing to it that everyone who wants a job can have one, providing good education, providing good medical care, providing adequate housing, fighting pollution, guaranteeing neighborhoods safe from crime, trying to even out differences in wealth between people.

22. Ideally, one would take the position of the median voter as the center of the distribution, but this is not possible with these data.

23. For example, see Judith Best, *The Case Against Direct Election of the President* (Ithaca: Cornell Univ. Press, 1975), p. 204; Peter Hain, *Proportional Misrepresentation: The Case Against PR in Britain* (Aldershot: Wildwood House, 1986), p. 40.

24. For example, increasing the number of 3-seat (rather than 4-seat or 5-seat) constituencies was justified in the Irish parliamentary debates on the grounds that "it is made easier for a party which may be called upon to shoulder the responsibility of government to get sufficient seats to enable them to undertake that task with adequate parliamentary support." *Dáil Debates*, vol. 108, col. 924 (October 23, 1947).

25. Even in a two-party system, there is the possibility of a grand coalition, for example in times of national crisis, as with Britain during World War II.

26. No calculation was made for parliaments with 16 or more parties (e.g., Germany after the 1930 election), both because of the expense of the calculation and because the results would have skewed any subsequent analysis.

27. On these, and other points raised below, see also André Blais and R. K. Carty, "The Impact of Electoral Formulae on the Creation of Majority Governments," *Electoral Studies* 6 (December 1987), 209–18.

28. This hypothesis is overly simple and ignores a number of possible confounding factors, including the possibility that a party might voluntarily leave government and may indeed even have made its intention to do so clear before the election. In this case, its exclusion from the subsequent cabinet, even if its vote went up, should not be counted as weakening the connection between elections and government formation. Unfortunately, taking account of these factors would require more detailed research than is possible here, so these statistical patterns should be taken as indicative rather than dispositive.

29. Gunnar Sjöblom, "The Role of Political Parties in Denmark and Sweden, 1970–1984," in Richard S. Katz (ed.), *Party Governments: European and American Experiences* (Berlin: de Gruyter, 1987), pp. 155–201.

30. Richard S. Katz, "Dimensions of Partisan Conflict in Swiss Cantons," *Comparative Political Studies* 16 (January 1984), 505–27.

Chapter 11. Districting: Apportionment and Gerrymanders

1. For example, two sections of the 1971 New York 35th Assembly district were connected by "LaGuardia Airport and the strip of land between Grand Central Parkway and Flushing Bay. The strip, which runs along the Parkway for some thirty blocks, is only a few feet wide in places. (In a sense, the 35th A.D. is contiguous only westbound. The eastbound lane of the Parkway is in another district.)" David I. Wells, "The Reapportionment Game," *Empire State Review* (February 1979), 8–14.

2. For a superb review of criteria specifically relevant to American districting cases,

see Bernard Grofman, "Criteria for Districting: A Social Science Perspective," *UCLA Law Review* 33 (1985), 77–184.

3. J. Patrick Boyer, *Election Law in Canada* (Toronto: Butterworths, 1987), p. 93.

4. See Robert G. Dixon, Jr., "The Court, The People, and 'One Man, One Vote'," and the "Commentary" by Malcolm E. Jewell, in Nelson W. Polsby (ed.), *Reapportionment in the 1970s* (Berkeley: Univ. of California Press, 1971), pp. 7–55.

5. This argument figures in American debates about electoral college reform. See Lawrence D. Longley and Alan G. Braun, *The Politics of Electoral College Reform* (New Haven: Yale Univ. Press, 1972).

6. The argument that rural voters are particularly virtuous is often attributed to supporters of rural overrepresentation. As John D. May points out, however, this argument was conspicuous by its absence from the 1973 Australian debate on the subject. "Rural Over-Representation: Pros and Cons in Recent Australian Debate," *Journal of Commonwealth and Comparative Politics* 13 (July 1975), 132–45, esp. note 8.

7. In the Australian debate, one argument raised in favor of rural overrepresentation was the importance of rural exports to the national economy. In a historical vein, an Austrian act of 1907 gave representation to a province in proportion to the average of the province's share of the national population and its share of the contributions to direct and indirect taxes. Andrew M. Carstairs, *A Short History of Electoral Systems in Western Europe* (London: George Allen and Unwin, 1980), pp. 125–26.

8. Aside from the Constitutionally mandated exceptions of the United States Senate (but not state senates) and the electoral college, exceptions for special purpose districts have been sanctioned by the Supreme Court (*Ball v. James* 451 US 355) (1980).

9. In the extreme, see *Karcher v. Daggett* 462 US 725 (1983) in which a plan with a total deviation of under 1% was rejected.

10. *Brown v. Thomson* 463 US 835 (1983).

11. John F. Banzhaf, "Weighted Voting Doesn't Work: A Mathematical Analysis," *Rutgers Law Review* 19 (Winter 1965), n. 31, 329–30.

12. *Whitcomb v. Chavis* 403 US 124 at 147 (1971).

13. R. L. Leonard, *Elections in Britain* (London: D. Van Nostrand, 1968), p. 18.

14. In Scotland, the boundaries of local authority areas are to be taken into account and in Northern Ireland, no ward may be divided between constituencies. This difference in standard has allowed the population disparity of Northern Irish constituencies to be held to about 10%, while the disparity for English constituencies has exceeded 30%. H. F. Rawlings, *Law and the Electoral Process* (London: Sweet and Maxwell, 1988), pp. 28–44.

15. Electoral Boundaries Readjustment Act, s. 13.

16. The South Island is assigned 25 seats (by the Electoral Amendment Act of 1965). This is divided into the "European population" of the South Island to produce the South Island's electoral quota. This quota is then divided into the "European population" of the North Island to obtain the number of North Island districts, and this number is divided into the North Island "European population" to obtain the North Island's electoral quota. From 1945 to 1950, the maximum allowable deviation was 750 individuals, and from 1950 to 1956 it was 10%.

17. Jean-Marie Cotteret et al., *Lois Electorales et Inégalités de Représentation en France 1936–1960* (Paris: Fondation Nationale des Sciences Politiques, 1960), p. 365.

18. Under the 1958 scheme, by contrast, the 8th district of Bouches-du-Rhône consisted of two separate pieces. Other examples of discontiguous constituencies were the 1st district of Meurthe-et-Moselle and the 6th district of Moselle.

19. L. no. 86–1197, 24 November 1986, art. 5.

20. Alistair Cole and Peter Campbell, *French Electoral Systems & Elections Since 1789* (Aldershot: Gower, 1989), p. 142.

21. *O'Donovan v. The Attorney General* (1961) I.R. 114.

22. Glácio Ary Dillon Soares, "Desigualdades Eleitorais no Brasil," *Revista de Ciêcia Politica* 7 (1973), 22–48.

23. R. K. Carty, "The Electoral Boundary Revolution in Canada," *American Review of Canadian Studies* 15 (1985), 273–87.

24. Leroy C. Hardy, "Considering the Gerrymander," *Pepperdine Law Review* 4 (1977), 256.

25. The district is the New Jersey 3rd. Illustrative of the colorful language associated with gerrymanders, the same apportionment plan also produced districts called "The Swan" and "The Fishhook." "New Jersey Map Imaginative Gerrymander," *Congressional Quarterly Weekly Report* (May 22, 1982), 1190–99.

26. See note 1, above.

27. One unintended consequence of a compactness standard may be to eliminate the use of naturally irregular geographical features like rivers as boundary demarcations.

28. See David Butler and Donald Stokes, *Political Change in Britain* (New York: St. Martin's, 1969), pp. 303–12 for a theoretical explanation and evidence that this kind of uniform swing is not unreasonable.

29. *Licht v. Quattrocchi* No. 82–1494 (R.I. Super. CT.), *aff'd*, 449 A.2d 887 (1982), cited in Grofman, "Criteria for Districting."

30. *Congressional Quarterly Weekly Report* (Feb. 27, 1982), 391.

31. *Congressional Quarterly Weekly Report* (Oct. 7, 1972), 2557.

32. Peter Mair, "Districting Choices Under the Single-Transferable Vote," in Bernard Grofman and Arend Lijphart (eds.), *Electoral Laws and Their Political Consequences* (New York: Agathon, 1986), pp. 289–307.

33. Gary King, "Measuring Political Gerrymandering," unpublished paper, March, 1989.

34. David R. Mayhew, "Congressional Representation: Theory and Practice in Drawing the Districts," in Nelson W. Polsby (ed.), *Reapportionment in the 1970s* (Berkeley: Univ. of California Press, 1971), pp. 249–85; Edward Tufte, "The Relationship Between Seats and Votes in Two-Party Systems," *American Political Science Review* 67 (June 1973), 540–54; Bruce E. Cain, "Assessing the Partisan Effects of Redistricting," *American Political Science Review* 79 (June 1985), 320–33.

35. Guillermo Owen and Bernard Grofman, "Optimal Political Gerrymandering," *Political Geography Quarterly* 7 (January 1988), 5–22.

36. John A. Ferejohn, "On the Decline of Competition in Congressional Elections," *American Political Science Review* 71 (March 1977), 168.

37. King, "Measuring Political Gerrymandering," pp. 25–26.

38. Mark E. Rush, *Does Redistricting Make a Difference?* (Baltimore: Johns Hopkins Univ. Press, 1993).

39. 412 US 755 (1973).

40. 478 US 30 at 50–51.

41. *Kirksey v. Board of Supervisors of Hinds County Mississippi* 554 F 2nd 139 at 152 (1977) cert denied 434 US 968; *Robinson v. Commissioners Court Anderson County* 505 F 2nd 674 (1974).

42. 42 U.S.C. § 1973b (1982).

43. *United Jewish Organizations of Williamsburg v. Carey* (1977) 430 US 144.

44. See *Shaw v. Reno* (1993) 113 S.Ct. 2819 and *Holder v. Hall* (1994) 114 S.Ct. 2581.

45. As Judge Gee put it concurring in *Kirksey*, "It is hard to avoid the conclusion that by *United Jewish Organizations* what the Court underwrites is a tribal, rather than republican, form of government," 155–56.

46. Larry Sabato, quoted in Bill Montague, "The Voting Rights Act Today," *American Bar Association Journal* 74 (August 1, 1988), 58.

47. Edward Still, "Cumulative and Limited Voting in Alabama: The Aftermath of *Dillard v. Crenshaw County*," paper presented at the 1988 annual meeting of the American Political Science Association, Washington, D.C., August 31–September 4, 1988; Richard L. Engstrom, Delbert A. Taebel, and Richard L. Cole, "Cumulative Voting as a Remedy for Minority Vote Dilution: The Case of Alamogordo, New Mexico," *Journal of Law and Politics* 5 (1989), 469–97. See also Richard L. Engstrom and Charles J. Barrilleaux, "Native Americans and Cumulative Voting: The Sisseton-Wahpeton Sioux," *Social Science Quarterly* 72 (June 1991), 388–93.

48. For a summary of this research, see R. Darcy et al., *Women, Elections and Representation* (New York: Longman, 1987). See also Karen Beckwith, "Candidature femminili e sistemi elettorali," *Rivista Italiana di Scienza Politica* 20 (April 1990), 73–103; Wilma Rule, "Does the Electoral System Discriminate Against Women?" *PS* 19 (Fall 1986), 864–67.

49. For a fuller description of some of these devices, see Arend Lijphart, "Proportionality by Non-PR Methods: Ethnic Representation in Belgium, Cyprus, Lebanon, New Zealand, West Germany, and Zimbabwe," in Grofman and Lijphart (eds.), pp. 113–23.

50. Derek W. Urwin, "Germany: Continuity and Change in Electoral Politics," in Richard Rose (ed.), *Electoral Behavior* (New York: Free Press, 1974), p. 137.

51. Ceylon Constitutions (Special Provisions) Act, July 16, 1954, § 3.

52. Schedule 1 to the Constitution, § 4. The four communities guaranteed representation are Sino-Mauritian, Hindu, Muslim, and General Population (other).

53. Lijphart, "Proportionality by Non-PR Methods," p. 120.

Chapter 12. The Nature of Electoral Choice

1. Richard S. Katz, "Party Government: A Rationalistic Conception," in Francis G. Castles and Rudolf Wildenmann (eds.), *Visions and Realities of Party Government* (Berlin: de Gruyter, 1986), pp. 31–71.

2. Based on U.S. Department of Commerce, Bureau of the Census, "1987 Census of Governments." The national figures include president and vice-president (2), senators (100), and members of the House of Representatives (435, plus one nonvoting delegate from the District of Columbia).

3. Figures for MPs, MEPs, and county and district council positions are from the *Municipal Year Book and Public Services Directory*, 1987. The estimate for parish councillors is extrapolated from the estimate of 57,000 for England in the mid-1960s reported by the Redcliffe-Maud Royal Commission on Local Government in England 1966–1969, Cmnd. 4040, vol. 3, p. 168.

4. Jan Sundberg, "Exploring the Basis of Declining Party Membership in Denmark: A Scandinavian Comparison," *Scandinavian Political Studies* 10 (1987), 17–38.

5. Constitution of the Fifth Republic, Article 6. This system was replaced by direct election in 1962.

6. *The Federalist*, no. 68.

7. See chapter 10.

8. In fact, these are not necessarily equivalent, as the partial renewal of the U.S. Senate every two years, notwithstanding a six-year senatorial term of office, illustrates.

9. See Robert W. Jackman, "Political Institutions and Voter Turnout in the Industrial Democracies," *American Political Science Review* 81 (June 1987), 414–15.

10. In 1990, Oklahoma voters approved a limitation of 12 years total service in the state legislature; Colorado voters limited governor, lieutenant governor, secretary of state, state treasurer, attorney general, and state senators to two consecutive four–year terms, members of the state house of representatives to four consecutive two–year terms, United States Senators to two consecutive terms, and United States Representatives to six consecutive terms; voters in California limited a wide variety of state executive officers plus state senators to two terms, and members of the state assembly to three terms. In 1991, Washington state voters rejected a similar proposal.

11. David R. Mayhew, *Congress: The Electoral Connection* (New Haven: Yale Univ. Press, 1974), p. 37.

12. For a full discussion of the issues involved in the term limitation debate, see Gerald Benjamin and Michael J. Malbin (eds.), *Limiting Legislative Terms* (Washington, DC: CQ Press, 1992).

13. The 15 states with recall provisions and the number of signatures required are Alaska, Arizona, Colorado, Louisiana, Michigan, Nevada, North Dakota, Oregon, Wisconsin (25% of the vote at the last general election); California (for statewide offices, 12% of the vote at the last general election; for state legislators, 20% of vote at the last general election); Georgia (statewide offices, 15% of registered voters; others, 30% of registered voters); Idaho (20% of registered voters); Kansas (40% of vote at last general election); Montana (statewide offices, 10% of registered voters; others, 15% of registered voters); Washington (25% or 35% of qualified voters, depending on office). Source: *Book of the States*, 1984–85, p. 170.

14. For example, see Sidney G. Tarrow, *Between Center and Periphery: Grassroots Politicians in Italy and France* (New Haven: Yale Univ. Press, 1977).

15. Myron Weiner, *India at the Polls, 1980* (Washington, DC: AEI, 1983), p. 65.

16. Karlheinz Reif and Hermann Schmitt, "Nine Second-Order National Elections — A Conceptual Framework for the Analysis of European Election Results," *European Journal of Political Research* 8 (March 1980), 3–44.

17. Jerrold G. Rusk, "The Effect of the Australian Ballot Reform on Split Ticket Voting: 1876–1908," *American Political Science Review* 64 (December 1970), 1220–38.

18. For some of the arguments raised in Australia, see J. F. H. Wright, *Mirror of the Nation's Mind: Australia's Electoral Experiments* (Sydney: Hale and Iremonger, 1980), pp. 24–30. For a contemporary communitarian view, see Benjamin Barber, *Strong Democracy* (Berkeley: Univ. of California Press, 1984).

19. G. J. G. Upton and D. Brook, "The Importance of Positional Voting Bias in British Elections," *Political Studies* 22 (June 1974), 178–90; Christopher Robson and Brendan M. Walsh, *Alphabetical Voting: A Study of the 1973 General Election in the Republic of Ireland* (Dublin: Economic and Social Research Institute, 1973); Colin A. Hughes, "Alphabetical Advantage in the House of Representatives." *Australian Quarterly* 42 (1970); Henry M. Bain and Donald S. Hecock, *Ballot Position and Voter's Choice* (Detroit: Wayne State Univ. Press, 1957); J. E. Mueller, "Choosing Among 133 Candidates," *Public Opinion Quarterly* 34 (Fall 1970), 395–402.

20. For a summary of the evidence, see Howard A. Scarrow, "Cross-Endorsement and Cross-Filing in Plurality Partisan Elections," in Bernard Grofman and Arend Lijphart (eds.), *Electoral Laws and Their Political Consequences* (New York: Agathon, 1986), pp. 248–54. The decline in roll-off with a party column ballot mirrors the much lower rate at which votes become non-transferable while a candidate of the same party still remains observed in Table 12.3 for Malta rather than Ireland.

21. Jack L. Walker, "Ballot Forms and Voter Fatigue," *Midwest Journal of Political Science* 10 (November 1966), 448.

22. Although the first round, in keeping with usual American parlance and the time of year at which the election is held, normally is called the "primary," it is in fact the first round of an SMM election. Thus, any candidate who receives more than half the vote in this "primary" simply is elected.

23. This is true even of systems with panachage (i.e., Switzerland and Luxembourg) since a preference vote expressed for a candidate is also a fractional vote for the list on which he or she appears.

24. Joel D. Barkan, "The Electoral Process and Peasant-State Relations in Kenya," in Fred M. Hayward (ed.), *Elections in Independent Africa* (Boulder: Westview Press, 1987), pp. 230; Joel D. Barkan and John J. Okumu, " 'Semi-Competitive' Elections, Clientelism, and Political Recruitment in a No-Party State: The Kenyan Experience," in Guy Hermet et al. (eds.), *Elections Without Choice* (New York: John Wiley, 1978), pp. 88–107.

25. Frank Dinka and Max J. Skidmore, "The Functions of Communist One-Party Elections: The Case of Czechoslovakia 1971," *Political Science Quarterly* 88 (September 1973), 395–422.

26. Richard S. Katz, "Intraparty Preference Voting," in Grofman and Lijphart (eds.), pp. 85–103.

27. Richard S. Katz, *A Theory of Parties and Electoral Systems* (Baltimore: Johns Hopkins Univ. Press, 1980).

28. For example, see Mayhew.

29. Nathaniel B. Thayer, *How the Conservatives Rule Japan* (Princeton: Princeton Univ. Press, 1969).

Chapter 13. The Electorate

1. Leon E. Aylsworth, "The Passing of Alien Suffrage," *American Political Science Review* 25 (February 1931), 114–16.

2. See *Collier v. Menzel*, 176 Cal App 3d 24, 221 Cal Cptr 110 (1985); *Pitts v. Black*, 608 F Supp 696 (S.D.N.Y., 1984).

3. Plebiscite Act, S.N.W.T. 1981 (3) c. 13, as amended by S.N.W.T. 1982 (1) c. 5.

4. Louisiana State Law Institute, *Project of a Constitution for the State of Louisiana with Notes and Studies* (Baton Rouge: 1954), III, 315.

5. *Cipriano v. City of Houma*, 395 US 701. In *Salyer Land Co. v. Tulare Water District*, 410 US 719 (1973), however, the Court ruled that property ownership could legitimately be used to establish a demonstrated interest in an election, and that this could be used to restrict participation in special purpose elections.

6. For example, although aborigines were generally disqualified from voting in Australia until 1967, those who met a property requirement could vote nonetheless.

7. *Holt Civic Club v. City of Tuscaloosa* 439 US 60, at 69–70.

8. Chilton Williamson, *American Suffrage from Property to Democracy, 1760–1860,* (Princeton, NJ: Princeton Univ. Press, 1960), p. 219.

9. Such arguments were falling into disrepute in the United States even as they were being enacted in Europe. One delegate to the 1853 Massachusetts convention, for example, quoted Tom Paine: "You require that a man shall have sixty dollars' worth of property or he shall not vote. Very well, take an illustration. Here is a man today who owns a jackass, and the jackass is worth sixty dollars. Today the man is a voter and he goes to the polls with his jackass and deposits his vote. Tomorrow the jackass dies. The next day the man comes to vote without his jackass and he cannot vote at all. Now tell me, which was the

voter, the man or the jackass?" [Cited in K. H. Porter, *A History of Suffrage in the United States* (Chicago: Univ. of Chicago Press, 1918), p. 109.]

10. Robert Justin Goldstein, "Political Repression and Political Development: the 'Human Rights' Issue in Nineteenth Century Europe," *Comparative Social Research* 4 (1981), 174.

11. Susan E. Marshall, "In Defense of Separate Spheres: Class and Status Politics in the Antisuffrage Movement," *Social Forces* 65 (December 1986), 327–51.

12. Archibald Hopkins, "Some Ideals of the Suffrage Shattered by Searching Analysis," *The Woman's Protest* 2, p. 3, cited in Marshall, pp. 332–33. A similar argument by Senator Joseph E. Brown of Georgia (1884) is quoted by V. O. Key in *Politics, Parties, and Pressure Groups* (New York: Thomas Y. Crowell, 1964), p. 613.

13. See Janet Siltanen and Michelle Stanworth, "The Politics of Private Women and Public Men," in Siltanen and Stanworth (eds.), *Women in the Public Sphere* (New York: St. Martin's Press, 1984), pp. 185–208; Mary G. Dietz, "Citizenship with a Feminist Face: The Problem with Maternal Thinking," *Political Theory* 13 (February 1985), 19–37.

14. An exception is the 1885 Canadian provision enfranchising sons of property owners at the rate of $300 worth of property per son.

15. Art. 70, sec. 1., translated in Herman G. James, *The Constitutional System of Brazil* (Washington, DC: Carnegie Institution, 1923), p. 231.

16. This table is based on total population rather than voting age or citizen population for two reasons: estimates of the first are more reliable than the others, and this approach allows the effects of changes in voting age to be observed. Small changes in the proportion of the population eligible to vote seen in the table often are the result of changes in the age distribution, the real value of property or tax requirements, or unusually high rates of immigration (e.g., the drop seen for Canada in the 1950s and 1960s).

17. Raphael Zariski, *The Politics of Uneven Development* (Hinsdale, IL: Dryden Press, 1972), pp. 29–31; Giovanni Sartori, "European Political Parties: The Case of Polarized Pluralism," in Joseph LaPalombara and Myron Weiner (eds.), *Political Parties and Political Development* (Princeton: Princeton Univ. Press, 1966), pp. 137–76.

18. See the remarks of Senator Hartke, 116 *Congressional Record* 6950, and especially the committee testimony cited by Benjamin Ginsberg, *The Consequences of Consent* (Reading, MA: Addison-Wesley, 1982), pp. 11–13.

19. Stein Rokkan, *Citizens, Elections, Parties* (New York: David McKay, 1970), pp. 31, 150.

20. W. J. M. Mackenzie, *Free Elections* (London: George Allen and Unwin, 1958), pp. 115–16.

21. Acts and Laws of Massachusetts, 1800, Ch. 74. For a brief account of the early history of voter registration in the United States, see Joseph P. Harris, *Registration of Voters in the United States* (Washington, DC: Brookings, 1929), ch. 3.

22. Harris, p. 66.

23. For example, see Richard G. Smolka, *Election Day Registration: The Minnesota and Wisconsin Experience in 1976* (Washington, DC: American Enterprise Institute, 1977), p. 7.

24. *Gallup Report*, no. 230 (November 1984), p. 11. Over the period from 1968 through 1984, the percentage of nonvoters citing nonregistration as their reason ranged between 28% and 42%. Other reasons that were mentioned by at least 10% of the nonvoters in at least one survey were: "Didn't like the candidates" (10%–17%); "Not interested in politics" (4%–10%); "Ill" (7%–15%); "New resident" (4%–10%); "No particular reason" (8%–13%).

25. Raymond E. Wolfinger and Steven J. Rosenstone, *Who Votes?* (New Haven: Yale Univ. Press, 1980), ch. 4.

26. Curtis Gans, "Voter Participation Revisited," *The FEC Journal of Election Administration* 16 (Summer 1989), 8–11.

27. Robert E. Scott, *Mexican Government in Transition* (Urbana: Univ. of Illinois Press, 1964), p. 225; Edward J. Williams and Freeman J. Wright, *Latin American Politics: A Developmental Approach* (New York: Mayfield, 1975), p. 316. On the other hand, the opposite problem, a register that is too permanent can be equally damaging to legitimacy. As one commentator put it, noting that Colombian identity cards seem never to be retired, "the truth is that in Colombia people die everywhere except in the Registry." Cited in Robert H. Dix, *The Politics of Colombia* (New York: Praeger, 1987), p. 110.

28. *Statistical Abstract of the United States*. For 1984, the estimate was 72.8%, while for 1988 it was 70.5%. Neither estimate makes allowance for voting age individuals who are not citizens or who are otherwise ineligible.

29. Scott, p. 226.

30. Alan Angell, Maria D'Alva Kinzo, and Diego Urbaneja, "Latin America" in David Butler and Austin Ranney (eds.), *Electioneering* (Oxford: Clarendon Press, 1992), p. 45.

31. André Blais and R. K. Carty, "Does Proportional Representation Foster Voter Turnout?" *European Journal of Political Research* 18 (March 1990), 167–81.

32. James W. Wilkie and David Lorey (eds.), *Statistical Abstract of Latin America*, 25 (Los Angeles: UCLA Latin American Center, 1987), p. 906.

33. Blais and Carty estimate an impact of 11.2% (p. 177).

34. The idea that suffrage expansion will result in a gradually declining reduction in turnout while the new voters become "acclimatized" is based on the arguments of Philip E. Converse in "Of Time and Partisan Stability," *Comparative Political Studies* 2 (July 1969), 139–71.

35. One possible explanation for the appearance of abnormally high turnout in New Zealand elections is that, although registration is in law compulsory, it is in fact not reliably so. If this is true, then many people who would in other countries have been registered and then counted as nonvoters in New Zealand would be missed altogether in turnout calculations based (as these are) on registered voters rather than the age-eligible population. This possibility was suggested to me by Jack Vowles, personal communication.

36. Mancur Olson, *The Logic of Collective Action* (Cambridge: Harvard Univ. Press, 1965).

37. Many of these arguments are developed more fully in Alan Wertheimer, "In Defense of Compulsory Voting," in J. Roland Pennock and John W. Chapman (eds.), *Participation in Politics* (New York: Lieber-Atherton, 1975), pp. 276–96.

38. Judd v. McKeon, 38 *Commonwealth Law Reports* (1926), 380.

39. Enrique C. Ochoa, "The Rapid Expansion of Voter Participation in Latin America: Presidential Elections, 1845–1986," in J. W. Wilkie and D. Lorey (eds.), *Statistical Abstract of Latin America*, 25 (Los Angeles: UCLA Latin American Center, 1987), p. 866.

40. Frederick W. Holls, *Compulsory Voting* (Philadelphia: American Academy of Political and Social Science, 1891), p. 8.

41. Otto Schmidt, "The Abolition of Compulsory Voting in the Netherlands: Some Empirical Findings," paper presented at the Joint Sessions of Workshops, European Consortium for Political Research, Strasbourg, France, March/April 1974.

Chapter 14. Candidacy

1. Austin Ranney, *Pathways to Parliament* (Madison: Univ. of Wisconsin Press, 1965). See also Michael Rush, *The Selection of Parliamentary Candidates* (London: Nelson, 1969);

Michael Gallagher and Michael Marsh (eds.), *Candidate Selection in Comparative Perspective: The Secret Garden of Politics* (London: Sage, 1988).

2. Herbert Kitschelt, citing an Austrian Socialist Party secretary. "Social Democracy and Liberal Corporatism: Swedish and Austrian Left Parties in Crisis," presented at the 1990 Annual Meeting of the American Political Science Association, San Francisco, August 29–September 1.

3. *FEC Reports on Financial Activity, 1987–88: U.S. Senate and House Campaigns, Final Report,* (September 1989).

4. David Butler and Dennis Kavanagh, *The British General Election of 1987* (Houndmills: Macmillan, 1988), p. 235.

5. Richard S. Katz and Peter Mair (eds.), *Party Organizations: A Data Handbook* (London: Sage, 1992).

6. Philip M. Stern, *The Best Congress Money Can Buy* (New York: Pantheon Books, 1988).

7. Ruud Koole, "The 'Modesty' of Dutch Party Finance," in Herbert E. Alexander (ed.), *Comparative Political Finance in the 1980s* (New York: Cambridge Univ. Press, 1989), p. 210.

8. Ignored here are public funding provisions in 8 Canadian provinces, the German and Austrian Länder, the Australian state of New South Wales, and 13 states (plus seven states that collect voluntary contributions through their state income tax systems), and a few localities in the United States. On the United States, see *Book of the States 1990–91,* pp. 259–60.

9. See W. J. M. Mackenzie, *Free Elections* (London: George Allen and Unwin, 1958), p. 149.

10. This provision was also included in earlier legislation. For example, in 1951, "The Conservative candidate in East Nottingham, a businessman, was charged by the Labour candidate of an adjoining constituency with having cut his factory's production and laid off workers for political purposes. The Conservative furnished the High Court with evidence of the falsity of the charge and was granted an immediate temporary injunction." Stanley Kelley, Jr., *Political Campaigning* (Washington, DC: Brookings Institution, 1960), p. 120.

11. *New York Times Co. v. Sullivan,* 376 US 254 (1964).

12. *Banks v. Lewis* (unreported), cited in H. F. Rawlings, *Law and the Electoral Process* (London: Sweet and Maxwell, 1988), pp. 185–86.

13. Spending limits imposed by the Federal Election Campaign Act Amendments of 1974 and earlier legislation (e.g., Publicity Act Amendments of 1911; Federal Corrupt Practices Act of 1925) were ruled unconstitutional in *Buckley v. Valeo* (424 US 1, 1976). The earlier limits were in any case largely ineffective because they limited the spending by individual committees, but not the number of such committees a single candidate could organize or inspire.

14. In 1988, the limits were $23,050 for the House, between $46,100 and $938,688 for the Senate, and $8.3 million for the presidency. These are regarded in law as limitations on contributions rather than as limitations on spending.

15. J. Patrick Boyer, *Money and Message: The Law Governing Election Financing, Advertising, Broadcasting and Campaigning in Canada* (Toronto: Butterworths, 1983), p. 73.

16. Pierre Avril, "Regulation of Political Finance in France," in Herbert E. Alexander and Rei Shiratori (eds.), *Comparative Political Finance Among the Democracies* (Boulder: Westview Press, 1994), pp. 85–96.

17. See Robin Kolodny, "The 1967 Republican Nomination: An Examination of the Organizational Dynamic," in Bernard Firestone (ed.), *Gerald R. Ford and the Politics of Post-Watergate America* (New York: Greenwood Press, 1991).

18. Howard R. Penniman (ed.), *New Zealand at the Polls: The General Election of 1978* (Washington, DC: AEI, 1980), p. 90. The limitation was £200 when introduced in 1895 and raised to £500 in 1948, NZ$1,500 in 1971, NZ$2,000 in 1975, NZ$4,000 in 1977, and NZ$5,000 in 1983.

19. Sec. 313. For the leading case law on the question of whether this section unconstitutionally infringed on the First Amendment rights of unions, see *United States v. CIO*, 335 US 106 (1948); *United States v. Painters Local 481*, 172 F 2d 854 (1949); *United States v. Construction & General Laborers Local 264*, 101 F Supp 869 (1951); *United States v. International Union UAW*, 352 US 567 (1957); *United States v. Lewis Food Co.*, 366 F 2d 710 (1966).

20. See *Pipefitters Local Union No. 562 v. United States*, 407 US 385 (1972).

21. Herbert E. Alexander, *Financing Politics* (Washington, DC: Congressional Quarterly Press, 1976), p. 117.

22. The limits were $50,000 for president or vice president; $35,000 for senator; $25,000 for representative. These limits were ruled unconstitutional. *Buckley v. Valeo* 424 US 1 (1976), at 54. The limit was reimposed in 1976 for presidential candidates accepting public funding.

23. These limits are FF500,000 for parliament, except in districts with fewer than 40,000 inhabitants where the limit is FF400,000, and FF120 million for the presidency.

24. *Newberry v. United States* 256 US 232 (1921); overruled in *United States v. Classic* 313 US 299 (1941).

25. See Susan B. King and Robert L. Peabody, "Control of Presidential Campaign Funding," in Harvey Mansfield (ed.), *Congress Against the President* (New York: Praeger, 1975), pp. 180–95; Jeffrey M. Berry and Jerry Goldman, "Congress and Public Policy: A Study of the Federal Election Campaign Act of 1971," *Harvard Journal on Legislation* 10 (February 1973), 331–65. One indication of the ineffectiveness of these requirements is that in 1968, seven United States senators reported that it had cost them nothing to be elected. Milton C. Cummings, Jr., and David Wise, *Democracy Under Pressure* (New York: Harcourt Brace Jovanovich, 1974), p. 274.

26. Khayyam Zev Paltiel, "Campaign Finance," in David Butler, Howard Penniman, and Austin Ranney (eds.), *Democracy at the Polls* (Washington, DC: American Enterprise Institute, 1981), pp. 138–172.

27. *National Republican Congressional Committee et al. v. Legi-Tech Corporation*, 795 F.2d. 190 (1986); *Federal Election Commission v. Political Contributions Data, Inc.* 753 F.Supp. 1122 (1990). See Brooks Jackson, *Broken Promise: Why the Federal Election Commission Failed* (New York: Priority Press, 1990), pp. 16–18.

28. Pilar del Castillo, "Financing of Spanish Political Parties," in Herbert Alexander (ed.), *Comparative Political Finance in the 1980s*, p. 182.

29. p. 7.

30. Representation of the People Act, 1983, ss. 121(1), 128(1).

31. Quoted in Rawlings, pp. 226–27.

32. Avril

33. David Butler and Austin Ranney (eds.), *Electioneering* (Oxford: Clarendon Press, 1992), p. 287.

Chapter 15. *Elections and Democracy*

1. Arend Lijphart, *Democracies* (New Haven: Yale Univ. Press, 1984), esp. pp. 214–16, 219.

2. Herbert Kitschelt, *The Logics of Party Formations* (Ithaca: Cornell Univ. Press, 1989).

3. See for example the report of the Labour Party's Plant Commission, published in 1991 as vol. 3 of *Guardian Studies*; Vernon Bogdanor, *What is Proportional Representation?* (Oxford: Oxford Univ. Press, 1984); Enid Lakeman, *Power to Elect* (London: Heinemann, 1982); Peter Hain, *Proportional Misrepresentation* (Aldershot: Wildwood House, 1986).

4. William Riker, *Liberalism Against Populism* (San Francisco: W. H. Freeman, 1982).

5. The German party law, with its requirements of internal democracy, is an example of this.

6. Michael Pinto-Duschinsky, *British Political Finance 1830–1980* (Washington, DC: American Enterprise Institute, 1981), p. 260.

7. Lani Guinier, "No Two Seats: The Elusive Quest for Political Equality," *Virginia Law Review* 77 (November 1991), 1413–514; "The Representation of Minority Interests," *Cardozo Law Review* 14 (April 1993), 1135–74.

8. For a classic statement with regard to firms, see Edward Chamberlin, *The Theory of Monopolistic Competition* (Cambridge: Harvard Univ. Press, 1938).

9. For example, see Angus Campbell, Philip E. Converse, Warren E. Miller, and Donald Stokes, *The American Voter* (New York: John Wiley, 1964).

10. On cognitive mobilization, see Russell J. Dalton, *Citizen Politics* (Chatham, NJ: Chatham House, 1988), pp. 18–24.

11. Attributed to "an intelligent Russian" in George Herbert, *Political Sketches of the State of Europe, 1814–1867*. My application of this aphorism to the Conservative Party is borrowed from an oral presentation by Jack Brand.

12. Bentham, *Radical Reform Bill*, p. 566.

13. This section draws heavily on Kris Deschouwer, "The Decline of Consociationalism and the Reluctant Modernization of Belgian Mass Parties," in Richard S. Katz and Peter Mair (eds.), *How Parties Organize* (London: Sage, 1994), pp. 80–108.

14. Piero Ignazi, *Dal PCI al PDS* (Bologna: Il Mulino, 1992).

15. Richard S. Katz and Luciano Bardi, "Preference Voting and Turnover in Italian Parliamentary Elections," *American Journal of Political Science* 24 (February 1980), 97–114.

16. For example, Joseph LaPalombara, *Democracy Italian Style* (New Haven: Yale Univ. Press, 1987).

17. See, for example, the numerous writings of Giorgio Galli and Gianfranco Pasquino.

18. "Centrism" in this context can only be defined relative to the particular political space.

19. On this debate, see chapter 3.

20. Leo J. Wollemborg, "The Political Scene: An Update," *Italian Journal* 7:2 and 3 (1993), 6.

21. Francis G. Castles and Peter Mair, "Left-Right Scales: Some 'Expert' Judgments," *European Journal of Political Research* 12 (March 1984), 73–88.

22. Royal Commission on the Electoral System, *Report of the Royal Commission on the Electoral System: Towards a Better Democracy* (Wellington: V. R. Ward, Government Printer, 1986). All paragraph references are to this report.

23. In 1975, Social Credit won 7.4% of the vote and the Values Party won 5.2%, each

winning no seats. In 1978, the Social Credit vote increased to 16.1%, which translated into one seat; in 1981, the Social Credit vote rose again to 20.7%, and the party won two seats (2.2%).

24. ¶ 2.1.

25. Wendy Frew, "New Zealand Perspective," *Australian Financial Review*, 10 July 1990. See also, *New Zealand Herald*, 25 October 1990.

26. *Australian Financial Review*, 2 May 1990, p. 12.

27. ¶ 2.224, 2.137, 2.1(b).

28. ¶ 2.159, 2.160.

29. Arend Lijphart, "The Demise of the Last Westminster System? Comments on the Report of New Zealand's Royal Commission on the Electoral System," *Electoral Studies* 6 (August 1987), 97–103.

30. ¶ 1.16.

31. ¶ 2.157.

32. ¶ 2.45, 2.159.

33. ¶ 2.41–45.

34. ¶ 2.116(c), 2.152.

35. ¶ 2.155 and following.

36. ¶ 2.126–127.

37. ¶ 4.17–21, 2.48.

38. ¶ 9.151.

39. ¶ 3.2.

40. ¶ 3.23.

41. See, for example, Samuel Finer, *Adversary Politics and Electoral Reform* (London: Anthony Wigram, 1975).

42. ¶ 4.29.

43. ¶ 2.47.

44. ¶ 2.116, 2.152.

45. ¶ 6.12.

46. ¶ 3.66.

47. ¶ 2.21.

48. E.g., ¶ 2.137.

49. ¶ 9.28.

50. ¶ 9.5.

51. ¶ 9.83.

52. ¶ 2.185.

Index